BERGBAUER
MYERS
KIRSCHNER

Dangerous Marine Animals

240

Reptiles 240

   Sea Snakes 240

   Crocodiles 250

   Turtles 252

   Komodo Dragon 255

256

Invertebrates 256

   Venomous Invertebrates 256

     Sponges 257

     Cnidarians 262

     Hydrozoans 264

     Fire Corals 273

     Siphonophores 277

     Jellyfishes 282

     Box Jellyfishes 292

     Sea Anemones 298

     Tube Anemones 306

     Disc Anemones 309

     Other Harmful Cnidarians 311

     Bristle Worms 312

     Cone Snails 317

     Blue-ringed Octopuses 326

     Flamboyant Cuttlefishes 333

     Nudibranchs 333

     Crown-of-thorns Starfishes 334

     Sea Urchins 338

     Flower Urchins 346

     Fire Urchins 350

     Lobsters and Crabs 354

     Hermit Crabs 355

     Mantis Shrimps 358

   Passively Poisonous Invertebrates .. 362

     Shellfish Poisoning 364

     Snail Poisoning 366

     Crab Poisoning 367

     Sea Cucumbers 370

Index 372

The Authors 382

Picture Credits 383

Introduction

Coastal waters throughout the world are inhabited by plants and animals that can harm humans in a variety of ways. A very few species – some sharks and crocodiles – can, and do on occasion, eat people. Nearly all other potentially harmful organisms hurt people only through self-defence, accidental contact or when eaten.

Animals inflict damage to humans primarily in three ways: by causing physical injury through biting, puncturing or cutting; by actively delivering venom or toxins into the body through mechanisms such as spines, fangs or stinging cells; and by being poisonous to eat. Under the right circumstances, nearly anything can be harmful. Any animal with strong jaws and sharp teeth, pincers or sharp spines, or that is large enough, can cause damage when provoked. This book covers only those animals that pose a danger to humans under normal circumstances – when swimming, diving or fishing, or when eating seafood normally considered edible. Species generally considered inedible are excluded from consideration whether they can be eaten or not.

The geographical scope of the book includes the coral reefs and coastal waters of the tropical Indo-Pacific, Caribbean and adjacent areas, and the warm-temperate waters of the Mediterranean, from the high-tide line to the maximum safe limits for recreational scuba-diving (40 m).

What makes an animal dangerous?

With the exception of feeding, territorial behaviour or cases of mistaken identity, fishes that injure humans do so defensively and are dangerous only because of the actions of humans. Injury is thus the result of accidental or intentional human behaviour. The same can be said for most marine reptiles except the Estuarine Crocodile, and for virtually all invertebrates.

Dangerous animals can be classified by the kinds of injuries they cause. Those that injure humans through physical trauma are termed **traumatogenic**. Fishes generally do this by biting, or by cutting or puncturing by means of sharp spines, blades or rough scales. Lobsters and crabs do so by means of pincers, while corals can cut with their sharp skeletons. A few species of

fishes use electricity to shock their prey as well as defend themselves. These are termed **electrogenic**. Many fishes, sea snakes and invertebrates use venom to kill prey and to defend themselves. Whether they deliver this by a spine, fang or stinging cells, all are termed **venomous**. Finally, many animals are entirely harmless unless eaten. They contain toxic substances or poisons and are thus termed **poisonous**. Some animals are dangerous in more than one way. For instance, some surgeonfishes have venom associated with certain spines, at least as juveniles, but we include them and other non-venomous surgeonfishes with the traumatogenic fishes because the primary danger they pose is through the cutting power of their caudal spines.

Venomous and poisonous animals

Toxic substances occur in many marine animals and fulfil a variety of functions. Offensively, they are used primarily to immobilise, capture or partially digest prey, or occasionally they may be used to attack an adversary. Defensively, they are used primarily as protection from predation. Some sessile animals, such as sponges, corals and sea squirts, use noxious compounds defensively against adversarial organisms ranging from predators to infectious fungi and bacteria, as well as offensively as a form of chemical warfare to kill and overgrow their neighbours. However, as these generally represent no danger to humans, they are beyond the scope of this book. Species that employ toxins or poisons are divided into two groups: actively venomous and passively poisonous marine animals.

Actively venomous animals possess a venom apparatus. This consists of specialised glandular tissue that produces and stores venom, as well as a mechanism that delivers the venom into the body of the victim. This mechanism is usually a spine or tooth, but can also be a bristle or jaw, pincers or a special type of cell called a nematocyst. In all cases, the venom is injected from the animal to its victim without having to pass through the intestinal tract. This type of venom absorption is described in medicine as parental. Each venom apparatus has various characteristics. In the Crown-of-thorns Starfish, for example, it is a simple spine surrounded with venomous tissue that is pushed back when it penetrates the skin. It can also be a distinct hard

Puffers are passively toxic. Consumption following incorrect preparation can result in fatal food poisoning.

spine, such as on stonefishes, which injects its poison into the wound like a hypodermic needle. And the venom apparatus can also be a sophisticated mechanism like the fangs of the sea snake, the elaborate venomous darts of the cone shells and the highly complex nematocysts of cnidarians.

Actively poisonous marine animals can use their venom offensively to catch prey or defensively to protect themselves against predators. And as with stinging animals, the venom is used for both purposes. None of the marine animals that uses its venom offensively would normally attack humans – we are simply not their typical prey. When humans are poisoned by marine animals, it is usually the result of unintentional contact or careless interaction with the animals and should be considered accidental.

Passively poisonous animals do not possess any specialised tissue to store venom, nor do they have any special mechanism to inject venom. Instead, venom absorption occurs enterally, via the intestinal tract of the victim. These types of envenomation are also known as food poisoning. Ciguatera and shellfish poisoning are caused when humans consume contaminated fishes. Species that are not poisonous by nature suddenly become so and thus pose a danger to humans. Passively poisonous puffer fishes have yet another mechanism for envenomation. in their natural habitat they are associated with various microbial strains that facilitate the concentration of highly poisonous tetrodotoxins in their bodies.

Venom composition

By definition, venom is never a pure substance but a mixture of substances, and may be highly complex or less so. The venoms of cone snails are particularly complex: in some species, more than

Bad reputation: Barracudas are powerful, lightning-fast predators. Fortunately, accidents involving them are extremely rare.

When exploring unfamiliar waters, taking the following precautions will reduce the chances of having a bad encounter with a dangerous animal:

When visiting the beach or rocky shore

• Inform yourself about the dangerous animals in the area you plan to visit. Learn where they are likely to be encountered and how to recognise them. Ask locals or other knowledgeable people about potential dangers.

• Never touch anything that is foreign or unknown.

• Wear beach shoes with sturdy soles when wading in shallow water or walking on rocky shores. Such footwear protects against injury from sharp rocks, as well as from sea urchins or fishes with venomous spines that may be buried in the sand.

• Avoid swimming at deserted beaches or at night. The setting may seem romantic, but if an emergency occurs there will no one around to help. Swimming in the ocean is riskier at night than during the day, as sea urchins are more exposed and jellyfishes cannot be seen until it's too late. Sharks and other predatory fishes such as puffers are often active at night, when they are also less likely to be seen and more likely to mistake you for food.

• Wear stinger suits of Lycra or neoprene in areas or seasons where there is an increased risk of encountering dangerous jellyfishes, such as in northern Australia during the summer.

• Do not swim close above sandy bottoms where a stingray could be buried. Close movement could startle it and cause it to lash out with its tail.

• When wading in calm sandy shallows, do the 'stingray shuffle' – shuffle your feet along the surface of the sand rather than take high steps. This will alert any nearby ray to move off and prevent it from being stepped on.

• Do not provoke dangerous animals or attempt to pet, play with or catch them.

• When handling fishes in an aquarium, always separate the venomous fishes using a panel or remove them with a scoop or net.

• Exercise care when handling venomous fishes. Always wear thick gloves and use tongs or pliers to remove a hook. Wash hands thoroughly after contact with animals that have poisonous skin.

• When diving into the water, always look first. Also be careful when jumping into shallows and wear sturdy beach shoes – a stonefish, devilfish or ray could be buried in the sand.

• Exercise care when encountering stranded jellyfishes since they can retain their stinging ability for days, long after they are dead. Their presence is also an indication that there are others in the water.

When scuba-diving

• Maintain proper buoyancy. Be careful when descending and, for both environmental and safety reasons, do not swim too close to the bottom to avoid accidental contact.

• Do not reach into hollows, crevices or holes without being able to see what is inside. Moray eels or other dangerous animals could be present and will bite if cornered.

• Always leave rays and other large fishes enough room to escape, particularly when they are lying near the entrances to caverns or under overhangs. A group of divers should never surround a large animal even if it is encountered in an open space.

• Exercise care with seemingly dead snakes. Sea snakes have been observed lying absolutely still for more than 15 minutes, moving only when disturbed by divers.

• Do not feed fishes, as accidents can occur in the blink of an eye. Moray eels, barracudas and other fishes often cannot differentiate between a human finger and a piece of food, particularly when excited, and surgeonfishes can cause injury with their sharp, blade-like spines.

Deadly dwarfs: Blue-ringed Octopuses are amongst the smallest octopuses, but produce a highly-toxic poison that they inject into potential predators or prey.

50 individual components have been isolated. The substances responsible for the effectiveness of the venom are referred to as toxins. Unlike venom, a toxin is not a mixture but rather a pure and defined substance. Venoms usually contain several toxins, many of which are kinds of protein. Certain components of venom can be largely or entirely non-toxic or ineffective, and the ratio of toxins to ineffective substances varies greatly depending upon the species. The venom of some species of sea snake, particularly sea kraits (*Laticauda* species, p.247), seems to consist only of toxins.

Course of envenomation
The severity of envenomation and resulting symptoms depends on several factors. The amount of venom introduced into the body plays a crucial role and can vary greatly. In many venomous species of snake, no venom is injected in up to half of the defensive bites and no symptoms arise. Even sea snake bites can result in no symptoms and thus have no consequences. If, on the other hand, the victim is hit full force by a bite and a large amount of venom is injected, the consequences may be extremely severe and result in death.

General and specific medical treatment
Symptoms of envenomation or poisoning do not follow a precise pattern, so there is no way of predicting the course or outcome. The symptoms can sometimes be extreme and result in serious health problems, and in other cases they are

Dangerous beauty: Lionfishes are actively poisonous fish. They use their long, venomous fin spines for defence.

hardly evident. Most poisons have no antidote, so treatment can be determined only according to the symptoms. Serious cases involving cardiovascular problems, imminent kidney failure or respiratory paralysis require intensive methods of treatment – appropriate first aid must be administered immediately and the victim transferred to hospital as soon as possible. If proper treatment is given, the chance of complete recovery, even in cases of severe poisoning, are very good thanks to advances in medicine. Cardiovascular functions can be stabilised, and artificial respiration can be used for days or even weeks in cases of respiratory paralysis. Dialysis is a life-saving method in cases of acute kidney failure. These techniques have led to a decline in the number of deaths through serious envenomation.

Antidotes

Antidotes are available for only a very few venoms, including those of sea snakes, stonefish (*Synanceia* species) and the Box Jellyfish *Chironex fleckeri*. Treatment with antivenom is considered a specific therapy. It is produced by immunising mammals (usually horses) with a minimal dose of the venom – just enough so that the animal does not become sick. The animal's immune system recognises the venom as being foreign and fights it by developing specific antibodies, which are removed and purified. The resulting antivenom is then used to treat the specific venom that was used to produce it. If the antivenom is produced through immunisation with a specific venom, it is called a monovalent antivenom, whereas if it was produced with a mixture of venoms, it is called a polyvalent antivenom. The latter is supposed to neutralise the venoms of an entire group of related species, such as venomous vipers of North Africa or elapid snakes of Australia.

It is a popular misconception that an injection of the right antivenom will be a life-saver and 'cure-all'. This is not the case. In some circumstances, in fact, the opposite can be true! Various factors and conditions limit the effects of antivenoms, and the risk of complication is high. The animal proteins they contain can cause severe side effects in humans, such as fever, painful joints and skin rashes, as well as acute circulatory shock, which can result in death. Without proper assessment of the risks and additional precautionary measures, the use of antivenom can be fatal, so it should be administered only in justified cases and only by qualified medical personnel. Furthermore, antivenoms are very expensive, have a short shelf-life and must remain cool. Often, an antivenom is not readily available. For example, the stone-fish antivenom is rarely available outside Australia. Despite these limitations, the use of an antivenom is often necessary to save a life, particularly when the victim has been bitten by a sea snake or stung by a box jellyfish. In the case of envenomation by a box jellyfish, first aid should be administered immediately by dousing the affected areas with household vinegar and removing any remaining tentacles. This prevents further envenomations by deactivating unfired stinging cells and preventing additional contact with them. The doctor will then decide if it is wise to administer antivenom.

Sword fighters: keeping a respectful distance is recommended. When threatened, rays may strike out with their whip-like tails and can deliver a potent injection of venom through a barbed spine at the tail's base.

First aid

Venom affects the body rapidly, with the effects usually evident very quickly and often intensely dynamic. Even venoms that cause little initial pain can produce serious effects within half an hour. Envenomation often occurs in remote areas miles away from a doctor or hospital. Immediate first aid is thus extremely important and may have to be carried out by the victim or a companion. The following measures can be used for all but the most trivial of accidents and envenomations.

Advice for envenomation by cnidarians (jellyfishes, box jellyfishes and men-of-war)

In cases of envenomation by cnidarians, rapid first aid is very helpful in limiting the degree of injury. On the other hand, incorrect or inappropriate first

aid can aggravate the injury. When the victim comes into contact with cnidarian tentacles and envenomation has occurred, numerous unfired nematocysts (stinging cells) remain stuck in the skin. Any disturbance can cause these to burst and release more venom, making the choice of first-aid measures extremely important. Appropriate first aid destroys unfired nematocysts and prevents them from injecting their venom. Over the last few years it has become evident that actions appropriate for some kinds of cnidarian stings may do more harm than good for stings by other kinds. For example, using vinegar on Box Jellyfish stings is still the best initial treatment for this species but is not suitable for stings by the Portuguese Man-of-war. There is no single method of treatment for all stinging animals. The recommended first aid for stings by various

Danger area: sea snakes are amongst the most poisonous snakes on Earth but most have much more placid dispositions than many of their poisonous relatives ashore.

Heavily armed: cnidarians like this jellyfish use poisonous nematocysts for hunting and defence.

cnidarians is described in their respective chapters. These methods reflect the latest medical knowledge. Never apply alcohol, do not flush the wound with fresh water and do not rub the skin, as these measures could cause the remaining nematocysts to discharge. Repeated envenomation through stinging animals often results in an increased sensitivity. In turn, this can result in extreme allergic reactions in later envenomations. Such reactions can cause circulatory collapse and asphyxiation.

Should the hot-water method be used?
The use of the hot-water method for fish poisoning is highly controversial. Extremely high temperature is supposed to denature the proteins in venom and thus disable them. The affected limb is thus immersed in hot water, or hot compresses are placed on the affected area. The water should not be too hot or there is a risk of damage to skin tissue similar to scalding. In the worst case, the victim could suffer additional injuries, leading to possible complications that hinder healing. Effectively disabling the venom using the hot-water method can really only work in areas with thin epidermis or with low tissue mass, such as fingers or toes. Aside from the fact that it has a rather questionable rate of success, the method is painful and psychologically strenuous for the victim, and for these reasons most experts now discourage its use.

Speed counts
Envenomation must be taken seriously, and time is of the essence – administer first aid immediately and get the victim to the closest doctor or hospital as quickly as possible. This is particularly true for stings by sea snakes, cone shells, stonefishes and the most dangerous cnidarians, as well as bites by blue-ringed octopuses.

Time is of essence – rapid treatment can save the victim's life. It is essential that the appropriate first-aid treatment is administered immediately and that the victim is transferred to the nearest doctor or hospital as quickly as possible.

What to do

• Remove the victim from the water immediately. Envenomation and severe pain can cause irrational reactions and, in some cases, unconsciousness, which can result in drowning. Always ensure your own safety when administering first aid.

• Keep the victim calm. Do not leave him alone, since injuries and even minor envenomation or poisoning can cause uneasiness and even panic.

• Immobilise the affected limbs and avoid movement, as this can cause pain and may facilitate the distribution of venom or lead to increased bleeding from wounds.

• Place fully conscious victims in the precautionary shock position. Shock can occur even in cases of light envenomation or injury. Place unconscious victims who are displaying spontaneous breathing in the recovery position. Do not leave the victim unattended.

• Remove rings, bracelets and necklaces. Affected areas often swell, increasing the possibility of constriction.

• Identify the offending animal. It is of the utmost important for first aid and further treatment to know which animal caused the envenomation or poisoning. Such knowledge is often the only way to make a reliable diagnosis and thus choose the correct treatment. Try to identify the animal without endangering oneself, either by capturing it or photographing it. This will be a great help to emergency and medical personnel.

• Seek medical attention as quickly as possible. This is especially important for injuries involving highly venomous animals (e.g. blue-ringed octopuses and sea snakes) as symptoms are often not immediately evident.

• Monitor vital signs. The cardiovascular system can be interrupted as a result of serious envenomation or shock. Monitor these vital functions at all times and, if necessary, administer artificial respiration and cardiac massage.

What not to do

A variety of household remedies are often used to treat cases of envenomation. These should not be taken seriously, as they are either useless or may even be harmful. The following 'remedies' should be avoided, even though they may be mentioned in travel guides or other literature:

• Do not use hot water on the bite or puncture wound or burn it with a cigarette or similar device. The chance of disabling the venom is extremely low and the risk of tissue damage very high.

• Do not pack the affected area with ice, as extreme cooling has a negative effect on the course of envenomation. In some documented cases, the disruption in blood circulation and frostbite, together with the effects of the venom, have led to extensive necrosis.

• Do not make incisions or excisions, or squeeze or otherwise manipulate the wound in an attempt to remove the poison. Doing so brings with it a risk of injuring muscles or tendons. Blood vessels can also be injured, thus allowing the venom to spread even more rapidly throughout the body. Furthermore, manipulating the wound also increases the risk of secondary infection.

• Do not suck the site of envenomation, as this is generally ineffective. The pressure created by sucking is not strong enough to remove the venom, which spreads quickly. Furthermore, extremely fine bites or punctures close up quickly, making suction impossible.

• Do not use household remedies. No tincture, herbal stock or similar potion is known to have a positive effect on acute cases of envenomation. Just as useless are occult and esoteric methods such as 'black stones', which are commonly used in many tropical areas.

• Do not apply a tourniquet – it not suitable for cases of envenomation and is useful only to stop heavy bleeding. By cutting off the flow of blood, a tourniquet can cause severe damage to tissue, and for this reason should be removed after 10 to 15 minutes. In cases of envenomation, a sudden and massive inflow of venom into the bloodstream would occur on removing the tourniquet, and the corresponding symptoms would soon become evident.

IF STUNG OR BITTEN BY A VENOMOUS ANIMAL

Venomous Fishes
Fishes with venomous spines or teeth

The Blotched Fantail Ray *Taeniura meyeni* has caused fatal injuries to divers. *Maldives, MB*

Stingrays
Order Myliobatiformes

Stingrays are among the few animals that deliver venom through a deep, knife-like stab wound. This is accomplished by a barbed spine located at the base of the tail. Species from five families pose a hazard to people who enter or fish in the warm, shallow marine waters covered by this book.

Behaviour
Most stingrays are bottom-dwellers that spend most of their time perfectly still, usually buried in sand and silt, sometimes in extremely shallow water. Often, the only things visible are the eyes and spiracles (openings similar to nostrils). They swim by undulating their large, wing-like pectoral fins and usually remain close to the bottom. Eagle and cownose rays are elegant swimmers with great

When photographing stingrays, always take care to leave open an escape route.

endurance that spend much of their time high in the water. They swim by synchronised flapping of their pectoral fins, which allows them to cover great distances. Stingrays feed largely on bottom-dwelling organisms, including worms, clams, shrimp, crabs and snails, and occasionally on fishes. In all species, the spine on the tail is used only for defence and never to capture prey. Despite this formidable weapon, stingrays do have enemies. Hammerhead sharks and some large groupers often feed on them and frequently have the encysted remains of spines in their stomach or body cavity walls. The loss of a spine is a temporary setback for a stingray, as it is soon replaced by a newly grown one. Like many sharks, rays give birth to fully developed young.

Appearance
All stingrays have a distinctive flattened round to quadrangular shape and a long, often whip-like tail. The pectoral fins are broadly fused to the head and torso in a structure collectively called the disc. Two nostrils are on the upper side of the disc behind the eyes, and the mouth and gills are on the lower side. Some small species are less than

Nearly invisible, this Southern Stingray has covered itself with a layer of sand. *Curaçao, RM*

A Southern Stingray takes food from a diver. *Grand Cayman, SMe*

A feeding ray attracts an entourage of fishes hoping to catch fleeing prey. *Egypt, MK*

30 cm wide, whereas larger species may reach more than 2 m or, in the case of the eagle rays, nearly 3 m in width.

Typical accidents

Most accidents occur when waders step on unseen rays in shallow water. Stingrays often bury themselves in sand or mud up to their eyes, making them practically invisible. Fishermen often catch rays in nets such as beach seines, or by hook and line. They risk injury when emptying the nets or attempting to remove a hook. When caught, rays whip their tails wildly, making them quite dangerous. Occasionally, eagle rays jump out of the water and land in a boat, where they flail about. Severe, sometimes fatal injuries have resulted.

Accidents with divers are quite rare. Divers are endangered when they get too close to a ray, particularly if they cut off an escape route. If the ray feels threatened, it will whip its tail as it attempts to flee. Nearly all fatal wounds are those to the torso that pierce vital organs or blood vessels. In some parts of the world, rays have been conditioned to humans by being hand-fed. Bloody fingers resulting from their clumsy table manners are the typical injury. Feeding rays outside of these well-established venues should never be attempted.

Prevention

Avoid wading in murky water, or shuffle your feet across the surface of the sand to create a disturbance. This may warn a ray of your presence and give it a chance to move away. When swimming, always maintain a safe distance from the bottom, as rays often bury themselves and can easily be overlooked. When diving, be careful when approaching a stingray, maintain a safe distance and do not touch it. Never swim close above a stingray, since the spines are on the upper side of the tail. A group of divers should never surround a ray, as if threatened it can whip its tail out at lightning speed, making it virtually impossible to dodge.

Venom

Stingray venom seems to be a mix of various toxic proteins that predominantly affect cardiovascular functions, in particular the heart muscle. Its precise composition has not been determined and there is no antivenom. The small American round rays (Urotrygonidae) and freshwater stingrays (Potamotrygonidae) seem to have the most potent venom, whereas some of the larger stingrays (Dasyatidae) seem to have weaker venom or possibly none at all.

The diver maintains a respectful distance from the tail of this Blotched Fantail Ray. *Maldives, MB*

Venom apparatus

Stingrays have one or more spines on the upper side of the tail. Each spine is flattened, tapered at the end, and serrated along the edges with rear-pointing barbs. The spines are made of a hard bone-like substance called vasodentin. Two grooves on the underside contain venom-secreting glandular tissue (indicated by the blue arrow). The entire apparatus is covered with a thin layer of skin called the integumentary sheath, where venom is concentrated. A stingray spine can inflict a deep stab wound that can be torn open further by the barbs when it is withdrawn or removed. When penetrating the skin, the surrounding sheath is torn and may be left in the wound with the venom. The spine – which in large rays may exceed 30 cm in length – may break off and remain stuck in the wound. The position, size and number of spines, as well as tail morphology, vary by family and species but basic spine morphology is similar. *(Photo Red Sea, MB; diagram after Halstead, 1970)*

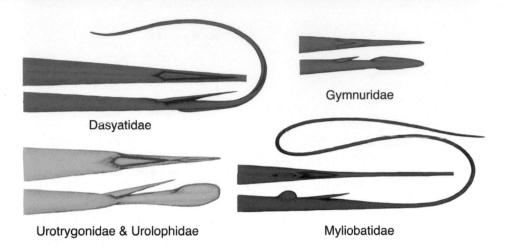

Dasyatidae

Gymnuridae

Urotrygonidae & Urolophidae

Myliobatidae

Envenomation and symptoms

A stingray's spines can cause deep and serious injuries. Acute pain is felt immediately, which rapidly increases in intensity and can last for several hours. The edges of the wound turn blue, and an oedema develops if it is bleeding. If the wound is not treated properly, secondary infection often occurs, which can result in tissue damage or death (necrosis). General symptoms such as nausea, diarrhoea, vomiting, sweating, circulatory problems and panic can occur. Injury to the torso can be fatal.

Treatment

First aid

Remove the victim from the water immediately. Remove any spines or spine fragments only if this can be done easily. Rinse the wound with sea water and provide appropriate first aid if it is bleeding. Seek medical attention, even if a wound seems to be minor and is relatively painless, as spine or tissue fragments could still be present and potentially cause secondary infection.

What not to do

Do not soak the wound in hot water. Do not apply a tourniquet and do not manipulate the wound in any way.

Ongoing medical management

An injury should be treated by medical personnel, even when it is slight and painless, since fragments of the spine and tissue could still be inside the wound. Spine fragments are easily seen on x-rays and must be surgically removed due to the danger of vascular injury which could lead to heavy bleeding. Treatment is otherwise like that for a stab wound.

Classification and distribution

Over 100 species of rays in ten families have barbed spines. Members of five families pose a hazard to people in the regions covered by this book. They can be identified by the length and shape of the tail, presence of fins and position of spines. In the species accounts, the size given refers to disc width.

Stingrays
Dasyatidae

Includes whiprays. Disc rhomboid to round; tail long, with one or more large venomous spines far from the base, giving them the greatest striking range. About 70 species, primarily on continental shelves, but in all tropical and temperate marine and estuarine waters. and a few in fresh water or pelagic. Genera distinguished by disc shape, tail morphology and distribution of thorn-like denticles. *Himantura*, *Dasyatis*, and *Pastinachus* with long whip-like tail, and a lower skin fold on the latter two; *Taeniura* and *Urogymnus* nearly round, the latter without a spine but covered in thorn-like denticles. Dangerous, many large species capable of causing severe injury or death.

IF INJURED

Urobatis
36 cm

Urotrygonidae

Himantura
150 cm

Pastinachus
180 cm

Dasyatis
210 cm

Urogymnus
100+ cm

Dasyatidae

Taeniura
180 cm

Aetobatus
270 cm

Gymnura
250 cm

Gymnuridae

Myliobatidae

RM/JR

American Round Rays
Urotrygonidae

Disc oval to nearly rhomboid, tail short and thick with well-developed fin and one or more venomous spines. About 15 species in coastal marine and estuarine waters of American tropics. Small but dangerous. Closely related to Potamotrygonidae of South America and Urolophidae of warm-temperate and tropical Australasia.

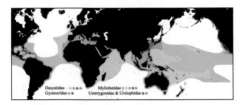

Range of the five major stingray families: Dasyatidae (excluding the pelagic stingray), Urotrygonidae, Urolophidae, Gymnuridae and Myliobatidae.

Butterfly Rays
Gymnuridae

Disc broader than long; tail short, whip-like, with or without a small venomous spine. About 11 species on continental shelves and adjacent tropical and temperate seas. Potentially dangerous.

Eagle Rays
Myliobatidae

Disc wide and wing-like with pointed tips; tail long and whip-like, with small dorsal fin and small venomous spines at base; snout protrudes, mouth near front. About 15 species in all tropical and temperate marine and estuarine waters. Spend most of their time above the bottom when not feeding. Potentially dangerous. The similar cownose rays (Rhinopteridae) have a blunt, indented snout, resembling a cow's nose. Most of the larger devil or manta rays (Mobilidae) have lost their spines, but a few retain them.

Sample cases

1) Fatality caused by a Blotched Fantail Ray *Taeniura meyeni* at Manado, Indonesia. A diver and his local guide descended to 15 m to watch a large black ray swimming about 3 m off the bottom. At that point the diver separated from the guide and descended to the ray from behind. He then grabbed the forward edge of a 'wing' with both hands and arms stretched forward. The ray whipped its tail up, causing the spine to hit the diver on his left side below the scapula and penetrate the heart and possibly a lung. Mike Severns, who was present as the guide surfaced with the body, described the slash on the man's back as unexpectedly large and looking as if the ray had struggled to free its spine. The guide told him that the man appeared to have mistaken the ray for a manta. He believed the diver was dead before they reached the surface and said that there was so much blood in the water he could not see well and became very frightened. He repeatedly described the quantity of blood in the water and was so badly shaken that he stopped diving altogether. *(Communicated by Mike Severns)*

2) The death of Australian wildlife personality Steve Irwin in 2006 after being spined by a large stingray was headline news worldwide. From the eyewitness and video accounts, it can be seen how the incident unfolded. As Steve was swimming close above the side of the ray, his photographer approached them from the front in order to get a dramatic sequence. This seems to have cut off the ray's perceived escape route, and it reacted by hitting the nearest person in its way. It behaved just like many other species Steve had interacted with, but in this case it seems he failed to anticipate the ray's reaction. It is also possible that there was a lapse in communication with his photographer, who may unwittingly have triggered the attack. Although it may not have made a difference, Steve's final act of pulling the spine from his chest could have caused him to bleed out and die before he could be helped. The species of ray involved is known locally as the Bull Ray, a name most often applied to *Taeniura meyeni* but also used for *Pastinachus sephen* and other large species. Unfortunately, no ray expert was consulted to view the video tape before it was destroyed.

Stingrays
Dasyatidae

Southern Stingray	150 cm
Dasyatis americana	*(59 in)*

Disc rhombic; tail smooth with lower fold of skin and 1 or more spines. **Biology:** in shallow coastal waters, from shoreline to over 25 m. Common in sandy areas of coral reefs. Feeds on bivalves, worms, crustaceans and small fishes. An active swimmer, migrates to temperate seas >15°C in summer. ♂'s mature at 51 cm width, ♀s at 75–80 cm. Litter size 3–5, neonates 17–18 cm. **Range:** Chesapeake Bay and Bermuda to se. Brazil, incl. all Caribbean.

Roughtail Stingray	210 cm
Dasyatis centroura	*(6.9 ft)*

Disc rhombic; midline of back and tail with irregular row of large tubercles; brown with scattered dark spots. **Biology:** inhabits estuaries and coastal waters, 1–274 m. Feeds on crustaceans, cephalopods and small fishes, incl. sharks. Reproduces once a year, with a litter size of 2–4. **Range:** C. Cod to s. Fl and Bahamas; Uruguay; Medit. and e. Atlantic from Bay of Biscay to Angola, incl. Canary and C. Verde Is.

Bluntnose Stingray	100 cm
Dasyatis say	*(60 in)*

Disc corners rounded; tail with dark upper and lower skin folds. **Biology:** in coastal waters, inlets and estuaries, 1–9 m. Not often seen in clear coral-reef waters. **Range:** NJ to Argentina, incl. Antilles.

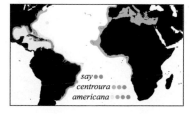

say ●●
centroura ●●●
americana ●●●

Bluespotted Stingray — 50 cm
Dasyatis kuhlii — *(20 in)*

Disc rhombic; top and bottom of tail with small skin folds; tan to grey with dark-edged pale blue spots; outer part of tail may be banded. **Biology:** inhabits sand flats of lagoon and seaward reefs, shoreline to 90 m. Common. May cover itself with sand. Feeds on sand-dwelling invertebrates. Neonates 16 cm. **Range:** S. Africa to Samoa, n. to s. Japan, s. to se. Australia and New Caledonia. **Similar:** *Taeniura lymma* (p.26) has oval disc, thick tail and larger blue spots.

Pink Whipray — >150 cm
Himantura fai — *(59 in)*

Disc rhomboid, uniformly tan to brownish pink; skin smooth; tail 3x disc length and smooth, with 1 functional spine. **Biology:** inhabits lagoon and seaward sand flats, intertidal zone to at least 200 m. Occasionally in large aggregations to feed and perhaps reproduce. **Range:** S. Africa (?) and India to the Tuamotus, n. to Marianas, s. to nw. Australia and New Caledonia. **Similar:** *H. jenkinsii* (below) has row of thorns and denticles along midline of back and tail.

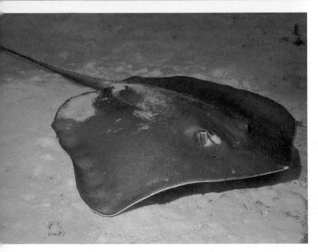

Jenkins' Whipray — 105 cm
Himantura jenkinsii — *(41 in)*

Disc rhomboid, spiracle large; row of thorns and denticles along midline of back and tail; usually one spine; olive-brown. **Biology:** on large expanses of sand near coral reefs to at least 30 m. Sometimes in groups, probably for courtship and mating. Common in Andaman Sea. **Range:** S. Africa to PNG, but patchy. **Similar:** *H. fai* (above) lacks row of thorns and denticles on back and tail.

D. kuhlii ●●●
H. fai ●●
H. jenkinsii ●●●

Mangrove Whipray   97 cm
Himantura granulata   *(38 in)*

Tail short, 2x disc width; disc oval with angular snout, upper surface with small granules; black with tiny white spots, tail mostly white. **Biology:** inhabits sand and rubble flats from mangrove-lined shores to a depth of 85 m. Neonates 28 cm. **Range:** Seychelles to Vanuatu, n. to Marianas, s. to Gt Barrier Reef.

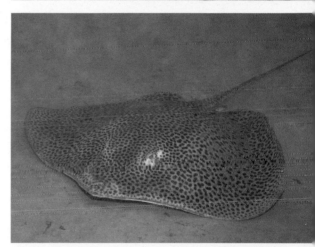

Honeycomb Stingray   150 cm
Himantura uarnak   *(59 in)*

Disc rhomboid; dark spots become reticulations when large. **Biology:** on sand or mud from estuaries to clear seaward reefs, 0.5–50 m. Large and potentially dangerous. Feeds on molluscs, crustaceans and fishes. Litter size 1–5, neonates 28 cm. **Range:** Red Sea to Fr. Polynesia, n. to s. Japan; migrant to e. Medit. **Similar:** Leopard Whipray *H. undulata* has leopard-like spots with pale centres (140 cm; India (?) to PNG).

Cowtail Stingray   183 cm
Pastinachus sephen   *(6 ft)*

Brown; a broad finfold under tail. **Biology:** on mud and sand bottoms of estuaries, coastal waters, and reefs, 1–60 m. Often among mangroves; penetrates fresh water. Large and potentially dangerous. Feeds on fishes, crustaceans, molluscs and worms. Neonates 18 cm. **Range:** Red Sea to Micronesia and New Caledonia.

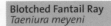

Blotched Fantail Ray   **164 cm**
Taeniura meyeni   *(65 in)*

Disc round; grey with irregular black blotches; to 154 kg. **Biology:** on sand near coral and rocky reefs, 3–500 m. Feeds on invertebrates and sand- and reef-dwelling fishes. Not aggressive, but has fatally wounded divers (3 deaths). Litter size 1–7. **Range:** Red Sea to Galápagos, n. to s. Japan, s. to S. Africa and L. Howe I.

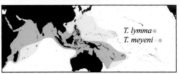

T. lymma ●
T. meyeni ●

Bluespotted Ribbontail Ray   **30 cm**
Taeniura lymma   *(12 in)*

Disc round, somewhat oblong; olive to brown with bright blue spots. **Biology:** inhabits sandy areas of coral reefs, often under ledges or in caves, 2–30 m. Sometimes partly buried. Active by day and night. Feeds primarily at night on molluscs, worms and shrimps. Often visits cleaning stations. Litter size 1–7. **Range:** Red Sea to Fiji, n. to Oman and Philippines, s. to S. Africa and e. Australia.

American Round Rays
Urotrygonidae

Yellow Stingray   **36 cm**
Urobatis jamaicensis   *(14 in)*

Disc oval; tail thick with well-developed fin and 1–2 spines. **Biology:** in coastal waters, 1–20 m. Common in seagrass beds and on nearshore reefs. Feeds on crustaceans and fishes. Raises front of its disc to mimic a crevice to attract prey. ♀s give birth in estuaries to 6 cm young. ♂s smaller than ♀s, mature at 16 cm width. **Range:** NC to n. S. America, incl. all Caribbean.

U. jamaicensis ●●
Urotrygon spp. ●

Eagle Rays
Myliobatidae

Spotted Eagle Ray	230 cm
Aetobatus narinari	(91 in)

'Wingtips' pointed; black with white spots or rings above, white below; tail very long with 1–5 spines; to 200 kg. **Biology:** frequents shallow, protected sand flats as well as outer reef slopes and open sea, surface to 80 m. Solitary, paired or in groups of up to 200. Roots in sand for molluscs and crustaceans. Timid. An active swimmer, sometimes leaping from water. Has caused injuries and fatalities when landing in boats. **Range:** circumtropical. **Similar:** in Indo-Pacific, a few *Aetomylaeus* species are easily distinguished by colour pattern.

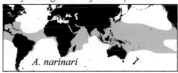

A. narinari

Juvenile Striped Eel Catfish *Plotosus lineatus* form ball-like schools. The bottom fish are feeding. *Bali, RM*

Eel Catfishes
Plotosidae

Catfishes are named for the conspicuous barbels around their mouths. There are over 3,027 species in 36 families. Most of them live in fresh water, but

IF INJURED

Treatment

First aid

Clean and disinfect the wound. If bleeding occurs, use a bandage. Seek medical treatment, since there is a high risk of secondary infection even with a minor injury.

What not to do

Do not use any hot-water treatment methods. Do not tamper with the wound.

Ongoing medical management

Although lidocaine soothes the pain, it only does so for a short period of time. The wound should be carefully cleaned to remove any foreign particles. Antibiotics and tetanus prophylaxis are recommended owing to the danger of secondary infection.

two families are predominately marine: the eel catfishes and the sea catfishes (Ariidae, p.31). Many species, including all of those in these two families, are armed with venomous spines. Wounds from the spines are extremely painful, long-lasting and, in rare cases, may be fatal. Even a 2-cm juvenile can cause a wasp-like sting. The 37 known species of eel catfishes inhabit tropical to warm-temperate marine and estuarine waters of the Indo-Pacific and southern Australia, and fresh waters of Australia and New Guinea. Some get quite large – up to 1.5 m in length (*Plotosus canius*) – and pose a danger to the fishermen who handle them. Only one species, the Striped Eel Catfish *Plotosus lineatus*, is widespread on coral reefs.

Behaviour

Eel catfishes feed on small bottom-dwelling animals, primarily crustaceans but also molluscs and fishes. Their barbels are used to find and flush out prey. They are sensitive to touch and have prolific taste buds that recognise the chemical signatures of various organisms. Divers generally see only juveniles, which school in conspicuous compact, undulating balls as they move along the bottom. These schools are most often encountered over sandy areas and among seagrasses, and form to

Venom apparatus

The venom apparatus of the Striped Eel Catfish consists of three large serrated spines, one each in front of the first dorsal and pectoral fins (shown in red), associated glandular tissue and axillary glands. The serrations consist of a series of sharp-edged oblique rings with a barb in front. Venom-producing glandular tissue runs along each side, is thickest on the outer third and is covered in skin. In addition, each pectoral fin spine has a venom-producing axillary gland above its base, which opens to a pore (blue arrow).

provide the juveniles protection by confusing predators. Further defensive measures include venomous spines. The fish seem to know they are safe, as they make little effort to move when disturbed. Adults occur in smaller groups or are solitary under shelter by day, and are seldom seen.

Appearance
Eel catfishes are elongate, with broad-based second dorsal and anal fins merging into a pointed tail fin. Four pairs of barbels surround the mouth, and a large serrated venomous spine is located in front of the first dorsal fin and each pectoral fin. Juveniles and sub-adults are black with a pale belly and two distinct white to yellowish stripes on each side. These fade in large adults, which reach a length of 33 cm.

Typical accidents
Usually only those who handle the fish – primarily fishermen and aquarists – get stung. Since schooling juveniles do not flee, they make a tempting target for a curious person to touch. This usually also results in a sting.

Prevention
Waders should keep an eye out for writhing dark balls and avoid them. Divers and snorkellers can get quite close but should avoid contact. Although eel catfishes are inoffensive, they will not hesitate to sting a hand inserted among them. Fishermen and aquarists should avoid handling them directly and be careful when landing the fish or emptying a net.

Venom
Little information is available. It appears to be proteinaceous, like most fish venoms. This substance, termed plototoxin, was extracted from the venom glands and injected into laboratory animals, which died swiftly. In laboratory tests, the venom had a corrosive effect on red blood cells as well as neurotoxic properties. There is no antivenom.

Envenomation and symptoms
A puncture is immediately followed by a violent stinging or throbbing pain, which may radiate up an affected limb and last over 48 hours. The area around the wound becomes ischaemic then cyanotic, and this is followed by redness and swelling.

Sample cases

1) While preparing a fresh specimen for a photograph, an ichthyologist was jabbed in the thumb by a pectoral spine. Three sharp tugs were needed to extricate the spine. The agonising pain became barely tolerable only after the thumb was placed in very hot water. After a four-hour soak, the thumb was removed and pethidine was administered. The digit remained unusable for two days. Another ichthyologist who had a similar experience was unable to use his thumb for over five months.

2) At the age of 15, one of the authors (RM) was stung on the thumb by a 2-cm juvenile that he had cupped in water in his hand. This was followed by an immediate sharp burning pain similar to that of a wasp sting. Within a few minutes, the thumb became quite swollen. An intense throbbing pain lasted for over an hour, followed by tenderness for at least a day.

In extreme cases there may be massive oedema of an entire limb and numbness around the wound. Shock may be indicated by faintness, weakness, nausea, rapid weak pulse, low blood pressure, clammy skin, respiratory distress or loss of consciousness; in rare cases, deaths have occurred. Severe wounds may take weeks to heal, and improper treatment may result in bacterial infections, gangrene and, possibly, tetanus.

Classification and distribution

The 37 known species of eel catfishes inhabit tropical to warm-temperate marine and estuarine waters of the Indo-Pacific and southern Australia, and fresh waters of Australia and New Guinea. Only one, the Striped Eel Catfish *Plotosus lineatus*, is widespread on coral reefs.

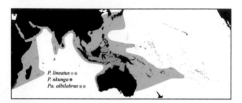

P. lineatus ●●
P. nkunga ●
Pa. albilabris ●●

Striped Eel Catfish	33 cm
Plotosus lineatus	*(13 in)*

Eel-like, 4 pairs of barbels; juveniles black with pale belly and 2 white stripes that fade with growth. **Biology:** inhabits estuaries, seagrass beds, and lagoon and coastal reefs, 1–60 m. Juveniles form dense ball-shaped schools. Adults in groups or solitary under ledges by day, in open at night. Feeds on small crustaceans, molluscs and fishes. Spawning occurs during the warmer months. Males construct nests under rocks and guard the large eggs (>3 mm). **Range:** Red Sea to Samoa, n. to s. Korea, s. to S. Africa and se. Australia. **Similar:** *P. nkunga* (S. Africa) has pale stripes; other species lack stripes.

Whitelipped Eel Catfish	134 cm
Paraplotusus albilabris	*(53 in)*

Eel-like, 4 pairs of barbels; dark brown, lips white; anterior nostril within upper lip; gets more elongate with growth. **Biology:** inhabits nearshore reefs and open coasts. Adults under ledges or in recesses, solitary or in small groups. **Range:** w. Indonesia to PNG, n. to Philippines, s. to sw. Australia and s. Gt Barrier Reef. **Similar:** many brown species in estuaries.

Sea Catfishes
Ariidae

Sea catfishes inhabit continental shelves and the lower reaches of rivers, primarily in the tropics. Most of the approximately 122 species are found in muddy coastal and estuarine waters. The largest species is 185 cm in length.

Behaviour
Sea catfishes feed on small bottom-dwelling animals that they detect and flush out with their barbels. Female sea catfishes spawn up to 55 very large eggs up to 25 mm in diameter. The male broods the eggs in its mouth for as long as two months and the newly hatched young for up to two weeks. Although rarely seen by divers, sea catfishes are often encountered by fishermen and many species are used as food.

Appearance
Sea catfishes are generally a drab silvery to brownish grey, have a rough bony plate on top of the head, a large forked tail and three large serrated venomous spines located in front of the dorsal fin and each pectoral fin. Although the venom is weak, wounds from the spines are extremely painful and susceptible to secondary infection. Permanent injury is possible.

Venom
The venom is not particularly potent and has not been studied.

Venom apparatus

The venom apparatus consists of three large serrated spines (shown in red) and associated glandular tissue, axillary glands (blue) and a locking mechanism. Venom-producing glandular tissue is more concentrated along the outer portion of the spines. The long second dorsal spine is serrated along its front and back edges, and

has a locking mechanism made from a modified first dorsal spine. In some species such as Hardhead Catfish, shown here, the tip may be elongate and flexible, and is often damaged. Each pectoral spine has an axillary gland above its base, which opens to a pore. A hollow tube runs through each spine but does not appear to be associated with venom. Dorsal and left pectoral spines are shown here from the top and side.

Treatment

First aid
Clean and disinfect the wound. If bleeding occurs, use a bandage. If foreign particles remain in the wound or pain persists for more than a few hours, seek medical treatment.

What not to do
Do not use any hot water-treatment methods. Do not tamper with the wound.

Ongoing medical management
Any foreign particles should be removed. Antibiotics and tetanus prophylaxis are recommended to prevent secondary infection.

Envenomation and symptoms
The relatively mild venom of sea catfishes produces pain that usually subsides within 30 minutes. However, large sea catfishes are capable of producing severe and extremely painful lacerations and puncture wounds that can easily become infected. No deaths have been reported.

Classification and distribution
Sea catfishes inhabit continental shelves and the lower reaches of rivers, primarily in the tropics. Most of the approximately 122 species inhabit muddy coastal and estuarine waters.

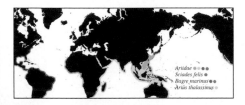

Hardhead Catfish	35 cm
Sciades felis	*(14 in)*

Dark blue-grey to brown, pale below; 2 pairs of chin barbels. **Biology:** over fine sand and mud bottoms of turbid coastal and estuarine waters. **Range:** NC to n. Yucatán; replaced by *S. assimilis* from e. Yucatán to Panama. **Similar:** most other species have 3 pairs of chin barbels and occur along tropical and warm-temperate coasts; Gafftopsail Catfish *Bagre marinus* has 1 pair of chin barbels, long filamentous dorsal and pectoral fin spines (100 cm; NC to s. Brazil, incl. w. Cuba); Coco Sea Catfish *B. bagre* has longer anal fin than *B. marinus* (55 cm; Colombia to Brazil).

Giant Sea Catfish	170 cm
Netuma thalassinus	*(67 in)*

3 pairs of chin barbels. **Biology:** Feeds primarily on crustaceans, occasionally on cephalopods, fishes, echinoids and detritus. A food fish. **Range:** Red Sea to PNG, n. to s. China, s. to se. Australia. **Similar:** many *Netuma* spp.; expert advice often required to identify to species level.

A Sapo Cano closely matches its surroundings and can easily be stepped on. *I. Cubangua, PH*

Venomous Toadfishes
Batrachoididae, subfamily Thalassophryninae

Toadfishes are large-headed, large-mouthed bottom-dwellers, and are armed with two or three stout dorsal fin spines and one to three pairs of opercular or sub-opercular spines. In members of the subfamily Thalassophryninae, these spines are hollow and venomous. Some of the non-venomous species can also inflict painful wounds or have toxic mucus (p.233). The venomous species are restricted to Central and South America, where they pose a hazard to fishermen and anyone wading in bare feet. In some areas they are eaten as a food fish.

Behaviour
Venomous toadfishes are ambush predators that spend much of their time buried in sediment. They spawn a few hundred relatively large eggs (5–6 mm), which are guarded by the male. Newly hatched juveniles remain near or on an adult, indicating further parental care.

Appearance
Venomous toadfishes have large, somewhat flattened heads with upward-directed eyes, large mouths and large, fan-like pectoral fins, and are scaleless. These features are adaptations for ambushing prey from below, and are also present in stargazers (p.166) and stonefishes (p.67). As described above, their dorsal fin spines and opercular spines are hollow and connected to large venom glands.

Typical accidents
Accidents most frequently occur when a wader steps on a buried toadfish. Those who handle toadfishes are occasionally stung, either when removing them from nets or preparing them for a meal.

IF INJURED

Treatment

First aid
Clean and disinfect the wound. If bleeding occurs, use a bandage. If foreign particles remain in the wound or pain persists for more than a few hours, seek medical treatment.

What not to do
Avoid hot-water treatments. Do not tamper with the wound.

Ongoing medical management
The wound should be carefully cleaned to remove any foreign particles. Antibiotics are recommended owing to the danger of secondary infection.

Prevention
Wearing shoes and shuffling one's feet along the bottom is advised when wading in shallow sandy or muddy areas frequented by venomous toadfishes.

Venom
The single study of the *Thalassophryne* venom indicated that it has both proteolytic and neurotoxic properties. There is no antivenom.

Symptoms
Intense radiating pain develops rapidly, followed by swelling, redness and heat, sensations said to be similar to a scorpion sting. Secondary bacterial infection is possible, and in one unusual case a victim remained ill for five months.

Classification and distribution
The subfamily Thalassophrynidae is restricted to continental shelves and rivers of Central and South America. Five species of *Thalassophryne* inhabit Atlantic coastal waters and one, *T. amazonica*, inhabits rivers of the Amazon Basin. Four species of *Daector* inhabit the eastern Pacific from Costa Rica to Peru, and one is found a Colombian river.

T. *maculosa* ◎
T. *megalops* ●
T. *montevidensis* ●
T. *nattereri* ◎
T. *punctata* ●
T. *amazonica* ◎
Daector spp. ◎

Venom apparatus

The stout dorsal and opercular spines of the Sapo Cano (shown in red) are hollow and connected basally to very large venom glands (blue). Pressure applied to the gland forces the venom through the spine. The detail shows the dorsal spine and left opercular spine with venom gland. *(Photo JR; diagram after Halstead, 1970)*

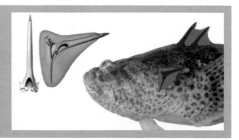

Sapo Cano	18 cm
Thalassophryne maculosa	*(7 in)*

Brown with dark mottling and pale, diffuse saddles; can adjust colours to match surroundings. **Biology:** inhabits sand and mud bottoms, shoreline to 200 m. Often partially buried. Feeds on small gastropods. **Range:** Colombia to Trinidad and coastal islands, incl. Aruba, Curaçao, I. Margarita and Tobago. **Similar:** *T. nattereri* has 3 dusky saddles (17 cm; Tobago to s. Brazil; below right); *T. megalops* has dark blotches (8 cm; G. of Darien, Panama, in 73–183 m).

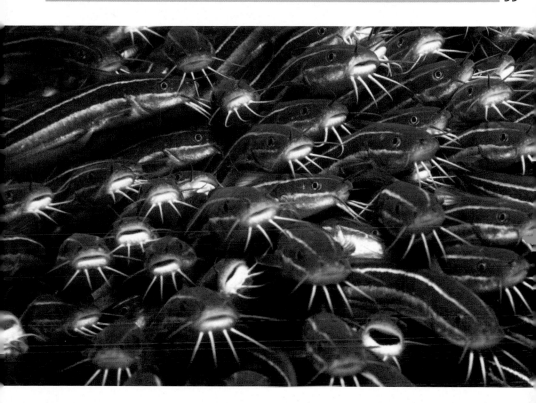

Scorpionfishes and their Relatives
Order Scorpaeniformes

What is a scorpionfish? To most divers, it is a well-camouflaged bottom-dwelling fish that is armed with venomous spines. Although accurate, this definition is far too simple. In reality, many scorpionfishes do not fit this description, and many species that do fit it are not scorpionfishes. In the broad sense, the name 'scorpionfish' has been applied to almost any of about 400 venomous species of the suborder Scorpaenoidei, but not to the 800 or so non-venomous species in the order Scorpaeniformes. Most of the venomous species were once lumped in one family, the Scorpaenidae, but have since been placed in families of their own. It is therefore more precise to reserve the scorpionfish name for the Scorpaenidae. Venomous scorpaenoid species range from cryptic bottom-dwellers to colourful mid-water swimmers, and they inhabit all seas to depths of over 2,200 m. Most have large bony heads armed with sharp spines, as well as stout venomous fin spines. All are carnivores. The species that are potentially dangerous to people visiting warm, shallow waters are distributed in seven families.

Rockfishes (Sebastidae)
Stocky, robust fishes with a large head and mouth. Primarily temperate to sub-arctic; many are important food fishes. Have internal fertilisation and bear live young. Venom not particularly potent but wounds can be quite painful. About 100 species, but only one, *Sebastiscus marmoratus*, inhabits coral reefs. It ranges from Japan to the northern Philippines (also the Sydney area, where possibly introduced) and is cultured for food in Japan.

Scorpionfishes (Scorpaenidae p.38)
Typically stout-bodied bottom-dwellers with large bony heads. Most species highly cryptic, with many skin flaps and tassels. Includes the colourful and conspicuous **lionfishes** (subfamily Pteroinae; p.53), which have greatly elongate fin spines and rays. About 140 species, most on rocky and coral reefs, others on soft bottoms. Many highly venomous. Some classifications include stonefishes, waspfishes and longfin waspfishes as subfamilies.

Stonefishes (Synanceiidae p.67)
Body type ranges from bulbous to typically fish-like. Includes stonefishes, **devilfishes** (subfamily Choridactylinae; p.75) and stingfishes. About 34 species, most on soft bottoms of shallow coastal waters and estuaries, a few on coral reefs. Most are highly venomous.

Longfin waspfishes (Apistidae p.65)
Typical fish-like shape with long wing-like pectoral fins, three chin barbels, small scales and no tassels. Three highly venomous species occur on soft bottoms.

Waspfishes (Tetrarogidae p.63)
Highly compressed, with dorsal fin originating in front of or over the eye and tiny, deeply embedded prickle-like scales. Inhabit coral reefs and shallow coastal and estuarine waters, with a few in fresh water. About 43 species, many highly venomous.

Velvetfishes (Aploactinidae p.81)
Similar to waspfishes, but with bristles instead of scales and unbranched fin rays. About 40 species in coastal and coral reef waters, all small and cryptic.

Orbicular Velvetfishes (Caracanthidae p.81)
Ovoid fishes covered with tiny tubercles. Five small species, living only in branching corals.

p37 overleaf: Examples of potentially dangerous scorpionfishes and their relatives. The fishes are proportionally scaled to the maximum size within the genus.

A Smallscale Scorpionfish among soft corals. *MB*

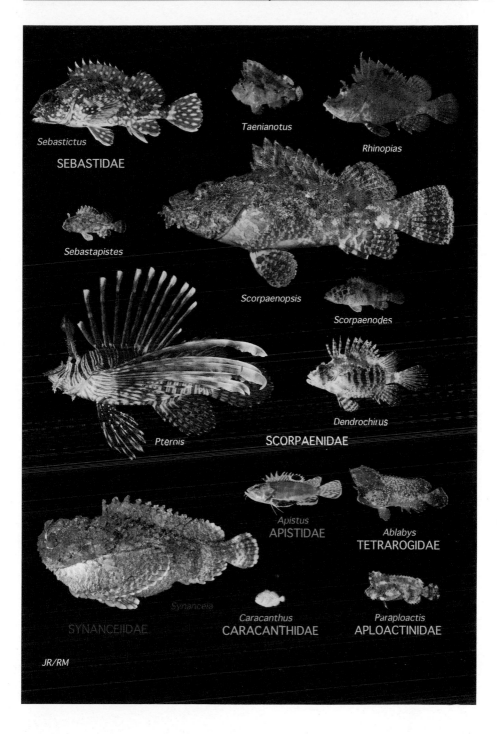

Taenianotus

Rhinopias

Sebastictus

SEBASTIDAE

Sebastapistes

Scorpaenopsis

Scorpaenodes

Pterois

Dendrochirus

SCORPAENIDAE

Apistus
APISTIDAE

Ablabys
TETRAROGIDAE

Synanceia

Caracanthus
CARACANTHIDAE

Paraploactis
APLOACTINIDAE

SYNANCEIIDAE

JR/RM

Scorpionfishes
Subfamily Scorpaeninae

Behaviour

Scorpionfishes are cryptic bottom-dwellers that often sit motionless for hours on end. Despite their sedate appearance, they can be astonishingly quick. They are ambush predators of fishes and crustaceans, relying on their camouflage to remain undetected. When prey gets within striking distance, it is sucked in by the vacuum created by the scorpionfish's cavernous mouth as it instantly opens and closes. Scorpionfishes typically swim in short bursts only when necessary. Many species emerge only at night to hunt by slowly stalking their prey. Scorpionfishes use their venomous spines primarily for defence, but some species use them on each other in territorial disputes. If approached too closely or prodded, scorpionfishes raise their spines in defence and may swim a short distance away or strike in a rapid burst. Most of the approximately 140 species occur on rocky and coral reefs, although some inhabit soft bottoms or deep mid-oceanic waters.

The cavernous mouth of this Smallscale Scorpionfish creates a vacuum that in sucks prey. *HF*

Appearance

Scorpionfishes have stout bodies, blunt heads with numerous short spines and protruding eyes, and large pectoral fins. They often have numerous fleshy tassels, especially on the head, and usually adapt their colour to match the surroundings. Typically, they are a mottled reddish brown. In some species the undersides of the pectoral fins are brightly coloured. These are flashed in a startling display that may deter predators by warning of the risk of envenomation, or distract them, thereby buying the scorpionfish time to escape. Depending on the species, scorpionfishes can measure anywhere between 3 cm and 50 cm in length.

Typical accidents

Scorpionfishes often remain unseen until it is too late. Most injuries to humans occur when they wade or jump into shallow water. Injuries to divers occur when they drift onto the bottom or place a hand on or near a scorpionfish. In regions where scorpionfishes are eaten, accidents occur when they are handled or cleaned. Scorpionfish venom remains potent for up to two days, especially when cooled. The thorn-like head spines do not contain venom, but can cause bleeding puncture wounds.

Prevention

When handling a scorpionfish, wear thick, sturdy gloves. Avoid direct contact with the spines altogether, since they can sometimes penetrate even leather gloves. When diving, be extremely careful before touching anything or making contact with the bottom. Use caution when closely approaching a scorpionfish and avoid prodding it.

Venom

Scorpionfish venom consists predominantly of various proteins. Laboratory analysis has revealed some of its effects and has isolated individual venom fractions. These effects include a rapid increase or drop in blood pressure and pulmonary oedema. The venom can also stimulate the body to release some of its own substances, such as acetylcholine, which acts on the junction between nerves and muscles, causing muscle spasms that result in pain.

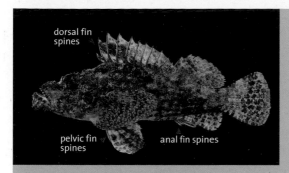

dorsal fin
spines

pelvic fin
spines

anal fin spines

The venomous dorsal spines are hidden by
tassels and disruptive coloration. *Red Sea, MB*

Venom apparatus

All of the fin spines (shown in red) are venomous. Depending on the species, there are 13
to 18 dorsal fin spines, usually three anal fin
spines and one spine in each pelvic fin, all
located along the front of the fins. Venom
(shown in blue) is produced by glandular tissue in longitudinal grooves along each side of
a spine, which is roughly T-shaped in cross section. Each spine is covered with a sheath-like
integumen from tip to base. When the spine is
thrust into a victim's flesh, this is compressed
or torn, allowing the venom to penetrate the
tissue. The venomosity of most scorpionfish
species is unknown and the spines of some,
such as the Leaf Scorpionfish *Taenianotus triacanthus*, may not be sharp enough to penetrate the skin or may not even be venomous.
*(Photo above left RM/JR; diagram above right
after Halstead, 1970)*

Envenomation and symptoms

When a spine penetrates the skin, the victim
immediately feels sharp pain. This can last for
several hours. Swelling usually occurs at the
injury site, and can spread to the entire limb and
last for several days. Secondary infection is possible but rarely occurs. General symptoms such
as nausea, sweating and heart palpitations are
also rare. There are no known cases of death as a
result of a scorpionfish sting. This does not
mean that it has never happened, but implies
that death by scorpionfish is exceptionally rare
or unrecognised.

Classification and distribution

Scorpionfishes occur in all tropical and warm-
temperate seas. The shallow-water species are
divisible into two subfamilies: the scorpionfishes (subfamily Scorpaeninae); and the
lionfishes (subfamily Pteroinae, p.53).

Tips for identification

Identifying scorpionfishes to species level can
be difficult, even for experts. Many vary greatly
in colour and ornamentation, so that individuals
of different species may more closely resemble
each other than those of their own kind.
Identifying some species, particularly certain
Scorpaenopsis, requires knowledge of such features as patterns of head spines, numbers of fin
rays and scale rows, and body proportions. In
some cases, identification by sight is possible
only by examining specimens. In areas where
there are only a few well-known species, this is
usually not necessary. For photographic identification, knowledge of the location is essential.

A beard of tassels helps disguise this Smallscale Scorpionfish. *Raja Ampat Is, RM*

Treatment

First aid

Leave the water immediately. If the pain and swelling are serious and persist for more than a few hours without abating, seek medical help.

What not to do

Do not apply a tourniquet, do not use the hot-water method and do not manipulate the wound in any way.

Ongoing medical management

Analgesic sprays have only a short-term effect. Clean and disinfect the wound to avoid secondary infection. If necessary, administer a tetanus prophylaxis. Complications from the wound seldom occur and can be treated in response to the symptoms.

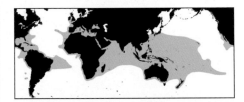

The bright pattern on the undersides of the pectoral fins of some species like this Flasher Scorpionfish is useful in identification. *Solomon Is, MB*

W. Atlantic Scorpionfishes

26 species, 16 in water shallower than 100 m but most of these rarely seen.

Spotted Scorpionfish	**45 cm**
Scorpaena plumieri	*(18 in)*

Underside of pectoral fin red and orange on outer part, black with white spots on inner. **Biology:** on sand, rubble, dead coral or among weeds of protected shallows as well as exposed reefs, 1–55 m. The most common scorpionfish in s. Florida and the Caribbean. When disturbed, flashes its brightly coloured pectoral fins. Its venom is potent. **Range:** NY and Bermuda through G. of Mexico and Caribbean to se. Brazil; St Helena, Ascension I.; also in E. Pacific.

Barbfish	**25 cm**
Scorpaena brasiliensis	*(10 in)*

Long, branched tentacle above eye; large dark spot above pectoral fin, underside with small dark spots; colour ranging from red to brown to yellow with small dark spots. **Biology:** on rubble and sand of protected inshore and seaward reefs, 1–91 m. Feeds on crustaceans and small fishes. Inflicts a painful sting. **Range:** VA through G. of Mexico and Caribbean to s. Brazil; not reported, but expected, from Bahamas. **Similar:** Plumed Scorpionfish *S. grandicornis* lacks dark spot above pectoral fin.

Mushroom Scorpionfish	**7.5 cm**
Scorpaena inermis	*(3 in)*

Light brown to red with pale mottling, reddish bands on pectoral fin; skin flaps over top of eye. **Biology:** on sand and under rubble, and in seagrasses beds, 0.4–73 m. May partially bury itself in sand. Feeds primarily on shrimps, also on other crustaceans and small fishes. **Range:** FL Keys, Bahamas and throughout Caribbean islands.

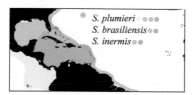

S. plumieri ●●●
S. brasiliensis ●●
S. inermis ●●

Mediterranean Scorpionfishes
Five Mediterranean species and another in the E. Atlantic.

Large-scaled Scorpionfish   50 cm
Scorpaena scrofa   (20 in)

First few dorsal spines very long with deeply incised membranes. **Biology:** on rocky bottoms, 10–300 m. Adults usually below 20 m. Moves to nearby sand at night to feed. A primary ingredient of the famous French soup bouillabaisse. **Range:** Medit., E. Atlantic from English Ch. to Senegal; Azores, Madeira, Canary Is, C. Verde Is.

Small Rockfish   20 cm
Scorpaena notata   (8 in)

Tentacle above eye poorly developed; a dark blotch at rear of spinous dorsal fin, usually red. **Biology:** on rocky, sand or mud bottoms, 5–700 m. Feeds on crustaceans and small fishes. **Range:** Medit., Black Sea, s. France to Senegal; Azores, Madeira, Canary Is. **Similar:** *S. porcus* has tiny white dots on lower body, is usually brown and has a well-developed tentacle above eye.

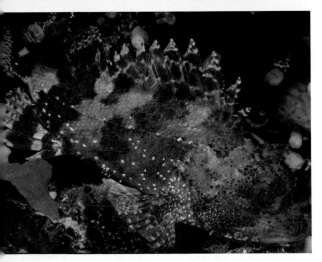

Black Scorpionfish   25 cm
Scorpaena porcus   (10 in)

Supraorbital tentacles long. **Biology:** on rock, sand or mud bottoms, 5–800 m. Feeds primarily at night. Breeds in late spring and summer. The eggs are embedded in a raft of transparent mucus. **Range:** Medit., Black Sea, s. Ireland to Senegal; Azores, Madeira and Canary Is.

notata ●●
porcus ●●●
scrofa ●●●

Indo-Pacific Scorpionfishes

More than 100 species, excluding lionfishes. The large reddish scorpionfishes most often encountered by
divers on well-developed coral reefs
are species of *Scorpaenopsis* – usually
S. oxycephala from the Red Sea to
Papua New Guinea, and *S. possi* from
most of Micronesia to French
Polynesia. On inshore coastal reefs of
the western Pacific, several species
may occur at the same site. For this
reason we include information on
snout length as well as scale row and
fin ray counts.

Tasselled Scorpionfish	36 cm
Scorpaenopsis oxycephala	*(14 in)*

Many tassels on head; snout long; scales
small, >62 rows; 19–20 pectoral rays; colour
highly variable. **Biology:** inhabits reef flats,
lagoons and seaward reefs, 1–43 m. Rests
on living corals, sponges, rubble, rock or
sand. The most common large scorpionfish
through most of its range. **Range:** Red Sea
to Gt Barrier Reef, n. to Taiwan. **Similar:**
S. papuensis (p.46) has larger scales (<55
rows), usually 19 pectoral rays; *S. possi*
(p.46), *S. ramaraoi* and *S. venosa* (p.46) have
shorter snouts, larger scales and fewer
pectoral rays (17–18).

Jenkins' Scorpionfish	51 cm
Scorpaenopsis cacopsis	*(20 in)*

Many tassels on head; snout long; colour
variable but usually reddish brown; the
largest species in genus. **Biology:** inhabits
rocky and coral reefs, usually in or near caves
or under ledges, 4–61 m. Feeds on fishes.
Highly prized food fish, uncommon in range
owing to overfishing. **Range:** Hawaiian Is.
Similar: Weedy Stingfish *S. cirrhosa*, *S. orien-
talis*, *S. oxycephala* (above) and *S. papuensis*
(p.46) share a long snout.

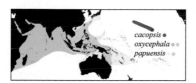

cacopsis ●
oxycephala ● ●
papuensis ●

Papuan Scorpionfish
Scorpaenopsis papuensis   25 cm (10 in)

Many tassels on head; snout long; usually 19 pectoral rays, 48–55 scale rows; often a white spot in pit behind eyes. **Biology:** inhabits coral and rocky areas from shallows to below 40 m. **Range:** Indonesia to Society Is, n. to the Ryukyus. **Similar:** *S. oxycephala* (p.45) has more pectoral rays and smaller scales, and is not found e. of PNG; *S. eschmeyeri*, *S. possi* (below), *S. ramaraoi* and *S. venosa* (below) have shorter snouts and fewer pectoral rays (17–18).

Raggy Scorpionfish
Scorpaenopsis venosa   24 cm (9.5 in)

Many tassels on head, usually a long, branched tentacle above eye; snout short, deep pit behind eyes; dorsal spines tall; usually 17 pectoral rays. **Biology:** mainly on open sand near reefs in protected coastal areas, 2–72 m. **Range:** se. Africa to e. Australia, n. to s. Japan; continental, not at mid-oceanic islands. **Similar:** other short-snouted species have shallower pit behind eyes.

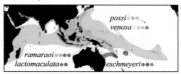

Spinycrown Scorpionfish
Scorpaenopsis possi   25 cm (10 in)

Many tassels on head; snout short; usually 17 pectoral rays. **Biology:** on rock and coral of channels and seaward reefs, 1–40 m. Feeds on fishes. Common from the Marianas to Fr. Polynesia. **Range:** Red Sea and E. Africa to Pitcairn Is, n. to Ryukyus; replaced by *S. eschmeyeri* from Gt Barrier Reef to Fiji. **Similar:** *S. venosa* (above) usually has long, branched tentacle above eye and deep pit behind eyes; *S. ramaraoi* has 18 pectoral rays (19 cm; Pakistan to New Caledonia, n. to Taiwan).

Bearded Scorpionfish   25 cm
Scorpaenopsis barbata   *(10 in)*

Snout short, its tip about an eye diameter in front of eye. **Biology:** inhabits areas of mixed sand and corals or among sea-grasses, 3–42 m. Feeds on fishes and crabs. **Range:** Red Sea to Arabian Gulf, s. to Somalia. **Similar:** other short-snouted species have larger scales and different head spine structure.

Flasher Scorpionfish   13 cm
Scorpaenopsis macrochir   *(5 in)*

Back slightly arched; may have colourful patches on skin; underside of pectoral fins yellow with orange- to red-edged black submarginal band. **Biology:** inhabits sand and rubble areas of reef flats and slopes, 0.3–80 m. Common. Enters brackish water. May bob head when disturbed. **Range:** Mauritius to Tuamotus, n. to Ryukyus. **Similar:** *S. neglecta* (below) has similar pectoral fin pattern, but less pronounced hump and a serrated bony ridge above the eyes.

Bandtail Scorpionfish   15 cm
Scorpaenopsis neglecta   *(6 in)*

Back slightly arched; underside of pectoral fins yellow with red-edged black submarginal band and black spots at fin base. **Biology:** inhabits open sand and mud bottoms of coastal reefs to 40 m. **Range:** Indonesia to nw. Australia, n. to s. Japan. **Similar:** Humpback Scorpionfish *S. gibbosa* is nearly identical (14 cm; E. Africa to Chagos Is and Mauritius).

Devil Scorpionfish   30 cm
Scorpaenopsis diabolus   *(12 in)*

Back highly arched; inner surface of pectoral fins with broad orange and yellow bands, also with many black spots in Hawaiian population. **Biology:** on rubble, sand, or coral of reef flats and lagoon and seaward reefs, 1–70 m. Feeds on small fishes. When disturbed, flashes bright undersides of pectoral fins. This is an effective warning that predators learn from experience. **Range:** Red Sea to Hawaii and Fr. Polynesia, n. to s. Japan. **Similar:** other humpbacked species have shorter snout, larger eyes and different pectoral fin flash patterns. Often misidentified as *Synanceia verrucosa* (p.71), which has warty skin and lacks pectoral fin flash pattern.

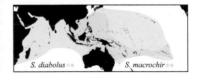

S. diabolus   *S. macrochir*

Decoy Scorpionfish   13 cm
Iracundus signifer   *(5 in)*

Front of dorsal fin resembles a small fish (inset). **Biology:** inhabits seaward reefs, 10–110 m. On sand and rubble under ledges, usually below 20 m. The only scorpionfish that uses its dorsal fin as a lure. When it wriggles the spines, the pigmented portion resembles a tiny fish that attracts the small fishes on which it feeds. **Range:** n. S. Africa, Mauritius; Taiwan, Ryukyus, Hawaiian Is; Coral Sea to Pitcairn Is.

I. signifer

Weedy Scorpionfish   23 cm
Rhinopias frondosa   (9 in)

All *Rhinopias* have a deep body, elevated eyes and upturned mouth. Tassels, colour and pattern variable, from yellow-brown to red to lavender, with or without bold circular markings. **Biology:** on rocks or reef patches of seaward reefs, 2–90 m. Creep along bottom on pectoral and pelvic fins, and may sway from side to side. Shed skin about every 13 days. **Range:** E. Africa to New Caledonia, n. to s. Japan. **Similar:** *R. aphanes* (below) has many spots, which are elongated into a paisley pattern.

Lacy Scorpionfish   23.5 cm
Rhinopias aphanes   (9.3 in)

Intricately branched tassels; colour from green to brown in bold paisley pattern. **Biology:** inhabits seaward reefs, 3–30 m. Mimics crinoids. **Range:** PNG to ne. Australia and New Caledonia. **Similar:** *R. frondosa* (above) has mostly circular spots and its tassels may be less developed.

R. frondosa ● ●
R. aphanes ●

Paddle-flap Scorpionfish   21 cm
Rhinopias eschmeyeri   (8.3 in)

Large paddle-like tentacle above eye, dorsal fin not incised, few tassels; colour from yellow to red and lavender. **Biology:** on open sand or among weeds of seaward reefs, 3–55 m. Shallow in areas of upwelling (<22°C). **Range:** Mauritius to Indonesia, n. to Philippines. **Similar:** *R. cea* (Easter Is. in 5 m), *R. xenops* (p.50) and some *R. frondosa* (above) have few tassels and branched tentacle above eye.

R. xenops ●
R. argoliba ●
R. cea ●
R. eschmeyeri ●

Strange-eyed Scorpionfish   20 cm
Rhinopias xenops   (8 in)

Tassels short; red to yellow with scattered pale and dark spots; front of dorsal fin slightly incised. **Biology:** seaward reefs, below 15 m in s. Japan and 36 m at Midway, but below 51 m to at least 124 m in main Hawaiian Is. **Range:** s. Japan and Hawaiian Is. only. **Similar:** *R. cea* and Japanese Scorpionfish *R. argoliba* have few tassels, *R. argoliba* is bright red with white streak below eye (17 cm; s. Japan and s. Coral Sea in 50–70 m).

Ambon Scorpionfish   12 cm
Pteroidichthys amboinensis   (4.8 in)

Huge tentacle above each eye; eyes high on head, mouth upturned; many branched tassels; colour variable, yellow to brown to red. **Biology:** on sand and mud bottoms, 3–50 m. Creeps along bottom with pectoral and pelvic fins. **Range:** Red Sea (?); w. Indonesia to Fiji, n. to Ryukyus, s. to Coral Sea. **Similar:** *Rhinopias* spp. have deeper bodies and smaller eye tentacles.

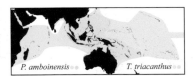

P. amboinensis   *T. triacanthus*

Leaf Scorpionfish   12 cm
Taenianotus triacanthus   (4.8 in)

Body deep and compressed, skin with prickly papillae instead of scales, dorsal spines feeble; usually yellowish green to brown, occasionally pink or white. **Biology:** on rubble, coral or rocks of sheltered and exposed reefs, 1–134 m. Mimics a leaf or blade of algae by swaying from side to side. Periodically sloughs off its outer layer of skin. Spines unlikely to cause a wound, possibly non-venomous. **Range:** E. Africa to the Galápagos Is, n. to the Ryukyu and Hawaiian Is.

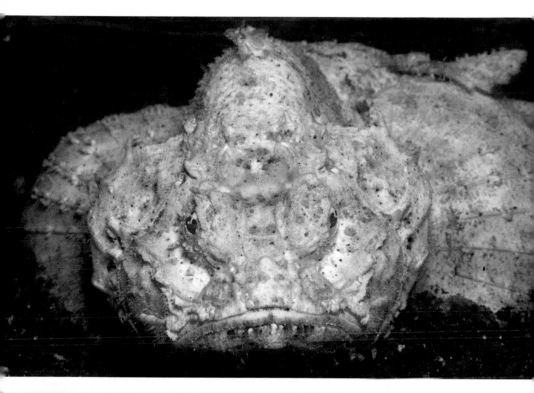

Lionfishes
Subfamily Pteroinae

Behaviour

Also called firefishes, turkeyfishes or zebrafishes, lionfishes are unmistakably elegant, with their wide, fan-like pectoral fins and tall, pennant-like dorsal spines. Unusually active for scorpionfishes, they spend considerable time well above the bottom. They move slowly and majestically with few fin movements or calmly hover, often in protected hollows. Lionfishes are encountered either singly or in small groups. They usually hunt at dusk with a calm, purposeful demeanor. Their typical hunting technique is to use their outstretched fins to manoeuvre a small fish into a corner. Once in a suitable position, their quarry is sucked into the mouth in the blink of an eye. At some popular dive sites, lionfishes have learned to take advantage of the disorienting effect of night divers' lights on prey. They may follow a diver like a pack of friendly dogs, grabbing snacks along the way.

With the exception of rare territorial disputes, lionfishes use their venomous fin spines solely for defence. They are generally fearless and will stand their ground or even move aggressively towards a diver who gets too close. Although there are several species of lionfish, two that are large and conspicuous are most often seen and well studied. These are *Pterois volitans* and *P. miles*, respectively known as the Red Lionfish and Common Lionfish. The discussion below applies to both species.

Appearance

With their wide, feathery pectoral fins, tall, pennant-like dorsal spines and contrasting colour pattern, lionfishes are truly majestic. The effect is enhanced by the motion of the fin membranes, which flutter as they move. Lionfishes are usually reddish brown with narrow white bars and banded pectoral fins, but some may be unusually red or even black with partially obscured white bars. With eyes set high on the head and a cleft in the upper jaw, they have a certain look of majesty, which is likely the inspiration for their name. Lionfishes are typically between 10 cm and 20 cm long, but may grow as large as 43 cm.

Lionfishes are fearless and will readily approach a diver. *Egypt, MB*

Typical accidents

Unlike most other fishes, lionfishes are not at all shy and may approach a diver closely as they maintain their course. It is not uncommon for a diver to be surprised by a lionfish that has come within touching distance. Injuries can occur if the diver attempts to drive it off, or accidentally bumps into it. If a lionfish thinks it is cornered, it may attack by arching its back and thrusting its spines forward. Some injuries are light, with little or no venom injected, but occasionally they may be serious. Most accidents from lionfishes seem to occur with captive fish, to hands put into an aquarium or when the animals are being handled. Even a tame pet lionfish may occasionally feel threatened and surprise its owner with a jab of its spine.

Prevention

The best protection is to maintain a respectful distance. Should a lionfish swim too close, move cautiously away. While most divers know to avoid contact, they should also be aware of a lionfish's potential for aggression. An arched back with spines pointing forward is a warning that may not be seen until it is too late. When working in an aquarium, a lionfish should either be removed with a net or separated by a barrier.

A Red Lionfish hunts with pectoral fins spread to block the escape of its prey. *Sulawesi, RM*

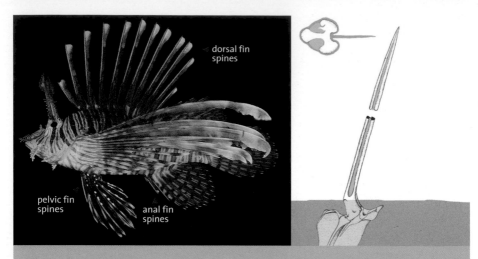

dorsal fin spines

pelvic fin spines

anal fin spines

Venom apparatus

The venom is contained in the rigid spines at the front of the dorsal, anal and pelvic fins (shown here in red). There are 12 to 13 in the dorsal fin, three in the anal fin and one in each pelvic fin. The flexible rays, including the feather-like rays of the pectoral fin, lack venom and are harmless. Each spine has a pair of lateral grooves along the outer two-thirds of its length; these contain glandular tissue that produces venom (blue). Both the spines and glandular tissue are covered by a thin membrane, which rips open when they enter the victim's tissue. This releases the venom from the gland into the wound. Since the spines are smooth, they generally do not break off, leaving the wound relatively clean.

IF INJURED

Treatment

First aid

Remove the victim from the water and try to calm him. Envenomation is not usually as serious as is often thought. If pain becomes excruciating, complications arise from swelling or infection sets in, see a doctor.

What not to do

Do not use any hot-water methods and do not apply a bandage. Do not dig into the wound.

Ongoing medical management

The injured person may overreact. If this is the case, use of a calming agent such as benzodiazepine is advisable. A lidocaine injection to treat the immediate pain usually results only in temporary relief. Due to the puncture form of the wound, there is no truly effective method of cleaning it. Should a secondary infection arise, antibiotics are recommended.

Venom

A lionfish's venom contains a high concentration of the neurotransmitter acetylcholinease, as well as a toxin (a protein) that sets acetylcholine free at the junction between nerves and muscles. This causes painful muscle spasms.

Envenomation and symptoms

Envenomation results in an immediate burning pain that rapidly spreads and may include the whole limb. The area surrounding the puncture site swells and the skin reddens. This oedema may last for several days and small blisters may form. General symptoms such as nausea, vomiting, heart palpitations and feelings of weakness are rare, and are usually physical reactions to the pain. Secondary infection is also rare. Although envenomation may be extremely painful, it is not as dangerous as is often supposed. Alleged fatalities are unconfirmed.

Distribution

There are 20 species of lionfish in five genera. Half are members of the genus *Pterois*, while

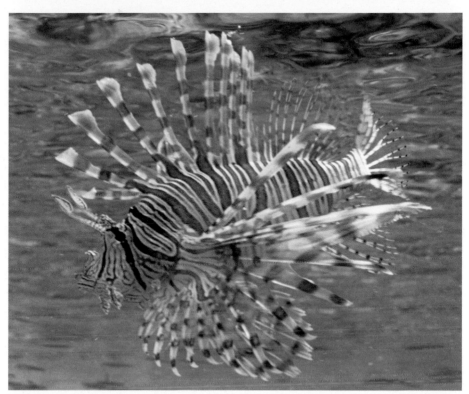

Lionfishes often swim well above the bottom, where divers can bump into them. *MB*

Sample cases

1) In an attempt to make a lionfish move, a woman put her hand into an aquarium. As she coaxed it, she was stung on the forefinger. The burning pain was so excrutiating that she went to hospital. Ice was used to cool the finger. Approximately 13 hours later, the hand remained swollen and painful, so a surgeon cut the finger along its entire length and washed the wound. The finger later stiffened as a result of a joint fibrosis. Even after a year and despite physiotherapy, movement of the finger was restricted. The underlying cause was not the envenomation but the innapropriate surgery. Furthermore, it was unnecessary as it was based on the false hypothesis that the deep surgical cut would assist the release of the venom. The healing of untreated stings usually takes place without complication.

2) While taking photographs, a diver remained nearly motionless as he crouched 2 m away from a large patch of reef on open sand. During this time, three lionfishes drifted curiously towards him from a coral head. As they hovered only a few centimetres away, he carefuly attempted to drive one off with a slight, calm hand movement. The lionfish responded by giving him a short, quick jab into the thigh with its foremost dorsal spine. Since the immediate pain was not great, the diver surfaced calmly. The pain had completely disappeared within a few hours, and the skin redness disappeared after one or two days. No treatment was undertaken and no complications arose during the swift healing process.

Both the Common Lionfish *Pterois miles* and Red Lionfish *P. volitans* sometimes have eyspots on leaf-like extensions of the tentacles above their eyes. *Red Sea, RM*

the remainder are smaller and less conspicuous. All are indigenous to the Indo-Pacific.

Mediterranean and North American invasions
The opening of the Suez Canal has enabled nearly 100 species of Red Sea fishes to expand their ranges into the western Mediterranean, where they now have stable breeding populations. The Common Lionfish *Pterois miles* is among them and is now established in rocky areas along the Israeli coast. In the US, the Red Lionfish *P. volitans* has been a popular aquarium fish for over 40 years and is imported primarily from the Philippines. Either by accident or design, this species is now resident in south-eastern US waters and throughout the Bahamas (red dots on map). The first individuals were observed in Biscayne Bay, Miami, in 1992 after the destruction of waterfront homes by Hurricane Andrew. Others soon appeared at dive sites off Palm Beach. In 2004, fisheries officials documented stable breeding populations on offshore wrecks as far north as North Carolina where winter waters remain above 15°C. Not surprisingly, a diver there has already been stung. The warm Gulf Stream has also

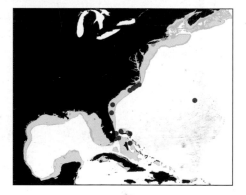

carried the species to Bermuda, and in the Bahamas it is spreading to the south and east. Juveniles have been found off Long Island and Rhode Island at the end of summer (orange dots), but these are doomed when the water cools in autumn. Individuals of several other ornamental species have also been found off south-eastern Florida, but so far none seems to be breeding successfully.

Red Lionfish	43 cm
Pterois volitans	*(16.9 in)*

Red to black with pairs of narrow white bars; 14 pectoral rays, mostly free and pennant-like. **Biology:** inhabits lagoon and seaward reefs from turbid inshore areas to offshore banks, shoreline to below 50 m. Common. Often hangs under ledges by day, but may also actively forage. Feeds primarily at night on small fishes, shrimps and crabs. Uses pectoral fins to corral prey. Attracted by divers' lights, which distract prey. Will stand its ground if harassed and may charge divers with dorsal spines pointing forward. Can inflict extremely painful wounds. **Range:** G. of Thailand to Marquesas and Pitcairn Is, n. to s. Japan and s. Korea, s. to n. NZ; introduced and established in se. US, Bahamas and Bermuda. **Similar:** *P. miles* (below) has 1 fewer soft dorsal and anal fin rays (10 vs 11 and 6 vs 7); other species have either 13 pectoral rays or few or no spots on soft dorsal, anal and tail fins.

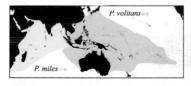

Common Lionfish	38 cm
Pterois miles	*(15 in)*

Red to black with pairs of narrow bars; 14 pectoral rays, mostly free and pennant-like. **Biology:** inhabits lagoons, bays and seaward reefs, shoreline to 60 m. Common near ledges, caves and in wrecks. Prey, hunting methods and defensive posturing as for *P. volitans* (above). Can also inflict extremely painful wounds. **Range:** Red Sea to Sumbawa, s. to S. Africa; recent migrant to w. Medit. **Similar:** *P. volitans* (above) has 1 more soft dorsal and anal fin rays.

Longspine Lionfish   40cm
Pterois andover   *(16 in)*

Rear dorsal spines taller than in other spp.;
13 pectoral rays, soft dorsal, anal and tail
fins with a few black spots. **Biology:** inhabits mud and fine-sand bottoms of estuaries and coastal waters, 3–30 m. Often near
logs and debris. This species still awaits
formal description. **Range:** Flores, Banda
Sea and Moluccas in Indonesia. **Similar:**
other species have shorter dorsal spines;
P. miles and *P. volitans* (p.57) have 14 pectoral rays and many black spots on soft
median fins; *P. kodipungi* and *P. russelli*
(below) lack spots on soft median fins.

Kodipungi Lionfish   35 cm
Pterois kodipungi   *(14 in)*

13 pectoral rays; soft median fins with few
or no black spots. **Biology:** on mud or fine-
sand bottoms of estuaries and coasts,
3–35 m. **Range:** Sumatra to Bali, Indonesia.
Similar: *Pterois* sp. (above) has longer dorsal
spines; *P. russelli* (below) has broader pale
bars; *P. miles* and *P. volitans* (p.57) have dark
spots on median fins and 14 pectoral rays.

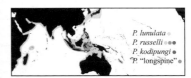

P. lunulata ○
P. russelli ○●●
P. kodipungi ●
P. "longspine" ●

Plaintail Lionfish   30 cm
Pterois russellii   *(12 in)*

Reddish brown with pairs of broad pale
bars; pectoral fin with spots or narrow
jagged bars merging into pale belly; usually 13 rays; soft median fins without black
spots. **Biology:** on open sand or mud bottoms, 5–60 m. **Range:** Red Sea to n.
Australia, n. to Philippines. **Similar:**
P. lunulata (p.59) has larger, highly visible
scales in 50–60 vertical rows; other clear-
tailed species have more heavily pigmented pectoral fins. The relationship
between this species, *P. lunulata* and
P. kodipungi (above) needs further study.

Japanese Lionfish
Pterois lunulata

30 cm)
(12 in)

Brown with pairs of broad pale stripes merging into pale belly; scales clearly visible; usually 13 pectoral rays; soft median fins with dark spots only in large adults. **Biology:** on rocky reefs and open sand or mud bottoms, 10–42 m. A food fish, marketed with spines removed. **Range:** s. China to Korea and n. Japan, possibly s. to Indonesia and New Caledonia. **Similar:** *P. russelli* (p.58) has smaller, less visible scales (65–80 rows) and unspotted median fins.

Clearfin Lionfish
Pterois radiata

24 cm
(9.6 in)

Pectoral rays white and mostly free and filamentous; base of tail with two thin white stripes. **Biology:** inhabits reef flats, lagoons and seaward reefs, 1–25 m. Solitary or in small groups in crevices, caves or under ledges by day, sometimes with *P. antennata* (below). Feeds primarily at night, mainly on small crabs and shrimps. Numbers variable: common in Red Sea, less common in most other areas. **Range:** Red Sea to Society Is, n. to Ryukyus, s. to S. Africa and New Caledonia.

Spotfin Lionfish
Pterois antennata

20 cm
(7.9 in)

Pectoral rays filamentous, connected basally by membrane with dark round spots. **Biology:** inhabits lagoon and seaward reefs, 1 m to at least 50 m. Usually under ledges and in holes, solitary or in small groups. Usually inactive during the day. Forages for shrimps and crabs in late afternoon and at night. Common. **Range:** E. Africa to Fr. Polynesia, n. to s. Japan, s. to se. Australia. **Similar:** *P. mombasae* (p.60) has shorter, partially banded pectoral rays.

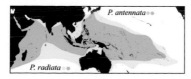

African Lionfish   19 cm
Pterois mombasae   *(7.5 in)*

Pectoral fin rays filamentous at ends, membrane with many dark spots. **Biology:** on hard bottoms of deep seaward reefs, 10 m to at least 60 m. Usually in areas rich in soft corals and sponges, rarely above 20 m. **Range:** Red Sea to PNG, s. to S. Africa and nw. Australia. **Similar:** *P. antennata* (p.59) has longer unbarred pectoral rays, fewer spots on pectoral fin membrane.

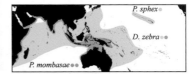

Hawaiian Lionfish   21 cm
Pterois sphex   *(8.3 in)*

Outer pectoral rays filamentous, membranes with spots in juveniles, concentric bands in adults. **Biology:** inhabits lagoon and seaward reefs. In caves or under ledges by day, usually upside down or vertical with head down. Roams the reef at night to feed primarily on small crabs and shrimps. The only *Pterois* in Hawaii. A sting on the hand was compared to having one's fingers repeatedly hit by a hammer. **Range:** Hawaiian Is. **Similar:** none co-occurring, *P. antennata* (p.59) of all sizes have dark round spots on pectoral fins.

Zebra Lionfish   20 cm
Dendrochirus zebra   *(7.9 in)*

Pectoral fin fan-like, some rays branched; body with light bars as in *Pterois*; longest dorsal spines taller than body. **Biology:** inhabits sheltered coastal reefs, 1–73 m. Typically on isolated coral heads, sponges or encrusted rocks, often hangs upside down. Feeds on crabs, shrimps and small fishes, in late afternoon and night. Males aggressively defend territories containing several females. Courtship and spawning occur at night. Spawns pelagically, leaving gelatinous mass of 2,000–15,000 eggs to drift in current. **Range:** central Red Sea and E. Africa to Samoa, n. to Ryukyus.

Shortfin Lionfish
Dendrochirus brachypterus   15 cm (5.9 in)

Pectoral fin fan-like, inner surface with concentric dark bands; usually brown, occasionally primarily yellow or red. **Biology:** inhabits reef flats and lagoon and coastal reefs, 2–80 m. Typically on isolated coral heads or weed-encrusted rocks, often hangs upside down. Solitary or in harems of up to 10. At night, actively roams the reef for small crustacean prey. **Range:** Red Sea to Samoa, n. to Ryukyus. **Similar:** *D. bellus* has larger scales and is red with broad pale bars (s. Japan, Taiwan and New Caledonia).

Green Lionfish
Dendrochirus barberi   16.5 cm (6.5 in)

Pectoral fin fan-like; greenish brown, eyes red. **Biology:** inhabits shallow sheltered reefs, 1 m to over 9 m. Common on inner reef flats. Usually perched at bases of coral heads and encrusted rocks, often upside down. Wounds reported to be extremely painful. **Range:** Hawaiian Is.

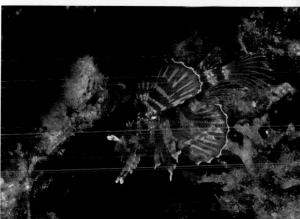

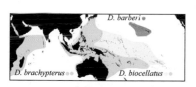

Two-spot Lionfish
Dendrochirus biocellatus   10.5 cm (4.2 in)

Soft-rayed dorsal fin with pair of conspicuous ocelli, inner pectoral fins with 3 concentric dark bands; long tentacle at corners of upper lip; dorsal spines shorter than body depth. Reaches 16 cm in s. Japan. **Biology:** inhabits areas of rich coral growth and clear water, 1 m to at least 40 m. Very secretive by day, but active and more exposed at night. **Range:** Mauritius to Society Is, n. to s. Japan; s. to nw. Australian continental shelf.

Blackfoot Lionfish   23 cm
Parapterois heterura   *(9 in)*

Pectoral fin fan-like, inner surface mostly black with electric-blue streaks; dorsal spines with filaments. **Biology:** inhabits mud and sand bottoms, 3–300 m. May partially bury in sediment. **Range:** G. of Aden to se. Africa; Indonesia to s. Japan. **Similar:** *P. macrura* (15 cm; w. India, below 75 m).

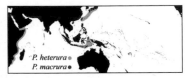

Bleeker's Lionfish   22 cm
Ebosia bleekeri   *(8.8 in)*

Centres of pale bars sometimes with 2 spots; pectoral fin fan-like, rays connected by membrane; adults with bony crest behind eyes, which becomes divided and may extend past first dorsal fin spines. **Biology:** on sand and mud in areas of moderate current, 10–85 m. A warm-temperate species, generally found in areas of cool upwelling in the tropics. **Range:** Indonesia to e. Australia, n. to central Japan. **Similar:** *E. falcata* has narrower crest (14 cm; E. Africa and s. India, below 47 m).

Pygmy Lionfish   12 cm
Brachypterois serrulata   *(5 in)*

Pectoral fins fan-like but smaller than in other lionfishes, dorsal fin low; cryptic with obscure bars. A link between lionfishes and other scorpionfishes. **Biology:** inhabits silty sand and mud bottoms of sheltered estuaries and coastal reefs, 3–40 m. Shelters in holes in sediment. **Range:** s. Red Sea to PNG, n. to s. Japan, s. to nw. Australia.

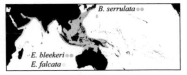

Waspfishes
Tetrarogidae

Waspfishes differ from scorpionfishes by the position of the dorsal fin, which originates in front of or over the eye, and by having tiny, deeply embedded prickle-like scales. Many of the species are highly venomous. Waspfishes inhabit primarily soft bottoms and feed on small fishes and crustaceans. At least 28 species occur in shallow tropical waters of the Indo-Pacific. Several others occur below 200 m or in temperate areas of South Africa, Australia and Asia, and a few inhabit fresh water. Waspfishes pose a danger primarily to fishermen as they remove them from nets. A few species are popular as aquarium fishes and with divers visiting 'muck' sites. Some experts consider waspfishes to lie within the scorpionfish family as their venom apparatus and venom are similar. Typical accidents, symptoms and treatment are also the same.

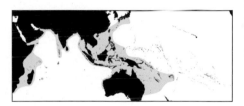

Like many waspfishes, the Cockatoo Waspfish (top and above) is variable in colour, sometimes with a sharply contrasting face. *Sulawesi, RM (top); HF*

Cockatoo Waspfish
Ablabys taenianotus
15 cm
(6 in)

Dorsal fin sail-like with 17–18 spines, anal fin with 4–5 rays; yellow to dark brown, face sometimes contrasting. **Biology:** on protected mud, sand or rubble bottoms, 1–80 m. Solitary or in pairs. Sways to mimic a dead leaf. **Range:** Andaman Sea to Fiji, n. to s. Japan; s. to se. Australia. **Similar:** *A. macracanthus* (below) has 15–16 dorsal spines, 7–8 anal rays; Redskinfish *A. binotatus* has 15 dorsal spines (e. Africa to Seychelles); dorsal fin of *Tetraroge* spp. starts above rear of eyes.

Spiny Waspfish
Ablabys macracanthus
18 cm
(7 in)

Dorsal fin with 15–16 spines, anal fin with 7–8 rays; dark brown to nearly white with dark face and chin. **Biology:** on mud or sand of coastal waters, 8–50 m. Solitary or in pairs, sways to mimic a dead leaf. **Range:** Maldives to Moluccas, n. to Ryukyus. **Similar:** Redskinfish *A. binotatus* has 5 anal rays; *A. taenianotus* (above) has 17–18 dorsal spines, 4 or 5 anal rays.

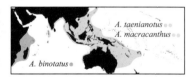

A. taenianotus
A. macracanthus
A. binotatus

Longspine Waspfish
Paracentropogon longispinis
10 cm
(4 in)

Dorsal spines deeply incised; 3 spines in series on cheek, the last 2 large; colour variable, in earth tones with fine mottling and blotches, face can be abruptly pale. **Biology:** on sand and rubble and in seagrass beds of coastal reefs, shoreline to 70 m. **Range:** s. India to New Caledonia, n. to Taiwan. **Similar:** *P. vespa* and at least 3 other species in genus, some of which may be same as this.

Whitebellied Rougefish | 8 cm
Richardsonichthys leucogaster (3 in)

Dorsal spines deeply incised, more so in front; eyes large, 2 pairs spines above upper lips, vertical row of large spines on pre-opercle. **Biology:** on mud and sand of coastal reefs, 3–90 m. Solitary. May partially bury itself. Dangerous. **Range:** E. Africa to New Caledonia, n. to s. China. **Similar:** juvenile *Paracentropogon longispinis* (p.64) may look similar.

R. leucogaster

Longfin Waspfishes
Apistidae

Longfin waspfishes are unusual scorpaenoids. They have typical fish-like bodies with small scales; three chin barbels; broad, rounded, soft-rayed fins; and long, wing-like pectoral fins used to flash a warning. They bury themselves in sediment by day and emerge at night to feed. The three known species are highly venomous. The venom apparatus and venom are similar to those of scorpionfishes, as are typical accidents, symptoms and treatment.

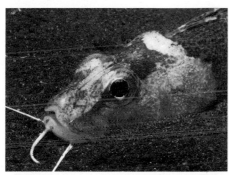

A. carinatus
A. caloundra
C. tridactyla

Longfin waspfishes typically lie partially buried. The chin barbels are used to locate hidden prey. *HF*

Bearded Waspfish | 18 cm
Apistus carinatus (7 in)

Front of jaw with 3 barbels; vertical fins boldly marked in black and white, a large black ocellus at rear of spinous dorsal fin, pectoral fins long, inner surface light green. **Biology:** on mud to fine-sand bottoms, shoreline to 60 m. Rests partially buried. Highly venomous. **Range:** Red Sea to PNG, n. to Japan, s. to e. Australia. **Similar:** *Apistops caloundra* has longer snout, denticulations on head (12 cm; w. Papua to n. and e. Australia); *Cheroscorpaena tridactyla* lacks chin barbels (n. Australia and s. New Guinea).

Stonefishes
Synanceiidae

Behaviour

Few people see stonefishes. They are masters of disguise, able to camouflage themselves so well that only the trained eye can spot them. They employ a simple but effective lie-in-wait hunting strategy. With incredible patience, they sit completely still, sometimes in the same spot for days. When a suitable fish, crab or shrimp gets close enough, the stonefish strikes with incredible speed: within 0.0015 seconds its huge mouth opens and the prey is sucked in to fill the ensuing vacuum. Then it's back to normal. The stonefish lies seemingly inanimate among corals, rock or buried in sand, its presence revealed only by the curve of its mouth or the twitch of an eye. Its venomous spines are revealed only when it is disturbed and used only in self-defence.

Appearance

The stonefish species usually encountered by divers, the Reef Stonefish *Synanceia verrucosa*, has a bulbous body and a large head with small, inconspicuous eyes. Its distinctive vertically oriented mouth is adapted for sucking in prey from above, and distinguishes it from most scorpionfishes, which have a mouth that projects forward (p.70). Its pectoral fins are large and fleshy, and its thick, scaleless skin is covered with wart-like growths. Thirteen to 14 sharp dorsal fin spines, as well as three anal fin spines and a single pelvic fin spine, lie hidden beneath warty sheaths. The globular shape, uneven skin and variable coloration render stonefishes nearly invisible by perfectly matching their surroundings. Although usually a reddish brown to grey, stonefishes resting among algae-covered stones or seagrasses may be greenish or even have algae growing on them.

Typical accidents

Finding a stonefish, either accidentally or intentionally, usually happens only by chance. Stonefishes are not shy and, when approached, show no fear and do not retreat. They trust their natural camouflage and simply stay put. Only rough prodding or persistent disturbance can prompt them to move, and when they do, it is usually less than a metre. Stonefishes are most common in the shallows and often lie buried in sand, sometimes with only their eyes exposed. They seem to prefer to be near the shelter of a ledge, rocks or coral, but occasionally occur on open sand or among seagrass. This is when they pose the greatest hazard to waders. When stepping directly on a stonefish, a wader's full weight drives the spines deep into the foot, causing a full load of venom to be injected. Injuries to fingers and hands occur when captive animals are handled or when divers nudge or prod the fish.

Prevention

Although the spines of a stonefish can penetrate the soles of most shoes, always wear footwear since it offers better protection than going barefoot. Always watch where you step. If wading in sandy areas, proceed slowly while shuffling your feet, as this may allow you to feel a buried stonefish and stop before you step directly on a raised spine. Likewise, divers and swimmers should look carefully before touching the bottom. Never play with or provoke these seemingly sluggish creatures, as they can move surprisingly fast.

A rock with eyes? This stonefish's camouflage is enhanced by algae growing on it. *Red Sea, MK*

Most accidents are the result of an unsuspecting wader stepping directly on a stonefish. *Bali, MK*

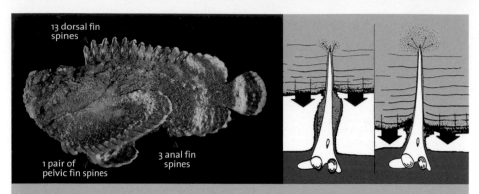

13 dorsal fin spines

1 pair of pelvic fin spines

3 anal fin spines

Venom apparatus

Stonefishes have the best-developed venom apparatus of all the Scorpaenidae. It consists of 12 to 14 dorsal fin spines, three anal fin spines and a pair of pelvic fin spines, each with asscociated venom glands. The spines (shown in red) are sharp and stout with a deep groove running up each side. Attached to each groove is an extremely large venom gland (blue), which terminates in a narrow duct that runs up the groove and opens at the spine tip. The spines are surrounded by a thick warty sheath of skin. The anal and pelvic fin spines are thinner and have smaller venom glands than the dorsal spines. Each dorsal spine contains approximately 0.03 mL of venom. When pressure is applied, the pale blue venom is expelled from the glands and into the wound. *(Photo JR/RM)*

IF INJURED

Treatment

First aid

Get out of the water immediately and seek medical help as quickly as possible.

What not to do

Do not wrap any bandages around the wound. Do not attempt to remove or cut out the spines or tissue, and do not attempt to cauterise the wound.

Ongoing medical management

An antivenom to treat stonefish envenomation does exist but is currently available only in Australia and dispensable only by a doctor. Whether it is dispensed at all and, if so, in what dosage depends on the severity and progression of the envenomation. One unit of the antivenom neutralises 0.01 mg of the stonefish venom. The spine's two venom glands contain 5–10 mg of venom. One vial of antivenom contains 2 mL and 2,000 units, meaning that it can neutralise 20 mg of venom. This corresponds to a sting by two to four stonefish spines.

Venom

Stonefish venom is a mixture of proteins of high molecular weight. A compound called stonustoxin has been isolated from the venom of the Estuarine Stonefish *Synanceia horrida*, and has a molecular sequence unlike any other known protein. In laboratory experiments, stonustoxin and the crude venom have both caused a rapid reduction in blood pressure, the effect of which can clearly be deadly. In contolled tests, the venom caused heart fluttering and atrioventricular blockage. Another compound in stonefish venom, the enzyme hyaluronidase, effectively enlarges intercellular gaps, which allows rapid dispersal of the venom.

Envenomation and symptoms

The immediate effect of a stonefish envenomation is severe burning pain, which can last for days. Swelling at the puncture site usually spreads extensively. Blisters may develop around it and small patches of tissue may die off. Further symptoms are nausea, vomiting and diarrhoea, as well as respiratory problems that can cause fainting. Although cases of envenomation leading to death within a few hours have been reported, this is rare.

Sample cases

A 49-year-old man had just finished a shore dive off the island of Espiritu Santo in Vanuatu. As he was walking in the knee-deep water 20 m from shore in barefoot-style fins, he screamed out in excruciating pain that he had just stepped on a sharp spike and saw what he thought to be a stonefish. He was then carried from the water and taken to the local hospital. On arrival 40 minutes later, his left foot exibited three puncture wounds and a large haematoma, and the foot and lower leg were red and extremely swollen. He described intolerable pain and paresthesias (pins and needles) ascending up the leg, decreased sensation in the foot, and greatly reduced movement of the foot and leg. Local pulses were not detectable and capillary refill of the toes was 5 seconds. His pulse rate was 108 beats/minute, blood pressure was 100/64 mm Hg and tympanic temperature was 37.2°C. He remained conscious but had difficulty swallowing.

None of the hospital staff had seen a case of stonefish envenomation. A nurse administered 5 mL of lidocaine with 1:1000 epinephrine into the wound, an action adverse to a wound containing a venom that reduces local circulation. The local physician started the patient on 50 mL of intravenous normal saline and 1 g of intravenous penicillin every six hours. A visiting undergraduate medical student on rotation consulted standard medical texts and immediately had the foot placed in hot water (45°C) for 30–90 minutes. After his second night in the hospital, the patient was unable to move his leg below the knee and had a temperature of 38.5°C. The foot had multiple fluid-filled blisters and the thigh had a large fluid-filled protruberance on its lateral surface and a distinct red line running up its medial surface. Macroscopic haematuria (blood in the urine) developed, with a white blood cell count of 20 billion/L.

The patient was evacuated to Port Villa, where he was kept on the same intravenous regimen, then to Brisbane, Australia, 24 hours later. It was considered too late to administer antivenom, so the patient was treated only with an antibiotic. He was discharged five days later with reduced swelling but was unable to bear weight on the foot. While still under medical care for a 4 cm ulcer 26 days after the sting, he returned home to Brazil, where he was able to walk within a few days and subsequently made a full recovery.

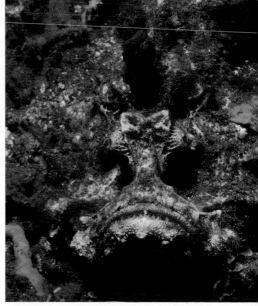

Stonefish sex

When stonefishes occur in groups, sex may be involved. In Australia, 25 to 30 Estuarine Stonefishes (right) were seen in an area of about 16 sq m. All but one were sitting on the mud bottom. Of those collected, the smallest were males, the largest were females and all were running ripe. Eggs released overnight in an aquarium were large (1.6 mm), which means large larvae and indicates a good potential for aquaculture. Why culture a potentially lethal fish? Read on... *(Above: Lombok, MK. Right: HF)*

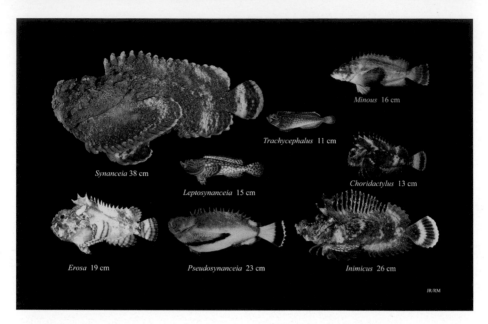

Minous 16 cm

Trachycephalus 11 cm

Synanceia 38 cm

Choridactylus 13 cm

Leptosynanceia 15 cm

Erosa 19 cm

Pseudosynanceia 23 cm

Inimicus 26 cm

JR/RM

Stonefish on the menu

Chinese gourmands pay top dollar to have a live stonefish prepared into a meal. Stonefish flesh is excellent to eat, but is not an aphrodisiac as some believe. Both the Reef Stonefish and the Estuarine Stonefish are sold live in Hong Kong. Aquaculture is the best hope for keeping these species from being over-harvested in the wild. The Estuarine Stonefish can tolerate a wide range of salinity and crowded conditions, so is the best candidate. *(Hong Kong, RM)*

Classification and distribution

The stonefish family, Synanceidae, includes at least 32 species in three subfamilies. Size and shape vary greatly. The subfamily Synanceinae includes one species each of the small stargazer-like *Leptosynanceia*, *Pseudosynanceia* and *Trachycephalus*, as well as two species of *Erosa* and four species of *Synanceia*. The devil-fishes (subfamily Choridactylinae, p.75) have pectoral fins designed for crawling and flashing a warning. The lower two to three rays are modified into finger-like appendages and the under-sides are often brightly coloured. In *Inimicus*, the eyes project above the head, the snout projects into an upturned mouth and most dorsal spines are free. In *Choridactylus*, the snout is blunt and all dorsal spines are connected by a membrane. The stingfishes (subfamily Minoinae, p.80) have barbels on the chin and only the lowermost ray of the pectoral fins is modified into a walking appendage. All species should be considered highly dangerous.

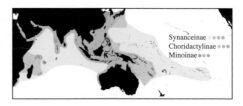

Synanceinae
Choridactylinae
Minoinae

Stonefishes
Subfamily Synanceinae

Reef Stonefish	38 cm
Synanceia verrucosa	(19 in)

Bulbous, with vertical mouth, tiny eyes and large fleshy pectoral fins; dorsal spines hidden beneath warty skin. **Biology:** on sand or rubble of reef flats, lagoons and seaward reefs, intertidal to 45 m. Often partially buried or in spaces under rocks or coral, may stay on site for months. Feeds on small fishes and crustaceans. Stonefishes occasionally shed skin, perhaps to rid themselves of fowling organisms. Recently shed individuals tend to have brighter colours. Wounds from this species and *S. horrida* (below) are extremely painful and potentially fatal without medical attention. **Range:** Red Sea to Fr. Polynesia, n. to s. Japan, s. to S. Africa. **Similar:** all other *Synanceia* have an obvious depression behind the eyes.

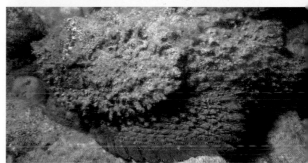

This fully grown adult Reef Stonefish *Synanceia verrucosa* can only be seen easily at close range. The fish, partially buried in the sand at the bottom of the southern plateau of the Elphinstone Reef in the Red Sea, sat motionless in the same spot for at least five days. Several groups of divers passed close by every day, without realising that the reddish-coloured clump was in fact a stonefish. If they noticed it at all, the divers believed it to be a protruberance of limestone covered with encrusting red algae.

S. verrucosa

Estuarine Stonefish 30 cm
Synanceia horrida (12 in)

Eyes elevated, with a bony knob above, deep saddle behind and connected by bony ridge (detail below). **Biology:** on mud, sand or rubble of estuaries and coastal reefs, 1–40 m. Often buried. Behaviour similar to *S. verrucosa* (p.71), but found on more turbid coastal reefs and flats. Responsible for most of the stonefish envenomations in Australia. **Range:** India to New Caledonia, s. to s. Queensland, n. to Ryukyus. **Similar:** other species lack the bony crest above the eyes and deep pit behind them; *S. alula* (below) has smaller pectoral fins with 11–12 rays.

Smallfin Stonefish 10 cm
Synanceia alula (4 in)

Intermediate in appearance to *S. horrida* (above) and *S. verrucosa* (p.71); has smaller pectoral fins with 11–12 rays (vs 15–19) and more closely spaced eyes. **Biology:** on dead coral and sand, 1–18 m. Poorly known and rare, but may be overlooked owing to confusion with other species. **Range:** Nicobar Is, n. Sulawesi, Flores, Hermit Is (n. PNG) and Solomon Is; likely throughout Indonesia and New Guinea.

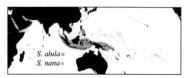

Red Sea Stonefish
Synanceia nana
13.5 cm
(5.3 in)

Shallow depression behind eyes; soft-rayed parts of fins with broad dusky margins; usually 14 dorsal spines (vs 13), 14 pectoral rays. **Biology:** on sand and dead coral, 3–10 m. Poorly known and considered rare, but may be overlooked owing to confusion with *S. verrucosa* (p.71). **Range:** Red Sea and around Arabian Pen. to Arabian G. **Similar:** *S. verrucosa* lacks depression behind eyes, has 18–19 pectoral rays and grows much larger.

North-west Stonefish
Erosa daruma
13 cm
(5.1 in)

Large, round head, velvet-like skin with small warts; variable in colour, often with banded pectoral fins and irregular pale patches resembling encrustations. **Biology:** inhabits mud or sand bottoms of coastal reefs, intertidal to 15 m. **Range:** nw. Australia only.

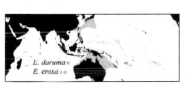

Monkeyfish
Erosa erosa
19 cm
(7.5 in)

Large, round head with spiny cheek, tapering body and large pectoral fins with pale spots. **Biology:** on soft bottoms of coastal waters, as shallow as 10 m in Japan and China, usually below 60–85 m elsewhere. A food fish in Japan. **Range:** s. China to s. Japan; Ambon; nw. Australia to New Caledonia and Tonga.

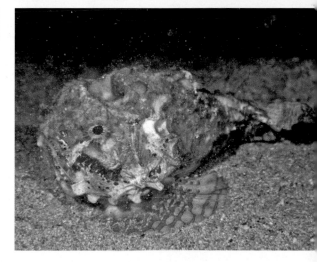

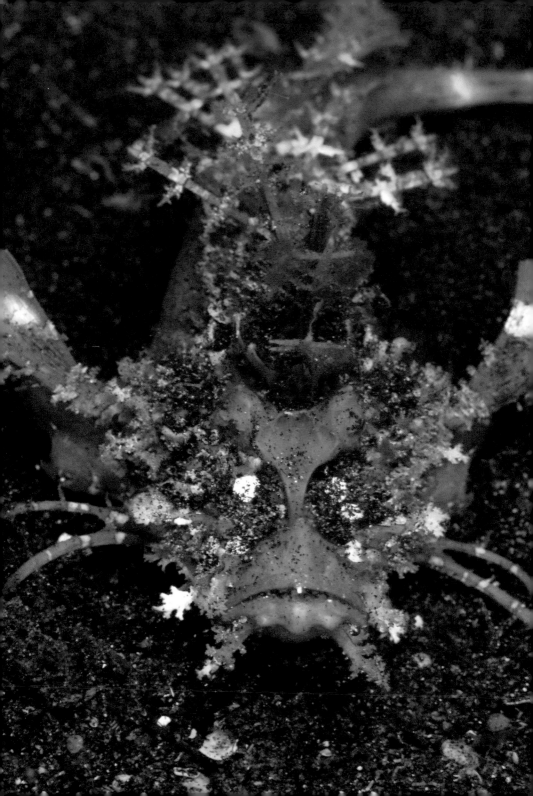

A Spiny Devilfish flashes its warning. Before it did so it was practically invisible. *Sulawesi, RM*

Devilfishes
Subfamily Choridactylinae

Behaviour

Devilfishes live in sand and rubble, where they often bury themselves so deep that only their eyes are exposed. From this position they ambush small fishes and crustaceans that venture too close. When they move, they crawl rather than swim, by using their two finger-like lower pectoral fin rays to pull themselves forward. This often leaves a distinct furrow in the sand. When resting, devilfishes keep their fins folded close to their bodies, allowing their cryptic colour to make them nearly invisible. When approached, devilfish do not move away but usually remain perfectly still until they feel threatened or are touched. Then they may suddenly spread their fins in a startling display that exposes the bright warning colours of the undersides of the pectoral fins and tail membranes. Devilfishes can be found from shallow reef flats to depths of over 100 m.

This unusually brightly coloured Spiny Devilfish may recently have shed its skin. *Sulawesi, HF*

Appearance

Like their close family relatives the stonefishes, devilfishes have upturned mouths and eyes set high on the head. Their 15 to 17 dorsal fin spines are taller and free-standing, with deeply incised membranes between all but the first three, and are adorned with numerous small tassels. This, combined with their habit of folding them at differing angles, breaks up their outline. The lower two rays of the pectoral fins are free and thickened into moveable finger-like appendages. The underside of the fins is brightly coloured in yellow, orange or white, in patterns distinctive to each species. The largest species of devilfishes grow to a length of 26 cm, which is somewhat smaller than the largest stonefishes.

Typical accidents

Most accidents occur when wading or jumping into shallow water. Accidents while diving can happen if the diver accidentally bumps into a devilfish or fails to heed its warning and provokes it. Devilfishes can move surprisingly fast and jab at a perceived threat.

An ovigerous female (left) may attract several males, which vie for her attention. The generally smaller suitors may spread their fins in an attempt to impress her or even dig her out of the sand. *Indonesia, HF*

Prevention

Although the spines of a devilfish can penetrate the soles of most shoes, always wear footwear since it offers better protection than going barefoot. Always watch where you step. If wading in sandy areas, proceed slowly while shuffling your feet, as this may allow you to feel a buried devilfish and stop before you step directly on a raised spine. Divers and swimmers should look

A Spiny Devilfish as typically found – mostly buried. *Satonda I., Indonesia, RM*

Treatment

First aid

Get out of the water immediately and seek medical attention as soon as possible.

What not to do

Do not apply a tourniquet or manipulate the wound in any way.

Ongoing medical management

Treat according to the symptoms. Clean and disinfect the wound to avoid secondary infection. Administer tetanus prophylaxis if necessary.

Venom apparatus

Devilfishes have a venom apparatus similar to that of stonefishes (p.68) but with much longer spines and smaller venom glands. They have 15 to 18 dorsal fin spines, three anal fin spines and a spine in front of each pelvic fin. The first few dorsal fin spines of the Spiny Devilfish *Inimicus didactylus* are shown here. As more cases of envenomation are documented, a positive identification based on a photograph or specimen could reveal differences in the potency between species and, eventually, aid in treatment. *(Sulawesi, RM)*

carefully before touching the bottom. If given a chance, a devilfish will flash its warning, and this should be heeded. Do not play with or provoke these creatures, as they can jab at a threat and move surprisingly fast.

Venom
Devilfish venom has not been studied and little is known about it. The severity of symptoms indicate that it may be similar to stonefish venom.

Envenomation and symptoms
Envenomation causes immediate and excruciating pain, which can increase in the hours after the sting. Oedema occurs at the site of the puncture wound and can extend to the entire limb. Swelling can last for days. General symptoms can include heart palpitations, weakness, nausea and sweating. Fatalities are not known to the authors, but given the close relationship between devilfishes and stonefishes, it should be considered a possibility.

Sample cases

1) While on a dive trip in the Solomon Islands, one of the authors (MB) witnessed the following typical case of envenomation. As his boat approached the shoreline, one of the young local assistants jumped into the knee-deep water to help pull it onto the beach. In the process he stepped on a Spiny Devilfish *Inimicus didactylus*. He immediately felt a burning pain as one of the dorsal spines penetrated deeply into his left heel. In the ensuing hours, his foot became quite swollen. In the days that followed, the swelling spread to his entire leg. He suffered from extreme pain, but other than a light feeling of weakness, he had no other general symptoms. A doctor cleaned and disinfected the wound. Three days later, the patient felt well enough to return to work. The devilfish, which he managed to kill with his paddle despite the extreme pain, is shown here. You can see the tip of the second and most of third dorsal spines exposed after the sheath of skin was pushed back by the force of penetration into the victim's heel. *(Solomon Is, MB)*

2) In another incident, this time at a depth of 10 m off Sulawesi, a diver settled on the sandy bottom to photograph an animal. In doing so, he didn't see a devilfish buried in the sand and was pricked by the spines. The symptoms and course of healing were similar to the Solomon Islands example. The general symptoms also included sweating and pallor. The wound was disinfected and healed with no complications. After just a few days, the underwater photographer was back on his feet.

Spiny Devilfish   19 cm
Inimicus didactylus   *(7.5 in)*

Inner surface of pectoral fins varying from white to yellow, orange or pink, upper 1–2 rays filamentous only in juveniles. **Biology:** inhabits open sand, mud or seagrass bottoms, 1 m to at least 80 m. Often lies buried up to its eyes waiting to ambush small fishes. When disturbed, flashes the brightly coloured undersides of its pectoral fins. The most common and widespread species. **Range:** Andaman Sea to Vanuatu, n. to s. Japan, s. to nw. Australia and New Caledonia.

Two-stick Stingfish   25 cm
Inimicus filamentosus   *(9.8 in)*

Upper 1–2 pectoral rays filamentous at all sizes (clearly visible in lower photo). **Biology:** inhabits open sand of lagoons, sheltered bays and deeper seaward slopes, 3–55 m. Often buried. Relatively uncommon. The only species of *Inimicus* in the w. Indian Ocean and Red Sea. **Range:** Red Sea to Maldives, s. to Mauritius. **Similar species:** Shortsnout Stinger *I. brachyrhynchus* has a narrow bright band on underside of its pectoral fins (26 cm; Singapore to Hong Kong); Japanese Stinger *I. japonicus* and Joubin's Stinger *I. joubini* have poorly defined flash patterns on the inside of their pectoral fins and are humpbacked with shorter snouts; *I. japonicus* is cultured for food (26 cm; s. China to central Japan and s. Korea), *I. joubini* has three finger-like lower pectoral rays (19 cm; Vietnam to Japan); Plainfin Stinger *I. cuvieri* has no pattern on the inner surface of pectoral fin (24 cm; G. of Thailand and Sunda Shelf to s. China).

I. didactylus

I. filamentosus

Caledonian Stinger
Inimicus caledonicus   22 cm (8.6 in)

Inner surface of pectoral fins pale with dark streaks that may form 2 broad bands. **Biology:** on open sand and in sparse seagrasses from shallows to deeper seaward slopes, 1–60 m. **Range:** Andaman and Nicobar Is and Gt Barrier Reef to New Caledonia.

Spotted Stinger
Inimicus sinensis   19 cm (7.5 in)

Inner surface of pectoral fins black with large pale to yellow spots, upper 2 rays in juveniles filamentous; snout somewhat elongate. **Biology:** on mud, sand or rubble, 5–90 m. Poorly known. **Range:** w. India to n. Australia, n. to Taiwan, s. to w. Australia.

Orangebanded Stingfish
Choridactylus multibarbus   13 cm (4 in)

Large, protruding eyes, blunt snout, lower 3 pectoral rays free; variable brown to orange, uniform or blotched; inner surface of pectoral fins bright yellow and black. **Biology:** on sand or mud, 1–50 m. **Range:** Red Sea to Philippines, n. to s. China. **Similar:** Three-stick Stingfish *C. natalensis* lacks dark margin on inner pectoral fin (13 cm; S. Africa and Mozambique, 35–75 m); *C. striatus* dark brown with thin white stripes, inner pectoral fin without marks (25 cm; G. of Aden to s. Oman, 26–41 m).

Stingfishes
Subfamily Minoinae

Stingfishes have prominent spines above the corners of the mouth and cheeks, large eyes and short chin barbels. They lack scales or tassels but are often covered in hydroids. The lowermost pectoral ray is modified into a walking appendage, and in some species the inner surface of the fin of is boldly coloured and flashed as a warning. Stingfishes inhabit soft bottoms of coastal waters. They are often buried by day, but hunt on the surface by night. They pose a danger primarily to fishermen. Twelve species are known; the Striped Stingfish is shown above. *(PNG, SM)*

Striped Stingfish	9 cm
Minous trachycephalus	*(3.5 in)*

Cheek red, pectoral fin banded on outside, with close-set pale yellow spots near base on inside. **Biology:** on mud or fine sand of coastal waters, 5–164 m. **Range:** Sri Lanka to New Calednia, n. to Taiwan. **Similar:** Painted Stinger *M. pictus* has dark streaks on the inner pectoral fins (G. of Thailand and Taiwan to n. Australia); Dwarf Stingfish *M. pusillus* has thin, feeble dorsal spines (s. Japan to Philippines, also New Caledonia).

M. trachycephalus
other species

Velvetfishes
Aploactinidae

Velvetfishes have tiny bristles instead of scales, unbranched fin rays, and skin that resembles velvet but feels like sandpaper. The dorsal fin originates over the eye and may be continuous, notched, or broken into isolated spines. The fin spines of some species are venomous, but there is uncertainty about the danger owing to confusion with waspfishes. Many species have blunt spines that seem incapable of injecting venom. About 40 species occur in the Indo-Pacific and range from 1 cm to 15 cm in length. Most are rare and highly cryptic. Velvetfishes pose little danger, but those who handle them should use caution.

Crested Velvetfish	10 cm
Ptarmus gallus	*(4 in)*

Deep-bodied, highly compressed, head without obvious spines; olive-brown with small, dark-edged pale spots, eyespots at corners of tail fin. **Biology:** on rubble and sand of lagoons and bays, 10–30 m. Solitary or in pairs, lies motionless. **Range:** Red Sea only. **Similar:** Crested Scorpionfish *P. jubatus* has dark speckles, lacks eyespots on tail (8cm; E. Africa).

Orbicular Velvetfishes
Caracanthidae

Spotted Coral Croucher	5.5 cm
Caracanthus maculatus	*(2.2 in)*

Pale grey with small reddish-brown spots. **Biology:** among branches of *Pocillopora eydouxi*, *Stylophora mordax* and certain *Acropora* corals, 3–15 m. Common. **Range:** E. Indies to Fr. Polynesia, n. to s. Japan. **Similar:** replaced by *C. madagascariensis* in Indian Ocean and *C. typicus* in Hawaiian Is.

Orbicular velvetfishes are small, compressed ovoid fishes covered with tubercles. The fin spines are probably venomous, but unlikely to deliver a sting unless the fish is squeezed. The five species occur exclusively in branching corals, where they wedge themselves when disturbed.

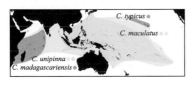

Queenfishes and Leatherjackets
Caringidae

Few people consider members of the jack family to be dangerous. However, one group, the queenfishes (*Scomberoides*), including the closely related leatherjackets (*Oligoplites*), have venomous dorsal and anal fin spines capable of causing painful wounds. They pose a danger only to those who handle them. Queenfishes are edible but are not as highly esteemed as most other jacks.

Behaviour
Adult queenfishes typically occur near the surface along sandy beaches. Juveniles of many species feed on the scales of small schooling fishes that are detached when they ram them with their mouths. They also may ram prey with their anal fin spines, in an unusual offensive use of venom. Juveniles of one species, the Leatherjacket *Oligoplites saurus*, are beneficial cleaners of larger fishes.

Appearance
Queenfishes are elongate, compressed silvery fishes with small, mostly embedded scales, a slender caudal peduncle and a strongly forked tail. Unlike most other jacks, the rear rays of the second dorsal and anal fins are broken into isolated finlets, and the spines of the first dorsal and anal fins are widely separated and isolated.

Prevention
Those who handle queenfishes should be aware of the danger posed by their fin spines and be cautious when handling them.

Typical accidents
Virtually all accidents are painful wounds to the hands inflicted when handling a caught fish.

Venom
The venom is relatively mild in comparison to that of many other fishes, and nothing is known of its chemistry, toxicology or pharmacology.

Symptoms
Wounds inflicted by adult fishes may be intensely painful for up to four hours, whereas those by juveniles feel much like a bee sting, with the pain lasting up to 30 minutes.

Distribution
Queenfishes are broadly distributed throughout coastal and coral reef waters of the Indo-Pacific. Their counterparts, the leatherjackets, inhabit

Venom apparatus

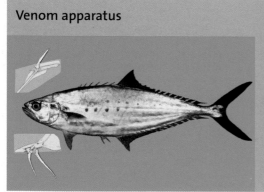

Queenfishes have five to seven short, isolated dorsal fin spines and two longer anal fin spines connected by a membrane (shown in red, with detail of spines and supporting bones at left). The spines are nearly rectangular in cross section and concave along their rear, with small grooves along their sides within the thin layer of covering skin. They are held erect by well-developed muscles and by a locking device in the anal fin. Shown here is the Doublespotted Queenfish *Scomberoides lysan*. (Photo JR; diagram modified from Halstead, 1970)

the Caribbean and tropical and warm-temperate coastal waters of the Americas and eastern Pacific.

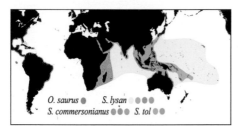

O. saurus ●   S. lysan ●●●
S. commersonianus ●●●   S. tol ●●

Treatment

First aid
Cleaning the wound is generally all the treatment that is necessary. Soaking in hot water is not recommended.

Doublespotted Queenfish   70 cm
Scomberoides lysan   (27.6 in)

Double row of 6–8 dark spots. **Biology:** inhabits shallow lagoons, bays and seaward reefs to 100 m. Juveniles in protected inshore waters and estuaries, adults solitary, usually near surface along beaches. Juveniles feed on scales torn from small schooling fishes, adults feed on small fishes and crustaceans. **Range:** Red Sea to Fr. Polynesia, n. to s. Japan. **Similar:** Other species of *Scomberoides* have a single row of pale spots.

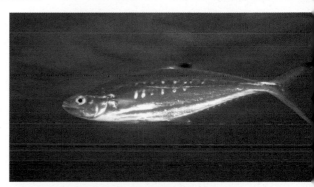

Talang Queenfish   120 cm
Scomberoides commersonianus (47 in)

Deep-bodied; single row of larger round spots. Dorsal and anal spines venomous. **Biology:** mid-water above reefs, to 30 m. **Range:** Red Sea and Arabian G. to e. Australia. **Similar:** Other species of *Scomberoides* have smaller spots.

Leatherjacket   30 cm
Oligoplites saurus   (12 in)

Tail yellowish; first 5 dorsal spines isolated; scales needle-like and embedded. **Biology:** mid- to surface waters along sandy beaches and in river mouths, often in turbid areas. Juveniles clean other fishes. **Range:** MA to Uruguay; all Caribbean except Bahamas; G. of California to Panama. **Similar:** *O. palometa* and *O. saliens* usually have 4 isolated dorsal spines (both from Central and S America).

The Streaked Weaver digs down into the sea bed. Often, only its eyes are showing. *MB*

Weevers
Trachinidae

Weevers are a small family of elongate bottom-dwellers that have venomous dorsal and opercular spines. They inhabit mud and sand bottoms of European, West African and Chilean seas from the shoreline to at least 300 m.

Behaviour
Weevers are ambushing predators of small invertebrates and fishes, and spend most of the daylight hours buried in sand with only their eyes and first dorsal fin exposed. When alarmed, they raise and sometimes vibrate the first dorsal fin. They stand their ground and may lunge aggressively at an intruder with surprising speed and accuracy. Their venomous spines are capable of causing extremely painful and occasionally incapacitating wounds. During late spring and early summer, weevers migrate to sandy shallows to spawn, where they pose a threat to waders. Despite their venomosity, weevers are good to eat and are fished commercially in parts of Europe, particularly France, where they are considered a delicacy.

Appearance
Weevers are elongate and somewhat laterally compressed, with eyes located far forward on top of the head, an upturned mouth, small scales, a single lateral line, and elongate second dorsal and anal fins. They have five to seven stout venomous spines in the first dorsal fin and one near the top of each gill cover.

Typical accidents
Most accidents occur when a wader steps on an unseen weever. This is most likely during the summer, when beachgoers and spawning weevers converge in shallow water. Accidents to divers and snorkellers occur when a weever strikes after being closely approached. Fishermen are often stung when trying to remove weevers from a net or hook. Since the venom remains potent until destroyed by cooking, the same risk extends to all those who handle them.

Prevention
Swimmers should wear stout beach shoes when wading in sandy shallows, particularly during the early summer when weevers may still occupy spawning areas. Divers should approach weevers with great care, always keep a safe distance and be on the lookout for aggressive behaviour. Anglers and fishermen are advised to handle weevers carefully, wear

thick gloves and use an appropriate tool such as pliers to remove a hook. Dead weevers should be handled with care since their venom remains potent until cooked.

Venom

Weaver venom contains a mixture of substances. These include proteins, which are clearly responsible for the toxic effect, as well as small molecules such as serotonin, which release histamine from the victim's own cells. These molecular substances are reputedly responsible for the pain that results from a sting. A protein called dracotoxin has been isolated from the venoms of both the Lesser Weever *Echiichthys vipera* and the Greater Weever *Trachinus draco*. Its effect is clearly directed against the cell membranes. An anti-serum to combat the draco venom has been developed, and has been used effectively in over two dozen known cases.

Envenomation and symptoms

A sting results in an immediate sharp pain that spreads rapidly through the surrounding area, increases in intensity, and is accompanied by redness and swelling, which may affect an entire limb. The pain slowly subsides within two to 24 hours, and is followed by tingling and numbness. The swelling may last for several

Treatment

First aid

Get the victim out of the water. Remove any pieces of spine that are easily accessible. Disinfect the wound with 40–70 per cent alcohol. Call a doctor, especially if severe symptoms or problems with healing are experienced.

What not to do

Do not tamper with the wound. Do not use hot water or a cigarette to burn the venom, as this only results in further injury. Do not rub soft soap or any other substance into the wound.

Ongoing medical management

Further treatment depends on the symptoms. The wound must be cleaned in order to avoid secondary infection. and a tetanus prophylaxis is recommended. The pain-reliever lidocaine provides only short-term relief. Strong analgesics such as morphine derivatives have virtually no effect. For treatment of patients who overreact to a sting, tranquillisers are recommended.

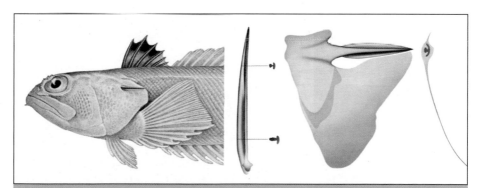

Venom apparatus

The venom apparatus consists of five to seven dorsal spines (detail with cross section above near right) and a backward-pointing spine at the top of each gill cover (detail with cross section above far right). The spines (shown in red) are T-shaped in cross section, with venom glands occupying the length of each lateral groove (blue), and are covered by a thin skin. The opercular spines have a broader, curved T-shaped top with correspondingly thicker venom glands, and may be flared up to 40° from the body plane. When a spine penetrates tissue, its sheath rips open and the venom is pressed into the wound.

Sample cases

1) While diving near Naples, a 31-year-old zoologist approached an unusually large weever (tentatively identified as the Lesser Weever *Echiichthys vipera*) partially buried in the sand. At first, the fish appeared to be undisturbed and allowed itself to be touched. Then, without warning, it turned to face the diver while aggressively vibrating its fins, and struck him on his right jaw. The wound initially bled profusely but without pain, then began stinging as the bleeding stopped. The pain rapidly increased and spread throughout the head and upper chest, severley hampering the diver's 200-m swim to shore. Within 15 minutes, respiration became difficult, then eased ten minutes later. On shore, the victim noticed that the speech and movement of others around him appeared greatly retarded as the pain and inflammation increased to the point where he asked to be shot. Injections of meperidine hydrochloride and morphine had no effect. Within five hours a severe burning sensation affected the skin of his chest. By the second day, much of his upper body became cyanotic as a massive haematoma developed over much of his face, head and upper chest. Breathing and swallowing became impaired and painful. On the fourth day, the victim was admitted to a major hospital, where he began to improve rapidly after two days. Treatment was symptomatic and included oxygen during the first two days; cold, moist compresses applied to areas of swelling; and intravenous solutions of vitamins, calcium and glucose. Opiates were administered but were ineffective. After ten days of hospitalisation, the swelling had disappeared but the discolorisation persisted, and the victim was discharged. Further recovery was uneventful. *(After Halstead, 1970)*

2) While wading in knee-deep water off a sandy Sicilian beach, a 45-year-old man stepped on a weever. He felt an immediate sharp pain and noticed a puncture wound on his left heel that bled slightly. Over the next two to three hours, the leg swelled as far as the knee and the pain shot up the entire leg. After about six hours, the pain slowly lessened. The swelling took several days to subside. The victim's condition improved over the following three to four days, and he recovered completely without treatment.

days. General symptoms such as fever, sweating and nausea may occur. In severe cases, shock has resulted in respiratory distress and cardiac palpitation. The puncture wound often bleeds for a short time and untreated wounds may succumb to secondary infection. Reported deaths are likely to be the result of secondary infection exacerbated by inappropriate treatment.

Streaked Weaver *Trachinus radiatus*.

Classification and distribution

Nine species of weavers are known, eight in the genus *Trachinus* and the other the Lesser Weaver *Echiichthys vipera*. One occurs in Chile, while the remainder inhabit the tropical and temperate eastern Atlantic, with four of these extending into the Mediterranean and two the Black Sea.

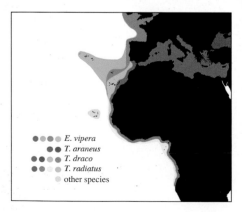

●●●● *E. vipera*
  ●● *T. araneus*
●●●●● *T. draco*
  ●● ● *T. radiatus*
      ● other species

Greater Weever
Trachinus draco 40 cm (16 in)

Blue and dark streaks horizontal on cheek, diagonal on sides; first dorsal fin with 5–7 spines, its outer part black. **Biology:** inhabits sand, mud or gravel bottoms, 1–150 m. Usually mostly buried by day, active and often free-swimming at night. Breeds in late spring and summer, spawns free-floating eggs. **Range:** Mauritania to Norway; Canary Is, Madeira, Mediterranean and Black seas. **Similar:** Spotted Weever *T. araneus* has row of 7–11 dark spots on sides, 7 spines on first dorsal fin (40 cm; Mediterranean and Black seas s. to Angola, incl. e. Canary Is).

Streaked Weever
Trachinus radiatus 50 cm (20 in)

Pale with small dark spots, some forming irregular circles, side of head often dark; first dorsal fin with 6 spines, its front ⅔ black. **Biology:** inhabits sand and mud bottoms, 2–150 m. More often in open than other weevers. **Range:** G. of Cadiz to Angola, Canary Is, Mediterranean. **Similar:** Lesser Weever *Echiichthys vipera* is pale with faint dark mottling above, has black first dorsal fin (15 cm; Scotland to Senegal, incl. all Mediterranean and Canary Is).

Striped Fangblenny *Meiacanthus grammistes. Palau, RM*

Fangblennies
Blenniidae, tribe Nemophini

As unbelievable as it may sound, there are fishes that have venomous fangs quite similar to those of some snakes – namely the fang-blennies, which are members of the genus *Meiacanthus*. These small, elongate, scaleless fishes have relatively small mouths that bear a pair of enlarged canine teeth in the lower jaw. Fortunately, they are innoffensive unless handled. However, their non-venomous relatives in the genus *Plagiotremus* are not so innocent. They feed on pieces of fins, skin and scales nipped from other fishes. They will also attack divers, but luckily all they can manage is a distracting nip. Many of them mimic species of *Meiacanthus* in order to get close to larger prey – these will ignore them, as the venomous *Meiacanthus* fangblennies feed on small invertebrates. A rule of thumb for divers is that, if it attacks, it's harmless. However, all fangblennies use their fangs for defence and should not be handled. We include a few of the 29 species of *Meiacanthus* here since they can give a painful bite like a wasp sting and are used in the aquarium trade. Fangblennies are indigenous to the Indo-Pacific. The largest reaches 12 cm in length.

Venomous fangs

The lower jaw (left side shown) contains a pair of enlarged grooved fangs (here in red), each behind a short row of small incisors and partially surrounded at its base by a venom gland (blue). The pressure of biting forces the venom up a groove along the front of the fang and into the wound. Each fang is replaceable; the replacement tooth sits behind it. Captive predatory fishes that were fed live *Meiacanthus* immediately spat them out and flexed their jaws in obvious discomfort. The effect of a bite on a human is similar to that of a wasp sting. *(Photo JR; diagram after Smith-Vaniz, 1976)*

Mimicry

Perhaps the most interesting aspect of fang-blennies is the phenomenon of mimicry. Most species of *Meiacanthus* are mimicked by a non-venomous species of fangblenny as well as by other species of fish. The *Meiacanthus* species serves as a model and is ignored by other fishes because it is harmless unless attacked. One kind of mimic is an identical-looking non-venomous fangblenny of the genus *Plagiotremus*. It feeds on the scales, skin and fins of other fishes and uses its disguise to approach and attack them. This is called aggressive mimicry.

Another kind of mimic uses its disguise to gain safety from predators that have learned through bad experience to avoid eating anything that resembles the model. This is called Batesian mimicry, after the researcher who first described it among butterflies. Batesian mimics of *Meiacanthus* include other fangblennies of the genus *Petroscirtes*, blennies of the genus *Ecsenius*, certain species of cardinalfish, and juveniles of certain species of monocle bream.

In some cases, two unpalatable species share the same colour pattern in order to increase the odds that predators will have a bad experience. This is termed Müllerian mimicry. If a species of *Petroscirtes* can give a painful enough bite to avoid predation in its own right, then it and its look-alike *Meiacanthus* species would be Müllerian mimics of each other. Any geographic variation in the colour of the model also occurs in the mimic. In nearly all cases the model is more abundant than the mimic, which helps to reinforce the mimicry.

Left, from top: Canary Fangblenny *Meiacanthus oualanensis*; its aggressive mimic, the Fiji race of the Bicolour Fangblenny *Plagiotremus laudandus flavus*; its Batesian mimic, a juvenile Bridled Monocle Bream *Scolopsis bilineatus*; a possible Müllerian mimic of the Striped Fangblenny *M. grammmistes*, the Shorthead Fangblenny *Petroscirtes breviceps*; Batesian mimic of *M. grammistes*, the Mimic Cardinalfish *Cheilodipterus nigrotaeniatus*. (Top 3 Fiji, lower 2 Indonesia, RM)

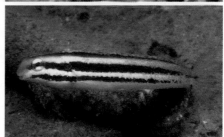

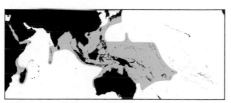

Distribution of *Meiacanthus* fangblenny species.

Yellowtail Fangblenny   11 cm
Meiacanthus atrodorsalis   *(4.2 in)*

Grey, grading to yellow towards rear; dark band on dorsal fin; 5 races, some with dark line through eye. **Biology:** inhabits lagoon and seaward reefs below the surge zone, 1–30 m. Hovers up to a metre above the bottom. **Range:** Philippines and Bali to Samoa, n. to Ryukyus. **Similar:** the species' mimic, Bicolour Fangblenny *Plagiotremus laudandus*, is more elongate (8 cm).

Canary Fangblenny   10 cm
Meiacanthus oualanensis   *(4 in)*

Uniformly yellow. **Biology:** inhabits lagoon and seaward reefs below the surge zone, 1–30 m. Hovers up to a metre above the bottom; feeds on zooplankton and small benthic invertebrates. **Range:** Fiji. **Similar:** Fiji race of aggressive mimic Bicolour Fangblenny *Plagiotremus laudandus flavus*; juvenile *Scolopsis bilineatus* (p.89).

Striped Fangblenny   12 cm
Meiacanthus grammistes   *(4.7 in)*

Head yellowish; white with 3 black stripes; black spots form band on dorsal fin. **Biology:** moderately common on protected reef slopes, 1–25 m. **Range:** Indochina to PNG and Gt Barrier Reef, n. to Ryukyus. **Similar:** Lined Fangblenny *M. lineatus* has more yellow, lacks spots (9.5 cm; Gt Barrier Reef); the mimics *Petroscirtes breviceps*, *Cheilodipterus nigrovittatus* and juvenile *Scolopsis bilineatus* (p.89).

Hairytail Fangblenny   6.5 cm
Meiacanthus crinitus   *(3.6 in)*

White with 3 black stripes. **Biology:** inhabits sheltered coastal reefs, 1–20 m. **Range:** Raja Ampat Is, W. Papua. **Similar:** the mimic *Cheilodipterus nigrovittatus* (p.89); other striped fangblennies.

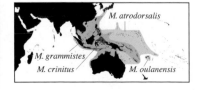

Scats
Scatophagidae

Scats are a small family of fishes that live in estuarine and protected coastal waters. The fin spines of juveniles are venomous. Scats are nearly square and compressed, with a small mouth, continuous dorsal fins and fine scales. They feed primarily on green algae and associated microfauna. The name *Scatophagus* means 'faeces-eater' and refers to their habit of eating human faeces. In many areas scats are used for food, and the more colourful juveniles are used as aquarium fishes. They pose a danger to humans only when handled. Symptoms of being spined are an intense shooting pain that is normally short-lived.

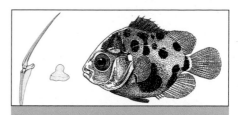

Venom apparatus

The dorsal, anal and pelvic fin spines of juvenile spotted scats (here in red) have paired grooves containing a thin strand of glandular tissue that disappears with age. Nothing is known of the venom. (Detail 2x life size.)

Spotted Scat	30 cm
Scatophagus argus	*(12 in)*

Quadrangular with concave head profile; silvery to dark grey with scattered black spots. Juveniles nearly black to golden brown with black spots and red margins. **Biology:** juveniles in brackish to fresh water, adults in shallow, turbid lagoons and coastal waters to 5 m. **Range:** Kuwait to Fiji and Tonga, n. to s. Japan, s. to New Caledonia; at least 3 geographic races may represent distinct species. **Similar:** African Scat *S. tetracanthus* has bars instead of spots (40 cm; E. Africa and Madagascar).

Spotbanded Scat	40 cm
Selenotoca multifasciata	*(16 in)*

Silvery with bars breaking into spots below. **Biology:** inhabits estuaries and river entrances. **Range:** Sulawesi to New Caledonia, s. to se. Australia. **Similar:** *Scatophagus* spp. have taller dorsal and anal fins.

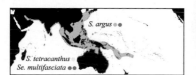

Rabbitfishes
Siganidae

Although they look harmless, rabbitfishes are well armed with stout venomous fin spines that have sharp cutting edges, making them hazardous to handle. In many parts of the world they are highly esteemed food fishes at all sizes, from tiny juveniles to adults. A few are even cultured, while some of the smaller and more colourful species are used in the aquarium trade. Rabbitfishes inhabit warm estuarine and rocky and coral reef waters of the Indo-Pacific, and have invaded the eastern Mediterranean through the Suez Canal.

Behaviour
Rabbitfishes are named for their voracious appetites and rabbit-like movements as they graze on algae and seagrasses. A few species also occasionally feed on tunicates and sponges. Rabbitfishes typically occur in small groups or pairs during the day. At night their skin takes on a disruptive pattern of dark and light areas, which renders them nearly invisible as they sleep exposed on the bottom. Rabbitfishes spawn on a lunar cycle, with peak activity in the spring and early summer, usually on outgoing tides at night or in the early morning. The early juveniles of some species form massive dark balls several metres in diameter as they approach shallow reef flats and estuaries for the first time. At this stage they are translucent and harmless, but within a few days they become fully pigmented and their spines become hard and venomous. Rabbitfishes use their venomous spines only in defence.

Appearance
Rabbitfishes are highly compressed oval to slender fishes characterised by a small terminal mouth with a row of small incisiform teeth, minute scales, and broad-based dorsal and anal fins with stout spines. Many species are quite colourful, while others are rather drab. The largest species attain lengths of up to 50 cm.

Many species of rabbitfish, including these Double-barred Rabbitfishes *Siganus virgatus*, occur in pairs. *Bali, RM*

IF INJURED

Treatment

First aid
Disinfect the wound and carefully remove any easily accessible foreign material. Seek medical attention if symptoms beyond pain and localised swelling become evident.

What not to do
Do not manipulate the wound in any way. Avoid immersion in hot water.

Ongoing medical management
Although rarely necessary, antibiotics may be used to prevent secondary infection.

Typical accidents
Rabbitfishes are shy and are not normally dangerous to divers or swimmers. The one exception is at night, when they sleep fully exposed and are nearly invisible owing to their disruptive nocturnal colour pattern. At this time there is a slight risk to waders and divers who make contact with the bottom. Throughout their range, rabbitfishes are valued as food, and the colourful species are part of the aquarium trade. Consequently, most accidents happen when they are handled. A little-known danger from larger species is their biting power. Their strong incisors can easily remove a plug of flesh from a fingertip.

Prevention
Divers should never touch a rabbitfish, particularly one that is sleeping, as it may suddenly lunge in an attempt to escape. At night they

Venom apparatus

Rabbitfishes have 13 dorsal fin spines preceded by an embedded forward-projecting spine, seven anal fin spines, and an outer and inner spine in each pelvic fin (shown in red). The spines vary in structure according to position, but all have a pair of grooves housing venom glands (blue) and are covered in a thin sheath of skin. Each dorsal fin spine has a pair of sharp lateral flanges behind the venom glands (oblique frontal view, A), while each anal fin spine has a sharp, broad keel along its rear edge (B). These spines are also slightly asymmetric in shape and position. They alternate between leaning slightly to the left or right of the midline, which increases their effectiveness as weapons. Each pelvic fin spine (C) has a keel on its inner edge. The embedded pre-dorsal spine (D) is cylindrical with a barbed tip. Although associated venom glands have not been found with the pre-dorsal spine, it produces wounds that are just as painful as the others, which indicates the presence of venom. When a spine enters flesh, its thin membrane tears and venom is forced into the wound. The razor-like flanges or keel cut the flesh further and increase the area exposed to venom. *(Photo: Siganus virgatus JR/RM)*

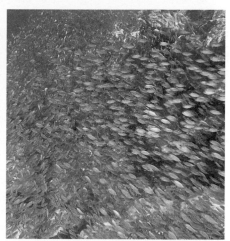

The disruptive colour pattern of this sleeping Forktail Rabbitfish *Siganus argenteus* makes it nearly invisible. *W. Papua, RM*

A large school of Mottled Spinefoot Rabbitfish *Siganus fuscescens* two days after arriving on the reef. *Sulawesi, RM*

should also avoid touching the bottom. Anyone wading on reef flats should don sturdy footwear. Fishermen and aquarists should be extremely careful when handling rabbitfishes and wear thick gloves if practicable. Be aware of the rabbitfishes' secret weapon: the forward-pointing spine in front of the dorsal fin, which does not fold backwards like the other spines. If the fish is alive, keep away from its mouth.

Envenomation and symptoms
Symptoms of envenomation are similar to those caused by many scorpionfishes. A wound is accompanied by an immediate sharp, burning pain, which may radiate to the entire limb and is followed by localised swelling. In parts of the western Pacific, rabbitfish wounds are feared almost as much as those produced by stonefishes, while in other areas the pain is reported to subside relatively quickly. This could be due to differences in potency between species. Although the pain may be extreme, other symptoms are rare.

Classification and distribution
All 31 known species of rabbitfish are indigenous to the Indo-Pacific and classified in the genus *Siganus*. The Forktail Rabbitfish *S. argenteus* has the longest larval stage and broadest distribution. Two species, the Dusky Spinefoot Rabbitfish *Siganus luridus* and Rivulated Rabbitfish *S. rivulatus*, have migrated into the eastern Mediterranean through the Suez Canal.

Invasion of the algae-eaters
The pelagic larval stage of rabbitfishes lasts three to four weeks. At a size of about 2 cm, larvae of the Fantail Rabbitfish *Siganus argenteus* transform into an elongate pre-juvenile stage that is lightly pigmented and lacks scales or venom. By the time they reach 6 cm, the pre-juveniles of this and other species gather into massive dark balls several metres in diameter and migrate to shallow reef flats, where they immediately begin to feed on algae. Within a few days they become fully pigmented and their spines become hard and venomous. These seasonal runs are a smorgasbord for predatory fishes, but by appearing in such large numbers the pre-juveniles assure the survival of some of their group. In some years, they are so numerous that the reef is stripped bare of filamentous algae and many starve to death before falling prey to predators. In the Philippines and Marianas, the pre-juveniles are heavily fished and preserved in brine for use as a condiment or side-dish.

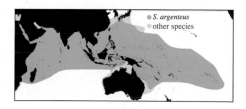

Rivulated Rabbitfish — 30 cm
Siganus rivulatus — (11.9 in)

Pale olive to mottled brown with faint orange lines on belly. **Biology:** inhabits shallow lagoon and protected seaward reefs, 1–15 m. Common. Usually in roving schools over weedy, sandy or dead coral bottoms. **Range:** Red Sea to G. of Aden, a recent migrant to e. Mediterranean.

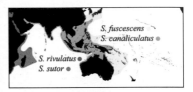

Lined Rabbitfish — 43 cm
Siganus lineatus — (17 in)

Deep-bodied; pale grey with orange stripes, breaking into spots around margins; a large yellow spot below rear of dorsal fin. **Biology:** in groups on protected reef slopes, 1–25 m. Sub-adults among mangroves and seagrasses. Aggregates at the mouths of channels to spawn. Spawns 9–10 days after new moon, with peaks Mar.–Jun. and Nov. Adults feed on algae and sponges from the dead bases of corals. Sleeps on open sand or rubble. **Range:** Maldives and Laccadives to Sri Lanka; Philippines to Vanuatu and New Caledonia.

Orange-spotted Rabbitfish — 42.7 cm
Siganus guttatus — (17 in)

Deep-bodied; pale grey with small, close-set yellow spots; a large yellow spot at rear base of dorsal fin. **Biology:** inhabits coastal reefs and estuaries to 12 m. Juveniles among seagrasses, adults in schools in river mouths, among mangroves and on coastal reefs. **Range:** Andaman Is to w. Papua, n. to the Ryukyus.

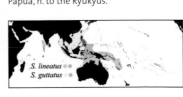

Coral Rabbitfish 30.5 cm
Siganus corallinus (12 in)

Deep-bodied; yellow with tiny pale blue spots, extent of which is variable. **Biology:** usually in pairs among corals of lagoon and coastal reefs to at least 6 m. Small juveniles feed on surfaces of seagrasses, progressing to coarse algae with growth. Adults often in pairs. **Range:** Aldabra to Vanuatu, n. to the Ryukyus; replaced by Three-blotched Rabbitfish *S. trispilos* in nw. Australia.

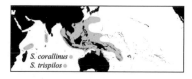

S. corallinus ●
S. trispilos ●

Masked Rabbitfish 38 cm
Siganus puellus (15 in)

Yellow with thin blue wavy lines; broad dark band through eye to chin. **Biology:** inhabits shallow, coral-rich areas of lagoon and seaward reefs to 30 m. Juveniles gather among branching corals. Adults in pairs along exposed coral slopes, where they feed on coarse algae and monaxid sponges. **Range:** Cocos (Keeling) to Gilbert Is and New Caledonia, n. to Ryukyus. Replaced by Blackeye Rabbitfish *S. puelloides* in Indian Ocean.

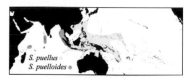

S. puellus ●
S. puelloides ●

Double-barred Rabbitfish 33 cm
Siganus virgatus (13 in)

Deep-bodied; yellow above, pale below with small blue spots on head and back, and oblique dusky bands through eye and above pectoral fin base. **Biology:** inhabits shallow coastal waters in areas of coral or sand with patches of rock or corals. Enters fresh water. Usually in pairs. Feeds on seaweeds. **Range:** s. India to w. Papua and NT, Australia, n. to Ryukyus. **Similar:** Scribbled Rabbitfish *S. doliatus* has narrow blue lines.

Gold-spotted Rabbitfish   45 cm
Siganus punctatus   *(17.8 in)*

Deep-bodied; pale grey to dark brown with
small, close-set, dark-edged orange spots.
Biology: inhabits clear lagoon and seaward
reefs, 1–50 m. Juveniles solitary or in small
groups in shallow reef areas. Adults usually
paired. Spawns around new or full moons,
or both. At Palau, spawns at low tide on
outer reef flat inshore of breaking waves.
Range: Cocos (Keeling) and w. Sumatra to
Samoa, n. to Ryukyu Is; replaced by *S. stellatus* (below) in Indian Ocean and *S. laqueus*
(below) in Red Sea.

Brown-spotted Rabbitfish   40 cm
Siganus stellatus   *(16 in)*

Deep-bodied; pale with close-set black
spots; nape olive-green, tail margin yellow.
Biology: inhabits coral-rich areas of lagoon
and seaward reefs, 1–40 m. Common.
Adults always paired, sub-adults in groups.
Covers large area while foraging for fila-
mentous algae and seaweed. **Range:** Red
Sea and G. of Aden.

Starry Rabbitfish   40 cm
Siganus laqueus   *(16 in)*

Deep-bodied; pale grey with close-set
brown to black spots; tail margin narrowly
yellow. **Biology:** inhabits coral-rich areas of
lagoon and seaward reefs, 1–40 m. Usually
in less than 10 m, often in areas of strong
currents. Common. Adults always paired,
sub-adults in groups. Covers large area
while foraging for filamentous algae and
seaweed. **Range:** E. Africa to Bali, s. to
Madagascar; replaced by *S. stellatus*
(above), which has a yellow tail, in Red Sea
and G. of Aden.

Streaked Rabbitfish
Siganus javus   **40 cm** *(16 in)*

Dark brown with pale spots, belly with pale reticulations; body profile like a rugby ball. **Biology:** estuarine and coastal waters, 1–40 m. Often in schools. Primarily continental. **Range:** Arabian G. to w. Australia, n. to Taiwan.

S. javus
S. vermiculatus

Foxface Rabbitfish
Siganus vulpinus   **23.7 cm** *(9.3 in)*

Long snout; yellow with white head and shoulder, broad black band through eye, black wedge on breast. **Biology:** inhabits coral-rich areas of lagoon and seaward reefs to 30 m. Juveniles and sub-adults in large schools among branching corals. At 10 cm, forms pairs and roams a small home range along upper edges of reef slopes. **Range:** Sumatra to Gilbert Is and New Caledonia, n. to Philippines. **Similar:** Onespot Foxface Rabbitfish *S. unimaculatus* has black blotch on sides (22 cm, Ryukyu and Ogasawara Is, s. to Rowley Shoals).

Magnificent Rabbitfish
Siganus magnificus   **23 cm** *(9 in)*

Long snout; head white with broad black eyeband, outer part of dorsal fin red, other fins yellow. **Biology:** inhabits open areas of protected coral reefs, 2–20 m. Adults paired. **Range:** Andaman Sea.

Traumatogenic Fishes
Fishes that injure by biting

Sharks and Shark Attacks
Reality vs myth

No marine animals are feared more than sharks. Popular film and print media have given them an almost universally bad and often malevolent image. This distortion of reality is in gross contradiction to the facts. Records of all shark attacks reported worldwide are kept by the International Shark Attack File (ISAF) of the Florida Museum of Natural History. They indicate that there are about 70 to 100 attacks per year, only five to 15 of which are deadly. In reality, the risk of dying from a shark attack is many times lower than the risk of being killed by either lightning or a falling coconut. If you stop to consider that each year millions of people swim, surf and dive in the oceans, the extremely low risk of being attacked by a shark is evident. For example, in the year 2000, in all continental US waters, there were only 54 unprovoked shark attacks, resulting in one death. The odds of being attacked by a shark are less than one-third that of drowning and less than one-tenth that of dying in a commerical airline crash.

Although the danger of a shark attack can never be eliminated, it can be minimised through education and awareness. With few exceptions, a fear of shark attack should never prevent you from entering the water. The reality is that sharks, not humans, are the victims. Each year millions of sharks are slaughtered through commercial and recreational fishing, most only for their fins. For every human killed by a shark, there approximately 10 million sharks killed by humans. Fortunately, during the last few years a turnaround has begun in the way the public views sharks, no longer perceiving them as monsters of the deep, but rather as fascinating predators that play a vital role in the ocean ecosystem.

Behaviour
All of the truly dangerous sharks (those species that have killed people) are large, strong swimmers over 2 m in length with teeth capable of removing limbs or causing severe lacerations. Like most sharks, they have very good sight and an excellent sense of smell, which allows some species to detect blood as dilute as one part per

The Tiger Shark is the most dangerous shark of tropical waters, where it is probably responsible for nearly half of all fatal attacks. *Bahamas, BW*

million. They are also able to detect underwater 'sounds' such as the vibrations given off by distressed fishes or swimmers from as far away as 3 km. Sharks have one sense that is unfamiliar to humans, namely the ability to detect electromagnetism. This is made possible by an array of specialised jelly-filled organs scattered about the head and mouth, called the ampullae of Lorenzini. These organs allow sharks to detect electric fields emitted by prey hidden in murky water or beneath sand and to use the earth's magnetic field to navigate the blue void of the open sea. This sense is best developed in the hammerhead sharks, whose distinctive lateral head flanges spread these organs over a wider area, enhancing their ability to triangulate sources of electromagnetism as well as scent.

All of the dangerous sharks typically remain in open water above the bottom and most must swim constantly in order to respire. Some frequent shallow coastal waters, while others remain far offshore or may even enter fresh water. The most dangerous sharks tend to feed on large prey that they must often cut into pieces. Many other species that have not been implicated in human fatalities are considered potentially dangerous because of their large size, anatomy and aggressive temperament. Even shark reproduction is often violent. The male holds the female by biting her, and twists his body into position to insert a clasper, a specialised external organ used to direct sperm into the female. All of the dangerous sharks give birth to a few fully developed young, grow relatively slowly and take several years to mature.

Appearance
The species of sharks most dangerous to humans have a spindle-shaped body with well-developed fins and massive jaws containing large, often serrated teeth. Mackerel sharks (Lamnidae), including the Great White, are distinguished by a conical pointed snout and crescent-shaped tail that has a pair of lateral keels along its base. Requiem sharks (Carcharhinidae) typically have somewhat flattened, usually rounded snouts, and elo~ upper-tail lobes. Some species s~~ Shark have distinctive, easily re~ tures, while others (particularly n~

The head flanges of this young Great Hammerhaed Shark *Sphyrna mokarran* enhance its ability to triangulate sources of scent and electromagnetism. *Bahamas, BW*

large genus *Carcharhinus*) may be quite difficult to identify. Hammerhead sharks (Sphyrnidae) are identical to requiem sharks except for their unique hammer-shaped heads. The fearsome-looking sand tiger sharks (Odontaspididae) have long, curved teeth that are fully visible even when the mouth is closed.

Shark attacks – when and where?

The steady rise in the number of shark attacks worldwide is due simply to the ever-increasing numbers of people in the water. The places where such attacks occur most frequently are simply those where the most people enter the water. The risk of shark attack has not increased and the fatality rate is actually falling owing to faster and better emergency treatment. The few real hotspots for shark attacks that have been identified are places where large, dangerous species habitually feed, either on their natural prey or on food unintentionally provided by man.

Who is at risk?

Anyone in the water is exposed to a slight risk of shark attack. During the past century, excluding maritime disasters, 51 per cent of unprovoked shark attacks were on swimmers, 31 per cent were on surfers and 13 per cent were on divers.

However, the lack of reliable statistics on the total numbers of each category entering the water makes it impossible to assign relative risk to those activities. Divers that see an approaching shark are better able to benefit from the animal's natural caution. A hunting shark will tend to attack unwary prey that is less likely to fight back, and sharks tend to respond to eye contact – in more than half the attacks on divers, the victim never saw the approaching shark. Although an attractant such as a wounded fish may increase the chances of a dangerous shark encounter, in 63 per cent of unprovoked attacks on divers there was no known attractant.

Unprovoked attacks

Four types of unprovoked shark attack have been identified. 'Hit-and-run' attacks occur when the shark gives one quick bite and immediately lets go. These attacks happen most frequently near the shoreline, usually inshore of a sandbar or on a reef flat where sharks feed. They are usually cases of mistaken identity due to turbid or turbulent water, which causes the shark to mistake a limb for its normal prey. Resultant injuries are seldom life-threatening and often limited to lacerations in a confined location. Swimmers, surfers and fishermen are the usual victims.

Tiger Shark *Galeocerdo cuvier.*

Specialised jaws and teeth

Both the upper and lower jaws of sharks can be protruded during feeding. Shark teeth are highly variable and are replaceable. Rows of replacement teeth lie folded behind the functional ones, so that when a tooth is lost a new one moves into place. Sharks that prey on animals too large to swallow whole have large teeth with serrated edges designed to shear, while those that prey on small animals have narrower teeth designed to grasp. Some sharks have multicuspid teeth (with many points) or knobbly teeth in cobblestone-like rows designed to crush hard-shelled invertebrates. Requiem sharks of the family Carcharhinidae exhibit a broad range of tooth types. The Tiger Shark has large, serrated, deeply notched teeth that form a saw-like blade in each jaw. When combined with lateral movements of the head and jaws, they can easily cut through the shell of a sea turtle, remove a limb or, if the shark is big enough, cut a human in two. Species of the genus *Carcharhinus* have narrower and more numerous teeth. The upper jaw teeth of the Grey Reef Shark are serrated for cutting, while those in the lower jaw are narrower and designed for grasping. A bite from this species may remove a large piece of tissue but not a limb, and no fatalities have resulted. The larger Bull Shark has wider teeth and has caused numerous fatalities. The narrow tricuspid teeth of the Whitetip Reef Shark are designed for grasping and directing small, slippery prey down its throat. A bite from this species results in numerous puncture wounds and some tearing, but not the removal of large pieces of tissue. *(Above photo by JR, all others by RM)*

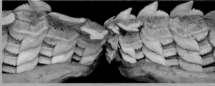

Rows of replacement teeth.

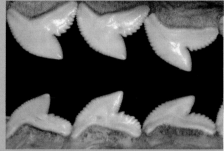

Tiger Shark *Galeocerdo cuvier.*

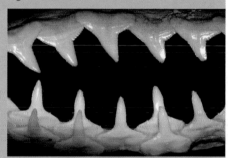

Grey Reef Shark *Carcharhinus amblyrhynchos.*

Whitetip Reef Shark *Triaenodon obesus.*

The Blacktip Reef Shark *Carcharhinus melanopterus* occasionally accidentally bites waders when it hunts in shallow water. *Maldives, MK*

IF INJURED

Treatment

First aid
Control any visible bleeding by applying direct pressure. Keep the victim calm, and if he is conscious keep him alert to ward off shock. Provide warmth. Carefully monitor breathing and cardiovascular activity, and provide resuscitation if necessary. Get emergency medical help as quickly as possible. Even seemingly minor cuts should be given medical treatment to prevent infection.

What not to do
Unless there is no other option, do not transport the victim yourself. Wait for professional help to arrive.

Ongoing medical management
Treatment and therapy vary according to the extent and type of injuries.

'Territorial defence' attacks are an intentional exhibition of dominance. These may be preceded by a clear antagonistic display termed 'threat-posturing' (p.105). This was first described for the Grey Reef Shark *Carcharhinus amblyrhynchos*. Prior to an attack, the shark swims in an exaggerated and clearly agitated manner, with its back arched and fins thrust forward, often in a rolling figure-of-eight pattern. The shark may then either flee, or suddenly rush and bite the victim. Such an attack may be stimulated by fear as well as territorial defence. Wounds from such attacks are usually severe but not life-threatening, owing primarily to the small size of the shark (under 1.8 m) and single bite. Several larger species have been observed to exhibit a similar display, but attacks have not been reported.

'Bump-and-bite' and 'sneak' attacks are less common than hit-and-run attacks, but are far more serious. These are typically the result of feeding behaviour but may also be due to antagonistic behaviour. Bump-and-bite attacks occur when the shark bumps the victim before biting, usually after a period of circling. Sneak attacks are less frequent and occur when the shark strikes without warning. Both of these kinds of attacks usually occur in deeper water beyond the surf zone, and involve divers and

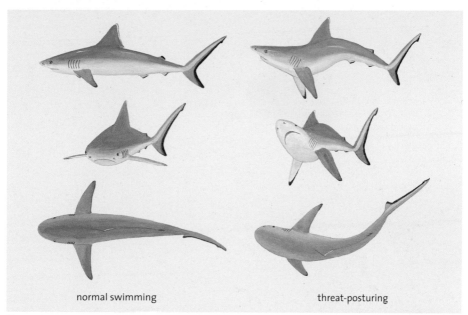

normal swimming   threat-posturing

Threat-posturing in the Grey Reef Shark. During normal swimming the shark's posture is relaxed. When threat-posturing, it is exaggerated and jerky. The shark may also swim in a rolling figure-of-eight pattern. This is a clear signal for a diver to back off, and may be followed by a single quick bite. *Illustration by EL*

swimmers as well as accident victims left floating in life vests. Bites from these attacks are usually quite severe and often fatal. Multiple bites and sustained feeding are not uncommon. Of course, if dead and wounded animals or people are present, there is an added stimulus to feeding. In cases involving the Great White Shark *Carcharodon carcharias*, the line between a hit-and-run and sneak attack is often blurred. There is usually only one bite, intended either to test or incapacitate the prey. When the shark realises that the victim is not the fatty seal it seeks, it often leaves. In one grizzly case, when the body of the victim was recovered, the severed head was held in place only by the wetsuit. However one categorises an attack by a Great White, its massive size and biting power cause far more damage than mistaken identity attacks by other sharks. Amazingly, most victims of such attacks survive as a result of quick medical intervention.

Shark attractants
The chances of being attacked by a shark may greatly increase when there is a feeding stimulus such as speared fish, or dead or wounded people, animals or animal parts in the water. Spearfishermen have been wounded by normally docile sharks that have become emboldened enough to steal their catch. During World War II, sharks were a major problem for survivors of torpedoed ships. The dead and wounded sometimes triggered feeding frenzies, during which sharks also preyed on the healthy, sometimes days after the disaster.

Not all causes of shark attacks are so obvious. More recently, in Recife, Brazil, a sudden and sustained increase in the number of attacks on surfers was traced to the opening of a sub-standard slaughterhouse 11 km up a river that emptied nearby. During a 14-year period, 34 surfers were victims of bump-and-bite attacks, 17 of them dying. Teeth left behind in surfboards were those of the Bull Shark *Carcharhinus leucas*. When the slaughterhouse was shut down, the attacks stopped. The dredging of a port in a nearby estuary was also blamed, because it disrupted the sharks' migration routes.

Prevention
The maritime disasters of World War II stimulated research aimed at finding a shark repellent. The few substances that showed promise were invariably impractical and nothing effective was found. While the odds of being attacked by a

Safety tips: guidelines to reduce the risk of shark attack

Swimmers and surfers
- Stay in groups, since sharks are more likely to attack an isolated individual.
- Avoid straying too far from shore, as this isolates you and places you further from assistance.
- Avoid the water during dusk, night or dawn, as this is when sharks most frequently move inshore to hunt and is also when they have their greatest sensory advantage.
- Stay out of the water if bleeding from an open wound or menstruating.
- Avoid unusually murky areas or the vicinity of harbours, channels, river mouths, storm drains or sewage outlets, especially after heavy rains. Sharks frequent these areas and may be attracted to dead animals or refuse that washes into the ocean.
- Avoid areas of fishing activity, either by humans or animals, especially if there are signs of feeding fishes, diving seabirds or marine life behaving erratically.
- If sharks are sighted, leave the water quickly and calmly.
- Do not wear shiny jewellery in the water since it may resemble the glint of a distressed fish. Even high-contrast swimwear or an uneven tan may increase the chances of an accident.
- Minimise erratic movements by avoiding excessive splashing and by keeping pets out of the water.
- Use caution and minimise the time you spend between sandbars or at a drop-off.
- Use beaches patrolled by lifeguards.

Divers and snorkellers
- Tow speared fishes, lobsters and dead or struggling marine life of any kind a safe distance from you and remove them from the water as soon as is practical.
- Leave the water as soon as possible after incurring a bleeding injury.
- If a potentially dangerous or unrecognised shark approaches, try to get close to the shelter of a reef or other structure.
- If a shark appears unusually curious, leave the water with calm, purposeful movements while facing it and avoiding open water.
- If a shark engages in threat-posturing (p.105), distance yourself from it immediately while maintaining eye contact.
- Do not pester or touch a shark resting on the ocean floor or corner a swimming shark.
- Do not attempt to feed or stimulate a shark.
- If seeking sharks, be aware of the area and resident species and treat them with caution and respect. Those seeking a close encounter with sharks should do so under the auspices of a well-established business with a safe track record.

Boaters
- Check for the presence of sharks before entering the water.
- Stay as close to the boat as possible, always keeping a lookout for sharks.
- Stay in a group.
- Post a lookout as high above the water as possible.
- Avoid swimming in deep or murky water.
- Do not throw any food waste overboard.

If marooned in open water
- Stay together as a group, facing outward.
- If bumped by a shark, strike it, preferably with an inanimate object as contact with the animal's rough skin can cause a bleeding injury.

The Tiger Shark, the most dangerous warm-water shark, may enter very shallow water to feed. This one is eating a dead whale. *Palau, ME*

shark are low, the threat can never be completely eliminated. However, by understanding when and where sharks aggregate and feed, and what can trigger an attack, one can minimise the risk by following certain safety tips. Those offered here are not hard-and-fast rules, simply guidelines, and there are many exceptions depending on the local situation. While it is probably a good idea for menstruating women to avoid areas accessible to sharks, there is no evidence that they are at increased risk while scuba-diving.

Injuries and symptoms

Shark bites range from small puncture wounds to the immediately fatal massive removal of body parts. Loss of blood and shock from otherwise survivable wounds can easily lead to unconsciousness and death. Most shark bites are survivable – the overall fatality rate for all bites is 23 per cent and falling. The rate is higher for bites from large sharks (33 per cent for the Tiger Shark) and lower for bites from smaller sharks.

Classification and distribution: which sharks are dangerous?

There are about 500 species of shark in 34 families. They evolved about 400 million years ago and, like their relatives the rays, have skeletons of cartilage instead of bone and five to seven pairs of slit-like gill openings. Sharks come in a

Sharks ranked by number of documented unprovoked attacks on humans

SPECIES	no.	%	no. deaths	%	no.	%
		ATTACKS – ALL ACTIVITIES			ATTACKS ON DIVERS	
Great White Carcharodon carcharias	232	37.3	63	46.3	48	33.8
Tiger Galeocerdo cuvier	86	13.8	28	20.1	21	14.8
Bull Carcharhinus leucas	75	12.1	23	16.9	7	4.9
unidentified requiem Carcharhinus spp.*	30	4.8	8	5.9	8	5.6
Sand Tiger Carcharias taurus	30	4.8	2	1.5	5	3.5
Blacktip Carcharhinus limbatus	28	4.5	1	0.7	5	3.5
Hammerhead Sphyrna spp.	17	2.7	1	0.7	1	0.7
Bronze Whaler Carcharhinus brachyurus	15	2.4	–	–	1	0.7
Spinner Carcharhinus brevipinna	15	2.4	–	–	–	–
Blue Prionace glauca	13	2.1	4	2.9	3	2.1
Blacktip Reef Carcharhinus melanopterus	11	1.7	–	–	2	1.4
Nurse Ginglymostoma cirratum	10	1.6	–	–	5	3.5
Lemon Negaprion brevirostris	9	1.4	–	–	3	2.1
Shortfin Mako Isurus oxyrinchus	9	1.4	2	1.5	3	2.1
Grey Reef Carcharhinus amblyrhynchos	6	1.0	–	–	5	3.5
Caribbean Reef Carcharhinus perezi	6	1.0	–	–	4	2.8
Silky Carcharhinus falciformis	6	1.0	–	–	2	1.4
Oceanic Whitetip Carcharhinus longimanus	5	0.8	1	0.7	4	2.8
Sandbar Carcharhinus plumbeus	5	0.8	1	0.7	2	1.4
Sevengill Notorhynchus cepedianus	5	0.8	–	–	2	1.4
unidentified mako Isurus spp.	3	0.5	–	–	1	0.7
Dusky Carcharhinus obscurus	3	0.5	1	0.7	1	0.7
Spotted Wobbegong Orectolobus maculatus	2	0.3	–	–	1	0.7
Whitetip Reef Triaenodon obesus	2	0.3	–	–	1	0.7
Galapagos Carcharhinus galapagensis	1	0.2	1	0.7	–	–
Leopard Triakis semifasciata	1	0.2	–	–	1	0.7
Porbeagle Lamna nasus	1	0.2	–	–	1	0.7
Tope Galeorhinus galeus	1	0.2	–	–	1	0.7
unidentified wobbegong Orectolobus spp.*	–	–	–	–	2	1.4
Silvertip Carcharhinus albimarginatus**	–	–	–	–	–	–
TOTAL	622		136		140	

* likely to include other species on list.

**divers aggressively rushed. Data based on ISAF figures through to 10 January 2007.

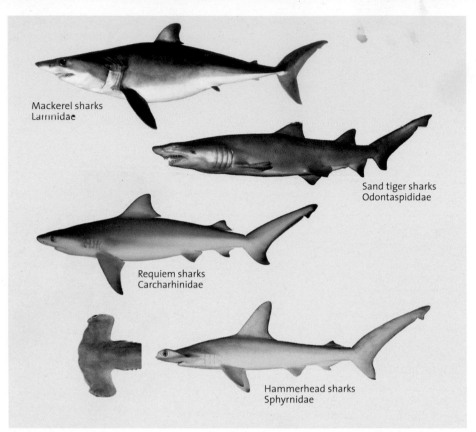

Mackerel sharks
Lamnidae

Sand tiger sharks
Odontaspididae

Requiem sharks
Carcharhinidae

Hammerhead sharks
Sphyrnidae

The four families of shark containing species identified in fatal attacks on humans. All of them have spindle-shaped bodies with well-developed fins and large jaws with large teeth. *JR and RM*

wide variety of shapes and sizes, and occur in all marine waters, from the surface to the abyss, and even in some major rivers. Of all these species of shark, only 28, or less than 6 per cent, have been identified in unprovoked attacks on humans. Only 12 species in four families have been implicated in fatal attacks. (The exact number cannot be determined owing to the difficulty of identification in certain groups.) All of them share a spindle-shaped body with well-developed fins, and large jaws that contain large, often serrated teeth. They typically spend their time actively swimming well above the bottom and nearly all occur in the warm-water regions covered by this book.

The Great White Shark tops the list of unprovoked attacks and fatalities, followed by the Tiger Shark and Bull Shark. These species are also ranked the same in attacks on divers. All of the remaining species identified in fatal attacks, aside from the Shortfin Mako, Sand Tiger and hammerheads, are requiem sharks (family Carcharhinidae), as are most of the species involved in non-fatal attacks. Members of this family account for 51 per cent of attacks and 50 per cent of fatalities, and are responsible for nearly all attacks and fatalities in tropical waters. Sixteen more species, including members of four other families, have been identified in non-fatal attacks. The Leopard Shark and Tope are members of the houndshark family (Triakidae) and live in temperate or deep tropical waters. The Sevengill Shark normally inhabits cold, deep water and is rarely encountered. The nurse sharks (Ginglymostomatidae) and wobbegongs (Orectolobidae) are bottom-dwellers with smaller mouths and small, grasping teeth that cause bruising injuries (p.121).

Sample cases

1) **Jensen Beach, Florida, June 2002, 1 pm.** A ten-year-old boy was playing in waist-deep water with a group of about 20 children. The surf was running about 60 cm and there were baitfish in the vicinity. The boy felt what he thought was a friend pulling his leg, then noticed a shark had bitten him, and immediately ran crying for help. Lifeguards stabilised him and quickly cleared the water. The boy was hysterical at first, but soon calmed and remained conscious but in pain. He was airlifted to the nearest hospital and treated. This was a typical case of hit and run by a small shark, likely a Blacktip. *(Based on a newspaper account.)*

2) **Maui, Hawaii, January 2002.** Conditions were clear and calm as a 35-year-old man and his girlfriend were snorkelling about 100 m offshore in water about 12 m deep. The couple had been watching a group of several turtles when they saw a 2 m Tiger Shark about 8 m away swimming directly towards them 'at an alarming speed'. They popped their heads out of the water and started to back away. When the shark was about 1.3 m away, the man noticed its mouth was open, so he curled into a ball. The shark bit him on the buttocks, then quickly released. He punched the shark on the snout as it lingered nearby and then it swam away. He didn't feel any pain as he was bitten, but felt a stinging sensation as he swam to shore. His shorts were tattered and he was bleeding from six lacerations, which required more than 50 stitches. *(Based on a newspaper account.)*

3) **Gulf Shores, Alabama, June 2002, morning.** Two men, CA, 44, and RW, 55, were swimming about 25–30 m from shore when CA felt something underneath him. Moments later, a 'large shark' bit his right hand and forearm, shredding it as he pulled free and swam to shore. RW saw his friend stagger out of the water and assumed he had run into jellyfish, when the shark suddenly came up beside him and bumped him. It then came up underneath him and bit his right hip. He fought back by hitting it. It let go but came back repeatedly as he swan to shore. Each time it charged, RW grabbed its nose and hit it, causing it to break away and circle for another strike. It ultimately chased him right onto the beach. CA's right arm had to be amputated above the elbow.

RW recovered from wounds to his right hip and arm. This was a typical bump-and-bite attack. The shark was not identified but was believed to be a Bull Shark. *(Based on a newspaper account.)*

4) **Enewetak Atoll, Marshall Islands, 1978, midday.** Two employees of a marine station, MD and PL, were scuba-diving along a lagoon pinnacle slope when they were approached by a 1.5-m-long Grey Reef Shark that had a mating scar on its back and was swimming in an agitated manner as if it were 'retarded'. MD responded by photographing the shark with a housed camera and flash. The shark immediately charged, knocked the camera loose, and bit MD on his right forearm and 'shook it'. PL, who was holding a pole-spear, tried to divert the shark's attention. The shark let go of MD and charged. As PL tried to fend it off, it bit him on the hand that was holding the spear, then left. The injured men struggled into their boat and radioed for help. They were given first aid at the local dispensary, then evacuated by air the next day to the US Naval Hospital in Guam for surgery. A substantial plug of muscle tissue had been removed from MD's forearm. It eventually healed, as did PH's less serious wound. In retrospect, the men realised they had witnessed a classic case of threat-posturing and should have backed away from the shark. *(Based on an interview of the victims by RM.)*

5) **Cactus Beach, South Australia, September 2000, 7:30 am.** Witnesses described how a 4–5-m-long Great White Shark fatally attacked a 25-year-old surfer about 200 m from shore. One witness described how the shark attacked several times. 'It just came in and attacked him, thrashing in a circular motion around him.... He seemed to get back on his board and was paddling back when the shark attacked again.' He described how the shark 'seemed to roll on its belly then it thrashed around a bit more then it seemed to release the surfboard...but there was nothing left of the guy'. Another witness said the shark 'created a whirlpool which dragged him down' and saw 'a flash of red' as a wave came over. He described the attack as 'very savage' and said 'the thing really wanted him and it wasn't going to let him go'. The attack lasted about 90 seconds and only three parts of the surfboard were recovered. This was a sneak attack in which the shark decided to eat its victim. *(Based on a newspaper account.)*

The Great White Shark is a massive species with huge serrated teeth. *HF (above); BW (below)*

Mackerel Sharks
Lamnidae

The five species of this family have spindle-shaped bodies with near-conical snouts, large, broad teeth, and crescent-shaped tail fins with a lateral keel on either side of their bases. All are sleek, warm-blooded swimmers of open water. Among them is the most dangerous shark of all, the Great White, which can attain the huge size of 3,220 kg. It prefers cool waters of 10–20°C and requires high fat-content prey to fuel its metabolism. Although it is responsible for more fatal attacks on humans than any other species, it rarely feeds on them. Attacks typically consist of a single bite, either as a test or due to mistaken identity.

Another dangerous member of the family that has fatally attacked humans is the Shortfin Mako *Isurus oxyrhinchus*, a swift, open-sea predator of tropical and temperate waters above 16°C that feeds primarily on fishes. The poorly known Longfin Mako *I. paucus* inhabits deep water, while the Salmon and Porbeagle sharks *Lamna ditropis* and *L. nasus* inhabit cold waters of 1–18°C. Neither has been implicated in attacks on humans.

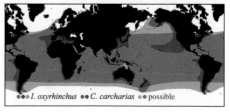

●●● *I. oxyrhinchus* ●● *C. carcharias* ●● possible

Great White Shark	6.2 m
Carcharodon carcharias	*(21 ft)*

Snout pointed, teeth triangular and ser-rated; grey above, abruptly white below. **Biology:** coastal and oceanic, surface to 1,300 m. Warm-blooded, prefers seas of 10–20°C, rarely near surface in tropics. Intelligent, with complex social structure. Juveniles feed on fishes, shifting to high fat-content marine mammals as adults. Adults coastal in temperate regions, gath-ering near seal colonies. Attacks prey by ambushing from below. Migrates across oceans (California to Hawaiian Is and S. Africa to W. Australia). Litters of 2–10 pups born at 110–160 cm after 12-month gesta-tion. ♂'s mature at 350–400 cm, ♀s at 450–500 cm. **Range:** circumglobal in all seas of *c.*10–24°C. **Similar:** Mako sharks have acutely pointed snout, smooth transi-tion between upper and lower body colours, and narrower, smooth-edged teeth.

Sand Tiger Sharks
Odontaspididae

This family includes only three species, all with a pointed snout, long, curved teeth that are clearly visible when the mouth is closed, small eyes, dorsal fins of near equal size at the rear of body, and a tail with a poorly developed lower lobe. They are relatively docile, but one species, the Sand Tiger *Carcharias taurus*, has bitten divers. Although it has been blamed for two fatalities, its bite wounds are not usually life-threatening since its fearsome-looking teeth are designed to grasp fishes. Embryos canni-balise their siblings, leaving one survivor in each uterus at the time of birth.

Sand Tiger Shark	4.3 m
Carcharias tauru	*(14 ft)*

Teeth long, curved and fully exposed. **Biology:** inhabits coastal waters, surf zone to 191 m. Usually near bottom, in or near caves, gullies and wrecks. Relatively slug-gish but strong. Feeds on fishes and inver-tebrates, aggregates to herd schooling fishes. **Range:** primarily warm-temperate waters in scattered coastal areas nearly worldwide. **Similar:** Small-tooth Sand Tiger *Odontaspis ferox* has narrower snout, more forward 1st dorsal fin, larger eyes.

Carcharias taurus • *Odontaspis ferox* •

The Tiger Shark *Galeocerdo cuvier*, the most dangerous warm-water shark, is a massive species with a broad head and large serrated teeth. It may enter very shallow water to feed. *Bahamas, BW*

Requiem Sharks
Carcharhinidae

This large, aptly named family includes most of the world's most dangerous species of shark. At least eight of its 54 species have fatally attacked humans and 15 have attacked divers. Requiem sharks are characterised by an elongate upper-tail lobe, often a broad and sometimes well-rounded snout, and blade-like teeth that are usually narrower in the lower jaw. Most are sleek and fast-swimming. Some species, including the largest, the Tiger Shark, are quite distinctive, while others, including many species of *Carcharhinus*, are difficult to identify.

The Tiger Shark is the most dangerous shark of tropical waters. It has been implicated in numerous fatal attacks, close inshore as well as in the open sea. The Bull Shark, widely regarded as the world's third most dangerous shark, is also responsible for many human fatalities, particularly among swimmers and surfers. It occurs in tropical coastal regions as well as inland fresh waters and, seasonally, in temperate regions. It has been found 2,896 km up the Mississippi and 3,540 km up the Amazon. The Oceanic Whitetip

Shark may be the most dangerous shark of tropical oceanic waters and is probably responsible for a large portion of fatalities among survivors of maritime disasters left floating in the open sea.

Requiem sharks are widely distributed in all tropical and temperate seas. Most species are primarily coastal, but a few are oceanic and some are exclusive to fresh water.

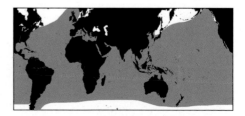

Tiger Shark — 7.4 m; 3,110 kg
Galeocerdo cuvier (24.3 ft; 6,856 lb)

Head broad, snout nearly square; upper sides with dusky bars; teeth serrated with distinctive notch. **Biology:** inhabits estuaries, coastal waters, offshore banks and coral reefs, 1–350 m. Usually deep during the day, shallow and close inshore at night, often in turbid areas near river mouths. Has very large semi-resident home range, may migrate as far as 3,430 km. Feeds on a wide range of prey, incl. sea turtles, porpoises, seabirds, sharks, rays, bony fishes, carrion and garbage. Highly dangerous but rarely aggressive towards divers. Gives birth during spring and summer. Litters of 10–82 pups born at 51–76 cm. Matures in 4–6 yrs, ♂s at 226–290 cm, ♀s at 250–350 cm. Fast-growing, lives to 45–50 yrs. **Range:** all tropical seas, seasonally in temperate seas (absent from Mediterranean).

Bull Shark — 3.4 m
Carcharhinus leucas (11.2 ft)

Stocky with broad, rounded snout, triangular dorsal fin; upper teeth triangular and serrated, lower teeth broad. **Biology:** inhabits marine and fresh waters of rivers, lakes, estuaries and coasts, 1–152 m. Usually near bottom. Migrates to temperate regions in summer. Feeds on wide variety of prey, incl. bony fishes, sharks, rays, invertebrates, sea turtles, marine and land mammals, seabirds and whale offal. Highly dangerous, ranked third in number of fatal attacks on humans. Generally not aggressive towards divers, but should be treated with respect. Litters of 1–13 pups born at 56–81 cm, usually in estuaries and rivers. Matures in 15–20 yrs, ♂s at 157–226 cm, ♀s at 180–230 cm. Lives over 25 yrs. **Range:** circumtropical.

G. cuvier ● C. leucas ●

Oceanic Whitetip Shark   3.5 m
Carcharhinus longimanus   *(11.5 ft)*

Stocky, with rounded snout, large, rounded
fins with white tips; upper teeth triangular
and serrated. **Biology:** oceanic, surface to
152 m over deep water. May visit adjacent
pinnacles and banks. Almost always
accompanied by Pilot Fish *Naucrates
ductor*, often shadows pilot whales. Feeds
on bony fishes, rays, cephalopods, seabirds,
turtles, crustaceans, gastropods, marine
mammals, carrion and garbage. Bold; may
persistently circle divers. Dangerous;
unprovoked fatal attacks reported. **Range:**
circumglobal in seas over 18°C.

Silky Shark   3.3 m
Carcharhinus falciformis   *(10.8 ft)*

Slender, small dorsal fin; greyish brown.
Biology: oceanic, 3–500 m, primarily over
deep shelf edges. Associated with tuna.
Feeds primarily on fishes, also on
cephalopods and pelagic crustaceans.
Swift and bold, but usually ignores divers.
May exhibit a threat posture. **Range:**
circumglobal in tropical and warm-
temperate seas.

C. longimanus ● ● C. falciformis ●

Silvertip Shark   3.0 m
Carcharhinus albimarginatus *(9.9 ft)*

Tips and rear margins of dorsal, pectoral
and tail fins white. **Biology:** usually along
deep drop-offs and banks, occasionally in
deep lagoons or channels, 2 m to >600 m.
Solitary or in groups, young more inshore.
Feeds on fishes, eagle rays and octopods.
Cautious, but can be aggressive. One confirmed bite incident. **Range:** Red Sea to
Equador, n. to s. Japan; primarily at oceanic
islands.

C. albimarginatus

Blacktip Shark   2.55 m
Carcharhinus limbatus   (8.4 ft)

Snout pointed. **Biology:** inhabits coastal
waters, shoreline to >30 m. Uncommon at
oceanic islands. ♀s migrate to inshore
nursery grounds. Feeds primarily on
schooling fishes. Not usually aggressive,
but responsible for at least one fatal attack
on a swimmer and may harass spearfishermen. Litters of 1–10 pups born at 38–72 cm
after 10–12 months gestation. ♂s mature
at 135–180 cm, ♀s at 120–190 cm. **Range:**
circumglobal in tropical and warm-
temperate seas.

Galapagos Shark   3.7 m
Carcharhinus galapagensis (12.1 ft)

Dorsal fin large, brownish grey. **Biology:**
inhabits rocky and coral reefs, primarily at
oceanic islands, 2–180 m. Usually near
bottom, may aggregate. Nursery grounds
below 25 m. Feeds primarily on fishes,
occasionally on invertebrates and garbage.
Inquisitive; may perform threat display.
Has fatally attacked a swimmer. **Range:**
circumtropical, patchy.

Sandbar Shark   2.4 m
Carcharhinus plumbeus   (7.9 ft)

Dorsal fin very large. **Biology:** primarily
coastal, from river mouths to continental
slope, 1–280 m. Usually near bottom; segre-
gates by size and sex. Mates in spring and
summer. Young in shallow nursery areas.
Feeds mostly on fishes, also on cephalopods
and crustaceans. Usually inoffensive, but
has bitten people, one fatality. Matures in
13 yrs at 1.4–1.8 m, lives to 30 yrs. **Range:**
circumglobal in widely scattered areas.

Gray Reef Shark   1.8 m
Carcharhinus amblyrhynchos   *(6 ft)*

Tail margin dusky, rear margin of dorsal fin
may be white. **Biology:** inhabits coral reefs,
1–274 m. Common in deeper atoll lagoons,
channels and along seaward reef drop-offs.
Active and social, may aggregate by day.
Strongly site-attached but with large
home range and may venture several kilometres offshore. Feeds primarily on reef
fishes, cephalopods and crustaceans. Dominant over Blacktip Reef and Whitetip Reef
sharks. Well known for threat-posturing
(p.105). Responsible for large portion of
shark bites to Pacific islanders. No fatalities
known but injuries often serious and debilitating. May be stimulated into feeding
frenzy by speared fish. Seems to become
less aggressive after long-term contact and
habituation towards humans. Litters of 1–6
born at 45–75 cm after c.1 yr gestation.
Matures in 7–7.5 yrs, ♂'s at 110–145 cm, ♀s at
120–137 cm. Lives to at least 25 yrs. **Range:**
Red Sea and S. Africa to Easter I., n. to
Taiwan, and Hawaiian Is.

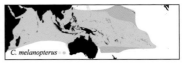

C. melanopterus

Blacktip Reef Shark   1.8 m
Carcharhinus melanopterus   *(6 ft)*

Fins and tail with black tips, sides with
light lateral streak. **Biology:** inhabits reef
flats and shallow lagoon and seaward
reefs, 0.2–75 m. A swift predator of reef
fishes and cephalopods. Fins and back
often exposed when in shallows. Timid and
difficult to approach. Avoids divers, but
occasionally bites a leg or foot of a wader
mistaken for prey. Litters of 2–4 born at
33–52 cm. ♂'s mature at 91–100 cm, ♀s at
96–112 cm. **Range:** Red Sea to Fr. Polynesia,
Hawaiian and Pitcairn Is. n. to s. Japan;
recent migrant to w. Mediterranean
(Tunisia to Israel).

Caribbean Reef Shark   2.95 m
Carcharhinus perezi   (9.7 ft)

Greyish brown, pale below, tail margin
slightly dusky. **Biology:** inhabits coral reefs
and clear coastal waters, 1 m to at least
45 m. The most common Caribbean reef
shark. Typically seen along slope edges.
May rest on bottom, pumping water over
gills while in sleep-like state. Feeds on bony
fishes. Relatively docile and approachable,
but has bitten divers. A favourite subject of
shark-feeding attractions. Has given birth
in captivity. Litters of 3–6 pups born at
70–73 cm every 2 yrs. Matures at
152–168 cm. **Range:** Bermuda, n. FL and Bay
of Campeche to s. Brazil, incl. all Caribbean.

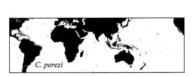
C. perezi

Lemon Shark   3.4 m
Negaprion brevirostris   (11.2 ft)

Dorsal fins nearly same size, snout broad,
teeth blade-like; yellow hue. **Biology:**
inhabits estuaries, bays, lagoons and seaward reefs, 1–92 m. Enters lower reaches of
rivers. Can rest on bottom. Young in nursery areas in mangroves and on shallow
flats. Adults with larger home ranges.
Aggregates off e. FL during winter. Feeds
primarily on fishes, also on crustaceans
and molluscs. May be aggressive when
stimulated. Has bitten humans and
attacked divers, but no fatalities. Litters of
4–17 pups born at 60–65 cm after 10–12-
month gestation. Matures in 6.5 yrs, ♂'s at
c.224 cm, ♀s at c.239 cm. Lives to at least 27
yrs. **Range:** NJ and Bahamas to s. Brazil, e.
to W. Africa; G. of California to Ecuador.
Replaced by Sicklefin Lemon Shark
N. acutidens in Indo-Pacific.

N. acutidens
N. brevirostris

Whitetip Reef Shark 1.75 m
Triaenodon obesus (5.7 ft)

Slender, with nasal flaps; tips of dorsal and tail fins white. **Biology:** inhabits lagoon and seaward reefs, 1–330 m. Often rests on sand in caves, channels or under ledges by day. Feeds on reef fishes and octopuses, primarily at night. Sometimes hunts in packs. Highly flexible, able to squeeze into narrow openings to reach prey. Returns to habitual daytime resting sites. Sometimes several may rest together in caves or under large tabular corals. Juveniles highly secretive, remaining among cover. Inoffensive unless provoked. Usually timid, but large individuals have been known to get aggressive around speared fish. Litters of 1–5 pups born at 52–60 cm after gestation of at least 5 months. Matures in 5 yrs, ♂'s at 104–105 cm, ♀s at 105–109+ cm. Adults grow 2–4 cm annually; lives to at least 25 yrs. **Range:** Red Sea to Panama, n. to s. Japan and Hawaii, s. to S. Africa.

Blue Shark 3.8 m
Prionace glauca (12.4 ft)

Slender with long snout, long pectoral fins, short dorsal fin; upper teeth triangular and serrated; blue above, white below. **Biology:** oceanic, surface to >350 m. Below thermocline in tropics, in high latitudes during summer. Migrates to follow prey and breed. Feeds primarily on pelagic fishes and squids. Cautious, but may be aggressive when stimulated. Has fatally bitten humans and attacked divers. Lives to at least 20 yrs. **Range:** circumglobal in seas of 7–25°C (usually 12–20°C).

Hammerhead Sharks
Sphyrnidae

The eight species of this family are identical to requiem sharks except for their unique hammer-shaped heads. By spreading the eyes and nostrils apart and increasing the space available for ampullae of Lorenzini, the head flanges may enhance the shark's stereoscopic vision as well as its ability to triangulate sources of scent and electromagnetism. The 'hammer is also used by the Scalloped Hammerhead to ram its stingray prey into the sand. A hammerhead has been implicated in at least one fatal attack on a human but the species is uncertain. The largest, the Great Hammerhead, is known to have attacked divers and another, the Smooth Hammerhead *Sphyrna zygaena*, has also bitten humans. Hammerheads are widely distributed in all tropical and temperate seas. They are primarily coastal, but some are also nomadic in the open sea.

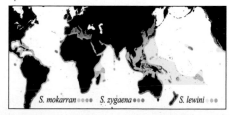

S. mokarran ●●●●   S. zygaena ●●●   S. lewini ●●

Great Hammerhead	6.1 m
Sphyrna mokarran	(20 ft)

Tall, curved dorsal fin; front of head nearly straight with median notch. **Biology:** coastal to semi-oceanic, inhabits continental and insular shelves, and lagoons and passes of coral atolls, shoreline to >80 m. Feeds on wide variety of prey, preferring stingrays, groupers and sea catfishes. Non-aggressive unless stimulated. Potentially dangerous, but attacks unverified. Litters of 6–42 born at 50–70 cm after 11 months gestation. ♂'s mature at 234–269 cm, ♀s at 250–300 cm. **Range:** circumglobal in tropical and warm-temperate seas.

Scalloped Hammerhead	4 m
Sphyrna lewini	(13.1 ft)

Front of head curved and notched. **Biology:** inhabits continental shelves and steep slopes of islands and banks, 1–275 m. Juveniles inshore, adults usually below thermocline in tropics. Feeds primarily on fishes, especially stingrays, occasionally on invertebrates. Non-aggressive unless stimulated. May display threat posture. Potentially dangerous but attacks unverified. Litters of 13–31 born at 42–55 cm after 9–10 months gestation. ♂'s mature at 140–165 cm, ♀s at 212 cm. **Range:** circumtropical. **Similar:** Smooth Hammerhead *S. zygaena* lacks median notch (4 m; primarily temperate coastal).

The Tasselled wobbegong *Eucrossorhinus dasypogon* has a record of biting divers. The two white spots are false eyespots just behind the real eyes. *W. Papua, RM*

Carpet Sharks and their Relatives
Order Orectolobiformes

These bottom-dwelling sharks are not capable of killing humans but some species can be bad-tempered and cause injury. They have small to medium-sized mouths with strong jaws full of needle-like teeth. Some members of two families, the wobbegongs (Orectolobidae) and nurse sharks (Ginglymostomatidae), can be bad-tempered and have attacked and injured humans. The single species of the Stegostomatidae family, the Zebra Shark, should be treated with caution owing to its large size and similar mouth and teeth. Other small species such as the longtail carpetsharks (Hemiscylliidae) may also nip if handled but are too small to cause significant injury.

Behaviour and life history
Orectolobiform sharks are typically bottom-dwellers that rest on sand or gravel of gullies or under ledges. Occasionally, they swim close above the bottom for considerable distances. Most feed on a variety of small animals, including crustaceans, molluscs and small fishes. Some even feed on sea urchins and sea snakes. Prey are sucked in and grasped with needle-like teeth. All of these sharks are usually docile and harmless unless provoked.

Wobbegongs are the most sedentary of the group. They rely on camouflage for protection as well as to ambush prey. They are also the members of this group most likely to remain unseen and surprise and injure a diver. Some species are reputed to have a rather short fuse. If touched or harassed, they may suddenly strike and hang on with a vice-like grip. Nurse sharks may also do this, but are more likely to avoid contact by swimming away. The Zebra Shark is less likely to bite but it does get large and has the equipment to cause injury.

Reproduction varies. Carpet sharks and most nurse sharks give birth to fully developed young, while the Zebra Shark and longtail carpet sharks lay egg cases.

Small mouths and teeth, and a vice-like grip

Wobbegongs have terminal mouths that can open surprisingly wide and are full of small, sharply pointed teeth (left). Nurse sharks (right) and the Zebra Shark have smaller mouths located under the snout and small, relatively broad multicuspid teeth in several functional rows. These sharks have a vice-like grip and, when they bite, they usually do not let go, even when removed from the water. They can survive out of the water for several hours and their jaws must be prised loose.

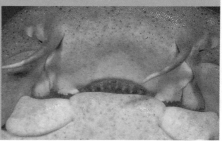

Appearance

All species in this group are elongate, with blunt snouts and small mouths, broad pectoral fins, two dorsal fins of almost equal size at the rear of the body, and long tails with only an upper lobe. The wobbegongs (Orectolobidae) are masterfully camouflaged with intricate spots and blotches that resemble crustose algae and seaweed. They are somewhat flattened, with a terminal mouth surrounded by branched tassels. Their eyes are small and nearly invisible with slit-like pupils. In some species, a pair of false eyespots behind the eyes completes the disguise. Many wobbegongs rest with their tail curled.

Nurse sharks (Ginglymostomatidae) have deeper bodies and are nearly cylindrical in cross section, with a smaller mouth under the snout, and are uniformly light brown to grey. The Zebra Shark (Stegostomatidae) differs from nurse sharks by having five ridges running along its upper body and a tail as long as the body. Juveniles are nearly white with black bars. As they grow, the bars break up into spots.

Typical accidents

Bites from carpet sharks are nearly always provoked, usually by a diver touching or harassing the animal. However, in some cases an unseen shark may bite a diver who accidentally surprises it. Fishermen can get bitten when removing a hook or releasing the shark from a lobster pot. The victim is invariably surprised by the

Sample case

Palm Beach County, FL, March 2002. A 39-year-old man was snorkelling about 270 m from shore in water about 5 m deep. He claimed that as he swam over a school of fish, a 90-cm Nurse Shark lunged at him and clamped onto his left arm. He grabbed the shark as he made his way to the surface for air. The shark held on as he struggled at the surface for about five minutes, before nearby boaters came to his rescue. The shark refused to let go, even after they were pulled from the water and its belly was slit open. On shore, paramedics had to use makeshift tools to prise the shark loose. The victim was given nitrous oxide to ease his pain but never lost consciousness. His arm was riddled with tooth marks but the only concern was infection. He was taken to hospital, where he was treated and released. Possibly the victim had thrust his arm into the school of fishes and the shark mistook it for an easy meal or an act of aggression.

During the day, Tawny Nurse Sharks *Nebrius ferrugineus* may share the same sleeping spots. *W. Papua, RM*

speed and manoeuvrability of the shark as well as its tenacity. In many cases the shark cannot be prised loose until the victim leaves the water and gets help. There have even been cases where the victim has driven himself to hospital with the shark still attached to his leg.

Prevention
Divers and snorkellers should never touch or harass a carpet, nurse or Zebra shark of any species. Being aware of your surroundings,

especially when close to the bottom where these sharks live, may prevent a bite due to accidental contact. Fishermen should be aware of the shark's manoeuvrability and tenacity, and take appropriate care or seek assistance when removing a hook or freeing a shark from a trap.

Injuries and symptoms
Wounds that result from carpet, nurse and Zebra shark bites are generally not serious and are limited to bruising and small punctures that may require sutures as well as antibiotics. For snorkellers, drowning is a distinct possibility in accidents involving large sharks,

Classification and distribution
The order Orectolobiformes contains about 35 species in seven families. All but one, the Whale Shark, are bottom-dwellers that have nasal barbels, relatively small mouths located in front of the eyes, two dorsal fins, and a tail fin with either a poorly developed lower lobe or none at all. Some of the nine species of wobbegongs (Orectolobidae) and three species of nurse sharks (Ginglymostomatidae) are known to attack humans. The single species of Zebra Shark (Stegostomatidae) has the potential to inflict damage owing to its large size and teeth.

IF INJURED

Treatment

First aid
Control any visible bleeding by applying direct pressure. Keep the victim calm. If the victim is conscious, keep him alert to ward off shock. Provide warmth. Carefully monitor breathing and cardiovascular activity, and provide resuscitation if necessary. Get emergency medical help as quickly as possible. Even seemingly minor cuts should be given medical treatment to prevent infection.

What not to do
Unless there is no other option, do not transport the victim yourself. Wait for professional help to arrive.

Ongoing medical management
Treatment and therapy varies according to the extent and type of injuries.

Wobbegongs
Orectolobidae

Indonesian Wobbegong	>125 cm
Orectolobus sp.	*(>49 in)*

Scattered branched tassels around mouth and sides of head. **Biology:** inhabits coral reefs in areas subject to cold upwelling (15–23°C). Known primarily from photographs. Very close to Spotted Wobbegong *O. maculatus*, a large temperate Australian species (3.2 m; 10.5 ft) reputed to be bad-tempered. **Range:** Komodo, Bali, w. Papua, possibly Philippines.

Tasselled Wobbegong	>125 cm
Eucrossorhinus dasypogon	*(>49 in)*

Dense branched tassels around mouth and sides of broad head. **Biology:** inhabits shallow coral reefs, 1–40 m. Usually on sand near or under coral heads by day with tail curled. Feeds on small fishes and, possibly, on invertebrates. Remains still when approached but known to bite. Newborns c.20 cm, matures at <117 cm. **Range:** tropical n. Australia and New Guinea.

E. dasypogon ●●
Orectolobus sp. ●●

Nurse Sharks
Ginglymostomatidiae

Tawny Nurse Shark	3.2 m
Nebrius ferrugineus	*(10.5 ft)*

Mouth small, prominent nasal barbels; grey to brown. **Biology:** inhabits lagoon and seaward reefs, 1–70 m. Typically rests on sand near or under corals by day, sometimes several in a pile. More active at night. Feeds on cephalopods, crustaceans, fishes, sea snakes and sea urchins. Prey are sucked in and then crushed; may break coral in process. Sluggish and harmless unless provoked. May bite and hang on tenaciously. **Range:** Red Sea and S. Africa to Tuamotus, n. to s. Japan, s. to New Caledonia.

Nurse Shark	3 m
Ginglymostoma cirratum	*(10 ft)*

Mouth small, teeth multicuspid; juveniles with scattered small dark spots. **Biology:** inhabits mangrove channels, sand flats, seagrass beds and rocky and coral reefs, 1–130 m. Juveniles among mangroves and on grass flats. Has small home range. Rests on sand bottom under ledges or in caves by day, sometimes several in a heap. Active at night. Feeds on invertebrates, small fishes and stingrays, which may be rooted from shelter and sucked in. May bite and hang on if harassed. Courtship involves synchronised parallel swimming. ♂ holds ♀ by pectoral fin and both roll upside down to mate. Litters of 20–30 born at size of 27–30 cm after 5–6 months gestation. ♂s mature in 10–15 yrs at 210 cm, ♀s in 15–20 yrs at 230–240 cm. **Range:** Sea of Cortez to central Peru; NC and Bermuda to s. Brazil, incl. all Caribbean, e. to G. of Guinea and Canary Is.

Zebra Shark
Stegostomatidae

Zebra Shark	2.35 m
Stegostoma varium	*(7.7 ft)*

5 ridges along back, tail as long as body; juveniles black with white bars. **Biology:** inhabits lagoons, channels and seaward terraces, 1–65 m. Uncommon, rare at oceanic islands. Juveniles rarely seen, possibly >50 m. Rests on sand or rubble facing current by day. Feeds primarily at night on molluscs, occasionally on crustaceans and small fishes. Docile, but potentially dangerous if abused. Young hatch from egg case at 20–26 cm; matures at 170 cm. **Range:** Red Sea and S. Africa to New Caledonia, n. to s. Japan.

Moray Eels
Muraenidae

Moray eels have a bad reputation, based not only on their ability to cause severe wounds but also on their fearsome looks and a persistent belief that they are venomous. While they are indeed able to inflict a crippling injury with their bite, the fear generated by their appearance and venomous reputation is largely unfounded. Of all the species studied to date, none has teeth designed to deliver venom, nor do they possess venom glands. A few species have serrated teeth and toxic skin. Venomous or not, a bite does carry with it the danger of secondary infection, so appropriate care should be taken. Ironically, the only fatalities attributable to a moray eel were caused by eating one. Although morays are widely used as food, in many locations the larger species are highly ciguatoxic (p.207).

Behaviour and biology
Moray eels inhabit all tropical and warm-temperate seas from intertidal rocky shores and estuaries to depths of more than 350 m. For the most part, they are nocturnal predators. During the day they usually remain hidden, with only their head protruding. At night they are more likely to be out in the open as they hunt with the aid of their highly developed sense of smell. Most species feed on fishes and octopods, but a few specialise in crustaceans. Their teeth vary in size and shape. Those that feed on fishes and octopods have dagger-like fangs designed for grasping and hanging on, while those that feed on crustaceans have conical or knobbly teeth well suited for crushing shells.

The rhythmic opening and closing of a moray's mouth is often misinterpreted as aggression but is only the act of breathing. Only if a moray holds its mouth wide open for a long time should it be considered a threat. Morays are normally docile and even large ones will usually avoid humans. However, most species will bite if provoked. Bites from large morays are often severe enough to require medical attention and can result in permanent injury or amputation.

Sexuality in morays varies. Some species are permanently male or female, while others are

A large Giant Moray *Gymnothorax javanicus* is capable of severely injuring a diver. *Red Sea, MK*

The wide gape of morays enables them to eat surprisingly large prey as well as cause severe injury to humans. This Green Moray is the largest species in the Caribbean. *Bonaire, RM*

hermaphrodites that either start life as females then change to males (protogynous), start life as males then change to females (protandrous), or are both sexes simultaneously. Morays have long larval stages and most are widely distributed.

Appearance
Moray eels are extremely long and somewhat compressed, with long dorsal and anal fins connected at the tip of the tail. The mouth has an extremely large gape and the gill openings are restricted to a pair of small holes. The skin is extremely tough, smooth and scaleless, and is covered by a protective layer of mucus. A few species are highly compressed and ribbon-like, while others are extremely narrow and snake-like with greatly reduced fins. Moray eels lack pectoral and pelvic fins, while eels of other families typically have small pectoral fins behind the gill openings. Sea snakes have easily visible, well-defined scales and no fins at all (p.241).

Typical accidents
Most injuries caused by moray eels occur when people are bitten on the hand as they reach into a hole. This is true particularly of lobster

Typically, all a diver sees of a moray is its head sticking out of a hole. One of the authors (MB) maintains a respectful distance from this Giant Moray. *MK*

fishermen, as lobsters often share their holes with morays. Injuries usually range from small, painful puncture wounds to more serious cuts that require sutures. Similar injuries occur when people intentionally pester or touch morays. One species in particular, the Blackcheek Moray *Gymnothorax breedeni*, is naturally aggressive. It has been known to bite camera housings or a hand or arm that would have been a safe distance from other species of similar size. Attacks by large morays over 1.5 m in length have resulted in permanently crippling and potentially life-threatening injuries, including severed fingers, tendons and blood vessels. These are often a defensive reaction to a provocation by the diver, such as being speared, but may also be an aggressive reaction to an attractant such as speared fish. The practice of feeding morays as a diving attraction can quickly become problematic, as they often mistake the feeder's hand for the food. Hand-fed morays lose their natural shyness and display behavioural changes such as swimming about in broad daylight and spontaneously approaching divers for a hand-out. This is uncharacteristic behaviour, and has resulted in divers being severely bitten. In one case, the arm of a young woman had to be amputated after it was bitten above the elbow.

Prevention
The best way to avoid injury from a moray eel is to treat it with respect and leave it alone. Do not feed or touch it and always maintain a safe distance, particularly if it is swimming in the open. Never reach into a hole without looking carefully. Do not hold wounded or dead fish in the hand or directly against your body. Never attempt to remove a hook from a moray that is still alive.

Injuries and symptoms
Even a bite by a small moray eel can be very painful and may require sutures. Secondary

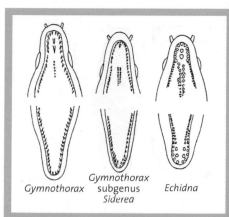

Spotted Moray *Gymnothorax moringua*.

Grey Moray *Gymnothorax griseus*.　　Chain Moray *Echidna catenata*.

A mouthful of daggers

Most species of moray eel, including those that most often injure people, have dagger-like fangs that are laterally compressed, have sharp edges and slant slightly backwards. Some may be inwardly depressible. Their arrangement and size varies by species and often changes with growth. The longest teeth are near the front and along the midline of the roof of the mouth. Those along the sides and back of the jaws may form a saw-like edge. In some cases there may be additional rows of smaller teeth. These teeth are designed to grasp struggling prey and force it down the throat. Although morays swallow most prey whole, their teeth cut deeply into soft tissue. The Spotted Moray *Gymnothorax moringa*, which feeds primarily on fishes, is a typical example. Some blunt-snouted species, like the Grey Moray *G. griseus* (subgenus *Siderea*) and the Chain Moray *Echidna catenata*, have short conical teeth. These are designed to break the shells of crustaceans. The Zebra Moray *Gymnomuraena zebra* has pebble-like teeth arranged like cobblestones. It feeds on bivalves and sea urchins, as well as crustaceans. Their large gape allows morays to eat surprisingly large prey.

Venomous or not?

Bites by the Whitemargin Moray *Gymnothorax albimarginatus*, a species with wide serrated teeth, are far more painful than the damage would indicate. This could be due to a venom or venom-like substance, although this has not been investigated. The Yellowmouth Moray *G. nudivomer* has toxic skin and mucus (p.136).

Whitemargin Moray *Gymnothorax albimarginatus*.

Sample cases

1) In a video recently posted on the Internet, a young diver is seen feeding Vienna sausages to a Giant Moray *Gymnothorax javanicus* about 1.6 m long. The eel is obviously excited as it swims about fully exposed, going from diver to buddy to photographer, rubbing up against them and poking its snout around as it tries to locate the food. An excited grouper and potentially dangerous Titan Triggerfish are also in the mix. The plastic bag is opaque and too large for the food to be easily extracted. Several minutes and a few sausages later, the eel finally grasps the diver's left thumb and hangs on. Within a few seconds, a popping sound is heard through an expanding cloud of blood. This is the thumb popping off. The next clip shows the hand with stitches in place of the thumb. This is followed by clips of the left foot with its index toe removed, the hand with the newly attached replacement 'thumb' and, finally, the smiling victim using his new thumb as he plays a video game.

2) In the late 1950s, at Johnston Atoll south of Hawaii, biologists conducted a quantitative sample of fishes by using the poison rotenone. A Giant Moray estimated to be well over 2 m long appeared to have been overcome and was lying in a sand channel. In order to handle it, one of the biologists speared it. As he surfaced with the eel in tow, it recovered. It immediately slithered up the shaft of the speargun and lunged at the diver's head. As he tried to protect himself, the eel grasped both parts of his left arm near his elbow. The wound required extensive surgery and the biologist never regained complete use of the arm. He was fortunate to have been operating from a military base where medical help was close at hand, otherwise he probably would have lost the arm.

Unprovoked attacks?

Both of the above incidents were obviously provoked. However, one of the authors (RM) is aware of a reliable source, a hypobaric doctor, who experienced an apparently unprovoked attack by the same species. In this case he described a very large eel that was apparently 'guarding' a sandy channel separating himself and another snorkeller from their boat, which was anchored in a shallow lagoon. The eel was swimming about over the open sandy bottom at a depth of perhaps 4 m. As each snorkeller swam past the eel to reach the boat, it chased him. One was bitten on the fin just as he reached the boat. One possible explanation for this aggressive behaviour is that the eel was a male in a reproductive state and overloaded with testosterone.

Treatment

First aid

Stop any bleeding, and clean the wound carefully without manipulating it. Get medical help to guard against infection.

What not to do

Do not manipulate the wound in any way.

Ongoing medical management

Clean and disinfect the wound thoroughly. Antibiotics and a tetanus prophylaxis may be necessary.

infection may also occur. As discussed above, attacks by larger morays can result in permanently crippling and potentially life-threatening injuries. These require immediate first aid, major surgery and rehabilitation.

Classification and distribution

There are approximately 185 species of moray eel. They are classified into two subfamilies, each with several genera distinguished by type and position of the teeth, as well as position of the fins and shape of the jaws, head and body. Most species encountered by humans are members of the subfamily Muraeninae. It includes *Gymnothorax*, *Muraena* and the hook-jawed *Enchelycore* and *Enchelynassa*. All of them except a few specialised *Gymnothorax* have long, dagger-like teeth, and nearly all injuries involve species of this group. Also included in this subfamily are the blunt-snouted Zebra Moray *Gymnomuraena zebra* and *Echidna*, the aptly named Ribbon Eel *Rhinomuraena quaesita* and White Ribbon Eel *Pseudechidna brummeri*, and the greatly elongate Longtail

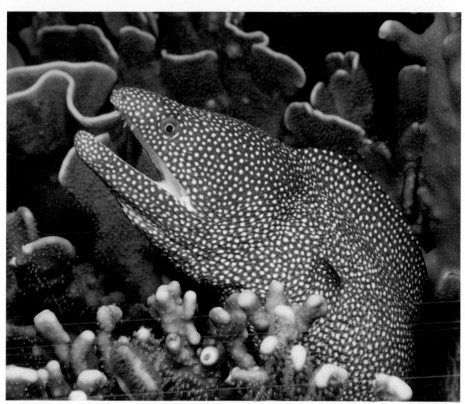

This Whitemouth Moray *Gymnothorax meleagris* is curiously looking out of its cave.

Moray *Strophidon sathete*. The snake morays of the subfamily Uropterygiinae are typically extremely long and nearly cylindrical, with fins restricted to the tip of the tail. They tend to be secretive and are seldom encountered.

Most Moray eels inhabit tropical inshore waters, but several inhabit temperate seas, slopes deeper than 200 m or fresh water. Morays have long pelagic larval stages and most species are widely distributed.

World distribution of moray eels.

How big do moray eels get?

The Longtail Moray *Strophidon sathete* is the world's longest eel, but it is narrow-bodied and two-thirds of its length is tail. The largest measured individual was 374 cm, but a 255-cm specimen weighed only 4.5 kg. The title of largest moray therefore belongs to the Giant Moray *Gymnothorax javanicus* – one taken by hook and line weighed 35.4 kg. Scientists who have collected specimens of up to 29 kg and 210 cm long claim the species gets substantially larger, to at least 250 cm. Since it becomes disproportionately thick at lengths of more than 150 cm, a weight of 50 kg is plausible. The largest Caribbean moray is the Green Moray *G. funebris*, which reaches a size of 189 cm and 15.2 kg. Reports of larger ones are unauthenticated. The thick-bodied Stout Moray *Muraena robusta* reaches a length of 186 cm but undoubtedly gets heavier than the Green Moray. It inhabits shallow waters of the cooler eastern Atlantic and southeastern US.

Atlantic Morays

Green Moray — 2.3 m; 28 kg
Gymnothorax funebris — (7.6 ft; 13 lb)

Uniformly green; 1–2 rows of large fangs on midline of upper jaw. **Biology:** inhabits brackish tidal creeks and coral and rocky reefs, 1–40 m. Avoids swimming in open. Feeds primarily on fishes and octopuses. Rare cases of unprovoked territorial aggression reported. Moderately common. The largest species in Caribbean. Can be ciguatoxic. **Range:** Bermuda, Bahamas and s. FL to s. Brazil, incl. all Caribbean.

Spotted Moray — 100 cm
Gymnothorax moringa — (36 in)

Small, variable, overlapping brownish-black spots on white background. **Biology:** inhabits rocky patches of inlets, seagrass beds, and rocky and coral reefs, 1–50 m. The most common moray of Caribbean reefs. Occasionally swims in open. **Range:** SC, Bermuda and Bahamas to s. Brazil, incl. G. of Mexico, all Caribbean; Ascension, St Helena, C. Verde Is.

G. funebris ●
G. moringa ●●

Purplemouth Moray — 84 cm
Gymnothorax vicinus — (33.5 in)

Pale with greenish-brown mottling and dark flecks; eyes yellow; much of inside of mouth and its corners purple. **Biology:** inhabits rocky and coral reefs, 1–75 m. Common, but usually hidden with only head visible. **Range:** n. G. of Mexico banks, Bermuda and Bahamas to s. Brazil, incl. all Caribbean.

G. vicinus ●●
E. catenata ●●

Chain Moray
Echidna catenata
71 cm
(28 in)

Head blunt, teeth conical to molar-like; irregular dark brownish-black blotches with network of narrow cream interspaces. **Biology:** inhabits rocky and coral reefs, intertidal zone to 20 m. Primarily in tide-pools and among interstices of shallow rocky and coral shorelines. Feeds primarily on small crabs. **Range:** Bermuda, Bahamas, s. FL and Yucatán to s. Brazil, incl. all Caribbean; Ascension, C. Verde Is.

Mediterranean Moray
Muraena helena
150 cm
(59 in)

Rear nostrils (above eyes) tubular; dark brown with highly variable golden-brown reticulations on sides, often forming rings that become spots on tail. **Biology:** inhabits rocky areas, intertidal zone to 105 m. Common. Feeds primarily on fishes and octopuses. In Canary Is more common in e. part with colder water. **Range:** Mediterranean and ne. Africa to Azores, Madeira and Canary Is. **Similar:** Fangtooth Moray *Enchelycore anatina* has strongly hooked jaws with multiple rows of long teeth (transatlantic, Caribbean, Mediterranean).

Dotted Moray
Muraena augusti
130 cm
(51 in)

Rear nostrils (above eyes) tubular; dark brown with tiny pale spots, may become pale on sides with dark specks, some forming vertical bars; eye always white. **Biology:** inhabits rocky areas, intertidal zone to 100 m. May alter colour slightly to match background. **Range:** Azores, Madeira and Canary Is only.

M. helena
M. augusti

Indo-Pacific Morays

Giant Moray   **2.4 m**
Gymnothorax javanicus   (7.8 ft)

Brown with black flecks forming leopard-like spots on sides. The largest moray, to over 35 kg. **Biology:** inhabits lagoon and seaward reefs, 1–46 m. Common in most areas. Feeds primarily on fishes, incl. juvenile Whiteip Reef Sharks, occasionally on spiny lobsters and octopuses. Normally docile and occasionally 'tamed' by dive guides, but has caused severe injury. Often ciguatoxic, fatalities have resulted. **Range:** Red Sea to Panama, s. to S. Africa; rare in Hawaiian Is, e. Pacific.

Yellow-edged Moray   **1.2 m**
Gymnothorax flavimarginatus   *3.9 ft*

Brown with fine yellow mottling, orange eye; fins of juvenile with yellow-green margin. **Biology:** inhabits reef flats and lagoon and seaward coral and rocky reefs, 0.3–150 m. Feeds on fishes and crustaceans. Common in many areas. Often ciguatoxic. A protogynous hermaphrodite. **Range:** Red Sea to Panama, n. to Ryukyus, s. to S. Africa and New Caledonia.

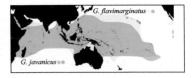

Blackcheek Moray	1.2 m
Gymnothorax breedeni	*3.9 ft*

Brown with large black patch from eye to corner of mouth and around gill opening. **Biology:** inhabits clear, current-swept seaward reefs, 4–25 m. Usually in porous coral rock with head protruding, often surrounded by small fishes. Unusually aggressive – will bite if approached too closely. **Range:** Comoros, Seychelles and n. S. Africa to Marquesas, n. to Caroline and Line Is; primarily oceanic.

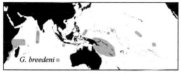

Honeycomb Moray	2.2 m
Gymnothorax favagineus	*(7.2 ft)*

White with black spots in honeycomb pattern. **Biology:** inhabits coastal reefs, 1–50 m. Occasionally in open in seagrasses. Feeds on fishes and octopuses by day and night. Occasionally aggressive. **Range:** s. Red Sea to Samoa, n. to Taiwan, s. to S. Africa. **Similar:** Black-spotted Moray *G. isingteena* has widelyspaced spots (180 cm; Indonesia to s. Japan).

Whitemouth Moray   120 cm
Gymnothorax meleagris   (47 in)

Dark brown with small white spots; inside of mouth white. **Biology:** in coral-rich areas of lagoon and seaward reefs, 0.3–36 m. Active by day and night; feeds primarily on fishes and crabs. A small fish, the Comet *Calloplesiops altivelis*, mimics the head of this eel protruding from a hole. Common in Mauritius and Hawaii. Often ciguatoxic. **Range:** s. Red Sea to the Galápagos, n. to Ryukyu and Hawaiian Is, s. to se. Australia.

Yellowmouth Moray   120 cm
Gymnothorax nudivomer   (47 in)

Brown with small white spots that become larger and ocellated towards rear; inside of mouth yellow. **Biology:** inhabits deep lagoon and seaward reefs, 1–165 m. Deep in equatorial areas. Solitary or in pairs, in holes by day. Preys on fishes at night. Displays yellow mouth as a warning. Skin mucus is toxic. **Range:** Red Sea to Fr. Polynesia and Hawaii, n. to the Ryukyus, s. to E. Africa.

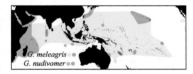

G. meleagris
G. nudivomer

Fimbriated Moray   80 cm
Gymnothorax fimbriatus   (32 in)

Pale olive with black spots, some forming irregular bars, head greenish. **Biology:** inhabits reef flats and lagoon and seaward reefs, 1–26 m. Probably nocturnal, not often seen by day. Feeds on fishes and crustaceans. **Range:** Seychelles and Mauritius to Society Is, n. to Ryukyus, s. to ne. Australia.

G. fimbriatus

Undulated Moray   110 cm
Gymnothorax undulatus   (44 in)

Dark brown with undulating light lines
and speckles; head olive-green. **Biology:**
inhabits reef flats and lagoon and seaward
reefs, 1 m to at least 50 m. Juveniles in tidepools. Among rubble, rocks and debris.
Common. Hunts at night for fishes, octopuses and crustaceans. A nervous species
that will readily bite. Often ciguatoxic.
Range: Red Sea to Panama, n. to s. Japan,
s. to S. Africa and Gt Barrier Reef.

G. undulatus

Grey Moray   65 cm
Gymnothorax griseus   (26 in)

Snout blunt, teeth conical; off-white with
black spots in pattern on head. **Biology:**
inhabits reef flats and coastal rocky and
coral reefs, 1–30 m. Common, often seen in
the open among seagrasses and rubble.
Hunts for small fishes and crustaceans,
sometimes in the company of goatfishes
and groupers. A simultaneous hermaphrodite. Releases up to 13,000 eggs per spawn.
Range: Red Sea to w. India, s. to S. Africa.

G. griseus

Peppered Moray   120 cm
Gymnothorax pictus   (47 in)

Snout blunt, teeth conical; white with tiny
black dots; juveniles with circles. **Biology:**
inhabits reef flats and shallow protected
areas, surface to 20 m. Common along
shorelines of fringing reefs. Primarily hunts
crabs and fishes, may leave water to capture grapsid crabs. **Range:** Red Sea to
Galápagos, n. to Ryukyu and Hawaiian Is,
s. to S. Africa and Gt Barrier Reef.

G. pictus

Greyface Moray — 66 cm
Gymnothorax thyrsoideus (26 in)

Snout blunt, teeth conical; brown with pale flecks and striking white eye. **Biology:** inhabits shallow coastal reefs, intertidal zone to 25 m. Common in coastal areas, uncommon on clear-water reefs. Often in small groups in holes. Non-aggressive. **Range:** Christmas Is and Indonesia to Tuamotus, n. to s. China and Ryukyus, s. to New South Wales.

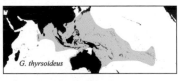

G. thyrsoideus

Barred Moray — 60 cm
Echidna polyzona (24 in)

Snout blunt, teeth conical; pale with dark bands that fade with age; juveniles with striking black bands on white. **Biology:** inhabits reef flats, clear lagoons and coastal reefs, intertidal zone to 15 m. Secretive; hides in crevices by day, hunts crabs and shrimps by night. Probes prey before striking. Non-aggressive. **Range:** Red Sea to Hawaii and Fr. Polynesia, n. to Ryukyus, s. to S. Africa and Gt Barrier Reef.

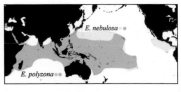

E. nebulosa

E. polyzona

Snowflake Moray
Echidna nebulosa   **75 cm** *(30 in)*

Snout blunt, teeth conical; cream with yellow spots in black blotches. **Biology:** inhabits reef flats and shallow lagoon and seaward reefs, intertidal zone to 39 m. Juveniles often in reef-flat tidepools. Primarily nocturnal, may leave water to hunt grapsid crabs on beach rock. Feeds primarily on crabs and mantis shrimps, occasionally on small fishes and cephalopods. A protogynous hermaphrodite. Common. **Range:** Red Sea to Panama, n. to Ryukyu and Hawaiian Is, s. to S. Africa and Fr. Polynesia.

Dragon Moray
Enchelycore pardalis   **92 cm** *(36 in)*

Jaws hooked, with multiple rows of long fangs, rear nostrils in long tubes; brown with dark-edged white spots. **Biology:** inhabits rocky and coral reefs, 12–50 m. Solitary and secretive. Feeds on fishes and octopuses. Gives impressive threat display with gaping jaws and erect dorsal fin. Rare in tropics, common in s. Japan. **Range:** scattered areas: e. Africa to Hawaii and Fr. Polynesia, n. to S. Korea, s. to Réunion and New Caledonia.

Viper Moray
Enchelynassa canina   **152 cm** *(60 in)*

Jaws hooked, with multiple rows of very long fangs, rear nostrils large with wide, jagged rim; dark reddish brown. **Biology:** inhabits shallow coral reefs, shoreline to 30 m. Primarily in porous reef of surge zone. Extremely secretive, rarely seen by day. Feeds at night on sleeping fishes. **Range:** Mauritius to Panama, n. to Hawaii, s. to Pitcairn; primarily at oceanic islands.

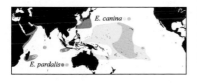

The jaws and teeth of this Spotted Spoon-nose Eel *Echiophis intertinctus* are designed for grasping and swallowing relatively large fishes.

Snake Eels
Ophichthidae

Snake eels do not have the same reputation as moray eels because most are small and only rarely encountered. However, a few of the larger ones have the equipment and disposition to be dangerous. There are around 290 species. They vary greatly in morphology, but most have a long cylindrical body with a pair of small pectoral fins behind the gill openings and a stiff, pointed tail tip. Most have long canine teeth used for capturing small fishes and crustaceans. Two even have a lure on their tongue to entice small fishes.

Snake eels inhabit sand and mud bottoms of all warm seas. They spend most of their time buried with only their head or eyes exposed, and can even move backwards beneath the sand. Those most often encountered by divers are small, harmless species that forage in the open. Some of the larger ones are robust-bodied ambush predators that have dagger-like teeth and enormous gapes. They can easily capture fishes of greater diameter than themselves and drag them beneath the sand, where they are swallowed whole. Although there are no reports of injuries to humans, the potential exists given the increasing interest in 'muck diving' and habit that photographers have of lying on the sand. The largest eel in the western Atlantic may be the King Snake Eel *Ophichthus rex*, which reaches at least 211 cm and possibly 335 cm in length! It lives in mud burrows in the Gulf of Mexico at depths of 16–366 m and is feared by fishermen.

World distribution of snake eels.

Stargazer Snake Eel — 1.56 m (5.1 ft)
Brachysomophis cirrocheilos

Eyes far forward, mouth large, lips fringed, roof of mouth with row of enlarged fangs; tan with dark specks and saddles. **Biology:** inhabits silty sand of coastal reefs, 0.5–38 m. Usually completely buried with only eyes exposed. More active at night, sometimes with head exposed. An ambushing predator of fishes and cephalopods. May bite if harassed. **Range:** Red Sea to PNG, n. to s. Japan, s. to Mozambique. **Similar:** *B. crocodilinus* and *B. henshawi* have eyes closer to tip of snout (Indo-Pacific).

Napoleon Snake Eel — 75 cm (30 in)
Ophichthus bonaparti

Nostrils hang over lower jaw, pupils as diagonal slits; head pale with dark-edged brown spots, becoming broad bars on body. **Biology:** inhabits silty to coarse sand of coastal, lagoon and seaward reefs, 1–20 m. Usually buried with eyes or head exposed, occasionally in open at night. An ambushing predator of small fishes and cephalopods. Will bite in self-defence. **Range:** E. Africa to Society Is, n. to s. Japan, s. to Gt Barrier Reef.

O. bonaparti
B. cirrhocheilos

Spotted Spoon-nose Eel — 152 cm (60 in)
Echiophis intertinctus

Eyes far forward, mouth large, pupils as diagonal slits; pale with dark spots. **Biology:** inhabits open sand, often near patch reefs. Actively forages by night. **Range:** NC to e. Brazil, incl. G. of Mexico and Antilles. **Similar:** Snapper Eel *E. punctifer* gets larger (122 cm; coastal nw. G. of Mexico and Cuba to s. Brazil).

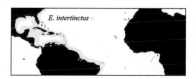

E. intertinctus

Great Barracuda: even a slightly opened mouth gives an idea of the impressive teeth.

Barracudas
Sphyraenidae

Barracudas have a reputation that is far worse than they deserve. Every day there are thousands of uneventful encounters between humans and barracudas. Attacks on humans are rare and nearly always the result of mistaken identity, self-defence or botched feedings. Unprovoked attacks in clear water simply do not happen. However, on the rare occasions that accidents do occur, they can be quite serious and life-threatening. All things considered, the threat of being attacked by a barracuda is far less than the threat of ciguatera poisoning when eating one (p.207).

Behaviour
Barracudas are voracious predators of other fishes and are able to strike with extraordinary speed. A large barracuda can easily cut a fish as wide as itself in two with a single quick bite, and equally its razor-sharp teeth can slice through any part of the human anatomy except large bones. Barracudas are not able to engage in long chases. An attack is a quick strike followed by a slower return to pick up the pieces. Only one species, the Great Barracuda *Sphyraena barracuda*, has been implicated in attacks on humans. It is curious and has the unnerving habit of

Blackfin Barracuda appear in swarms.

silently approaching and following a diver. In areas where they have been hand-fed, Great Barracuda can be a danger to anyone holding or wearing an object that can be mistaken for food. Likewise, such objects on anyone in murky water can invite an attack. The Great Barracuda is typically solitary but also occurs in groups. Juveniles inhabit protected inshore and estuarine waters, particularly mangrove-lined inlets. As they grow, they move out to coastal and offshore waters. The Great Barracuda reaches a length of at least 1.8 m and a weight of 46.7 kg. Only the Guinean Barracuda *S. afra* gets as large or larger, reaching 2.05 m and 50 kg. Most other species of barracuda occur in large schools during the day and disperse at night to feed.

Appearance
Barracudas are elongate, streamlined silvery fishes characterised by a pointed head with a projecting lower jaw and large mouth armed with long knife-like teeth. They have two widely separated dorsal fins, pelvic fins located well behind the pectoral fins, a forked tail, small cycloid scales and a well-developed lateral line.

Typical accidents
Most accidents occur in murky water and are the result of mistaken identity. Barracuda quickly

Razor-sharp teeth

The business end of a Great Barracuda consists of flattened, knife-like teeth with extremely sharp front and back edges. They can easily cut a large fish in two. The largest teeth are along the midline of the roof of the mouth, and hold the prey, while those along the sides of the jaws form an unbroken saw-like blade that cuts. This 1.6-m-long barracuda had been conditioned to take fish from humans. It was destroyed after it mangled the hands of two tourists. *(Guam, TA)*

Sample cases

1) At a marina in Florida, a diver who had dropped into the water to clean the hull of a boat was immediately bitten on the arm by a large Great Barracuda, then released. She nearly died of loss of blood and needed extensive surgery and months of recuperation to regain use of the arm. She had routinely cleaned hulls at the same location for years without incident.

2) In some areas, divemasters hand-feed barracuda. While a few professionals have perfected their techniques, incidents still occur. At a popular Guam site, a 1.6-m-long Great Barracuda conditioned to being hand-fed mistook a disposable camera for a meal and mangled several fingers in the process. After a second incident the barracuda was destroyed by one of the divemasters. Fish feeding continues at the site, but only to harmless species.

strike at anything that resembles a struggling fish. The glint of light on jewellery or the face of a watch can be confused with a silvery fish separated from its school and trigger an attack. Such incidents should be considered unintentional. 'Intentional' attacks occur when a barracuda attempts to steal a fish from a spearfisher or mistakes the hand for the dinner when being fed. There are no reliable reports of truly unprovoked attacks. Accidents also occasionally occur when fishermen handle live barracudas.

Prevention
When swimming or diving, do not wear shiny jewellery and do not attempt to feed or touch a barracuda. Be extremely careful when handling a barracuda of any species.

Injuries and symptoms
Most injuries caused by barracudas are deep lacerations to the fingers, hand or arm. Severe cases have included potentially life-threatening arterial bleeding as well as severed tendons and fingers.

Classification and distribution
Barracudas inhabit all tropical and warm-temperate seas. There are at least 21 species, all in the genus *Sphyraena*. The Great Barracuda has the broadest distribution. It inhabits all tropical seas but is rare in the eastern Pacific. All other species are confined to single biogeographic regions. The medium-sized species tend to have chevron-shaped marks on their upper sides, while the smaller ones are unmarked or have one or two narrow horizontal stripes.

IF INJURED

Treatment

First aid
Treat injuries like any bleeding wound, then seek medical attention if sutures are required.

What not to do
Do not self-treat wounds beyond first aid.

Ongoing medical management
Wounds should be properly cleaned and repaired by a medical professional. Prophylaxis should be taken to prevent infection.

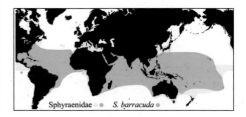

Sphyraenidae ● S. barracuda ●

Great Barracuda 1.8 m; 46.7 kg
Sphyraena barracuda (5.9 ft; 103 lb)

Upper sides with dusky bars, lower sides often with a few dark spots; tail emarginate, each lobe often with a dark blotch and white tip. **Biology:** inhabits estuaries and coastal and offshore waters, 1–198 m. Juveniles common in estuaries, often in groups. Adults usually solitary, occasionally in groups. Hovers in open water above or near reefs. Curious but not dangerous unless provoked or attracted by shiny objects in murky water. Has caused severe injuries. Notoriously ciguatoxic in Caribbean, but widely eaten elsewhere even though occasionally toxic. **Range:** all tropical seas, but rare in e. Pacific.

Blackfin Barracuda 1.4 m
Sphyraena qenie (4.6 ft)

Sides with dark chevrons; tail dusky to black, slightly emarginate. **Biology:** in large, semi-stationary schools above current-swept points or in deep lagoons or channel entrances, 1–50 m. May occur at these sites for months. Probably disperses at night to feed. Has been caught in open sea hundreds of kilometres from land. **Range:** Red Sea to Panama, n. to Micronesia, s. to S. Africa and Fr. Polynesia; rarely in Hawaii. **Similar:** Pickhandle Barracuda *S. jello* has dusky-yellow tail, prefers more turbid areas; other chevron species have lighter tails.

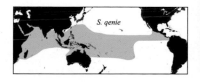

A large Titan Triggerfish *Balistoides viridescens* in an aggressive posture. *Bali, RM*

Triggerfishes
Balistidae

Triggerfishes have only recently been recognised as a hazard to humans. Three of the largest Indo-Pacific species are known to attack and sometimes cause significant injury to divers. Even small species may attack swimmers and inflict a painful bite. When eaten, triggerfishes also pose the danger of ciguatera poisoning (p.207).

Behaviour

All triggerfish are diurnal. At night or when alarmed, they wedge themselves in a hole by erecting the first dorsal fin and the spine-like pelvic girdle. They can be removed only if one is able to reach in and depress the small second dorsal spine, the 'trigger' that unlocks the first one. Triggerfishes normally swim by undulating their second dorsal and anal fins, sometimes while tilted to one side. For strong bursts of speed they use their tail in a rapid sculling motion.

Most triggerfishes are solitary carnivores that prey on a wide variety of benthic animals, including crustaceans, molluscs, sea urchins and other echinoderms, corals, tunicates and fishes. Others feed mainly on zooplankton and large pelagic animals such as salps and jellyfishes, or on benthic algae. Some triggerfishes blow jets of water on sand to expose hidden prey or reach the vulnerable undersides of sea urchins. The Grey Triggerfish *Balistes capriscus* has been observed biting the erect penis of a Loggerhead Turtle as it attempted to mate. Triggerfishes are haremic, with males having a large territory that encloses the territories of several females. They spawn on a lunar cycle, usually within a day or two of the full moon, new moon or both. The eggs are laid in a nest, which is aggressively guarded by the female. At these times, some of the larger species will attack and bite an intruding diver. At

If a Titan Triggerfish chases other fishes from a patch of sand, it is guarding a nest. *Red Sea, MK*

Nest-guarding

Female triggerfishes make a nest for their eggs in the form of a shallow crater in sand and rubble. Nests of large species may reach a metre in diameter and up to 20 cm deep, and are usually located on a sandy slope or in a channel subject to currents. In some areas, nests of several females may be closely spaced within a male's territory. Spawning is on a lunar cycle timed to coincide with the strongest currents, which carry the newly hatched larvae out to sea. The tiny eggs, under 0.6 mm in diameter, are clumped together in a spongy mass attached to rubble in the centre of the nest and usually hatch during the first night after being spawned. Only active nests are guarded by the female. She patrols the area 1–2 m above the nest, and will chase intruders away and occasionally enter the nest to blow water on the eggs. When a diver gets too close, many triggerfish species will feign an attack by rushing out, then sharply turning away. This is an obvious warning that should be heeded. In the case of the Titan, Yellowmargin and Blue triggerfishes, the next rush may be an attack in which the fish forcefully hits or bites whatever body part is closest and may hang on and pull. A Titan Triggerfish may continue to press an attack as far as 30 m from its nest.

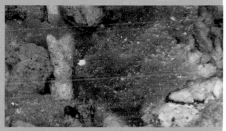

The pink eggs of a Yellowmargin Triggerfish. The female guarding this nest was agitated but did not attack. *W. Papua, RM*

On the warpath – a Yellowmargin Triggerfish attacks the photographer. It rammed the camera, then attempted to bite his legs. *Palau, RM*

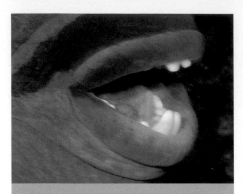

Powerful jaws, massive teeth

The triggerfish mouth is relatively small, but its jaws are powerful and the teeth of many species are very large. They are designed for crushing well-armoured prey and can break almost any shell or coral branch small enough to be grasped. The four teeth in the middle of the jaws are the largest and slant slightly forward. The true size of the teeth – nearly 4 cm in a large Titan Triggerfish – is revealed only when the lips are pulled back. *(Bali, RM)*

any time, a large Titan Triggerfish *Balistoides viridescens* may spontaneously attack a diver that violates its 'personal space' of about 2 m diameter.

Appearance
Triggerfishes have relatively deep, compressed bodies and large angular heads, and are covered

with large armour-like scales. The eyes are set high on the head, an adaptation that keeps them a safe distance from spiny prey. They move independently, giving triggerfishes the ability to scan for predators as they search for prey. The second dorsal and anal fins are broad-based with flexible rays. The first dorsal fin consists of a thick spike-like spine followed by two smaller ones, and fits into a groove. The large spine may be locked upright and depressed only by lowering the smaller second 'trigger' spine. The pelvic fin is reduced to a spiny knob. The mouth is relatively small but the jaws are quite powerful and contain large teeth designed for crushing hard-shelled prey. The largest Indo-Pacific species, the Titan Triggerfish, reaches a length of 75 cm. The eastern Stone Triggerfish *Pseudobalistes naufragium* reaches a metre in length.

Typical accidents
Most injuries occur when a diver gets too close to a triggerfish that is guarding its eggs. Close proximity to a large Titan Triggerfish at any time can also lead to an attack. An attack by it or the Yellowmargin or Blue triggerfishes usually results in a painful bruise but can also lead to a wound serious enough to require medical attention. An attack by smaller species such as the Lagoon Triggerfish *Rhinecanthus aculeatus* can result in a small, painful welt. Injuries to humans also occur when triggerfishes are being handled. Bites to fingers by the smaller species, even through a glove, have resulted in plugs of flesh being removed. One species, the Grey Triggerfish *Balistes capriscus*, has been known to bite a diver's fingers spontaneously in an attempt to make a meal of them.

Prevention
Divers and snorkellers should not approach a triggerfish that is seen chasing other fishes or seems agitated. A feigned attack is a warning that should be taken seriously, and you should retreat immediately. Try to place fins or some object between you and the attacker. Do not attempt to remove a triggerfish from its hole as it can turn and give a serious bite.

Injuries and symptoms
Wounds caused by triggerfishes vary greatly in severity, ranging from small welts to lacerations that require medical treatment. In one case, a hit to the head by a Titan Triggerfish caused a concussion. The victim, a divemaster, had to be rescued by her guests.

Treatment

First aid
Rinse the wound with sea water and then disinfect it. Seek medical help to eliminate the risk of secondary infection.

What not to do
Do not manipulate the wound in any way.

Ongoing medical management
Lacerations large enough to require sutures require medical help. Treatment with antibiotics and a tetanus prophylaxis are recommended in order to prevent secondary infection.

Sample cases

1) At a depth of 18 m at the Blue Corner, Palau, the author (RM) observed a large Yellowmargin Triggerfish *Pseudobalistes flavimarginatus* chasing a smaller triggerfish from the vicinity of its nest. RM approached to take a photograph. At a distance of 3 m, the fish attacked, banging the camera with considerable force. It then immediately hit his fins and attempted to bite his legs as he took evasive action and backed away quickly. It did not break off until RM was at least 15 m from the nest and nearly halfway to the surface.

2) Off Oahu, Hawaii, the author (RM) attempted to capture a Pinktail Triggerfish *Melichthys vidua*, which had taken shelter in a small hole, leaving its tail visible. As he reached in to depress its dorsal fin, it managed to turn around and bite his thumb through the cotton glove he was wearing. The wound bled profusely for a short time. On surfacing, RM found that a plug of tissue about 8 mm in diameter and reaching well beneath the skin had been excised and was attached by only a shred of skin. The thumb was unusable for a few days and the resulting crater took weeks to heal.

3) While snorkelling in the shallow lagoon of Tumon Bay, Guam, the author's (RM) nine-year-old daughter was hit on her foot by an adult Lagoon Triggerfish *Rhinecanthus aculeatus*. The attack left an oval welt about 1 cm long but the skin was not broken. RM and his daughter immediately left the area without determining if there was a nest. The area is next to most of the island's tourist hotels. Hotel managers reported that complaints by guests of attacks by this species seem to occur in clumps spanning a few days. It is highly likely that these clumps coincide with periods of nest-guarding.

Classification and distribution

Triggerfishes inhabit all tropical and most warm-temperate seas. There are at least 34 species in 11 genera. All species have a long larval stage, and some have a long pelagic pre-juvenile stage or associate with floating seaweed or debris, so tend to be broadly distributed. Including two circumglobal species, there are 29 in the Indo Pacific and seven in the Atlantic, one of which is also in the Mediterranean and Black seas.

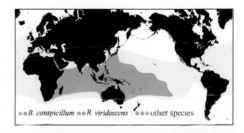

●●*B. conspicillum* ●●*B. viridescens* ●●●other species

Clown Triggerfish	30 cm
Balistoides conspicillum	*(12 in)*

Black with large white spots below, yellow reticulations on back. **Biology:** inhabits clear seaward reefs, 1–75 m. Usually on coral-rich reef margins and terraces. Juveniles usually in caves below 20 m. Uncommon, usually solitary. Feeds on wide variety of invertebrates. Nests in small depression in rubble and sand on exposed terraces. Will usually back off from an active nest when confronted by a diver. A highly prized though aggressive and extremely territorial aquarium fish. Ciguatoxic in some areas. **Range:** E. Africa to Line Is and Samoa, n. to s. Japan. Photo shows ♀ guarding eggs.

Titan Triggerfish 75 cm; 11 kg
Balistoides viridescens (25 in; 24 lb)

Olivaceous with complex pattern, scale margins pale, dark band above upper lip. **Biology:** inhabits lagoons and seaward reefs, 1–40 m. Usually solitary. Feeds on wide variety of invertebrates, incl. corals, molluscs, crustaceans, sea urchins and worms, as well as some algae. Becomes aggressive towards divers when guarding eggs or if approached too closely, and attacks by hitting or biting. May cause serious injury. Ciguatoxic in some areas. **Range:** Red Sea to Fr. Polynesia, n. to s. Japan.

Yellowmargin Triggerfish 60 cm
Pseudobalistes flavimarginatus (24 in)

Tan with pink face; fin margins yellow. **Biology:** inhabits deep lagoons, channels and sandy notches of seaward reefs, 2–50 m. Spawns within 1–2 days of new and full moons. Nests in sandy areas exposed to currents. ♀s aggressively guard eggs. May attack or back off. May be ciguatoxic. **Range:** Red Sea to Fr. Polynesia, n. to s. Japan.

P. fuscus ●●
P. flavimarginatus ●●

Blue Triggerfish 55 cm
Pseudobalistes fuscus (22 in)

Blue with yellow spots in Pacific, yellow reticulations in Indian Ocean; juveniles <4 cm tan with dark saddles. **Biology:** inhabits lagoons, bays and semi-protected seaward reefs, 1–50 m. Prefers areas of sand and rubble near patch reefs or scattered coral heads, also in seagrass beds. Spends much time blowing sand to expose invertebrates, often with an entourage of other fishes waiting to dart in for a meal. Wary, but may be aggressive and attack divers when guarding an active nest. Common in Red Sea and Indian Ocean, uncommon in much of w. Pacific. **Range:** Red Sea to Fr. Polynesia, n. to s. Japan.

Grey Triggerfish 30 cm
Balistes capriscus *(12 in)*

Olive-grey with narrow blue reticulations and spots. **Biology:** inhabits inlets, estuaries and coastal and offshore rocky and coral reefs, 3–30 m. Feeds on bottom-dwelling invertebrates, especially molluscs. Aggressive and opportunistic, has been known to attack the penis of a mating sea turtle and fingers of divers. Solitary or in small groups. Juveniles drift with floating *Sargassum* weed. Ciguatoxic in some areas. **Range:** tropical and temperate Atlantic, Mediterranean and Black seas.

Queen Triggerfish 60 cm
Balistes vetula *(24 in)*

Olive-yellow with blue lines and spots; 2nd dorsal fin and tail fin with filaments. **Biology:** inhabits sand and rubble areas of coral reefs, 2–53 m. Feeds on invertebrates, especially the sea urchin *Diadema antillarum*. Uncommon since population crash of *Diadema*. Ciguatoxic in some areas. **Range:** tropical and warm-temperate Atlantic, MA to Argentina, incl. Bermuda, Ascension I., Azores and C. Verde Is.

B. capriscus ● B. vetula ●●

Black Triggerfish 35 cm
Melichthys niger *(13.8 in)*

Black with white line at bases of dorsal and anal fins, blue lines often between eyes. **Biology:** inhabits seaward reef slopes, 1–75 m. Often high above bottom. Feeds on zooplankton and detached algae. Uncommon in many areas but super-abundant around isolated mid-oceanic islands. May engage in feeding frenzy-like behaviour, so possibly hazardous to wounded shipwreck victims. **Range:** all tropical seas.

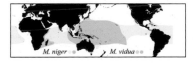
M. niger ●● y M. vidua ●●

Pinktail Triggerfish
Melichthys vidua

35 cm
(13.8 in)

Black, dorsal and anal fins clear with broad black margins, tail white to pink. Planktonic stage up to 13 cm; fins of juveniles orange-brown. **Biology:** inhabits clear seaward reef slopes, 4–60 m, up to 3 m above bottom. Feeds on detached algae, invertebrates and fishes. **Range:** E. Africa to Hawaii and Fr. Polynesia, occasionally in e. Pacific, n. to s. Japan, s. to New Caledonia. **Similar:** Indian Triggerfish *M. indicus* has white margin around tail fin (24 cm; E. Africa to w. Indonesia).

Orange-lined Triggerfish
Balistapus undulatus

30 cm
(12 in)

Green with curved orange stripes; adult ♂ lacks stripes on snout. **Biology:** inhabits coral-rich areas of lagoon and seaward reefs, 1–50 m. Feeds on fishes, corals, algae and benthic invertebrates. Excavates a shallow nest in sand or rubble of channels. Aggressive in captivity. **Range:** Red Sea to Fr. Polynesia, n. to s. Japan, s. to New Caledonia.

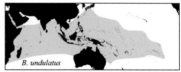

B. undulatus

Lagoon Triggerfish
Rhinecanthus aculeatus

25 cm
(10 in)

Tan above, white below with distinctive black patttern on sides. **Biology:** inhabits reef flats and shallow lagoons, 1–4 m. Feeds on benthic invertebrates, fishes and algae. Usually wary but may attack in defence of an active nest. Spawning peaks within a day of full moon. **Range:** e. Africa to Hawaii and Fr. Polynesia, n. to s. Japan. **Similar:** Wedge-tail Triggerfish *R. rectangulus* (s. Red Sea to Fr. Polynesia); Picasso Triggerfish *R. assasi* (Red Sea to Arabian G.).

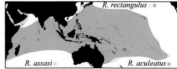

R. rectangulus
R. assasi
R. aculeatus

A Starry Puffer *Arothron stellatus* nearly 1 m long leisurely hovers above the reef. Its huge lower jaw teeth are clearly visible. *Chuuk, RM*

Puffers
Tetraodontidae

Many species of puffer have long been recognised as being poisonous but few people would consider them dangerous to those who enter the water. However, in the Indo-Pacific at least three species have been implicated in attacks on humans that have led to significant injury. These are discussed here, while other aspects of the family and further species are covered in more detail in the section on poisonous fishes (p.198).

Behaviour
Also called 'blowfishes', puffers have both defensive and offensive weapons. Their common names refer to their ability to inflate themselves by drawing water into a specialised chamber near the stomach. When fully inflated, they are too large, hard and prickly to be eaten by many predators. Their toxicity and often bitter taste also renders them unpalatable. Consequently, they tend to be slow-moving and easy to approach. Puffers propel themselves with sculling motions of their dorsal and anal fins, and manoeuvre with fine motions of their pectoral fins, which allows them to rotate or move backwards. Although diet may vary among the species, they tend to feed on a wide variety of plants and animals, including many hard-shelled forms that are crushed by their powerful beaks. Any puffer will use its beak in defence, but many species tend to be aggressive and some will attempt to eat parts of prey larger than themselves, including humans.

Appearance
Puffers are oblong and globular in shape, with short-based dorsal, anal and pectoral fins, and

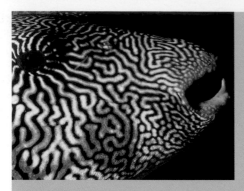

Powerful beak

Puffer teeth are fused into a formidable beak with a median suture. The family name Tetraodontidae is derived from the Latin for 'four-toothed'. The beak is used to break off pieces of food as well as to crush hard-shelled prey. The bite of some large species, including the Starry Puffer shown here, is powerful enough to remove a finger or toe. In the photo above, a Pacific Cleaner Shrimp *Lysmata amboinensis* performs dental hygiene on *Arothron mappa*. *(Above: Bali, RM. Right: Red Sea, MB)*

eyes set high on the head. They have a tough, highly flexible skin with short prickles instead of scales, and lack fin spines, pelvic fins and ribs. Their teeth are fused into a powerful beak with a median suture. The largest species attain at least 1 m in length.

Treatment

First aid
Rinse the wound with sea water and then disinfect it. Seek medical help for deep wounds or if a minor wound does not heal normally.

What not to do
Do not manipulate the wound in any way.

Ongoing medical management
Lacerations large enough to require sutures require medical help. Treatment with antibiotics and a tetanus prophylaxis are recommended in order to prevent secondary infection.

Typical accidents
Most wounds from puffers occur when the fish are handled. A bite from a large puffer may result in a deep, jagged cut with loss of some skin and flesh. In northern Australia, a very large and aggressive species, the Ferocious Puffer *Feroxodon multistriatus*, has been implicated in unprovoked attacks on humans. In one case, a girl wading in the shallows lost three toes. In other tropical areas there are several early 20th-century accounts of male mutilation attributed to aggressive puffers. In Singapore, this is said to be partly the reason for the puffer's reputation as an aphrodisiac.

Prevention
When handling a live puffer, great care should be taken to avoid contact with the mouth. When swimming off remote tropical beaches, use caution, particularly in northern Australia. This advice applies during the night as well as day since many puffers are active after dark. Given many puffers' predilection for bite-sized appendages, skinny-dipping is not advised.

Starry Puffer
Arothron stellatus   100 cm
                     (39 in)

White with close-set black spots; sub-adult also with dusky patches; small juveniles orange with curving black lines. **Biology:** inhabits lagoon and seaward reefs, 2–52 m. Rests on sand or hangs in mid-water in channels and above drop-offs. Juveniles in sandy areas of protected inner reefs. Solitary. Feeds on sea urchins, starfishes, crabs, hermit crabs, sponges, corals, fire corals and algae. May bite! **Range:** Red Sea and Arabian G. to Fr. Polynesia, n. to S. Korea and s. Japan, s. to S. Africa and n. New Zealand.

Ferocious Puffer
Feroxodon multistriatus   90 cm
                          (36 in)

Snout long, eyes set high on head; pale with oblique brown bands above, brown spots below, these thicker in juveniles, finer and broken in large adults. **Biology:** inhabits coastal reefs and sandy bottoms from shoreline to deep offshore trawling grounds. The most dangerous and aggressive puffer, known to attack swimmers and waders spontaneously. Has severed toes. **Range:** n. Australia from NW Cape to central Queensland.

Silver Puffer
Lagocephalus sceleratus   96 cm
                         (38 in)

Elongate; back greenish brown with small dark spots, ocelli and dusky saddles, a broad, mirror-like silver band on sides, belly white. **Biology:** inhabits mud and sand bottoms, juveniles may occur along shoreline, adults 18 m to over 100 m. May occur in schools. Feared by swimmers and divers in W. Australia. Can bite through fish-hooks and bone. Also extremely toxic. **Range:** Red Sea to Samoa, n. to s. Japan. (See p.199.)

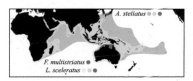

Porcupinefishes
Diodontidae

Porcupinefishes are basically puffers whose short prickles (actually modified scales) have evolved into long, sharp spines and whose teeth are completely fused so the beak lacks a suture. They share the ability of puffers to inflate themselves but have the added protection of the spines. A large inflated *Diodon* is an impenetrable fortress capable of choking a large shark to death. The beak-like jaws are used to crush the hard shells of prey such as molluscs, crustaceans or sea urchins, and can inflict a severe bite. Porcupinefishes tend to be more nocturnal than puffers and their eyes are larger. In many areas porcupinefishes are eaten or dried and sold as curios. In some regions they may be poisonous owing either to concentrations of tetrodotoxin or ciguatoxin (pp.198 and 207). Porcupinefishes inhabit all tropical and warm-temperate seas. Nineteen species in six genera are known.

Typical accidents
Although such occasions are rare, swimmers and unwary divers have been bitten. This danger may be more likely at night, when species of *Diodon* are more active but less likely to be seen. Puncture wounds may result when an inflated porcupinefish is handled.

Treatment

First aid
Treatment is the same as for wounds caused by pufferfishes (p.154), and should be directed toward repair of the wound and the prevention of infection.

Prevention
When swimming off tropical beaches, exercise caution and defer to local knowledge, particularly at night. There is no safe way to handle a porcupinefish except with a net or other device. Divers should not harass a porcupinefish or cause it to inflate, since this places harmful stress on the animal.

Porcupinefish weapons

The massive dental plates of the beak are a porcupinefish's only offensive weapon. In addition to the spines, they are also effective defensive weapons but rarely pose a danger to humans unless the fish is handled. The spines are either three-rooted and rigid (in burrfishes: *Chilo-* *mycterus*, left, and *Cyclichthys*), two-rooted and moveable (in *Diodon*, right), or a combination of the two. The moveable spines normally lie backwards but stand erect when the fish is inflated. The long spines of a large *Diodon* can cause deep puncture wounds but are not venomous. The shorter spines of burrfishes cause less serious superficial wounds. (*Southern FL, RM; SM*)

Porcupinefish
Diodon hystrix
80 cm
(31.5 in)

Spines long and depressible; tan with dark spots, white below. **Biology:** inhabits lagoon and seaward reefs, 2–50 m. Juveniles pelagic. Adults often along reef margins. Usually inactive under ledges or in crevices during the day, occasionally hovers high in the water. Common. Feeds primarily at night on molluscs, crabs, hermit crabs, sea urchins and sand dollars. Known to bite swimmers opportunistically. **Range:** circumglobal in tropical and warm-temperate seas. **Similar:** *Chilomycterus reticulatus* (p.158) has short fixed spines.

Long-spine Porcupinefish
Diodon holocanthus
29 cm
(10.5 in)

Spines long and depressible; pale with large brown blotches and smaller black spots, decreasing in number with age. **Biology:** inhabits lagoon and seaward reefs, 1–100 m. More often over open bottom than other species. Juveniles pelagic to a size of at least 7 cm. More common in cooler warm-temperate waters than in tropical seas. **Range:** circumglobal in tropical and warm-temperate seas.

D. hystrix   other species

Black-blotched Porcupinefish
Diodon liturosus
50 cm
(20 in)

Spines depressible, shorter than in *D. hystrix* (above); tan above with large, pale-edged dark blotches. **Biology:** inhabits coastal and seaward reefs, 5–90 m. Usually inactive under ledges or in crevices by day. Forages at night on hard-shelled invertebrates. More common around continental islands than oceanic islands. **Range:** s. Red Sea to Fr. Polynesia, n. to s. Japan. **Similar:** *D. holocanthus* (above) has dark blotch bridging eyes and longer spines.

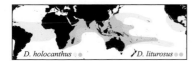

D. holocanthus   D. liturosus

Spotfin Burrfish   70 cm
Chilomycterus reticulatus   (28 in)

Spines short and rigid; pale brown, usually with widely scattered small dark spots. **Biology:** inhabits shallow protected areas to exposed seaward reef slopes, 1–141 m. Usually in shelter by day. **Range:** circum-global in tropical and warm-temperate seas, but absent from Red Sea, Arabian G., and most of central Pacific and Caribbean. **Similar:** *Diodon hystrix* (p.157) has longer, depressible spines and more black dots.

Striped Burrfish   25 cm
Chilomycterus schoepfi   (10 in)

Spines rigid, mustard-yellow; pale brown with narrow dark brown lines and 3 dark ocelli on sides and dorsal fin base. **Biology:** inhabits shallow protected areas, 1–9 m. Common in seagrass beds and coastal lagoon reefs. **Range:** w. Atlantic, coastal New England (rare n. of SC) to ne. Brazil; absent from W. Indies. **Similar:** Web Burrfish *C. antillarum* has web-like network of dark lines, Bridled Burrfish *C. antennatus* has small dark spots (both in seagrass beds and protected inshore reefs from FL and Bahamas, W. Indies and n. coast of S. America).

Birdbeak Burrfish   15 cm
Cyclichthys orbicularis   (6 in)

Brown with clusters of dark spots; spines short and rigid. **Biology:** inhabits protected areas of sand and rubble of coastal reefs, 2–20 m. Inactive by day under corals and rocks or in large sponges. Feeds on crabs, molluscs and worms. Uncommon. **Range:** Red Sea and Arabian G. to ne. Australia, n. to s. Japan, s. to S. Africa.

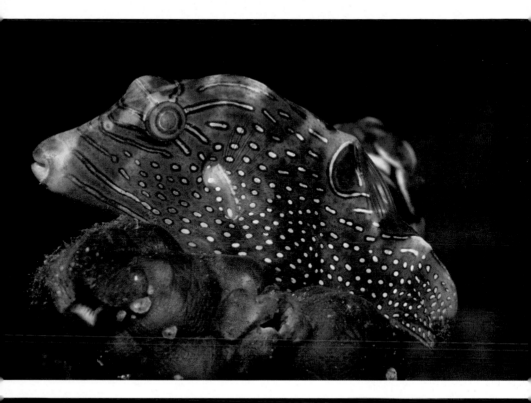

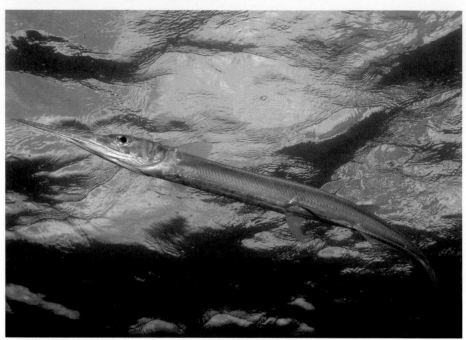

The largest needlefish, the Houndfish *Tylosurus crocodilus*, hovers just beneath the surface. *Guam, RM*

Needlefishes
Belonidae

Treatment

First aid
Try to immobilise both the victim and the impaled fish. If possible, cut off the body of the fish where it is softest just behind the head. This will kill the fish and prevent further damage from its movements.

What not to do
Do not try to remove the needlefish. If the needlfish becomes separated from the wound, flush the exposed parts with salt water. Do not mainpulate the wound.

Ongoing medical management
All parts of the impaled fish must be surgically removed and the wound cleaned and repaired appropriately according to the damage done. Administer antibiotics to fight infection.

Behaviour
Needlefishes are surface-dwelling predators of small fishes. They occasionally descend a few metres to visit cleaning stations and spawn by attaching large adhesive eggs to floating debris. To escape predators they launch themselves from the water with considerable speed and use the lower lobe of their tail to skitter above the surface. At night, they occasionally hurl themselves towards lights and have impaled fishermen. Underwater, needlefishes are generally harmless. At certain dive sites where they have become conditioned to accepting food, there are no reports of problems. Their teeth are not sharp-edged like those of barracuda and at worst could cause only small puncture wounds.

Appearance
Needlefishes are extremely elongate silvery fishes with jaws that resemble needle-nosed pliers armed with needle-like teeth. They have small, spineless dorsal and anal fins, and a

A living spear

When closed, the spear-like jaws of a rapidly moving needlefish are sharp enough to impale a human. Large species such as the Houndfish shown here have caused fatalities. The needle-like teeth are relatively harmless.

slightly forked tail, usually with an elongate lower lobe. The largest species, the Houndfish *Tylosurus crocodilus*, reaches over 135 cm in length and a weight of 7.1 kg.

Typical accidents

Accidents involving needlefishes are rare, but they can be fatal. They usually occur at night when a needlefish startled by a light launches itself out of the water and hits someone. In one case, a ten-year-old boy was fatally impaled in the right eye as he pulled in a beach seine. In 2005, off Oahu, Hawaii, a 19-year-old man spearfishing at night barely survived being impaled in the chest. In a rare daytime accident on Guam, a young woman was impaled in the shin by a small needlefish while waterskiing.

Prevention

When on a small open boat at night, avoid lingering in the immediate vicinity of a bright light.

Symptoms

An impaled needlefish is a serious condition that requires immediate medical attention. Symptoms vary according to the extent of the injury. A needlefish impaled in the heart or brain can cause instant death. Damage to other vital organs can be agonising and life-threatening. Even a flesh wound caused by a small needlefish will soon become infected if not properly treated.

Classification and distribution

Needlefishes inhabit the surface waters of all tropical and temperate seas. There are 34 species in ten genera ranging from 38 cm to over 135 cm in length. Some species are found inshore above reefs while others remain over deep oceanic waters.

Belonidae ●   *T. crocodilus* ●

Houndfish	1.35 m
Tylosurus crocodilus	(4.4 ft)

Snout becomes thicker with red tinge near tip with age. **Biology:** inhabits coastal waters, usually along upper edge of reef margin. Descends from surface to visit cleaning stations. Has fatally impaled fishermen. **Range:** circumtropical. **Similar:** Agujon *T. acus* (100 cm; Indo-Pacific) and Red Sea Houndfish *T. choram* (120 cm; Red Sea to G. of Oman) are nearly identical; Banded Needlefish *Strongylura leiura* is smaller with longer jaws (80 cm; Indo-Pacific); Keeled Needlefish *Platybelone argalus* (45 cm; circumtropical) has a flattened tail base and is often in groups.

The Sabre Squirrelfish *Sargocentron spiniferum* is the largest species in the family. *Palau, RM*

Squirrelfishes
Holocentridae, subfamily Holocentrinae

Behaviour
Squirrelfishes are nocturnal predators that typically hover near or under ledges during the day, often in small groups. At night they disperse over the reef to feed primarily on benthic invertebrates (mostly shrimps and crabs) and small fishes. At this time they often exhibit a colour pattern slightly different from that seen in the day. They are relatively easy to approach during the day, but at night they tend to swim more rapidly and avoid a diver's light. They are completely inoffensive and harmless unless handled.

Appearance
Squirrelfishes are moderately elongate, compressed fishes with bony heads and large, coarse scales. The margin of the pre-opercle (forepart of the cheek) has a bony edge with a prominent sharp spine at its corner. The related soldierfishes (subfamily Myripristinae) have a serrated pre-opercle that lacks the prominent spine. Squirrelfishes are primarily red with some combination of white, silver, yellow or orange. Many have white stripes. The red shows up as black in the low light of night.

Typical accidents
Squirrelfishes are excellent to eat and are heavily fished, particularly in the Indo-Pacific, where they are caught primarily by spear and gill nets. Accidents often occur when the fish are

Treatment

First aid
Disinfect the wound with alcohol (40–70 per cent).

What not to do
Do not manipulate the wound in any way.

Ongoing medical management
If secondary infection becomes evident, consult a doctor for treatment with antibiotics.

Squirrelfish weapons

The prominent pre-opercular spine is the squirrelfish's primary defensive weapon. It is best developed in the Sabre Squirrelfish *Sargocentron spiniferum* (right). The dorsal, anal and pelvic fin spines are also sharp and stout, and are equally capable of inflicting painful puncture wounds.

handled, and usually result in a small knife-like cut or puncture wound caused by the pre-opercular spine or the fin spines. The rough scales can also leave shallow cuts.

Prevention
When handling a squirrelfish wear sturdy gloves and avoid the pre-opercular spines. Care should also be taken to hold the fish firmly with its dorsal, anal and pelvic fin spines folded.

Symptoms
A puncture from the pre-opercular spine of at least one species, the Sabre Squirrelfish *Sargocentron spiniferum* (also known as the Long-jawed Squirrelfish), is followed by an immediate sharp pain, which may become throbbing and shoot up the arm. The severity and long-lasting nature of the pain is indicative of a venom, but

there do not seem to be any other symptoms of envenomation. The sharp edge of the spine can leave a somewhat open wound. Puncture wounds from the fin spines or spines of other species are less severe.

Classification and distribution
Squirrelfishes of the subfamily Holocentrinae inhabit all tropical and many warm-temperate seas. The are 32 species in three genera. The related soldierfishes (subfamily Myripristinae) consists of 36 species in five genera.

Soldierfish species like these Bigscale Soldierfishes *Myripristis berndti* lack the prominent pre-opercular spine of squirrelfishes but have sharp fin spines and scale margins that can cut when handled. *Palau, RM*

Sabre Squirrelfish 45 cm
Sargocentron spiniferum (18 in)

Pre-opercular spine extremely long; red with white scale margins; spinous dorsal fin uniformly red, other fins orange. **Biology:** inhabits lagoon and seaward reefs, 1–122 m. Solitary or in small groups hovering under ledges, tabular corals or in caves by day. Forages at night on crabs, shrimps and small fishes. **Range:** Red Sea and S. Africa to Hawaiian, Marquesan and Ducie Is, n. to s. Japan, s. to se. Australia and Rapa.

Silverspot Squirrelfish 25 cm
Sargocentron caudimaculatum (10 in)

Red with white scale margins, base of tail pale with large white spot. **Biology:** inhabits deep lagoon and seaward reefs with rich coral growth, 2–50 m. Solitary or in small groups in the vicinity of holes or ledges by day. The white tailspot gets reddish during night, when it hunts for small fishes and crabs. **Range:** Red Sea and s. Oman to Fr. Polynesia, n. to s. Japan, s. to S. Africa and Gt Barrier Reef.

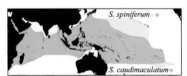

Crown Squirrelfish 17 cm
Sargocentron diadema (6.7 in)

Red with narrow white stripes; dorsal fin mostly black with curved white stripe. **Biology:** inhabits sub-tidal reef flats and lagoon and seaward reefs, 2–60 m. Typically near crevices and caves or under ledges by day. Roams over open sand at night to feed on gastropods, polychaetes and small crustaceans. Solitary or in groups. Has invaded the w. Mediterranean. **Range:** Red Sea and Oman to Fr. Polynesia, n. to Ryukyu and Hawaiian Is, s. to se. Australia.

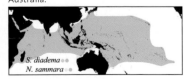

Spotfin Squirrelfish — 32 cm
Neoniphon sammara — (12.6 in)

Silvery with narrow white stripes; front of dorsal fin with large reddish-black spot. **Biology:** inhabits reef flats, lagoons and seaward reefs, 2–45 m. Common and less secretive than other squirrelfishes. Hovers in small groups near branching corals, rocks or ledges by day. Disperses at night to feed on small fishes and crabs. Not shy. **Range:** Red Sea to Fr. Polynesia, n. to s. Japan, s. to S. Africa and Gt Barrier Reef.

Longjaw Squirrelfish — 22 cm
Neoniphon marianus — (8.6in)

Orangey pink with yellow stripes; spinous dorsal fin yellow with white tips and white band. **Biology:** inhabits seaward reef slopes, 1–70 m. Rare in shallow waters, common below 30 m. Usually under ledges or in holes by day. Disperses at night to feed on shrimps and small crabs. **Range:** FL Keys, Bahamas and G. of Mexico banks through Caribbean to Trinidad.

Squirrelfish — 46 cm
Holocentrus adscensionis — (18.5 in)

Orangey pink with pale stripes; spinous dorsal fin pale yellow; soft dorsal and tail fin lobes lengthen with age. **Biology:** inhabits coastal to offshore reefs, usually in groups in crevices and holes by day, 1–90 m. Disperses at night to feed on small crustaceans. **Range:** VA and Bermuda to s. Brazil, incl. G. of Mexico and all Caribbean; Ascension, St Helena and G. of Guinea. **Similar:** Longspine Squirrelfish *H. rufus* has white tips on dorsal spines (46 cm; NC to n. S. America).

All that is normally seen of a stargazer are its eyes and grin. *Sulawesi, MB*

Stargazers
Uranoscopidae

Behaviour
Stargazers are predatory fishes that lie buried in the sand, waiting to ambush prey that swims by.

Treatment

First aid
Disinfect the wound with alcohol (40–70 per cent).

What not to do
Do not manipulate the wound in any way.

Ongoing medical management
If secondary infection becomes evident, consult a doctor for treatment with antibiotics.

Usually only their eyes and lips are visible. Many species have a worm-shaped lure growing out of the lower jaw, which they wiggle to attract small fishes. Prey lured by this 'bait' become victims of their own curiosity. Some species also have a pair of electric organs behind the eyes that may be used to stun passing prey as well as for defence (p.195). Stargazers use their enlarged pectoral fins to anchor themselves in place and will not move if prodded or even if they have taken a baited hook. If dug from the sand, a stargazer immediately reburies itself, using its pectoral fins to shovel its way under. In some parts of the world, stargazers are used for food.

Appearance
Stargazers are club-shaped, with a massive flat-topped bony head and tapering body, small first

IF INJURED

Stargazer weapons

Most stargazers have a pair of large cleithral (shoulder) spines with associated glandular tissue. Although this tissue is claimed to be venomous, no venom has ever been isolated. Laboratory animals injected with a tissue extract and people accidentally spined showed no symptoms of envenomation. The small dorsal fin has weak spines. Some species have electric organs behind the eyes, but the shock is relatively weak (p.195). *(Photo: U. sulphureus, JR)*

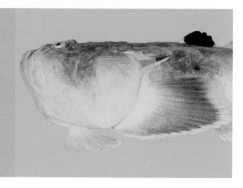

dorsal fin, broad-based second dorsal and anal fins, and large pectoral and tail fins. Their eyes are widely spaced and set on top of the head, and the mouth is wide and upturned with fringed lips that resemble teeth. Small teeth hidden behind the lips secure prey, which is then swallowed whole. Most species have a stout conical spine at the top of each gill cover that points obliquely backwards.

Typical accidents

Stargazers typically pose a danger only to fishermen, who may be poked by the large shoulder spine or shocked when removing a hook or emptying a net (see p.195). There is a remote possibility of a wader being spined, but there are no records of this. Even a diver who accidently lies on a stargazer will probably never know it because the fish is unlikely to do anything.

Prevention
Do not touch a stargazer or dig it from the sand.

Symptoms
A 'sting' is painful but is not accompanied by any other symptoms.

Classification and distribution
Stargazers inhabit continental shelves and major island slopes of all tropical and temperate seas. There are over 50 species in eight genera.

Whitemargin Stargazer	38 cm
Uranoscopus sulphureus	(15 in)

Shoulder spine large and exposed; tan with dark flecks or blotches, may have 2 broad dusky saddles; pectoral fin with pale margin; red lure in lower jaw. **Biology:** inhabits sand bottoms of coastal waters, 1–150 m. Primarily continental, rarely at oceanic islands. This is the species most often seen by divers. Its venomosity is unknown.
Range: Red Sea; Indonesia to Samoa, n. to Marianas, s. to Gt Barrier Reef and Tonga.
Similar: Marbled Stargazer *U. bicinctus* has 2 broad dusky bands on sides (27 cm; s. Japan, Indonesia, and nw. Australia).

The large and aggressive Sohal Surgeonfish *Acanthurus sohal* patrols its feeding territory. *Egypt, RM*

Surgeonfishes
Acanthuridae

Surgeonfishes are named for the pair of retractable scalpel-like blades located at the base of the tail in most species. When the tail is flexed to one side, the forward-pointing blade on the opposite side pops out. The unicornfishes and sawtails, also in this family, have two or more pairs of permanently deployed sharp fixed blades instead, and some species have venomous fin spines as well. These weapons pose a danger to humans only when surgeonfishes are captured or handled. This danger is well known to the aquarists who keep them, as well as to those who catch and eat them.

In the Caribbean, Blue Tang often gather in large numbers to overwhelm the defences of territorial damselfishes. Within 20 to 30 seconds the damselfishes' patch of edible algae is stripped bare and the surgeonfishes move on. *Curaçao, RM*

Behaviour and biology

Surgeonfishes are conspicuous and abundant on shallow coral reefs. The family includes herbivores that graze algae from hard or sandy surfaces, as well as plankton-feeders that swim high above the bottom. Some species feed primarily on detritus, dead organic matter mixed with filamentous and single-celled algae, and form a key link in the ciguatera food chain (p.207). All species are active only during the day and shelter in the reef at night.

Surgeonfishes use their blades offensively against one another in struggles for dominance as well as defensively against predators. Some surgeonfishes are highly territorial, while others form large roving schools in order to raid the territories of more dominant species.

Surgeonfishes typically spawn at dusk on a lunar cycle, either in large groups or in pairs. Their specialised larval stage is armed with

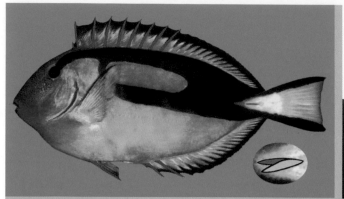

Surgeonfish weapons

Spines The fin spines of the Palette Tang *Paracanthurus hepatus* (shown in red, above), some species of the genus *Naso* and the Japanese Sawtail *Prionurus scalprum* (both above right) have been reported to be venomous. Those of the sawtail are an inverted 'T' shape in cross section, with glandular tissue in the lateral grooves. The post-larval stages of some, if not all, species have enlarged venomous second dorsal, second anal and pelvic fin spines (e.g. Convict Surgeonfish *Acanthurus triostegus*, above) but no venom has been isolated. *(Photos: JR)*

Blades The paired caudal blades differ between subfamilies (right). The true surgeonfishes (Acanthurinae) have a single pair of scalpel-like blades, which fold into a groove; the unicornfishes (Nasinae) have one or two pairs of sharp, fixed keel-like blades; and the sawtails (Prionurinae) have three to four pairs of fixed blades. The location of the blades is well marked by bright colours in many species, but inconspicuous in others. *(Photos: RM)*

Surgeonfishes: single pair of retractable blades.

Unicornfishes: two pairs of fixed blades.

Sawtails: three to four pairs of fixed blades.

Small species such as these Convict Surgeonfishes (above) gather in large numbers to overwhelm the defences of larger, more dominant ones such as the Lined Surgeonfishes (right), here engaged in a territorial dispute. *Guam, RM; Palau, PM*

enlarged fin spines and may last up to 60 days and reach a size of 6 cm. Surgeonfishes have long lifespans ranging from 25 to 45 years.

Appearance
Surgeonfishes are ovoid to elongate and compressed, and have small mouths containing small, blade-like incisiform teeth, continuous dorsal fins, tough skin with minute scales, and one or more pairs of sharp blades at the base of the tail. The surgeonfishes proper (subfamily Acanthurinae) are deep-bodied and have a single pair of retractable blades, while the unicornfishes (subfamily Nasinae) and sawtails (subfamily Prionurinae) are more elongate and have two or more pairs of fixed blades. Many species are quite colourful but others are rather drab.

Typical accidents
Surgeonfishes are popular food fishes usually caught by net or spear, and several species are important in the aquarium trade. Most accidents are slash or puncture wounds to the hand. Accidents to people in the water are unlikely.

Sohal Surgeonfish *Acanthurus sohal*.

The Monrovia Surgeonfish *Acanthurus monroviae* occurs in the Mediterranean only as a rare stray. It is found in large groups off the west coast of Africa. *Cape Verde Is, MK*

Prevention
When handling surgeonfishes, wear sturdy gloves and avoid contact with the caudal area or fin spines. When diving, avoid feeding them.

Symptoms
Slash wounds made by the caudal blades of surgeonfishes produce an immediate intense stinging or throbbing pain, accompanied by profuse bleeding and severe local swelling. The pain may radiate to the entire appendage and persist for days, but diminishes in intensity within 12 hours. Nausea has also been reported. Puncture wounds caused by fin spines are usually less severe.

Classification and distribution
Eighty species in three subfamilies are known. The true surgeonfishes (Acanthurinae; 53 species) occur in all tropical seas, with 49 species in the Indo-Pacific and four in the Atlantic. The unicornfishes (Nasinae; 19 species) are only in the Indo-Pacific. The sawtails (Prionurinae; seven species) occur in scattered subtropical and tropical areas subject to cold upwelling. Most species have broad distributions owing to a long larval stage.

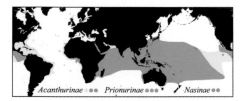

Acanthurinae ●● *Prionurinae* ●●● *Nasinae* ●●

IF INJURED

Treatment

First aid
Apply pressure to stop the bleeding. Remove any accessible foreign matter, then bind the wound.

What not to do
Do not cauterise or manipulate the wound. Avoid immersion in hot water.

Ongoing medical management
Seek medical care if sutures are required, and take measures to prevent secondary infection.

Case study

A spearfisherman was severely slashed on the hand by the caudal spine of an Orangeband Surgeonfish *Acanthurus olivaceous* as he was trying to remove it from a spear. Profuse bleeding ensued immediately, followed by severe swelling within about an hour. Swelling and drainage of the wound continued for about ten days. Treatment consisted of daily soaking in warm water containing Epsom salts, followed by the application of bactericidal cream. Healing took about three weeks.

Surgeonfishes
Subfamily Acanthurinae

Blue Tang — 36 cm
Acanthurus coeruleus — (14.5 in)

Dark brownish blue to pale blue with dark pinstripes; juveniles yellow. **Biology:** inhabits rocky and coral reefs, 2–60 m. Common, occasionally in seagrass beds or on deep sponge bottoms. Feeds on filamentous algae. Aggregates with other surgeonfishes to raid algae patches guarded by damselfishes. **Range:** SC to se. Brazil, Bermuda and Ascension I.; juveniles to NY.

Ocean Surgeonfish — 36 cm
Acanthurus bahianus — (14.3 in)

Pale to dark brownish blue, often with orange pectoral fins and pale tail base. **Biology:** rocky and coral reefs, 1–25 m. Often grazes on algae coating rubble and sand. Aggregates with other surgeonfishes to raid damselfish territories. **Range:** SC to se. Brazil, Bermuda, Ascension I. and St Helena.

A. bahianus ● ● ●
A. chirurgus ● ● ●
A. coeruleus ● ● ●
A. monroviae ● ● ●

Doctorfish — 35 cm
Acanthurus chirurgus — (13.5 in)

Blue to brown with dark bars, may have pale tail base. Caudal blade considered venomous. **Biology:** rocky and coral reefs and deep sponge bottoms, 1–70 m. Juveniles use seagrass beds and mangroves as nurseries. Often grazes algae from the surfaces of rubble and sand. Aggregates with other surgeonfishes to raid damselfish territories. **Range:** SC to se. Brazil, Bermuda, Ascension I. and W. Africa; juveniles to MA.

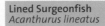

Lined Surgeonfish   38 cm
Acanthurus lineatus   *(15 in)*

Yellow with black-edged blue stripes; belly lavender. **Biology:** a common inhabitant of outer reef flats and margins of exposed seaward reefs, 1–6 m. Highly territorial. Spawns throughout the year, with peak in the summer. Matures in 1–7 years, lives to age of 18–45 years. An important food fish in Pacific islands. Caudal blade reported as venomous. **Range:** E. Africa to the Marquesas and Tuamotus, n. to s. Japan, s. to New Caledonia; strays to Hawaii.

Sohal Surgeonfish   40 cm
Acanthurus sohal   *(16 in)*

Pale with narrow black stripes, median fins black with blue edges. **Biology:** a common inhabitant of outer reef flats and exposed reef margins, 0–10 m, usually <3 m. Males aggressively defend small, well-defined feeding territories, which include a harem of females. Spawns at new moon shortly after sunrise. **Range:** Red Sea to Arabian G. only.

A. sohal ●●
A. lineatus ●●

Convict Surgeonfish   27 cm
Acanthurus triostegus   *(10.6 in)*

Pale grey with 6 narrow black bars. **Biology:** inhabits hard-bottom areas of lagoon and seaward reefs, 1–90 m. Usually in large aggregations, sometimes with other small surgeonfishes. Swarms to gain access to feeding territories of other herbivores. **Range:** E. Africa to Panama, n. to s. Japan, s. to Kermadec and Rapa Is. **Similar:** Black-barred Surgeonfish *A. polyzona* has 9 thick bars (Comoros to Mauritius).

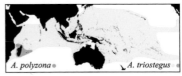

A. polyzona ●
A. triostegus

Achilles Tang   25 cm
Acanthurus achilles   *(10 in)*

Black with bright orange-red spot over
caudal spine, white and red trim on dorsal
and anal fins, outer tail fin red with white
margins. **Biology:** inhabits clear seaward
reefs, primarily in surge zone, 1–4 m. Territorial but occasionally in small groups. Feeds
on filamentous and delicate leafy algae.
Hybridises with *A. nigricans* (below).
Range: Micronesia to Cabo San Lucas,
Mexico, n. to Hawaiian Is, s. to New
Caledonia and Ducie I.

Whitecheek Surgeonfish   21 cm
Acanthurus nigricans   *(8.4 in)*

Black with bright orange-red spot over
caudal spine, white and red trim on dorsal
and anal fins, outer part of tail fin red with
white margins. **Biology:** inhabits sheltered
and seaward reefs, 1–67 m. Territorial, feeds
on filamentous algae. Hybridises with
A. achilles (above) and *A. leucosternon*
(below). **Range:** Cocos (Keeling) to Panama,
n. to Ryukyu and Hawaiian Is. **Similar:**
Japanese Surgeonfish *A. japonicus* has
longer cheek spot, red trim on dorsal and
anal fins (20 cm; n. Sulawesi to s. Japan).

Powder Blue Surgeonfish   23 cm
Acanthurus leucosternon   *(9 in)*

Blue with black face, yellow dorsal fin
and pale blue to white anal fin and tail.
Biology: inhabits clear reef flats and upper
reef slopes, 1–25 m. Solitary or in groups, occasionally in huge aggregations. **Range:** E.
Africa to s. Indonesia, n. to Laccadives and
Burma. Hybridis with *A. nigricans* (above)
are a darker blue and lack pale area under
chin.

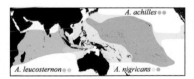

Orangeband Surgeonfish — 35 cm
Acanthurus olivaceus — (14 in)

Grey to black with blue-rimmed orange shoulder band, often abruptly pale in front; juveniles yellow, becoming mustard-yellow then grey with growth. Caudal blade reported as venomous. **Biology:** lagoon and seaward reefs, 2–46 m. Usually over rubble with sand patches, often in groups. Feeds on algal film. **Range:** Cocos (Keeling) to Hawaii and Tuamotus, n. to s. Japan, s. to Lord Howe I.; replaced by *A. reversus* in the Marquesas.

Doubleband Surgeonfish — 31 cm
Acanthurus tennenti — (12 in)

Grey to black with two black shoulder bands, a pale blue-ringed blue to black oval over caudal blade. **Biology:** inhabits lagoon and seaward reefs, 1 m to over 20 m. Usually over rubble with sand patches, often in groups. Feeds on algal film. **Range:** E. Africa to s. Indonesia, n. to Burma. Hybridises with *A. olivaceous* (above) in Bali.

A. olivaceus
A. tennenti ● ● — A. reversus ●

Blackstreak Surgeonfish — 40 cm
Acanthurus nigricauda — (15.7 in)

Olive grey with narrow black shoulder band and long black streak through caudal blade; outer edge of pectoral fin yellow; base of tail white, rest of tail white to dark brown. **Biology:** clear lagoon and seaward reefs, 1–30 m. Usually over open rubble and sand patches, often in groups with other dark surgeonfish species. Feeds on algal film. **Range:** E. Africa to Tuamotus, n. to s. Japan, s. to Gt Barrier Reef; replaced by Dusky Surgeonfish *A. gahhm* in Red Sea.

A. gahhm ● ●
A. nigricauda ●

Yellowfin Surgeonfish — 62.5 cm
Acanthurus xanthopterus (24.5 in)

Grey brown to purplish brown; yellow mask through eyes, pectoral fins mostly yellow, base of tail often white. **Biology:** inhabits lagoon and seaward reefs, 3–90 m. Juveniles in shallow inshore areas. Often in loose groups. Feeds primarily on filamentous algae and the diatom and detritus film on sand, occasionally on hydroids and animal material. The largest species of *Acanthurus*. **Range:** E. Africa to Panama, n. to s. Japan and Hawaii. **Similar:** *A. dussumieri* and *A. blochii* (below), and *A. mata* (p.178), have darker pectoral fins.

Eyestripe Surgeonfish — 54 cm
Acanthurus dussumieri (21 in)

Brown with narrow blue pinstripes; tan band through eye; caudal blade white; tail blue with small black dots. **Biology:** inhabits seaward reefs, 4–131 m. Feeds primarily on surface film on sand, occasionally on hard surfaces. Solitary or in small groups. **Range:** E. Africa to Hawaiian and Line Is, n. to s. Japan. **Similar:** Ringtail Surgeonfish *A. blochii* has stripes on tail, dark blade.

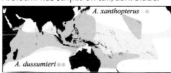

Mimic Surgeonfish — 29 cm
Acanthurus pyroferus (11.4 in)

Adults brown to nearly black with red breast, outer pectoral fin and tail margin yellow; juveniles yellow or grey with blue trim. **Biology:** inhabits lagoon and seaward reefs, 2–60 m. Solitary or in groups feeding with other surgeonfishes. Juveniles mimic the angelfishes *Centropyge flavissima* and *C. vrolikii*. **Range:** Cocos (Keeling) to Tuamotus, n. to s. Japan; replaced from sw. Indonesia to Maldives by *A. tristis*, which is dark grey to black.

Roundspot Surgeonfish 42 cm
Acanthurus bariene (16.5 in)

Snout becomes bulbous with age; brown with blue trim, dorsal fin tan, lips white; round spot behind eye. **Biology:** inhabits clear coastal and seaward reefs, 6–50 m. Usually solitary or in small, loose groups. **Range:** E. Africa to the Solomon Is, n. to Ryukyus, s. to Gt Barrier Reef.

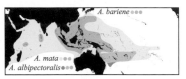

Elongate Surgeonfish 50 cm
Acanthurus mata (19.6 in)

Bluish brown with thin pinstripes and yellow eyepatch; occasionally with white bar on tail base. Caudal blade considered venomous. **Biology:** occurs in aggregations in open water of deep lagoons, bays and seaward reef slopes, 5 m to over 30 m. Often in turbid water, near shelter of caves or wrecks. Feeds primarily on zooplankton. Becomes pale at cleaning stations. **Range:** s. Red Sea to Fr. Polynesia, n. to s. Japan, s. to S. Africa and Gt Barrier Reef. **Similar:** Whitefin Surgeonfish *A. albipectoralis* has white pectoral fins (Gt Barrier Reef to Samoa).

Whitespotted Surgeonfish 28 cm
Acanthurus guttatus (11 in)

Dark brown with 2 pale bars in front, small white spots behind. **Biology:** inhabits the surge zone of clear seaward reefs and rocky shores, 0.5–5 m. Usually in large aggregations in turbulent water, where its white spots help conceal it among bubbles. Feeds primarily on filamentous algae and some calcareous algae. **Range:** Seychelles to Hawaiian, Marquesan and Pitcairn Is, n. to the Ryukyus.

Striped Bristletooth	26 cm
Ctenochaetus striatus	(10 in)

Blue-grey with brown to orange pinstripes, these becoming spots on face. Caudal blade possibly venomous. **Biology:** inhabits reef flats and lagoon and seaward reefs, 1–30 m. Common, solitary or in schools, often with other small surgeonfishes. Feeds on blue-green algae and diatoms growing on hard surfaces and sand. A key link in the ciguatera food chain (p.207), occasionally toxic. **Range:** Red Sea to Fr. Polynesia, n. to s. Japan, s. to S. Africa and Gt Barrier Reef.

Goldring Bristletooth	24 cm
Ctenochaetus strigosus	(9.5 in)

Dark brown with pale pinstripes, these becoming spots on head; yellow ring around eye. Caudal blade possibly venomous. **Biology:** inhabits lagoon and seaward reefs below surge zone, 1–113 m. Abundant. **Range:** Hawaiian Is and Johnston Atoll; replaced by similar species in rest of Indo-Pacific.

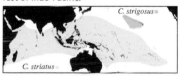

Palette Surgeonfish	26 cm
Paracanthurus hepatus	(10 in)

Brilliant blue with black palette pattern; tail with yellow wedge; belly of adults yellowish in Indian Ocean. Fin spines and caudal blade reported as venomous. **Biology:** inhabits clear, current-swept areas of seaward reefs, 2–40 m. In loose groups up to 3 m above the bottom. Feeds on zooplankton. Shelters in groups among branches of large *Pocillopora* corals or crevices. **Range:** E. Africa to Line Is, n. to s. Japan, s. to se. Australia.

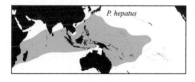

Pacific Sailfin Tang   40 cm
Zebrasoma veliferum   *(15.7 in)*

Deep body with sail-like dorsal and anal fins; brown with pale bars beneath thin orange bars and spots. **Biology:** inhabits deep lagoons and semi-protected seaward reefs with moderate to rich coral growth, 1–30 m. Usually in pairs or small groups. Juveniles solitary, often hidden among corals. **Range:** Christmas I. and Malaysia to Hawaiian and Pitcairn Is, n. to s. Japan; replaced by *Z. desjardinii* (below) in Indian Ocean.

Indian Sailfin Tang   40 cm
Zebrasoma desjardinii   *(15.7 in)*

Deep body with sail-like dorsal and anal fins; brown with pale bars, overlaid with thin orange bars above and spots below. **Biology:** inhabits deep lagoons and semi-protected seaward reefs with moderate to rich coral growth, 1–30 m. Usually in pairs or small groups. Juveniles solitary, often hidden among corals. **Range:** Red Sea and S. Africa to Java.

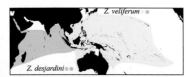

Z. veliferum

Z. desjardini

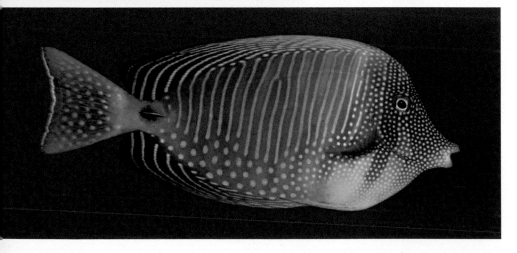

Sawtails
Subfamily Prionurinae

Indonesian Sawtail	47.5 cm
Prionurus chrysurus	*(18.5 in)*

Dark brown with dark grey bars and yellow tail. **Biology:** inhabits areas of cold upwelling (16–23°C), often with strong currents, 12–30 m. Difficult to approach. All other species in the genus are from either cooler warm-temperate or tropical areas subject to cold upwelling. **Range:** Komodo and Bali only. **Similar:** Scalpel Sawtail *P. scalprum* is grey with white tail.

Unicornfishes
Subfamily Nasinae

Elegant Unicornfish   45 cm
Naso elegans   *(17.5 in)*

Grey with orange dorsal and anal fins with blue trim and orange caudal blades; ♂ with elongate tail filaments. **Biology:** inhabits reef flats and lagoon and seaward reefs, 1–90 m. Common, adults sometimes in groups. Large ♂'s occasionally territorial. Pair-spawns. Feeds primarily on leafy brown algae, incl. *Sargassum*. **Range:** Red Sea to Bali, n. to Andaman Sea, s. to S. Africa; replaced by *N. lituratus* (below) in Pacific.

Orangespine Unicornfish   46 cm
Naso lituratus   *(18 in)*

Same as *N. elegans* (above) except dorsal fin black. **Biology:** inhabits reef flats and lagoon and seaward reefs, 1–90 m. Common, adults occasionally in groups. Large ♂'s occasionally territorial. Pair-spawns. Feeds primarily on leafy brown algae, incl. *Sargassum*. **Range:** G. of Thailand to Hawaiian and Pitcairn Is, n. to s. Japan.

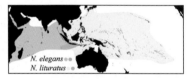

N. elegans
N. lituratus

Bluespine Unicornfish   70 cm
Naso unicornis   *(28 in)*

Olivaceous with blue caudal spines; horn and tail filaments grow with age. **Biology:** inhabits shallow lagoon and seaward reefs, 1–80 m. Common, often in exposed surge areas. Usually occurs in groups and feeds on coarse leafy algae, including *Sargassum*. A major food fish in many areas. **Range:** Red Sea to Fr. Polynesia, n. to s. Japan and Hawaii, s. to S. Africa and se. Australia.

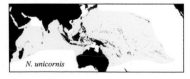

N. unicornis

Whitemargin Unicornfish 100 cm
Naso annulatus (39 in)

Grey to black, tail with white margins and membranes; juveniles with white tail base; tail lobes of ♂'s filamentous. **Biology**: in groups in open water above reef slopes. Juveniles in clear lagoons as shallow as 1 m, adults usually below 25 m off steep seaward slopes. Feeds on large zooplankton. **Range**: Red Sea to Marquesas and Tuamotus, n. to s. Japan and Hawaii; Clipperton I. in E. Pacific.

Sleek Unicornfish 75 cm
Naso hexacanthus (30 in)

Olive-grey, usually tan below; edges of preopercle and operculum black. **Biology**: inhabits deep lagoon and seaward reef slopes, 6–137 m. Common, usually in groups above reef slopes. Feeds on large zooplankton. Courting ♂'s flash white patch and bars on upper body. **Range**: Red Sea to Fr. Polynesia, n. to s. Japan and Hawaii, s. to se. Australia.

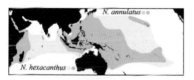

Bignose Unicornfish 75 cm
Naso vlamingii (30 in)

Dark brown with narrow dark bars and spots and blue trim; can instantly turn mostly blue. **Biology**: inhabits deep lagoon and seaward reef slopes, 4–50 m. Usually in groups a few metres above the reef. Feeds on large zooplankton. Often turns pale blue when visiting cleaning stations. Courting ♂'s flash blue areas. **Range**: E. Africa to Tuamotus, n. to s. Japan; strays to Galápagos.

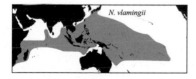

Goliath Groupers *Epinephelus itajara* usually frequent a home cave or wreck. *Southern FL, RM*

Giant Groupers
Serranidae, subfamily Epinephelidae

Groupers are robust-bodied bottom-dwellers that live in a wide range of habitats from the shoreline to depths of over 400 m. Two species, the Giant Grouper *Epinephelus lanceolatus* and the Goliath Grouper *E. itajara*, reach the immense size of at least 320 kg, large enough to swallow a small adult human. While there are no verifiable reports of this having occurred, there are plausible accounts of groupers having taken people in their mouths. Several other species of grouper reach a size of 100 kg or more, and some have caused death to humans by drowning. A more common threat posed by groupers is that of ciguatera poisoning (p.207).

Behaviour and biology
Groupers are voracious carnivores that stalk and swallow their prey whole. They eat primarily crustaceans, fishes and cephalopods, but the largest ones also eat stingrays and young sea turtles and sharks. In general, a grouper will eat anything that moves that it is able to swallow. Large groupers may hover well above the bottom, sometimes tilted to one side.

Most groupers are hermaphrodites, but the largest species remain either male or female throughout life. Small species may mature in as little as a year, while large ones may take four to seven years. Groupers are long-lived, with many having lifespans of 20 to over 40 years. The largest species grow relatively fast. In an extreme example, a Giant Grouper held captive in China and overfed grew from 30 cm to 1.6 m and a weight of 150 kg in just five years. It died of arteriosclerosis! Many groupers migrate to favoured sites, where they aggregate to spawn. Their small eggs (under 1 mm) are pelagic, and the planktonic larval stage lasts up to several weeks. Groupers readily take a baited hook and large species are vulnerable to overfishing.

Grouper weapons

A grouper's primary threat is its sizeable mouth, which it uses to swallow large prey whole. Several rows of small, sharply pointed teeth are used to secure prey and jockey it into position. The primary threat extremely large groupers pose to humans is drowning, either by holding them underwater or from the force of a collision. A secondary hazard is that of being punctured and scratched by the grouper's numerous teeth. The few divers who have been taken in a grouper's mouth and lived tell their story suffered cuts and scratches to themselves and their gear.

Appearance

Groupers have large rounded heads with large mouths, relatively small eyes and low, broad-based dorsal and anal fins. Most species are slightly compressed and oval in cross section. Groupers are distinguished from fishes of related families by having a continuous lateral line, two or three flattened opercular spines and small ctenoid scales. They have several rows of small, sharp conical to needle-like teeth. Species of *Plectropomus* and *Mycteroperca* also have one or more pairs of conspicuous canine teeth.

Typical accidents

There are numerous reports of people in remote places being eaten by Giant Groupers, but none can be confirmed. However, there are at least two well-documented cases of people being taken in the mouth of a Goliath Grouper and escaping. At least two cases of drowning have been caused by groupers. In one, a Potato Grouper *Epinephelus*

tukula looking for a handout collided with a diver holding a bag of fish to his chest. The diver had just entered the water and was hit with enough force to knock the wind from him. He immediately sank to the bottom in 12 m and drowned. In 2006 in the Florida Keys, a free-diver who illegally speared a Goliath Grouper drowned when his wrist became entangled in the line attached to the spear. His body was found tethered in the cave to which the grouper had retreated.

Prevention

Use common sense – do not corner any fish larger than yourself and do not closely approach a grouper that is massive enough to swallow you. If you feel you are being stalked, retreat and get close to others. There are no known cases of a grouper stalking a group of people. Never feed large fishes except in a controlled and sanctioned venue. If you are taken into a grouper's mouth, fight like hell to escape. If an arm is outside the mouth, try to gouge an eye.

Classification and distribution

Groupers inhabit nearly all tropical and warm-temperate seas. The two species large enough to swallow a human are broadly distributed, with one in the Indo-Pacific and the other in the east Pacific and Atlantic. Other species weighing 100 kg or more are found in many regions.

Treatment

First aid

Cardio-pulmonary resuscitation (CPR) should be administered immediately to anyone brought to the surface unconscious. Cuts should be disinfected with alcohol (40–70 per cent).

Ongoing medical management

Victims of near-drowning should be held in a medical facility for observation for at least 24 hours. Secondary infections should be treated with antibiotics under the care of a physician.

IF INJURED

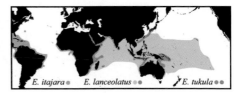

E. itajara ●   *E. lanceolatus* ● ●   *E. tukula* ● ●

Giant Grouper   2.6 m; 320 kg
Epinephelus lanceolatus   *(9 ft; 705 lb)*

Bold juvenile pattern breaks up with growth. The largest bony reef fish. **Biology:** inhabits estuaries, coastal and offshore reefs, 3–100 m. Usually has a home cave or wreck. Solitary and wary. Feeds on fishes, large crustaceans, small sharks and turtles. Large individuals can be ciguatoxic. Possible fatal attacks on humans. Rare, nearly wiped out by fishing. Juveniles secretive. **Range:** Red Sea to Fr. Polynesia and Hawaii, n. to Ryukyus.

Juvenile *Epinephelus lanceolatus.*
Illustration: EL

Goliath Grouper   2.4 m; 315 kg
Epinephelus itajara   *(7.9 ft; 691 lb)*

Mottled brown with small black spots. **Biology:** inhabits mangrove creeks and rocky and coral reefs, 1–100 m. Juveniles primarily in estuaries. Territorial, often near home cave or wreck. May show a threat display by opening mouth and raising dorsal fin. Feeds primarily on spiny lobsters, also on fishes, stingrays and young turtles and sharks. Known to stalk and try to eat humans. Migrates up to 100 km to aggregate and spawn at end of summer. ♀s mature in 4–6 yrs at 110–115 cm, ♂s in 6–7 yrs at 120–130 cm. Lives over 37 yrs. Endangered in many areas by overfishing, now protected in US. **Range:** FL, Bermuda and G. of Mexico to s. Brazil; e. Pacific and e. Atlantic.

Potato Grouper   **2.0 m; 110 kg**
Epinephelus tukula   *(6.6 ft; 240 lb)*

Light grey with large, dark blotches.
Biology: inhabits pinnacles, drop-offs, deep
lagoons and wrecks, 3–150 m, usually in
clear, coral-rich areas. Solitary or in small
groups. Uncommon and highly localised.
Feeds on fishes, crustaceans and
cephalopods. Easily approached, but
potentially dangerous to inexperienced
divers. The main attraction at the Gt
Barrier Reef's Cod Hole. **Range:** Red Sea to
Gt Barrier Reef, n. to s. Japan, s. to S. Africa
and Mauritius; distribution patchy.

Other Giant Fishes

Some normally inoffensive fishes can be dangerous simply because of their large size and behaviour. For example, there are cases of Manta Rays leaping from the water and landing on small boats, killing or injuring the occupants. Mantas also occasionally get their cephalic lobes entangled in rope, possibly in an attempt to scrape off parasites. One of the authors (RM) witnessed such an occasion when one hooked itself on a group's dive flag, forcing its holder to let go. After the dive, the flag was found about a kilometre away with the Manta still attached.

When a large fish of any species is cornered and bolts for freedom, it can pose a danger to anyone in its way. Blunt force can easily cause unconsciousness or drowning. During a spearfishing derby on Guam, a young free-diver drowned after having the wind knocked from him by a large Bumphead Parrotfish. It bolted as the diver tried to manhandle it to the surface. Some large fish can cause unexpected injury with their teeth.

Manta Ray	6.7 m width; 1,400 kg
Manta birostris	*(22 ft; 3,086 lb)*

Flaps at sides of mouth flexible. **Biology:** inhabits surface to mid-waters of lagoons and seaward reefs, usually near channels during outgoing tides, 1–50 m. Often visits cleaning stations. Solitary or in groups of up to 50. Dangerous only when leaping. **Range:** circumtropical. **Similar:** devil or box rays *Mobula* spp. are smaller and differ by having inflexible head flaps.

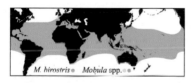

Bumphead Parrotfish	1.3 m
Bolbometopon muricatum	*(4.3 ft)*

Steep head profile with large pink hump on forehead; young with more normal head and white spots. **Biology:** in closely knit groups on coral-rich outer reef flats and lagoon and seaward reef slopes, 1–50 m. Feeds on algae and living corals. Sleeps in groups in crevices. Wary and rare in most areas. The largest parrotfish, to at least 70 kg. **Range:** Red Sea and E. Africa to Fr. Polynesia, n. to Taiwan.

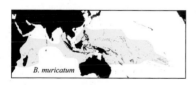

The outline of the left electric organ of this male Leopard Torpedo Ray *Torpedo panthera* is clearly visible as it swims above the bottom. *Red Sea, MB*

Electric Rays
Order Torpediniformes

Behaviour

Electric rays live on sand or mud bottoms of coastal shelves and slopes. They are ambush predators that are well disguised by their cryptic coloration or habit of partially burying themselves in sediment. They feed mainly on small fishes and invertebrates, which they stun with an electrical charge, then swallow whole. Their electrical discharge is also used to deter predators. Like many animals with an effective defence, they are reluctant to move and do not flee an approaching diver. Occasionally they swim well above the bottom by beating the tail from side to side rather than undulating the disc. Electric rays are born live and fully developed, so the newborns resemble miniature versions of their parents.

Appearance

Electric rays have round to oval bodies with fused pectoral fins, thick tails and small, close-set eyes that rise above the front of the disc. Most species have two dorsal fins on the tail, which ends in a rounded, paddle-shaped fin and lacks any form of armament. The mouth and gills are located on the underside, and the shape and position of the nostrils and mouth varies by family. Rows of teeth line the mouth; those in the back may be pavement-like and are used for dispatching and crushing prey. In many species the outline of the electric organs is visible through the skin. Most species are cryptically coloured, but some have bold spots or reticulations. The largest species, the Atlantic Torpedo Ray *Torpedo nobiliana*, reaches a length of about 1.8 m.

Leopard Torpedo Ray *Torpedo panthera*.

Electric organs

The kidney-shaped electric organs (outlined here in blue) are located on either side of the head and take up most of the forward part of the disc. They extend from top to bottom and are made of highly modified muscle tissue that can generate and store electricity. The power of the electric discharge varies. The numbfish *Narcine bancroftii* (Narcinidae) produces 14–37 volts, while other numbfishes (*Diplobatis* spp.) and torpedo rays (*Torpedo* spp.; Torpedinidae) may discharge up to 230 volts. Because sea water conducts electricity, the electric organs are effective only at very close range. *(Photos: JR. Artwork: RM)*

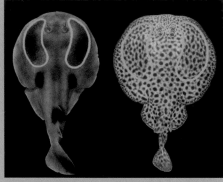

Narkidae
Heteromarce hentuval

Torpedinidae
Torpedo fuscomaculata

Typical accidents

Divers and waders occasionally get acquainted with an electric ray's special capabilities when they touch or prod one. This results in an unpleasant jolt. Electric rays are often taken as bycatch in nets and are occasionally hooked. Fishermen may be shocked as they sort the catch or remove a hook. Disorientation and unconsciousness have been reported, but there are no known cases of divers getting into trouble. As the ray needs time to 'recharge', a second jolt is easily avoided.

Prevention

Do not touch an electric ray!

Symptoms

The shock is powerful but normally results in nothing more than a sharp jolt, which has been likened to a strong blow from a fist. Occasionally, the shock may cause momentary disorientation and, in very unusual cases, brief unconsciousness.

Treatment

First aid

Other than the unpleasant jolt, there are usually no side effects and no need for first aid. It is not known if a shock will have any effect on a pacemaker.

Ongoing medical management

Generally not necessary.

Classification and distribution

Electric rays inhabit soft bottoms of continental and major island shelves and the slopes of most temperate and tropical seas, from the shallows to depths of over 1,000 m. The 66 known species are divided into four families and are distinguished by position and shape of the nostrils, mouth and teeth, as well as shape of the body, tail and fins. Numbfishes (Narcinidae; 27 species) of the Atlantic and Indo-Pacific are banjo-shaped with two relatively large dorsal fins and distinctive folded lips. Sleeper rays (Narkidae; ten species) of the Indo-Pacific are similar, but they lack 'lips' and may have one, two or no dorsal fins. Torpedo rays (Torpedinidae; 28 species), found worldwide in tropical and temperate seas, have wider discs that may be nearly square. The bizarre Coffin Ray *Hypnos monopterygium* of Australia is in a family of its own (Hypnidae). It has a rectangular disc, followed by a small secondary disc that is formed by its pelvic fins, which surround a very short tail with small fins. Most species of electric ray have restricted ranges owing to their limited abilities to disperse. However, a few temperate species are relatively bouyant and even semi-pelagic, and so have broader distributions.

Torpedinidae
Narcinidae
Narkidae
Hypnidae

IF INJURED

Torpedo Rays
Torpedinidae

Leopard Torpedo Ray	100 cm
Torpedo panthera	*(39 in)*

Disc round with straight front; pale tan to ochre with white stellate spots. **Biology:** on sand or mud near coral reefs, 0.5–55 m. Usually buried. Not shy, may move slowly away when disturbed. Common. Moves deep during winter. Can feed on surprisingly large prey, incl. scorpionfishes. **Range:** Red Sea and Arabian G. only. **Similar:** many species distinguishable by colour pattern.

Marbled Torpedo Ray	130 cm
Torpedo sinuspersici	*(51 in)*

Disc round with straight front; brown with close-set pale, stellate spots that often form reticulate pattern. **Biology:** on sand or rubble bottoms of coral or rocky reefs, 2–200 m. Often buried. Feeds on fishes, crustaceans and molluscs. Usually solitary. Aggregates during mating season. Gives birth in shallows, has litter of 9–22 pups. **Range:** Red Sea and Arabian G. to Sri Lanka, s. to S. Africa.

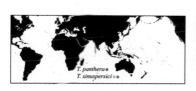
T. panthera ●
T. sinuspersici ●●

Numbfishes
Narcinidae

Indonesian Numbfish   **>31 cm**
Narcine sp.   *(>12.3 in)*

Disc oval, narrower in front; brown with small and large darker spots. **Biology:** on sand or mud near coral reefs, 20–63 m. An undescribed species, known only from a few specimens and photographs. **Range:** s. Indonesia, Java to Komodo only. **Similar:** many species, distinguishable by colour pattern.

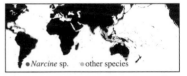

● *Narcine* sp.   ● other species

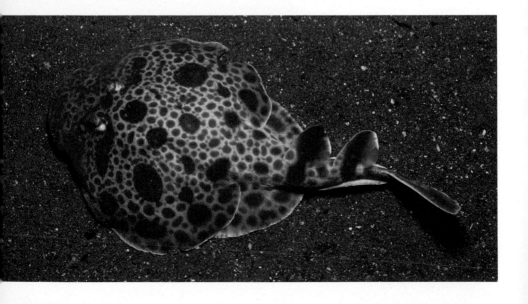

Electric Stargazers
Uranoscopidae, genus Astroscopus

Three species of stargazer have a pair of electric organs behind the eyes that they use for both defence and stunning prey. When touched, these organs are powerful enough to give a painful shock, but no lasting side effects have been reported. Most stargazers are protected by a pair of stout shoulder spines, but those in *Astroscopus* are weak. More detailed information on the family is given on p.166.

Southern Stargazer	44 cm
Astroscopus ygraecum	*(17.3 in)*

Shoulder spine blunt and covered in skin, electric organs behind eyes (outlined in blue in photo); greyish brown with small, dark-edged white spots, fins dark with pale margins and stripes. **Biology:** inhabits sand bottoms of estuaries and coastal waters, 2–40 m. **Range:** coastal waters from Chesapeake Bay to n. S. America. **Similar:** replaced by Northern Stargazer *A. guttatus* n. of C. Hatteras, Brazilian Stargazer *A. sexspinosus* in se. Brazil, and Pacific Stargazer *A. zephyreus* in tropical e. Pacific.

A. ygraecum ●
A. guttatus ●
A. zephyreus ●

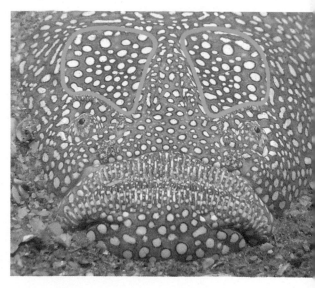

Passively Poisonous Fishes
Fishes that are poisonous to eat

Poisonous Fishes

While eating spoiled seafood of any kind can make one seriously ill, there are a great many species that are highly poisonous regardless of their condition. Those that are most frequently poisonous can easily be avoided once they are recognised. However, a large number of normally edible species, particularly tropical varieties, can suddenly become toxic and are not so easily avoided. There are several kinds of fish poisoning; three are common and widespread, while most others infrequent to rare.

Widespread and frequent causes of poisoning:
- **Tetrodotoxic fishes** contain deadly tetrodotoxin in their organs and tissues. The toxin is produced by bacteria that are acquired through diet or the environment (p.198).
- **Ciguatoxic fishes** accumulate ciguatoxin in their tissues through the food chain. This and related toxins are produced by microscopic dinoflagellates and concentrate in top marine predators (p.207).

The poisonous Blackspotted Puffer *Arothron nigropunctatus* has a readily recognisable globular body and is easy to approach. *Maldives, MB.*

- **Scombrotoxic fishes** acquire high concentrations of histamines produced by bacterial action – in other words, spoilage. Tunas, mackerels and Mahimahi are all high risk (p.229).

Infrequent causes of poisoning:
- **Palytoxic fishes** are normally edible species that rarely contain deadly palytoxin, produced by dinoflagellates and certain soft corals. Originally described as clupeotoxin after fatal poisonings caused by eating herrings, sardines and anchovies (p.227).
- **Crinotoxic fishes** are those that have a toxic, often bitter-tasting skin and mucus (p.233).
- **Hallucinogenic fishes** produce hallucinations when eaten. The causative substance seems to be concentrated in the brains of various fishes, particularly goatfishes of the genus *Upeneus* (p.230).

Other kinds of fish poisoning may occur after eating snake mackerels (gempylotoxism; p.231), which are extremely oily and cause diarrhoea, or fish eggs (ichthyootoxism), or fish blood (ichthyohaemotoxism). Even in recent years, mysterious cases of severe and fatal poisoning remain unsolved, particularly those involving sharks or shark liver.

Tetrodotoxic Fishes
Tetraodontidae

Many members of the Tetraodontidae family, which includes puffers and their relatives, are extremely poisonous. Despite – or rather because of – this, the Japanese regard them as a delicacy. This culinary speciality is called *fugu*, a dish of raw puffer meat cut into extremely thin slices. It does not have an unusual taste, but that is not what makes it a delicacy. The desire is to experience a slight, controlled poisoning. The moderate consumption of *fugu* results in a minor tingling and burning sensation on the tongue and roof of the mouth, with a numbness in the mouth area. This also happens in other mucus membrane areas such as those associated with the genitalia, hence *fugu*'s aphrodisiac reputation. To savour this highly prized dish, diners need to be very careful of the quantity they ingest. If more than just a little is eaten, the tingling could develop into a severe or even deadly poisoning.

Behaviour and life history

Puffers are named for their ability to inflate themselves. When danger threatens, they can gulp water into a special chamber near the stomach and inflate like balloons. They then become too large, hard and prickly to be eaten by many predators. Their toxicity and often bitter

This small Whitespotted Puffer was found inflated and nearly stranded on a tidal flat. Perhaps it had just escaped a predator. *Red Sea, RM*

taste also renders them relatively unpalatable. Puffers can be quite aggressive and will readily bite when handled. Some species are dangerous to waders and swimmers, and are capable of severing a finger or toe (p.153). Puffers are portly yet highly manoeuvrable swimmers. Like a helicopter, they are able to turn around in one spot or move backwards. Most species normally remain near the bottom and prefer calm, sheltered areas. They feed on a wide variety of plants and animals, including many hard-shelled forms that they crush with their powerful beaks.

Little is known of puffer reproduction. Temperate species spawn during the warmer months. The warm-temperate Grass Puffer *Takifugu niphobles* swarms beaches at high tide to spawn and leave its eggs in wet sand and rubble. The small coral reef-dwelling Valentini Puffer *Canthigaster valentini* is haremic, with males overseeing territories containing up to seven females. Each female deposits her eggs in a tuft of algae. The toxic eggs hatch into pelagic larvae in three to five days, and the pelagic stage lasts seven to 16 weeks. Puffers occur in all tropical to temperate seas, as well as in estuaries and the lower reaches of many tropical rivers. Some species are pelagic.

Appearance

Puffers are easily identified by their oblong globular shape, with short-based dorsal, anal and pectoral fins and eyes set high on the head. The gill opening is restricted to a small slit in front of the pectoral fin. Puffers have a tough, highly flexible skin with short prickles instead of scales, and they lack fin spines, pelvic fins and ribs. Their teeth are fused into a powerful beak with a median suture. The largest species attains at least 1 m in length.

The poison and its occurrence

The substance responsible for pufferfish poisoning is tetrodotoxin (TTX), named after the puffers from which it was extracted. It is a small molecule whose structure was determined in 1963. It works by binding to the external part of a nerve's sodium channel, thereby blocking its impulse. This interrupts muscle contraction and causes paralysis. Severe poisoning results in complete paralysis of all voluntary muscles,

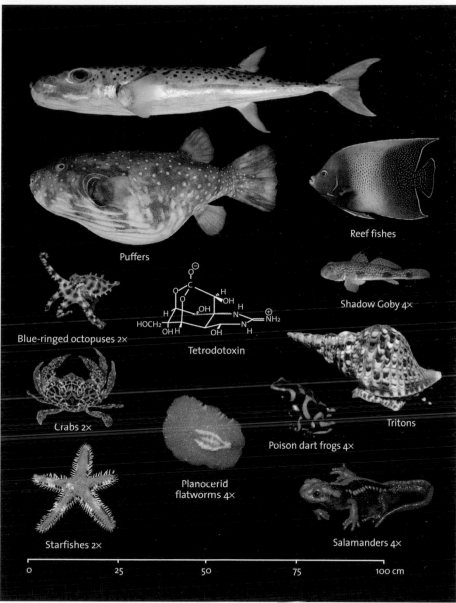

Tetrodotoxin (TTX) occurs in a wide variety of marine and terrestrial animals. Many puffers are extremely toxic (e.g. *Lagocephalus sceleratus* at top), while others are variable in their toxicity (e.g. *Arothron* spp.). The Shadow Goby *Yongeichthys criniger* and some crabs (e.g. *Zozymus* spp.) are often highly toxic, while other normally edible reef fishes (e.g. *Pomacanthus semicirculatus*), some starfishes (*Astropecten* spp.) and several gastropods may occasionally be toxic. Blue-ringed octopuses (*Hapalochlaena* spp.) incorporate TTX in their salivary glands and use it as a venom to paralyse their crustacean prey. Planocerid flatworms, poison dart frogs (*Dendrobates* spp.) and many salamanders also contain high levels of TTX. *RM, JR*

Treatment

First aid

As soon as signs of poisoning appear, immediately force vomiting. Only when the poisoning is at an advanced state should vomiting be avoided, as paralysis of the mouth and throat muscles (which appears as a difficulty in swallowing) leads to a danger of vomit entering the windpipe and lungs. If breathing becomes impaired or stops, use artificial (mouth-to-mouth) resuscitation. Emergency medical care is mandatory as the victim must be artificially ventilated throughout the course of paralysis.

which stops respiration and causes death by asphyxiation. TTX is one of the most effective natural poisons, with an average lethal dose of 0.009 mg per kilogram of the victim's body weight. It is surprisingly widespread in nature, being found in a wide range of marine animals as well as a few terrestrial ones. It is the same toxin found in blue-ring octopuses, various crabs, horseshoe crabs, gastropods, flatworms, a starfish, poison dart frogs, salamanders and newts. It is not produced by the animals themselves, but rather by various kinds of bacteria. The animals incorporate the bacteria in their tissues, either through diet or other environmental contact. Puffers, in common with most other toxic species, use the toxin passively as a defence against predators. However, blue-ring octopuses (p.327) and, perhaps, the Flamboyant Cuttlefish *Metasepia pfefferi* (p.333) incorporate it in their salivary glands and use it actively by biting, both offensively to capture prey as well as defensively.

Distribution of poison within puffers

The poison is distributed throughout the fish. The highest concentrations tend to be in the internal organs, particularly the liver and sex organs, and the skin. Spawned eggs may also be toxic. Toxicity varies greatly, not only between species but within the same species. Puffers in one location may be highly toxic while others of the same species in a neighbouring area may contain very little toxin. Toxicity may also vary by season. Females of many species often have a higher poison content in the ovaries during their reproductive period.

Typical cause of poisoning

Poisoning occurs only when the puffer is eaten. *Fugu* dishes served in special restaurants and prepared by licensed chefs are nearly always safe. Poisoning usually occurs when a puffer is prepared by those unaware of the danger or by an unlicensed amateur. In 1996, several cases in the US were caused by puffers illegally imported and improperly prepared.

Symptoms

The first symptoms usually appear 10 to 20 minutes after ingestion. They start with a slight tingling and burning in the mouth area. This then extends to the limbs, and finally a feeling of numbness is experienced. In cases of major poisoning, the following progressive symptoms occur: difficulty in swallowing, speaking and breathing, a dazed state, a feeling of weakness, difficulty in walking, and falling blood pressure. The victim normally remains completely conscious but is unable to communicate and soon cannot move a muscle or even blink. Total paralysis of the breathing muscles results in death by asphyxiation. The involuntary muscles of the heart are normally unaffected, so it continues beating until starved of oxygen. In Japan, a 61 per cent fatality rate was reported during a ten-year period. Folklore of people 'coming back from the dead' may be the result of sub-lethal

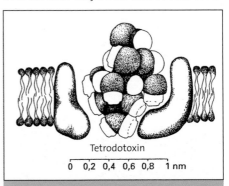

Tetrodotoxin

0   0,2 0,4 0,6 0,8   1 nm

Tetrodotoxin (TTX) is a small molecule that binds to the external part of a nerve's sodium channel, thereby blocking its impulse. This interrupts muscle contraction and causes paralysis. In severe cases, complete paralysis of all voluntary muscles stops respiration, resulting in death by asphyxiation. The average lethal dose is 0.009 mg per kilogram of the victim's body weight. *(After Mebs, 2002)*

This Starry Puffer *Arothron stellatus* bears the fresh scars of a shark bite. The superficial nature of the wound indicates that the predator immediately released its grip. *Palau, PM*

cases of tetrodotoxin poisoning. In some cases, victims who clung to life barely breathing and with low heart rates were declared dead, placed in coffins or even buried before experiencing a 'miraculous' recovery.

Prevention
The simplest and safest way to avoid pufferfish poisoning is to not eat any kind of puffer. Those who absolutely must try it should do so only in a Japanese restaurant specifically licensed to prepare *fugu*. Under no circumstances should any one other than a licensed *fugu* chef make a meal of any species of puffer. Puffers are easily recognisable and anyone who catches one should release it. Anyone who handles a puffer should wash their hands thoroughly before touching food or the mouth. Since species other than puffers may occasionally be toxic, anyone fishing or shopping for fish should be familiar with which local species are safe. There is no way to detoxify a tetrodotoxic fish.

Therapy and ongoing medical treatment
There is no antidote for tetrodotoxin. The treatment must be carried out based entirely on the symptoms. The stomach should definitely be pumped out. Thereafter, the patient, even if only slightly poisoned, should be kept under close observation for 12 hours. If breathing difficulties set in, the patient should be intubated and put on a respirator. Improvement depends on the severity of the poisoning but usually occurs within 24 hours when spontaneous respiration returns. Complications are rare and most often due to aspiration pneumonia (from inhaling vomit or saliva) or renal failure due to hypotension. Where healing takes place without complication, there are no residual effects.

Classification and distribution
The puffer family Tetraodontidae includes about 105 species in 19 genera and two subfamilies. The tobies or sharpnose puffers (subfamily Canthigasterinae) includes 30 small species (under 19.5 cm), all in the genus *Canthigaster*. They inhabit primarily coral reefs and warm-temperate coastal waters. The rest (subfamily Tetraodontinae) vary in shape and range from under 6 cm to over 1 m in length. They occur in all tropical to temperate seas, as well as estuaries and many tropical rivers. Most species inhabit shallow coral reefs and coastal waters, but some

Sample case

NSW, Australia. While camping, a family caught over 20 small puffers. They were cleaned, gutted and soaked in sea water overnight. The next day they were boiled in sea water, then eaten. Shortly after the meal, as the family was breaking camp, one member, a 14-year-old boy, felt numbness in his lips, a swelling sensation of his tongue and general lightness. About 45 minutes after the meal he vomited, then had problems swallowing and became very cold. He was taken to hospital, where he arrived cyanotic (blue) and apnoeic. He was intubated, ventilated and transferred to a major hospital. Although fully conscious, he was unreactive, areflexive and had flaccid paralysis. His pupils were dilated but his pulse and blood pressure were normal. Artificial respiration was continued throughout the course of paralysis. After 12 hours of complete paralysis, he was able to move his eyelids and communication was established. Within two hours he was able to move his lips and tongue, and 24 hours after the meal, respiration was restored followed by full vital capacity within a few hours. The puffer the boy ate was identified as Prickly Puffer *Contusus richei*. Other family members suffered milder symptoms or none at all and two brothers vomited. A young injured crow in the family's care, which was given one fish, staggered about and then dropped dead within a few minutes. *(After Mebs, 2002)*

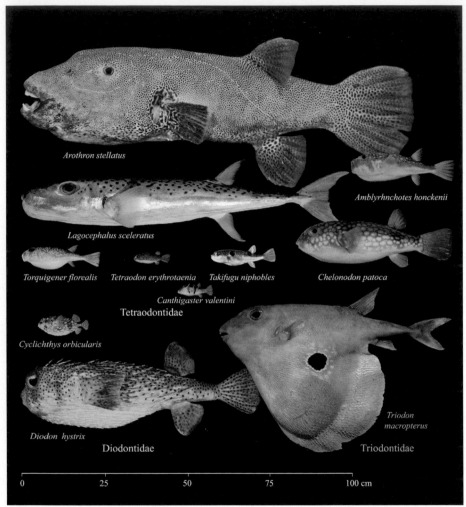

Arothron stellatus

Amblyrhnchotes honckenii

Lagocephalus sceleratus

Torquigener florealis   *Tetraodon erythrotaenia*   *Takifugu niphobles*

Chelonodon patoca

Canthigaster valentini

Tetraodontidae

Cyclichthys orbicularis

Diodon hystrix

Triodon macropterus

Diodontidae

Triodontidae

| 0 | 25 | 50 | 75 | 100 cm |

Diversity in size and shape among the puffer families. Representative genera are true to scale. *RM, JR*

occur in deep water (100–480 m) and others are entirely pelagic. The species used primarily for *fugu* dishes, members of the genus *Takifugu*, inhabit subtropical to temperate Southeast Asian coastal waters. See also p.153 for information on puffers that have caused injuries by biting. The strange Threetooth Puffer *Triodon macropterus* has a single tooth in the lower jaw and is in a family of its own (Triodontidae). It inhabits the waters above coastal slopes of the Indian Ocean and western Pacific at depths of about 100–450 m. Although ths species is sold fresh and eaten in Japan, it is considered toxic in other areas. Porcupinefishes and burrfishes, the so-called 'spiny puffers (family Diodontidae) are occasionally toxic, presumably from tetrodotoxin but also from ciguatoxin (pp.156 and 207).

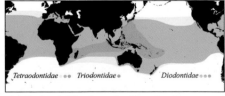

Tetraodontidae •• *Triodontidae* • *Diodontidae* •••

Distribution of the three families of puffer.

Bluespotted Puffer — 80 cm
Arothron caeruleopunctatus (32 in)

Brown to grey with small, close-set pale blue spots forming rings around eyes. **Biology:** inhabits coastal reefs, channels and seaward reef slopes, 2–45 m. Uncommon, usually seen hovering close above corals or under overhangs. Solitary and slow-moving. **Range:** Réunion and Maldives to Marshall Is, n. to Ryukyus. **Similar:** *A. mappa* (p.204) has lines radiating from eyes; *A. stellatus* (p.155) is pale with black spots.

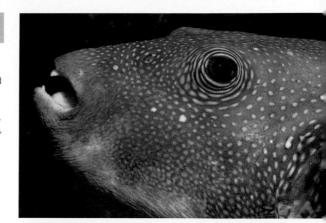

Whitespotted Puffer — 50 cm
Arothron hispidus (19.7 in)

Brown with white spots (rarely reticulations) and rings around eyes and pectoral fin base. **Biology:** inhabits lagoons, bays and seaward reefs with moderate coral growth, 1–50 m. Common, often rests on rubble or sand. Eats sponges, tunicates, polychaetes, crabs, corals, molluscs, sea urchins, algae and detritus. **Range:** Red Sea to Panama, n. to s. Japan. **Similar:** Reticulated Puffer *A. reticularis* has lines on belly and face, inhabits turbid in-shore reefs and estuaries (30 cm; India to Fiji).

caeruleopunctatus • 　　　 hispidus •

Striped Puffer — 31 cm
Arothron manilensis (12.2 in)

Basic colouring beige to light brown or greyish green, with vertical dark stripes. **Biology:** Generally found in lagoons and reefs, on sand, mud and seagrass, 1–17 m. **Range:** Borneo and Bali, and from the Philippines to Samoa, n. to Ryukyus, s. to NSW and Tonga.

Map Puffer   60 cm
Arothron mappa   (23.6 in)

Pale to blotched with fine black spots or reticulations forming lines that radiate from eyes. **Biology:** inhabits lagoon and seaward reefs, 4–40 m. Solitary. Feeds on sponges, tunicates, gastropods and algae. **Range:** E. Africa to Samoa, n. to s. Japan, s. to New Caledonia and Tonga.

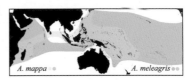

Guineafowl Puffer   32 cm
Arothron meleagris   (12.6 in)

Black with small white spots, occasionally partly to nearly completely yellow. **Biology:** inhabits lagoon and seaward reefs, 1–73 m. Solitary. Usually in clear water, rare on coastal reefs except in e. Pacific. Feeds primarily on the branch tips of corals, also on sponges, gastropods, zoanthids and algae. **Range:** E. Africa to Panama, n. to s. Japan, s. to New Caledonia.

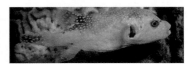

Blackspotted Puffer   29.5 cm
Arothron nigropunctatus   (11.6 in)

Pale cream to brown, grey or mostly yellow with widely scattered small black spots. **Biology:** inhabits coral-rich areas of coastal, lagoon and seaward reefs, 1 m to at least 35 m. Solitary. Feeds primarily on corals, to a lesser extent on sponges, tunicates, zoanthids and algae. **Range:** E. Africa and G. of Aden to Line and Cook Is, n. to s. Japan. **Similar:** Masked Puffer *A. diadematus* has dark band through eyes (30 cm; Red Sea).

Milkspotted Puffer — 33 cm
Chelonodon patoca — (13 in)

Olivaceous with oblong white spots and
pale yellow to white belly. **Biology:** inhabits
the lower reaches of rivers, estuaries and
coastal rocky and coral reefs, in fresh and
marine waters, 4–50 m. **Range:** Arabian G.
to New Caledonia, n. to Ryukyu and Bonin
(Ogasawara) Is.

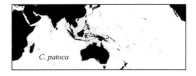

Bandtail Puffer — 18 cm
Sphoeroides spengleri — (7.1 in)

Elongate; olivaceous above, with a double
row of round dark spots on sides. **Biology:**
inhabits seagrass beds, inlets and coastal
to offshore reefs, 1–20 m. Common in
weedy protected areas. Solitary or in loose
aggregations. Feeds primarily on small
benthic invertebrates. Toxic, has caused
fatalities. **Range:** MA, Bermuda and n. G. of
Mexico to se. Brazil; e. Atlantic.

Checkered Puffer — 30 cm
Sphoeroides testudineus — (11.6 in)

Pale with greenish-brown blotches over-
lain with small dark spots. **Biology:** inhabits soft bottoms of estuaries, seagrass beds
and protected coasts to 44 m. Common in
mangrove creeks. Solitary or in groups. May
partially bury itself. Feeds primarily on
shellfishes. Lethally toxic. **Range:** ne. FL,
Bahamas and w. Yucatán to se. Brazil, incl.
all Caribbean.

Large predatory fishes at the top of the reef fish food chain, like this Twinspot Snapper *Lutjanus bohar*, tend to be the most highly ciguatoxic species. *Palau, RM*

Ciguatoxic Fishes

Ciguatera is a food poisoning contracted by eating normally non-toxic species of fish. The toxins responsible have been found in over 400 species, including many popular ones traded worldwide. This makes ciguatera the most common fish poisoning. About 50,000 people are affected globally each year, 20,000 of them in the Caribbean and most of the rest in the tropical Pacific islands region commonly known as the 'South Seas'. In Puerto Rican waters, ciguatera is so widespread that the territory imports approximately 85 per cent of its fish.

Ciguatera originates almost exclusively in tropical coral reef waters rather than in subtropical areas. It becomes a problem in other regions when edible fishes are imported from the tropics. The USA and Canada collectively experience about 2,300 cases of ciguatera poisoning a year. In the USA, ciguatera is the most commonly reported type of food poisoning caused by a natural toxin. The highest number of cases occurs in Florida, where many of the fish are caught locally.

The ciguatera food chain

Ciguatoxic fishes do not produce the poison themselves. It is produced by one or more species of microscopic single-cell dinoflagellates, a type of algae. The chief culprit is *Gambierdiscus toxicus*, a species nearly large enough to be seen by the naked eye. It produces not only ciguatoxin, but the similar maitotoxin. In the Caribbean, another species, *Ostreopsis lenticularis*, is also considered responsible for ciguatera poisoning. These dinoflagellates do not live as phytoplankton in open water, but are attached to the upper surfaces of larger algae. The herbivorous fishes that eat them along with their normal algae food sequester the toxins. Although the toxins do not affect the fishes, they are either not metabolised or are metabolised so slowly that they accumulate in their tissues. A predator that eats a herbivore accumulates its lifetime load of toxins and in turn may be eaten by a larger predator. The toxins thus concentrate at the top of the food

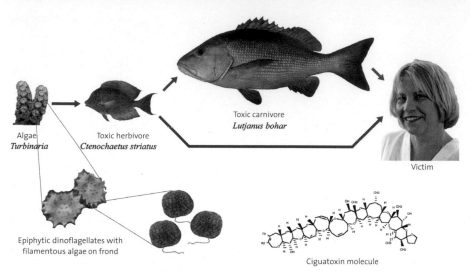

Toxic carnivore
Lutjanus bohar

Algae
Turbinaria

Toxic herbivore
Ctenochaetus striatus

Victim

Epiphytic dinoflagellates with
filamentous algae on frond

Ciguatoxin molecule

The ciguatera food chain. Ciguatoxin is produced by the dinoflagellate *Gambierdiscus toxicus*, which lives among filamentous green algae and other tiny epiphytes on the surfaces of macroalgae. These are eaten by herbivorous fishes, which sequester the toxin. Large predatory fishes that eat the herbivores accumulate their lifetime load of toxins. People are more likely to become poisoned when they eat a large predator with a high concentration of toxin, but may also become ill by eating a herbivore with enough toxin. Surgeonfishes of the genus *Ctenochaetus* are specialised for scraping filamentous algae from various surfaces and are particularly prone to becoming toxic. The snapper *Lutjanus bohar* is notoriously toxic throughout much of the Indo-Pacific.

chain, and large piscivorous predators such as barracudas, groupers, snappers, jacks and moray eels tend to be the most frequently and highly toxic species. The toxins also become much more concentrated in certain internal organs, particularly the liver and gonads, than in the flesh.

Ciguatoxin and related poisons are often present in lower concentrations throughout the reef food web. Invertebrates such as molluscs and crustaceans, as well as small herbivorous fishes, are also occasionally toxic. Pelagic fishes that have only a minor connection to the coral reef are almost always safe. In most areas, only predatory coral reef fishes tend to be affected to the extent that they pose a danger to humans.

The poison and its effect

Ciguatoxin is among the most powerful of natural toxins – only 10 picograms can cause extreme illness. It is a biologically highly active, complex polyether molecule that is fat-soluble and comes in various forms. It attacks the sodium channels of the nerve membranes, causing them to open. This results in continuous agitation, which eventually damages the peripheral nerve sheath and leads to permanent blockage of the

nerve. Ciguatera poisoning causes long-term and often permanent debilitation but is rarely fatal. Fatality rates range from under 0.1 per cent in parts of the Caribbean to 12 per cent in extreme cases in the Pacific.

Other toxins are also associated with ciguatera. Water-soluble maitotoxin is an extraordinarily long polyether chain, and is the largest known poison molecule that is not a protein. Biologically, it is extremely active and far more toxic than ciguatoxin. Maitotoxin attacks the calcium channels of the nerve membranes, activating them and causing muscle contractions and eventual paralysis. Maitotoxin was first found in surgeonfishes. Another toxin related to ciguatera is scaritoxin, which was first isolated from parrotfishes.

Occurrence and outbreaks

Ciguatera originates almost exclusively in tropical coral reef areas. Its occurrence is highly variable by location as well as through time, but tends to be more prevalent in disturbed environments. The dinoflagellates that produce the toxin are 'pioneer organisms' that are among the first to colonise an empty surface. A new shipwreck, the dredging of a channel, construction of

In French Polynesia, the Napoleon Wrasse *Cheilinus undulatus* is frequently toxic and banned from sale. However, in many other areas this highly prized fish is safe to eat and endangered through overfishing. *MK*

a wharf or even the passage of a severe storm can provide just the surface needed. Fishes that are normally safe to eat may suddenly become toxic some time after an unseen bloom of dinoflagellates. In many areas of the Pacific, the problem became acute following the construction of military facilities during World War II.

The occurrence of ciguatera can also be quite limited. It is not unusual for the same species of fish to be toxic in one location but safe even in an adjacent bay or the opposite side of an island. Variation in movements, longevity and feeding habits among and between species make the likelihood of poisoning highly unpredictable. However, it is more typical for ciguatera to be found in an extensive area. Sometimes whole islands are affected, and occasionally outbreaks may take on epidemic-like proportions. Over 400 million people now live in ciguatera-prone

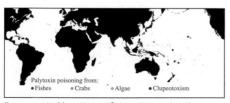

Documented locations of ciguatera poisoning.

areas and are especially at risk. Moreover, in recent decades ciguatera poisoning has spread to distant countries as a direct result of the importation of fish from tropical seas. It has even turned up in cultured fishes that were fed fishmeal made from ciguatoxic fishes.

Association with seafood

The word ciguatera is derived from *cigua*, the Spanish name for a small snail that poisoned explorers in Cuba in the 1500s. In the Pacific, ciguatera may have been the cause of death of the *Bounty*'s surgeon died following a fish feast. Of course, native peoples have long been aware of ciguatera. The Marshallese have given it the colourful name 'step and a half', which refers to the distance victims typically travel between bouts of diarrhoea.

By 1988, research showed that over 110 species of fish could potentially be ciguatoxic, but today the toxin has been found in over 425 species of fishes as well as in a few invertebrates. Although not all of the animals carrying the toxin are prized edible fishes, most are. A large number of them are clearly responsible for most cases of ciguatera poisoning. Large groupers, barracudas, jacks, snappers, moray eels, wrasses and triggerfishes are particularly liable to be toxic. Some goatfishes, parrotfishes, surgeonfishes and even

From the late 1960s to early 1970s, several tonnes of large Giant Moray Eels, as well as livers of reef sharks, were taken fromJohnston Atoll for ciguatera research by the Hawaii Institute of Marine Biology. The effort resulted in the isolation and identification of the ciguatoxin molecule. *RM, CA*

butterflyfishes are also occasionally toxic. Unfortunately, it is impossible to determine the exact cause of many cases of fish poisonings, and it is likely that some species blamed for ciguatera poisoning contain other toxins instead.

Tips for avoiding ciguatera poisoning

– Know how to identify chronically toxic species and avoid them.
– Seek local knowledge of which areas are safe and which kinds of reef fishes are safe to eat.
– Do not eat fishes from areas known to have frequently toxic catches.
– Avoid predatory reef fishes over 2 kg as well as certain species as small as 0.9 kg.
– Avoid smoked reef fishes.
– If eating out, try to determine what kind of fish is being served.
– Never eat the internal organs – the viscera, liver, gonads or eggs – of any coral reef fish.
– Anyone who has a history of ciguatera poisoning should be particularly cautious as this lowers the threshold for recurrence.

Absurd beliefs and unreliable testing

As is so often the case with toxins and poisoning, there are a host of household remedies and old wives' tales that suggest ways of detecting ciguatera. For instance, it is said that a copper coin will not turn green if it is laid on the meat of a ciguatoxic fish, or that a silver coin will not turn black if it is cooked with the fish. There is also the belief that flies will not settle on a toxic fish. These are all myths and dangerous nonsense. It also impossible to discern the toxin by checking the colour of the teeth, gills or other features of the fish. In some areas, a cat or dog may be fed some of a particularly prized suspect fish. This is also unreliable, as symptoms often appear hours after ingestion and cats will readily vomit their meal before too much toxin can be absorbed.

It took millions of dollars and decades of research to identify and isolate ciguatoxin and related compounds. A 'mongoose test' to assay for the presence of ciguatera was developed by the University of Hawaii. This involved feeding controlled amounts of tissue (usually the liver) to captive mongooses. This, of course, is an impractical method for normal use. In the 1990s, a rapid enzyme immuno-assay for detecting ciguatoxin was developed and test-marketed as a simple and easy-to-use kit. Unfortunately, it proved to be unreliable and did not receive US Food and Drug

Sample cases

1) **Fiji, June 2006.** After eating dinner at a high-end dive resort, a female guest woke in the night with diarrhoea, itchy hands and aching, 'heavy' legs. Her feet felt odd on the bathroom tiles. In the morning, the cold water 'burned' as she washed her hands and tasted metallic and carbonated. That day a local dive instructor and other staff developed similar symptoms. At dinner that evening a diver collapsed and broke out in a cold sweat, and had tingly hands, a slow pulse and shallow breaths. After dinner another guest developed diarrhoea, aching muscles, sweating and itchiness. All those that had eaten fish were affected. More than a month later, the first to be affected continued to experience mild itching, tingling of the hands and feet, and sensitivity to cold and fatigue, and at least two others suffered similar ongoing effects. Subsequent investigation indicated the fish served was a Narrow-barred Spanish Mackerel *Scomberomorus commerson*. *(After Undercurrent, August 2006)*

2) **Saipan, c.1949.** A group of 57 Filippino workers fell ill after eating a large moray eel. Within 30 minutes, some of the victims were unable to talk. This was followed by numbness and tingling about the lips and tongue, as well as the hands and feet. Later, they became comatose and developed various neurological symptoms, including muscular paralysis and convulsions. Seventeen were severely intoxicated and two died. A photograph of the victims with the eel was taken before it was eaten. Although its tail is out of the frame, it appears to be a Giant Moray *Gymnothorax javanicus* about 1.5 m long (it was originally identified as a Yellow-edged Moray *G. flavimarginatus*). *(After Halstead, 1967, on Khlentzos, 1950)*

Administration approval. In the future, a more reliable kit might be able to provide a degree of protection. At this point there is no practical and reliable way of knowing if a fish is ciguatoxic or not. There is also no way to detoxify a ciguatoxic fish. The toxin is heat-resistant, so cooking has no effect. Neither does boiling and pouring off the water since the toxin is fat-soluble.

Precautionary measures

The sole reliable method to determine whether a fish is toxic is through impractical and expensive laboratory tests. So for now, the best method for determining if a fish caught in tropical marine waters is safe to eat is to make use of reliable general and local knowledge. Always be aware of which kind of fish you are eating. Predatory reef fishes over 2 kg should be avoided, as should fishes of certain species as small as 0.9 kg in some locations. Never eat the internal organs – the viscera, liver, gonads or eggs – of any coral reef fish. Anyone who catches their own fish should be aware of which areas are considered safe. Smoked reef fishes such as barracudas, groupers, jacks, snappers and moray eels should be avoided because smoking removes only water and will concentrate the toxin. Offshore pelagic species such as tuna and Mahimahi are safe, as are deep-dwelling bottom fish species that live exclusively below 100 m. In the Caribbean, the open-water Yellowtail Snapper *Ocyurus chrysurus* is safe to eat.

Symptoms

The first symptoms of ciguatera poisoning may appear anytime within a few minutes to over 24 hours after ingestion, although they usually appear within the first six hours. Nausea, vomiting, diarrhoea and abdominal cramps are often the first signs of poisoning. The victim often feels a prickling or burning sensation around the lips and mouth, followed by a numbness that extends through the arms to the fingertips and down the legs to the toes. Further symptoms include dizziness, cramps, weakening reflexes, a dazed state, coordination problems, sight disturbances, headaches, joint and muscle pain and fatigue, as well as itching of the inner surface of the hands and soles of the feet. A special characteristic of ciguatera poisoning is an acute sensation of cold and the reversal of the sensations of heat and cold. Hot coffee has been described as cold, and ice cream has been called hot. Circulatory problems including low blood pressure, and heart rhythm instability such as a rapid or slow heartbeat, may occur.

Symptoms are varied and complex, and may differ owing to the combination and strength of gastrointestinal, neurological and cardiovascular distress. Some cases may exhibit one set of symptoms while others may show a different set. In some cases, symptoms resemble those of the outbreak of severe influenza. The course of poisoning may also differ by region. Most gastrointestinal symptoms clear up after about ten hours but the neurological symptoms usually last one to two months. In severe cases, they can persist for several months to years owing to permanent nerve damage. Fatalities are rare and usually the result of respiratory distress. The mortality rate is less than 0.5 per cent but in some areas may be as high as 12 per cent. People who have previously suffered ciguatera poisoning are vulnerable to a more severe recurrence.

Diagnosis
The complex and varied symptoms of ciguatera poisoning make it difficult to diagnose, particularly in areas far removed from coral reefs where

Treatment

First aid
As soon as the first symptoms appear, vomiting should be provoked if it has not already occurred. Seek immediate medical attention. In areas where ciguatera may not be well known, contact the Ciguatera Hotline, which in turn can alert the appropriate medical personnel (US 305/361-4619 or 305/661-0774].

What not to do
Do not drink any alcohol or eat nuts or oil which can exacerbate the symptoms.

Ongoing medical management
The only effective treatment is the intravenous infusion of mannitol within 72 hours of poisoning. A dosage of 1 g/kg body weight added to 0.9 NaCl or Ringer's solution is recommended. (Mannitol injection, 25 per cent: 12.5 g/50 cc vial = six vials for a 75 kg person infused with 700 cc D5W or 0.9 NaCl infused at a rate of 250–350 cc/hour over three to four hours.) Re-treatment may be necessary if symptoms recur owing to further absorption of toxin through the gastrointestinal tract. Continuous vomiting should be countered with the absorption of sufficient fluids and electrolytes to prevent circulatory collapse. Mannitol is believed to compete with ciguatoxin at the cell membrane or render it inert, and to increase its elimination through urine. After 72 hours it is ineffective. Long-term therapy depends on the symptoms and is generally ineffective. Corticosteroids, vitamin B6 supplements, calcium gluconate, pyridoxine and atropine may help stroke-like conditions but do not resolve neurological problems.

medical personnel may be completely unfamiliar with it. There is no diagnostic laboratory test. Successful diagnosis relies on the patient's history of ingestion followed by gastrointestinal and strange neurological symptoms. The presence of other victims with variable symptoms who shared the same meal is a strong indicator. The best clinical sign of ciguatera poisoning is when ice applied to the tongue or fingertips causes a burning sensation.

Shark-meat poisoning – a new toxin?
Poisoning from eating sharks is usually associated with the liver and has been attributed to extreme concentrations of vitamin A. However, there are some cases of severe and fatal poisoning from eating the flesh.

In Madagascar in 1993, about 200 people were severely poisoned after eating the flesh and, in some cases, the liver of a 100-kg Bull Shark *Carcharhinus leucas*. All who had eaten the meat became ill within ten hours. They developed neurological symptoms typical of ciguatera, but generally lacked gastrointestinal symptoms. Many became unconscious and comatose. When a team of doctors arrived at the local hospital five days after the meal, 15 of the victims had died after days of seizures and respiratory and cardiovascular problems. Ultimately, 50 of the 188 who were hospitalised died and five to 18 others died at home.

Testing of remains of the shark's liver revealed two possible fat-soluble toxins that are apparently different from ciguatoxin but whose structure could not be determined. They have been given the names carchatoxin A and B. Similar fatal cases involving fewer people have been reported in the past. In one case, the victims ate the liver of a Tiger Shark *Galeocerdo cuvier*. Whatever the reason, shark liver can be dangerously toxic and should never be eaten. The flesh of large coastal sharks of any species should also be avoided.

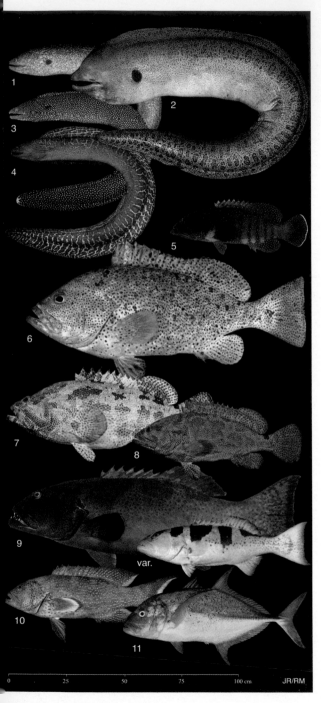

High-risk species

Over 425 species of fishes have been implicated in ciguatera poisoning. Most of these are food fishes that may be safe to eat in most areas. However, large individuals of a few species are frequently toxic almost anywhere. Large predators, particularly moray eels, groupers, jacks, snappers and barracudas, as well as a few wrasses and omnivorous triggerfishes, are particularly liable to be toxic. Sharks are occasionally toxic. A few herbivores, including surgeonfishes, rabbitfishes, parrotfishes and rudderfishes, may also be toxic in high-risk areas.

Indo-Pacific

The species shown here are frequently toxic in certain areas. A few should be avoided altogether, while others are safe at smaller sizes nearly everywhere. Local knowledge is essential if any of these species are to be safely eaten. The specimens shown are scaled near their maximum sizes. Full species accounts are given where indicated.

1. **Yellow-edged Moray** *Gymnothorax flavimarginatus* (p.134): often toxic.
2. **Giant Moray** *G. javanicus* (p.134): dangerously toxic when over 3 kg.
3. **Whitemouth Moray** *G. meleagris* (p.136): often toxic.
4. **Undulated Moray** *G. undulatus* (p.137): often toxic.
5. **Peacock Grouper** *Cephalopholis argus* (p.216): often toxic in Hawaii.
6. **Speckled Grouper** *Epinephelus cyanopodus* (p.216): occasionally toxic.
7. **Brown-marbled Grouper** *E. fuscoguttatus* (p.217): often toxic.
8. **Camouflage Grouper** *E. polyphekadion* (p.217): toxic in some areas.
9. **Blacksaddled Coralgrouper** *Plectropomus laevis* (p.217): frequently toxic.
10. **Lyretail Grouper** *Variola louti* (p.218): occasionally toxic.
11. **Bluefin Trevally** *Caranx melampygus* (p.218): occasionally toxic.

var.

0   25   50   75   100 cm   JR/RM

1. **Green Jobfish** *Aprion virescens* (p.220): toxic in some areas.
2. **One-spot Snapper** *Lutjanus monostigma* (p.219): toxic in some areas.
3. **Twinspot Snapper** *L. bohar* (p.219): often dangerously toxic.
4. **Orangefin Emperor** *Lethrinus erythracanthus* (p.220): occasionally toxic.
5. **Longface Emperor** *L. olivaceus* (p.220):occasionally toxic.
6. **Napoleon Wrasse** *Cheilinus undulatus* (p.221): toxic in some areas.
7. **Ringtail Wrasse** *Oxycheilinus unifasciatus* (p.221): often toxic in Hawaii.
8. **Pacific Steephead Parrotfish** *Chlorurus microrhinos* (p.222): toxic in high-risk areas.
9. **Striped Bristletooth** *Ctenochartus striatus* (p.179): toxic in high-risk areas.
10. **Orangeband Surgeonfish** *Acanthurus olivaceus* (p.176): occasionally toxic.
11. **Great Barracuda** *Sphyraena barracuda* (p.145): occasionally toxic.
12. **Narrow-barred Spanish Mackerel** *Scomberomorus commerson* (p.223): occasionally toxic.
13. **Titan Triggerfish** *Balistoides viridescens* (p.150): occasionally toxic.

Florida and the Caribbean

Great Barracuda *Sphyraena barracuda* are notoriously toxic and banned from sale in most areas (pp.145). Other frequently toxic species include large Green Morays *Gymnothorax funebris* (p.132), several groupers (*Mycteroperca bonaci, M. tigris* and *M. venenosa*; pp.223–224), jacks (*Caranx latus, C. hippos*; p.224) and snappers (*Lutjanus cyanopterus* and *L. jocu*; p.225; *L. apodus* and *L. aya*), the Hogfish *Lachnolaimus maximus* (p.226) and the Queen Triggerfish *Balistes vetula* (p.151). In ciguatera-prone areas, Spotted Morays *Gymnothorax moringua* (p.132), Nassau Groupers *Epinephelus striatus*, Goliath Groupers *E. itajara* (p.187), and any unusually large groupers of other species, jacks, snappers, porgies and parrotfishes may occasionally be toxic.

JR/RM

Indo-Pacific region
Groupers
Serranidae

Peacock Grouper	60 cm
Cephalopholis argus	*(23.6 in)*

Dark brown with blue spots, up to 6 pale bars at rear of body; tail round. **Biology:** inhabits shallow lagoon and seaward reefs with rich coral growth and clear water, 1–50 m. Often under ledges or on reef margins. Feeds primarily on fishes. Juveniles in protected coral thickets, adults often in pairs or small groups. Often toxic in Hawaii, occasionally toxic in Fr. Polynesia. **Range:** Red Sea to Marquesas and Pitcairn Group, n. to s. Japan; introduced to Hawaii.

Speckled Blue Grouper	120 cm
Epinephelus cyanopodus	*(47 in)*

Juveniles with bright yellow fins, back and tail base, becoming grey with age. **Biology:** inhabits lagoon and seaward reefs, 2–150 m. Uncommon, usually around isolated coral heads. Feeds primarily on fishes, incl. snake eels, occasionally on crustaceans. Toxic in some areas. **Range:** S. China Sea to Kiribati, n. to Ryukyus, s. to Lord Howe I. Replaced by Blue-and-yellow Grouper *E. flavocaeruleus* in Indian Ocean (90 cm).

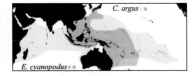

Brown-marbled Grouper
Epinephelus fuscoguttatus   **95 cm**
(37 in)

Eyes bulge slightly, head profile slightly concave; short, dark dashes in colour pattern. **Biology:** inhabits lagoon pinnacles, channels and outer reef slopes, usually in coral-rich areas, 1–60 m. Wary and difficult to approach. Feeds on fishes, crabs and cephalopods. Uncommon. Toxic in some areas. **Range:** Red Sea to Line Is, n. to Ryukyus, s. to New Caledonia. **Similar:** *E. polyphekadion* (below) has convex head profile, lacks dark dashes.

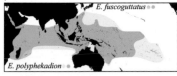

Camouflage Grouper
Epinephelus polyphekadion   **75 cm**
(30 in)

Head profile convex; black blotch on upper caudal peduncle. **Biology:** inhabits lagoon and seaward reef slopes with rich coral growth, 1–46 m. Often along the base of fringing reefs close to caves or crevices. An ambushing predator, primarily of small fishes. Curious and approachable in unfished areas. Toxic in some areas. **Range:** Red Sea to Line and Gambier Is, n. to s Japan, s. to se. Australia and Rapa.

Blacksaddled Coralgrouper
Plectropomus laevis   **125 cm**
(49 in)

Conspicuous canine teeth; 2 phases, blue spot phase reddish brown with darker saddles and small blue spots, blacksaddled phase white and yellow with black saddles (p.212). **Biology:** inhabits coral-rich areas of channels and clear lagoon and seaward reefs, 4–90 m. A roaming predator that feeds primarily on fishes. Frequently toxic. **Range:** S. Africa to Mangareva, n. to Ryukyus. **Similar:** Squaretail Coralgrouper *P. areolatus* has larger, dark-edged spots (73 cm; Red Sea to Samoa).

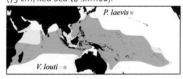

Lyretail Grouper   81 cm
Variola louti   *(31.9 in)*

Lunate tail; pectoral, dorsal, anal and tail fins with yellow rear margins. **Biology:** inhabits lagoons, channels and seaward reefs, 1–150 m. A predator of fishes and crustaceans. Common. Occasionally toxic. **Range:** Red Sea to Marquesas and Pitcairn Group, n. to s Japan, s. to se. Australia. **Similar:** White-edged Lyretail Grouper *V. albimarginata* has narrow white and black tail margin.

Jacks
Carangidae

Giant Trevally   1.65 m; 86.6 kg
Caranx ignobilis   *(5.4 ft; 191 lb)*

Steep head profile; silvery to blackish with dark specks, pale vertical streaks. **Biology:** inhabits lagoon and seaward reefs, 5–80 m. Solitary or in small groups along reef edges and slopes. Juveniles in schools over sandy inshore and estuarine areas. Feeds primarily on fishes and crustaceans. Large individuals may be toxic. Uncommon. **Range:** Red Sea to Fr. Polynesia, n. to Arabian G. and s. Japan, s. to New Caledonia.

Bluefin Trevally   100 cm
Caranx melampygus   *(39 in)*

Olivaceous silver with tiny black and blue flecks above, and blue fins. **Biology:** inhabits lagoon and seaward reefs, 1–190 m. Common, solitary or in small groups. Patrols reef edges and slopes. Feeds primarily on reef fishes, occasionally on squids. Often shadows goatfishes and moray eels in search of prey. Large individuals may be toxic. **Range:** Red Sea to Panama, n. to s. Japan and Hawaii.

Greater Amberjack   1.88 m; 81 kg
Seriola dumerili   *(6.2 ft; 178 lb)*

Lacks scutes; greyish silver, may have purplish hue. **Biology:** seaward reefs, 20–360 m. Occasionally enters shallow bays. Feeds on schooling fishes. A prized gamefish. Often toxic in Hawaii, occasionally toxic elsewhere. **Range:** most tropical and warm-temperate seas, incl. the Caribbean.

C. lugubris ••   S. dumerili ••

Snappers
Lutjanidae

Twinspot Snapper   80 cm
Lutjanus bohar   *(31.5 in)*

Reddish grey with darker fins **Biology:** inhabits lagoons, channels and seaward reef slopes, 1–70 m. Solitary or in small groups. A voracious predator of smaller reef fishes, participates In feeding frenzies with sharks. Notoriously ciguatoxic in some areas. Juveniles mimic the damselfishes *Chromis flavaxilla* and *C. ternatensis* to approach prey more closely. **Range:** Red Sea to Fr. Polynesia, n. to s. Oman and Ryukyus, s. to S. Africa and Gt Barrier Reef.

Onespot Snapper   55 cm
Lutjanus monostigma   *(21.5 in)*

Pastel grey to silvery with yellow fins; a small dark spot on lateral line may disappear in large adults. **Biology:** inhabits lagoon and seaward reefs, 5–60 m. Solitary or in small groups, common in wrecks and along reef margins with caves and overhangs. Feeds on fishes, mainly at night. May be ciguatoxic in some areas. **Range:** Red Sea to Fr. Polynesia, n. to Ryukyus, s. to Mozambique.

L. bohar ••

L. monostigma ••

Green Jobfish 110 cm; 20.2 kg
Aprion virescens *(43 in; 44.5 lb)*

Elongate with blunt snout, conspicuous canine teeth and forked tail; grey, olivaceous above. **Biology:** solitary or in small groups in mid-water along slopes of deep lagoons, channels and seaward reefs, 3–180 m. A voracious piscivore that also feeds on octopuses and crustaceans. Flesh highly esteemed but occasionally toxic. Wary, difficult to approach. **Range:** Red Sea to Fr. Polynesia, n. to Arabian G. and Ryukyus, s. to se. Australia.

A. virescens

Emperors
Lethrinidae

Orangefin Emperor 70 cm
Lethrinus erythracanthus *(27.6 in)*

Steep head profile; brown with orange fins. **Biology:** inhabits deep lagoon and seaward reefs, 18–120 m. Solitary. Feeds on molluscs, sea urchins, starfishes and crinoids. Toxic in some areas. **Range:** Red Sea to Tuamotus, n. to Rykyus, s. to New Caledonia.

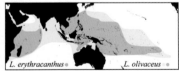

L. erythracanthus • *L. olivaceus* •

Longface Emperor 100 cm
Lethrinus olivaceus *(39 in)*

Elongate snout; olive-grey, may have orange face, often assumes mottled pattern. **Biology:** inhabits lagoon and seaward reefs, 1 m to over 20 m. Common, usually solitary, occasionally in small groups. Feeds on fishes and crustaceans. Toxic in some areas. **Range:** Red Sea to Samoa, n. to s. Japan, s. to New Caledonia. **Similar:** Smalltooth Emperor *L. microdon* (70 cm; Red Sea to PNG) nearly identical but has fewer scale rows above lateral line (4½ vs 5½) and shorter snout.

Wrasses
Labridae

Napoleon Wrasse	1.7 m; 68 kg
Cheilinus undulatus	*(5.5 ft; 150 lb)*

♂s with hump on forehead. **Biology:** inhabits lagoon and seaward reefs, 1–60 m. Hides and sleeps in home cave. Feeds on armoured invertebrates, incl. molluscs and toxic sea urchins and Crown-of-thorns Starfish *Acanthaster planci*. Toxic in some areas. Decimated in many areas by cyanide fishing driven by high demand for live fishes in SE. Asian restaurants. **Range:** Red Sea to Fr. Polynesia, n. to Ryukyus, s. to New Caledonia.

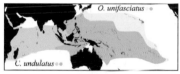

Ringtail Wrasse	46 cm
Oxycheilinus unifasciatus	*(18 in)*

Olive-green with red streaks on face, pale band behind eye, pale bar near base of tail. **Biology:** inhabits clear lagoon and seaward reefs, 1–160 m. Favours coral-rich and rubble areas, where it often hovers well above bottom. Bold and inquisitive. Feeds primarily on fishes. Toxic in some areas, especially Hawaii. **Range:** Cocos (Keeling) to Hawaiian, Marquesan and Tuamotus Is, n. to Ryukyus, s. to New Caledonia and Rapa.

Parrotfishes
Scaridae

Pacific Steephead Parrotfish	70 cm
Chlorurus microrhinos	*(28 in)*

Large adults with vertical forehead. **Biology:** inhabits lagoon and seaward reefs, 1–35 m. Juveniles solitary, adults occasionally in groups. Large individuals can be toxic in high-risk areas. **Range:** e. Indonesia to Line and Pitcairn Is, n. to Ryukyus. **Similar:** *Bolbometopon muricatum* (p.189) is dull dark green, gets much larger, and has not been implicated in ciguatera.

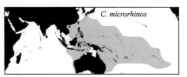

Tunas and Mackerels
Scombridae

Dogtooth Tuna	2.2 m; 131 kg
Gymnosarda unicolor	*(7.2 ft; 291 lb)*

Silver; sizeable mouth with large canine teeth; tips of dorsal and anal fins white. **Biology:** solitary or in small groups in mid-water along lagoon, channel or seaward reef slopes, 1–100 m. A voracious predator of fishes, particularly fusiliers and other planktivores. Large adults occasionally toxic. **Range:** Red Sea to Fr. Polynesia, n. to s. Japan, s. to New Caledonia.

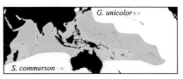

Narrow-barred Spanish Mackerel 2.45 m; 45 kg
Scomberomorus commerson (8 ft; 100 lb)

Compressed; silver with dusky bars.
Biology: solitary or in small groups in mid-water along deep lagoon and seaward reef slopes, 1–200 m. A common coastal pelagic species that migrates long distances. Feeds primarily on sardines, anchovies and fusiliers. May approach divers, but never lingers. A highly valued food fish. Occasionally toxic in some areas. **Range:** Red Sea to Fiji, n. to Korea and Japan, s. to S. Africa and se. Australia; migrant to e. Mediterranean.

Caribbean region

Groupers
Serranidae

Black Grouper 133 cm; 65 kg
Mycteroperca bonaci (52 in; 143 lb)

Dark brown with network of pale reticulations and fine dark spots. **Biology:** juveniles inhabit mangroves and inshore reefs, adults on rocky and coral reefs, 3–100 m. Often drifts above bottom. Juveniles feed mainly on crustaceans, adults on fishes. Common in most areas. Matures as ♀s at 50 cm, transforms to ♂s at 96–100 cm. Lives to at least 19 yrs. **Range:** central FL (juveniles to MA), G. of Mexico and Bermuda to s. Brazil.

Tiger Grouper 100 cm; 10 kg
Mycteroperca tigris (39 in; 22 lb)

Reddish brown with oblique pale bars on back, close-set spots on head and irregular blotches on belly. Can change intensity, hue and pattern. **Biology:** inhabits rocky and coral reefs, 10–40 m. Common on clear offshore banks and island reefs, rarely on coastal reefs. Feeds mostly on fishes. Matures as ♀s in 2 yrs at 28 cm, transforms to ♂s at 37–45 cm. Reaches 42 cm in 9 yrs. **Range:** s. FL, Bahamas, Bermuda, and n. G. of Mexico banks to s. Brazil.

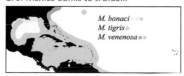

M. bonaci
M. tigris
M. venenosa

Yellowfin Grouper — 100 cm; 18.5 kg
Mycteroperca venenosa (35 in; 41 lb)

Pale with elongate dark blotches or all dark, both patterns with small dark spots, pectoral fin margins always yellow; more red when deep. **Biology:** juveniles in sea-grass beds, adults on rocky and coral reefs and deep soft bottoms, 2–137 m. Common in Caribbean. Feeds almost exclusively on fishes, occasionally on squids. Often toxic. Spawns at Bermuda in Jul., in FL Keys in Mar., in e. G. of Mexico Mar.–Aug., at Jamaica Feb.–Apr., and off Puerto Rico in Apr. Matures as ♀s at 54 cm. **Range:** NC, Bermuda and n. of G. Mexico banks to se. Brazil.

Jacks
Carangidae

Horse-eye Jack — 80 cm; 16 kg
Caranx latus (31.5 in; 35.3 lb)

Eyes large; tail yellow, small dark spot on upper edge of gill cover. **Biology:** in schools along beaches and outer reef slopes, 1–50 m. Enters fresh water. Common. Feeds primarily on fishes, also on invertebrates. Large individuals may be ciguatoxic. **Range:** NJ and Bermuda to se. Brazil; Ascension I. and e. Atlantic. **Similar:** Crevalle Javk *C. hippos* gets larger, and has dark spot on lower base of pectoral fin.

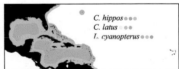

C. hippos ●●●
C. latus ●●
I. cyanopterus ●●●

Snappers
Lutjanidae

Cubera Snapper	160 cm; >57 kg
Lutjanus cyanopterus	*(63 in; >126 lb)*

Steely to brownish grey; may have narrow pale bars above. Largest snapper in region. **Biology:** inhabits coral and rocky reefs, 12–55 m. Juveniles shallower, among mangroves, may enter fresh water. Adults usually near rocky ledges. Feeds mainly on fishes, often ciguatoxic. Wary. Spawning aggregations form off FL and Belize in Jun. and Jul. Toxic in many areas. **Range:** NS (rare n. of FL), Bermuda and n. G. of Mexico to Brazil.

Dog Snapper	90 cm; 14 kg
Lutjanus jocu	*(35.4 in; 31 lb)*

Pale grey to reddish brown with narrow blue stripe and pale triangular bar under eye. **Biology:** inhabits rocky and coral reefs and wrecks, 5–30 m. Juveniles in brackish to fresh water. Usually solitary near shelter along outer edges of shelves. Feeds primarily on fishes, also on benthic invertebrates. Occasionally ciguatoxic. A spawning aggregation seen off Belize in Jan., ♀s ripe off Jamaica in Mar. and Nov., and in ne. Caribbean in Mar. **Range:** FL (juveniles to MA), Bahamas and n. G. of Mexico to se. Brazil; St Paul's Rocks, Ascension I.

Porgies
Sparidae

Jolthead Porgy	**68 cm; 10.6 kg**
Calamus bajonado	*(26.8 in; 23 lb)*

Body deep in front, snout convex, mouth large; silvery blue, corners of mouth red. **Biology:** inhabits seagrass beds, sand patches and flats of coral reefs, 3–180 m. Adults usually solitary. Feeds primarily on molluscs, crabs and sea urchins. Occasionally ciguatoxic. **Range:** RI (rare) to s. Brazil, incl. Bahamas and W. Indies. **Similar:** several spp. distinguished by details of head colour.

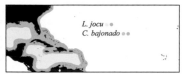

L. jocu
C. bajonado

Wrasses
Labridae

Hogfish	**100 cm; 9 kg**
Lachnolaimus maximus	*(39 in; 20 lb)*

Body deep; large ♂'s with concave snout profile, pale with purple forehead. **Biology:** inhabits sheltered inshore to offshore reefs, 2–60 m. Common on open bottoms with abundant gorgonians. Feeds primarily on molluscs, also on crustaceans and sea urchins. Highly esteemed for food but occasionally toxic in some areas. Lives up to 23 yrs. **Range:** NC and Bermuda to n. Brazil, incl. all Caribbean.

L. maximus

Palytoxic Fishes and Clupeotoxism

Some cases of severe and usually fatal fish poisoning once attributed to ciguatoxin have been shown to be caused by palytoxin, an extremely potent compound found in anemone-like zoanthid soft corals (p.311), dinoflagellates and, possibly, bacteria. Like ciguatoxin, palytoxin enters the food chain and finds its way to the dinner table. It is also heat-stable and cannot be neutralised by cooking, removed from flesh or detected outside of the laboratory. Fortunately, it is considerably less widespread than ciguatoxin and cases of poisoning are rare.

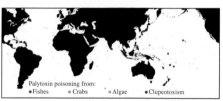

Locations of some documented cases of palytoxin poisoning and clupeotoxism.

Palytoxin in the food chain
Palytoxin was first isolated from the zoanthid soft coral *Palythoa caesia*. It is now known to be synthesised by the bottom-dwelling dinoflagellate *Ostreopsis siamensis*, and also probably by pelagic dinoflagellates and bacteria. Palytoxin has been found in worms, crustaceans and fishes that either feed on *Palythoa* or are associated with it, and in fishes that feed on or come in contact with dinoflagellates. An entire class of fish poisoning, clupeotoxism, named after clupeoid fishes (sardines, herrings and anchovies), has recently been found to be due at least in part to palytoxin.

The poison and its effect
Palytoxin is among the most potent of natural compounds. When intravenously injected into mice, the lethal dose is only 10 nanograms per kilogram (LD$_{50}$, meaning the amount required to kill 50 per cent of test animals). Palytoxin disrupts cell membranes by increasing their permeability for sodium and potassium but not calcium. This causes uncontrolled contractions of skeletal muscles, severe muscular pain, seizures and respiratory distress.

Occurrence and outbreaks
Palytoxin poisoning in humans is rare and sporadic. It most often results from eating certain fishes and crabs, but has also occurred after the victims ate edible algae. Among fishes, two groups account for most cases: clupeoid fishes and certain reef fishes. Among clupeoid fishes, poisoning (termed clupeotoxism) typically occurs during the warm and rainy months of the year from fish caught in turbid or brackish areas. The species involved include the Atlantic Thread Herring *Opisthonem oglinum* in the Caribbean, and the sardines *Herklotsichthys*

quadrimaculatus, *Sardinella marquesensis* and other members of the genus *Sardinella* in the Indo-Pacific. Often the victims most severely affected had eaten the viscera, and in some cases the fishes had been dragged through sediment after being caught in a beach seine. This means the toxin most likely occurs in both pelagic and benthic dinoflagellates and enters the fish though its diet or by contamination. Possible clupeotoxism has also been reported in the Mediterranean.

Palytoxin has been found in smoked Shortfin Scad *Decapterus macrosoma* (a mackerel-like jack of the family Carangidae) exported from the Philippines, and in freshwater puffers. Among reef fishes, it has been found in the Pinktail Triggerfish *Melichthys vidua* (p.152), Scrawled Filefish *Alutera scripta* (p.229), and the butterflyfishes *Chaetodon capistratus* and *C. sedentarius*. In the Ryukyu Islands, Japan, one of two people who ate the parrotfish *Scarus ovifrons* died from palytoxin poisoning. In Guam, two people died after eating seaweed bought at a local supermarket. Palytoxin was found in a sample of the seaweed from the victim's home but not in the remainder that was pulled from the store's shelf. Contamination during harvesting by contact with *Palythoa* or bottom sediments may have been the cause.

Precautionary measures
The easiest way to avoid palytoxin poisoning is by not eating any of the fishes or other marine life that have been implicated in poisoning. If you are compelled to catch and eat sardines, seek local knowledge of when and where they are safe before doing so. Thoroughly clean and gut fishes, and clean seaweed and other marine life.

Symptoms
Among the first symptoms of palytoxin poisoning is a sharp metallic or bitter taste in the

mouth immediately after eating. This is soon followed by many of the gastrointestinal and neurological symptoms associated with ciguatera poisoning: nausea, vomiting, diarrhoea and abdominal cramps, numbness, tingling, vertigo and low blood pressure. Further symptoms that rapidly ensue include dryness of the mouth, nervousness, violent headaches, dilated pupils, hypersalivation, feeble pulse, tachycardia (rapid heartbeat), chills, clammy skin, respiratory distress, progressive muscular paralysis, seizures, convulsions and coma. Death has occurred in as little as 15 minutes but can take several days. There has been no calculation of the fatality rate but it is very high, possibly over 50 per cent.

Diagnosis
The sharp metallic or bitter taste, followed by rapid and severe neurological symptoms and signs of cardiovascular collapse, are diagnostic. A sample of the suspect meal should always be saved for testing.

First aid and treatment
Immediate medical attention is essential. Treatment is entirely symptomatic: stabilisation and maintenance of the victim's vital signs for as long as possible. There is no specific treatment or cure.

Sardines
Clupeidae

Goldspot Sardine   **14 cm**
Herklotsichthys quadrimaculatus   (5.5 in)

Two brassy spots at top and rear of gill cover. **Biology:** inhabits sheltered inshore reefs and mangroves. In dense schools by day, dispersing at night to feed on zooplankton. Lives about 1 yr. **Range:** E. Africa to Samoa, n. to s. Japan; introduced to Hawaiian Is. **Similar:** Several similar spp. lack brassy spots on gill cover, and inhabit primarily estuarine and brackish waters.

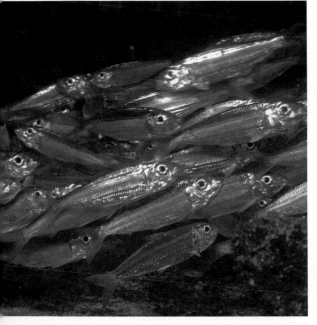

H. quadrimaculatus

Filefishes
Monacanthidae

Scrawled Filefish	91 cm
Aluterus scriptus	*(36 in)*

Highly compressed with large, broom-like tail; olivaceous with blue spots and lines. **Biology:** on coastal and offshore reefs, 2 m to at least 80 m. Juveniles in open sea around drifting objects. Feeds on a wide variety of attached organisms, incl. algae, seagrasses, hydrozoans, gorgonians, colonial anemones and tunicates. **Range:** Circumtropical.

Scombrotoxic Fishes
Histamine poisoning

High-risk species
The species shown here are highly susceptible to histamine poisoning. It is essential to keep them well iced or refrigerated. They are scaled to near their maximum sizes, except for Yellowfin Tuna, which reaches its largest size in subtropical waters.

Coryphaenidae
1. **Mahimahi** *Coryphaena hippurus*: 2 m, 39.9 kg (6.5 ft, 88 lb).

Scombridae
2. **Wahoo** *Acanthocybium solandri*: 2.1 m, 71.9 kg (6.9 ft, 158.5 lb).
3. **Indian Mackerel** *Rastrelliger kanagurta*: 38 cm (15 in).
4. **Frigate Tuna** *Auxis thazard*: 50 cm (20 in).
5. **Kawakawa** *Euthynnus affinis*: 38 cm (15 in).
6. **Skipjack Tuna** *Katsuwonus pelamis*: 100 cm, 20.5 kg (39 in, 45.2 lb).
7. **Yellowfin Tuna** *Thunnus albacares*: 1.95 m, 176.4 kg (6.4 ft, 389 lb).
8. **Narrow-barred Spanish Mackerel** *Scomberomorus commerson*: 2.45 m, 45 kg (8 ft, 99 lb).

Rapid spoilage of silvery pelagics

Scombroid fish poisoning is a type of rapid spoilage common in certain groups of fishes. It is included here only because it is second in importance to ciguatera. Visitors from temperate regions are often unaware how fast it occurs in the tropics. Silvery pelagics such as tunas and mackerels, as well as Mahimahi, are especially susceptible to this form of poisoning. They are often caught by boaters and dive-boat crews who troll for them. Sardines, herrings, anchovies and bluefish from temperate regions are also susceptible to this form of spoilage.

The poison

Scombroid fish poisoning is caused by unusually high concentrations of histamine (50–400 mg/ 100 g of fish). Histamine is produced by bacterial breakdown of the amino acid L-histidine, which is present in high concentrations in certain fishes. In humans, it is a hormone released in allergic reactions, and when ingested, it produces the same symptoms.

Prevention

All seafood must be properly iced or refrigerated immediately after, if not before, death. Fish must be frozen for long-term storage. A peppery taste is a classic sign of high histamine content. If this is detected, stop eating immediately.

Symptoms

Symptoms occur anywhere from a few minutes to a several hours after the meal. They are classic allergy symptoms: a red skin rash, facial flushing, sweating, and oral burning or blistering. Occasionally, nausea, vomiting, abdominal pain, diarrhoea or hypotension (low blood pressure) may occur. Even without treatment, symptoms disappear within 12 to 24 hours.

Treatment

Antihistamines should be given to treat allergy symptoms. Appropriate drugs should be used to treat gastrointestinal symptoms.

Hallucinogenic Fishes
Goatfishes

On rare occasions, hallucinations have been reported after eating a fish. In Hawaii, for example, disturbed sleep and hallucinations can result from eating the brain of the Bandtail Goatfish *Upeneus arge* (family Mullidae). Locals call this fish Weke-pahulu, which means 'ghost goatfish' or 'nightmare goatfish'. Toxicity is said to vary by season. Avoid eating the brains and other internal organs of all fishes, as they tend to concentrate toxins of all kinds.

Bandtail Goatfish	30 cm
Upeneus arge	*(12 in)*

Pale with pair of brown to yellow lateral stripes, tail with 10–12 dark bands. **Biology:** inhabits sheltered sand bottoms, often in turbid areas, shoreline to 31 m. In small groups that actively move over bottom. Feeds on sand-dwelling invertebrates. **Range:** E. Africa to Hawaiian and Tuamotu Is, n. to Yaeyamas. **Similar:** Several similar spp. have stripes on body and bands on tail; they should also be considered potentially hallucinogenic.

• *U. arge*
• other species

Gempylotoxic Fishes
Purgative snake mackerels

Snake mackerels of the family Gempylidae have extremely oily flesh that typically causes diarrhoea when eaten. Native peoples use them as a purgative; no other serious effects are known. The causative factor is not affected by cooking or any other process. The Oilfish *Ruvettus pretiosus* is particularly known for this. It inhabits depths of 100–700 m in mid-water above steep slopes, seamounts and banks of tropical and warm-temperate seas. It is occasionally caught by hook and line. Most other species in the family are oceanic species that remain deep during the day but rise to the surface at night as they follow the vertical migration of plankton and prey on the fishes and squids that feed on them. They are typically elongate with barracuda-like heads and teeth, and delicate black skin and flesh. Some are often safe to eat, at least in small quantities, but others can cause diarrhoea. They are often caught by trolling at night.

1. **Oilfish** *Ruvettus pretiosus*: 2.5 m, 80 kg (8.2 ft, 176 lb); circumglobal, 100–700 m.
2. **Snake Mackerel** *Gempylus serpens*: 100 cm (39 in); circumglobal, surface to 200 m. *(Guam, RM)*

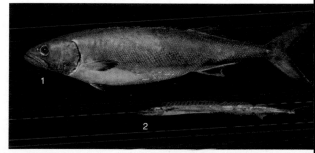

When stressed, trunkfishes like this Yellow Boxfish *Ostracion cubicus* secrete the highly toxic substance ostracitoxin, which can kill other fishes. *Rinca, PM*

Crinotoxic Fishes
Toxic skin and mucus

A large number of fishes have toxic or bitter-tasting skin or mucus that is used as a defence against predators or parasites. They do not represent the same health hazard as many other toxic fishes, because they are easily identified and are consistently toxic, rather than infrequently and sporadically toxic. Unlike ciguatoxin and many other poisons, crinotoxins are primarily external, confined to the skin and outer surface rather than in the flesh. Many of the toxins are also easily destroyed by cooking. It is not surprising that in many parts of the world certain crinotoxic fishes are widely and safely eaten. These fishes are included here because they are potentially dangerous to those who may handle them improperly or prepare them as food.

Occurrence of crinotoxins

Crinotoxins have evolved independently in many groups of fishes. They are best known in

The Yellow Boxfish *Ostracion cubicus* has several colour forms. Shown left: adult male (top), juvenile female (middle), young juvenile (below).

the grouper-like soapfishes (Grammistidae) and trunkfishes (Ostraciidae), but are also present in certain moray eels (Muraenidae, p.127), toadfishes (Batrachoididae; p.33), clingfishes (Gobiesocidae), gobies (Gobiidae) and soles (Soleidae). Repellent substances have also been reported from the skin of puffers (Tetraodontidae; p.153), eel catfishes (Plotosidae; p.28), filefishes (Monocanthidae; p.229) and scorpionfishes (p.36), but little is known of their function or toxicity. In most cases, evidence of toxicity is empirical – in other words, mucus or crude extracts clearly repel or kill other animals or cells exposed to them, but their identity and chemical structure remain unknown.

Production of crinotoxins

Among soapfishes, trunkfishes and moray eels, the crinotoxins are produced in specialised ampule-shaped cells, called club cells, embedded throughout the skin. Trunkfishes also have additional well-developed toxin-secreting glands around the inner portion of their lips. In toadfishes, soles and, possibly, marine catfishes,

Treatment
Only the symptoms can be treated.

toxins are secreted by cells associated with glands that open to pores. These are located above the pectoral fin base in catfishes, and in the same place as well as near the bases of the pectoral fin rays in toadfishes. In soles, they are located along the bases of the dorsal and anal fin rays. In soapfishes, soles and trunkfishes, the toxin can be released at will, typically when the fish is stressed. In trunkfishes, the toxin appears to require activation by the living fish since freshly killed trunkfish are often non-toxic.

Effect of crinotoxins
The toxicity of the Greater Soapfish *Rypticus saponaceus* was discovered by a young biologist when he speared one and placed it in his swimming trunks. A burning pain developed in his

Some toxic toadfishes, like this Whitespotted Toadfish *Sanopus astrifer*, advertise their toxicity with a striking colour pattern. *Belize, JN*

urethra but disappeared soon after the fish was removed. Aquarists have long been aware that other fishes should not be transported or stored in a confined space with either soapfishes or trunkfishes as they will often die within a few minutes. In the stable confines of a well-managed aquarium, this does not seem to be a problem. Soapfishes are apparently unaffected by their own mucus, but trunkfishes injected with the mucus of other trunkfishes die. Crude extracts of soapfish mucus were found to be lethal when injected into mice. The active ingredient, grammistin, is proteinaceous.

The toxin associated with the Yellowmouth Moray *Gymnothorax nudivomer* (p.136) was discovered when a biologist washing a specimen noticed that his hands, which had coral cuts, started tingling. It is also a protein and has a molecular weight of over 100,000. Although the eel's mucus is 46 to 188 times as toxic as soapfish mucus, it does not have a bitter taste or seem to be repellent. Its role may be to deter parasites.

The toxin from the Moses Sole *Pardachirus marmoratus*, also probably a protein, is clearly a defence against predators. In an experiment, a hungry Whitetip Reef Shark rejected a tethered sole and would not even clamp its jaws on it.

All of these toxins are lethal to other fishes and are haemolytic, meaning that they destroy blood cells. Most are unstable and lose their toxicity with cooking or freezing. However, the trunkfish toxin ostracitoxin is not destroyed by either and is lethal to fish and blood cells in concentrations of as little as one part per million.

Prevention
Do not handle crinotoxic fishes in ways that allow them to come into contact with cuts or sores, and thoroughly wash everything they touch. Avoid eating them, but if you must do so, cook them thoroughly.

Symptoms
Contact with crinotoxic fishes may result in skin irritations, particularly a burning pain in mucus membranes such as the urethra or tingling around cuts and abrasions. There are no definitive reports on the effects of eating them. Serious effects caused by eating trunkfishes appear to be due to ciguatoxin rather than ostracitoxin, which does not occur in the flesh. In some areas, local people grill crinotoxic fishes in their own 'shell'. One of the authors (RM) has eaten the Two-banded Soapfish *Diploprion bifasciatus* without any ill effects, or knowledge of its toxicity at the time.

Toadfishes
Batrachoididae

Broad-headed, narrow-bodied fishes. Some have venomous dorsal fin spines (p.33), while others produce toxic mucus.

Coral Toadfish	20 cm
Sanopus splendidus	*(8 in)*

Head transversely striped, many chin barbels; fins with yellow margins. **Biology:** inhabits clear-water coral reefs, 8–25 m. On sand under coral heads or in crevices. **Range:** Cozumel and Cancún, Mexico, only.

Soapfishes
Grammistidae

Small grouper-like fishes that produce the bitter toxin *grammistin* in their mucus.

Arrowhead Soapfish	15 cm
Belonoperca chabanaudi	*(6 in)*

Dark grey to black with yellow saddle behind dorsal fin. **Biology:** inhabits coral-rich areas of steep outer reef slopes, 4–50 m. Typically hovers near entrance of small cave or crevice. Skin bitter-tasting. **Range:** E. Africa to Samoa, n. to Ryukyus, s. to New Caledonia.

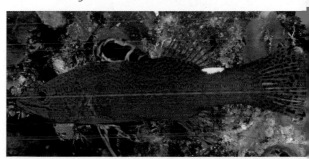

Two-banded Soapfish	14 cm
Diploprion bifasciatus	*(5.5 in)*

Yellow with black bar through eye, broad black bar through mid-body; occasionally black with yellow fins. **Biology:** inhabits rocky and coral reefs, 1–18 m. Usually near caves and crevices. **Range:** Maldives to PNG, n. to s. Japan, s. Lord Howe I. **Similar:** Yellowfin Soapfish *D. drachi* is grey with a yellow face and black band through dorsal fin (14 cm; Red Sea, G. of Aden).

Sixline Soapfish   27 cm
Grammistes sexlineatus   (10.6 in)

Black with narrow white stripes that break up into dashes with age. **Biology:** reef flats, lagoons, channels and seaward reefs, 1 m below 40 m. Sub-adults common, but secretive in or near holes. Adults move to quite deep water. **Range:** Red Sea to Fr. Polynesia, n. to s. Japan.

Spotted Soapfish   35 cm
Pogonoperca punctata   (14 in)

Brown with black saddles and tiny white spots. **Biology:** inhabits clear seaward reef slopes, 15–120 m. Hovers near entrance of sand-bottomed holes. **Range:** Indonesia to Marquesan and Society Is, n. to s. Japan. **Similar:** Snowflake Soapfish *P. ocellata* has more numerous close-set white spots (33 cm; Comoros to Maldives).

Greater Soapfish   33 cm
Rypticus saponaceus   (13 in)

Head profile concave, mouth upturned; grey to brown with small pale blotches; juveniles with pale dorsal stripe. **Biology:** inhabits seagrass beds and coral reefs, 1–55 m. Usually sits tilted on sand near or under overhangs. Solitary. Feeds at night on small fishes. Common. **Range:** Bermuda and s. FL to Brazil, incl. all Caribbean and tropical Atlantic islands. **Similar:** Whitespotted Soapfish *R. maculatus* is tan with a few white spots (se. USA).

Clingfishes
Gobiesocidae

Urchin Clingfish	5 cm
Diademichthys lineatus	*(2 in)*

Reddish brown with cream stripe on sides and midline. **Biology:** inhabits lagoon and seaward reefs, 1–20 m. Solitary or in small groups. Free-swimming, often among sea-urchin spines. **Range:** Oman and Mauritius to New Caledonia, n. to Ryukyus.

Small elongate fishes with pelvic fins modified into a suction disc. At least two of the 120 species have toxic skin.

Soles
Soleidae

Peacock Sole	30 cm
Pardachirus pavoninus	*(12 in)*

Dark spots and ocelli with yellow flecks; mouth below snout. **Biology:** Inhabits sandy areas near reefs, 1–40 m. Usually completely buried except for eyes and nostrils. Secretes a milky toxin from pores at the base of dorsal and anal fins. **Range:** Sri Lanka to Tonga, n. to s. Japan. **Similar:** Moses Sole *P mar moratus* has less distinct pale spots and reticulations (26 cm; Red Sea to Sri Lanka).

Flatfishes with eyes on the right side.

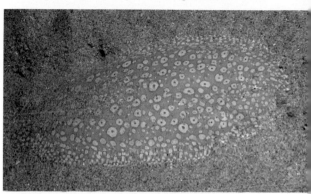

Trunkfishes
Ostraciidae

Honeycomb Cowfish	40 cm
Acanthostracion polygonius	*(16 in)*

Short horns in front of eyes; honeycomb pattern of polygons, colour variable, usually blends with background; juveniles orange with small black spots. **Biology:** inhabits seaward reef slopes, 3–75 m. Feeds on sponges, soft corals, tunicates and shrimps. Solitary. Uncommon off e. FL. **Range:** NJ and Bermuda to Brazil, absent from G. of Mexico.

Box-like, with large bony scales fused into a hard shell with holes for the mouth, eyes, gill opening, fins and tail. Secrete highly poisonous ostracitoxin when stressed.

Scrawled Cowfish   45 cm
Acanthostracion quadricornis *(18 in)*

Short horns in front of eyes; yellowish tan
to pale grey with blue spots and streaks.
Biology: inhabits seagrass beds and inshore
to offshore reefs, 3–80 m. Feeds on sessile
invertebrates, incl. sponges, anemones,
gorgonians, tunicates and worms. Solitary.
Range: MA, Bermuda and n. G. of Mexico to
Brazil.

Spotted Trunkfish   45 cm
Rhinesomus bicaudalis   *(18 in)*

No horns in front of eyes; white with small
round black spots, often large, irregular, diffuse brown patches. **Biology:** inhabits rocky
and coral reefs, 2–50 m. Sometimes under
ledges and near small holes. Feeds on
tunicates, sea cucumbers, sea urchins,
starfishes, crustaceans, molluscs and seagrasses. Solitary. **Range:** FL Keys, Bahamas
and s. G. of Mexico to Brazil; Ascension I.

Smooth Trunkfish   30 cm
Rhinesomus triqueter   *(11.6 in)*

No horns in front of eyes; grey with complex pattern of black, white and yellow-
brown patches, the center of each plate
pale or with round white spot; rarely
orange with pale spots in nw. G. of Mexico
and G. of Honduras; small juveniles black
with white spots. **Biology:** inhabits sand
and rubble patches of coral reefs, 3–50 m.
Sometimes under ledges and near small
holes. Common. Solitary or in small groups.
Feeds on benthic invertebrates, incl. molluscs, crustaceans, worms, tunicates and
sponges. **Range:** MA, Bermuda and n. G. of
Mexico banks to Brazil.

Longhorn Cowfish
Lactoria cornuta

46 cm
(18.1 in)

Long horn in front of each eye; straw-yellow with pale blue spots in centre of each plate. **Biology:** inhabits sand and rubble bottoms of protected lagoon and coastal reefs, 1–50 m. Solitary. Feeds on benthic invertebrates exposed by blowing away sand. **Range:** Red Sea to Marquesas and Tuamotus, n. to S. Korea. **Similar:** other cowfishes have spine in centre of back and shorter horns.

Yellow Boxfish
Ostracion cubicus

45 cm
(18 in)

Juveniles yellow with black dots, becoming mustard-yellow with growth; ♂'s pale metallic blue with protuberance above upper lip. **Biology:** inhabits lagoon and seaward reefs, 1–35 m. Usually near shelter. Solitary. Feeds on benthic invertebrates. **Range:** Red Sea to Tuamotus, n. to Ryukyus, s. to n. New Zealand, rarely in Hawaii; replaced by *O. immaculatus* in s. Japan. **Similar:** Shortnose Boxfish *Rhynchostracion nasus* is paler (30 cm; E. Africa to Fiji); Long-nose Boxfish *R. rhinorhynchus* has larger protuberance higher on snout (28 cm; E. Africa to Philippines and n. Australia).

Spotted Trunkfish
Ostracion meleagris

15 cm
(6 in)

Juveniles and ♀s black with white dots; ♂'s metallic blue with orange ocelli on sides (only dark spots in Hawaii and e. Pacific). **Biology:** inhabits clear lagoon and seaward reefs, 1–30 m. Usually near shelter. Solitary. Feeds primarily on tunicates, sponges and algae. **Range:** E. Africa to Panama, n. to Ryukyu and Hawaiian Is. **Similar:** several Indo-Pacific spp. with distinctive colours and limited ranges.

Reptiles

The Yellow-lipped Sea Krait is the species most often seen by divers. *Lombok, MK*

Sea Snakes
Subfamilies Hydrophiinae and Laticaudinae

Most people consider snakes to epitomise venomosity, yet the majority of species lack venom and are quite harmless. However, nearly all of the species that live in the ocean are highly venomous. Fortunately, most of them have placid dispositions and even the most aggressive ones pose little danger to humans unless roughly handled or removed from the water. In parts of Asia, sea snakes are hunted and sold for food and traditional medicines.

There are three families of snakes with species that occur in marine waters. The term 'sea snake' properly refers only to those members of the family Elapidae, which have paddle-like tails and are adapted to life in the sea. The 'true sea snakes' of the subfamily Hydrophiinae are entirely aquatic, while the sea kraits of the subfamily Laticaudinae are amphibious and must return to land to lay their eggs and digest their food. Non-venomous water snakes and other land snakes of the family Colubridae may occur in salt marshes or mangrove swamps but not in the open sea. A non-venomous file snake (family Acrochordidae; p.248) also inhabits estuaries and coastal marine waters.

Behaviour and life history
Sea snakes evolved from their terrestrial counterparts and thus possess lungs and must surface to breathe. They are also excellent divers that can stay under water for more than two hours, although they typical do so for 30 minutes or less. Some species can dive to depths of 103 m. Sea snakes avoid the bends by surfacing only briefly. When they do so, their heart rate increases to facilitate rapid gas exchange. They also have physiological adaptations that inhibit gas exchange between their lungs and blood when diving. Up to 20 per cent of the oxygen they need can be absorbed from the surrounding water through their skin. Excess salt is expelled through a gland under the tongue.

Venom apparatus

Sea snakes typically have one pair of short, hollow fangs near the front of the mouth on the maxillary bone (upper jaw). Each fang is connected by a venom duct to an elongate venom gland extending beneath and behind the eye. Occasionally, there may be two or three functional fangs on each side of the jaw and up to three spare ones folded behind. When the snake bites, venom is forced through the fangs and into the wound. The fangs of sea snakes sit further back in the mouth than those of vipers, are much shorter and are fixed rather than moveable. *(Modified from Halstead, 1970)*

Sea snakes are usually seen poking in reef crevices or holes on soft bottoms as they hunt for prey – typically eels or other small fishes. A few species feed exclusively on fish eggs. A bite from a sea snake quickly paralyses and kills its prey, which is devoured whole. True sea snakes never leave the water unless stranded, while sea kraits come ashore to lay their eggs, warm up or digest their food. One may expect sea snakes to be free of predators, but this is perhaps true only of the Yellow-bellied Sea Snake *Pelamis platurus*, which also has toxic skin. Other species are regularly preyed upon by sea eagles, ospreys, herons and sharks, particularly the Tiger Shark. The Estuarine Crocodile, large moray eels and even a sea anemone and swimming crabs are also known to feed on sea snakes.

True sea snakes copulate in extended sessions that may last more than one breathing cycle, and bear their offspring live in the water. Sea kraits copulate in the water or on land and lay their eggs on land. Gestation typically takes three to nine months. Sea snakes grow fastest

when young – up to 43 cm per year. Male Olive Sea Snakes *Aipysurus laevis* mature in three years, females in four. In this and most other species, females grow larger than males.

Most sea snakes generally ignore divers, allowing them to get within centimetres without feeling threatened or disturbed. Often a diver can touch or handle the snake without getting much of a reaction except that it may pull away and resume its normal activity. Some true sea snakes can be curious and may approach or even wrap themselves around a diver before moving off. A few species can be quite short-tempered and aggressive, and will attempt to bite if molested. This is particularly true for courting males.

Appearance
Sea snakes are easily distinguished from eels by having clearly visible scales with a smooth, mucus-free surface, and by lacking fins and gill openings. Also, like land snakes, they often flick out their tongue (although only the tip) to taste the water, something eels are incapable of. Unlike their terrestrial counterparts, sea snakes have laterally compressed paddle-like tails and

All sea snakes have a laterally compressed paddle-like tail. Some, like this Yellow-bellied Sea Snake, may also have somewhat laterally compressed bodies with a ventral keel. *Maldives, HV*

nostrils on top of their snouts. Some sea snakes are somewhat laterally compressed while others, along with the sea kraits, are cylindrical through most of the length of their bodies. In most species the head is about the same width as the neck. Some species are rather uniform in diameter, but in others the neck narrows to a very small head. Depending on the species, sea snakes range from 50 cm to 2.7 m in length. An exceptionally large Yellow-lipped Sea Krait measured 3.6 m long. In most species, females grow larger than males, but in a few the reverse occurs. Some species are uniformly coloured, often olive to dark blue-black, while many are banded. Some have saddles, spots or a combination of markings, and one is black with a yellow belly. Some species can be variable in colour, ranging from uniform to blotched or banded.

Curious sea snakes sometimes approach divers but should never be grasped or handled except by experts. Here, an Olive Sea Snake explores a diver. *Coral Sea, LI*

Typical accidents

Accidents occur almost exclusively to fishermen, who get bitten when sorting their catch. When taken out of water, sea snakes may react aggressively, whereas in the water they are usually quite docile. The only documented cases of divers being attacked and bitten that the authors are aware of involved researchers who handled the snakes. In all cases the short fangs did not penetrate their wetsuits. It is extremely rare for swimmers or beachgoers to be bitten. In fact, in some parts of the world children routinely play with the local sea snakes without getting bitten. As with land snakes, sea snakes can withold venom at will. In some species, more than 70 per cent of defensive bites are 'blank', with no venom being delivered.

Prevention

Never attempt to touch or handle a sea snake. All except for three egg-eating species (p248) are potentially lethal and those are not easily distinguished from the others. Although divers often touch sea snakes without being bitten, it is advisable to leave them alone and keep a safe distance. Occasionally, sea snakes approach a diver or wrap themselves around an arm or leg. If this happens, remain calm, avoid sudden movements and do not try to remove the snake as this could provoke a bite. Only two species, *Aipysusrus laevis* and *Astrotia stokesii*, have fangs long enough to penetrate a typical wetsuite.

Venom

Sea snake venom is similar to that of their terrestrial counterparts of the family Elapidae, which includes cobras, mambas, kraits, taipans and coral snakes. It is typically rich in neurotoxins and in some species consists only of toxins and no enzymes. The primary purpose of the venom is to immobilise and kill prey quickly – a job best done by fast-acting neurotoxins. These chemicals interrupt the signals between nerves and muscles, thus leading to muscular paralysis. In addition to neurotoxins, some venoms contain highly active phospholipases, enzymes that attack muscles which release the pigment myoglobin. This can result in kidney failure, cardiac arrhythmia and respiratory failure.

Envenomation and symptoms

Bites from sea snakes are relatively painless and often go unnoticed. Initial symptoms are no different than what one would expect from the mechanical effects of being punctured by the fangs. In rare cases, massive envenomation can result in rapid collapse and shock – not to be confused with fainting, which is temporary. In most cases of serious envenomation, symptoms of muscle pain and stiffness appear within 30 minutes of the bite. The victim usually avoids movement and remains in a cramped position. Other common symptoms are paralysis in the facial muscles, resulting in droopy eyelids and difficulty in swallowing and speaking. This may be accompanied by vomiting and visual disturbances. Bites from species whose venom contains phospholipases result in the release of myoglobin from the breakdown of muscle fibres. This usually occurs three to six hours after envenomation, turns urine dark brown and can cause

Treatment

First aid

Remove the victim of a sea snake bite from the water immediately and seek medical attention. Keep the victim as still and calm as possible. If the bite occurs on a digit or limb, apply a pressure bandage (crêpe bandages work best) at the site of the bite and for some distance in both directions (if the bite is on a finger, bandage the arm to the elbow). Restrain the limb, since muscular action spreads the venom. Leave the bandage on until professional medical help is at hand. Even in cases of fatal envenomation, the bite itself can be relatively painless. All bites must therefore be considered potentially life-threatening.

What not to do

Do not apply a tourniquet or cut, suck or manipulate the wound.

Ongoing medical management

Treatment is according to the symptoms. If there is a sign of respiratory paralysis, stabilise the victim's cardiovascular system. Respirators or dialysis can be used to keep the patient alive through respiratory or kidney failure, even without the use of an antivenom. Antivenoms developed for certain species of sea snake are available in Australia and some other parts of the world. Tiger Snake Notechis scutatus antivenom or polyvalent antivenom may be substituted if sea snake antivenom is not available. However, antivenoms for cobras and land kraits are not particularly effective. Administering an antivenom is no substitute for first aid and does entail some risk. Antivenom must be given according to the symptoms and only by qualified medical personnel, and can be effective as long as two days after envenomation. Adrenalin and antihistamines should be used in the event of allergic reactions to the serum in the antivenom.

take up to two days. Patients who survive may suffer permanent disability owing to muscular wastage and kidney damage. Although most sea snake venoms are powerful, the chance of surviving a bite is good if adequate treatment is achieved quickly. Not every bite from a sea snake results in envenomation and in some species up to 70 per cent of bites are 'dry'. Low doses of venom can result in less severe symptoms.

Species and distribution

At least 75 species of snake in three families occur in marine or estuarine waters. The only truly marine snakes that are venomous are members of the family Elapidae, which includes cobras, mambas, kraits, taipans and coral snakes. They are divided into two groups: the fully aquatic true sea snakes (subfamily Hydrophiinae), which give birth to live young; and the amphibious sea kraits (subfamily Laticaudinae), which lay eggs on land. The true sea snakes include 56 species in 16 genera. All are fully marine except Hydrophis semperi, which inhabits Lake Taal in the Philippines. The Yellow-bellied Sea Snake Pelamis platurus is a pelagic inhabitant of nearly the entire Indian Ocean and tropical eastern Pacific. In summer, it can stray as far north as southern Siberia. All others have more restricted distributions from the Arabian Peninsula to Fiji.

The sea kraits include eight species, all in the genus Laticauda. Seven are marine and one, L. crockeri, inhabits a freshwater lake in the Solomon Islands. The centre of diversity for sea snakes is the Indo-Australian region, with 30 species in Malaysia and Indonesia and 32 species in northern Australia.

Some species of sea snake occur in a variety of habitats, from estuaries and murky coastal waters to coral reefs and deep muddy bottoms, while others are restricted to a particular habitat. One of three species of non-venomous file snakes (family Acrochordidae) also inhabits estuaries and coastal marine waters. There are no sea snakes in the Red Sea, Atlantic or Mediterranean.

kidney failure. Serious envenomation affecting the entire skeletal muscles also leads to massive release of potassium from the muscle tissue, which can cause cardiac arrhythmia. Paralysis of the respiratory muscles can lead to apnoea (inability to breathe), resulting in asphyxiation. Death often occurs within 12 to 24 hours but can

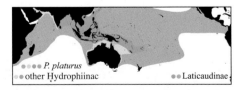

Distribution of Yellow-bellied Sea Snake Pelamis platurus, other true sea snakes and sea kraits.

Sea Snakes
Subfamily Hydrophiinae

Yellow-bellied Sea Snake   <110 cm
Pelamis platurus   (<43 in)

Head elongate, slightly depressed, 49–69 mid-body scale rows; black above, yellow below, end of tail yellow with large black spots; fangs tiny, to 1.5 mm. ♀ gets larger than ♂. **Biology:** pelagic, occasionally washed ashore. Primarily at or near surface, occasionally below 35 m. Most often in areas of surface slicks, occasionally with drifting seaweed. Feeds on wide variety of small fishes. Possibly mimics a floating stick to attract prey, which is grabbed by whipping its head sideways. Moults by coiling around itself and rubbing. Gives birth to 2–8 live young about 25 cm long. May bite if provoked, has even bitten a surfer. Venom highly toxic but yield low. Has caused human fatalities. **Range:** S. Africa to Panama, n. to Arabian G. and s. Japan.

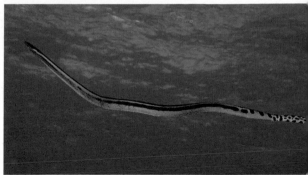

Horned Sea Snake   <123 cm
Acalyptophis peronii   (<48 in)

Slender forebody, robust hindbody and ventral keel towards rear, scales stongly keeled and overlapping on head and forebody, in 21–31 mid-body rows; cream to brown, often with double pale bars. **Biology:** inhabits sandy areas of coral reefs. Feeds primarily at night on gobies. Bites if provoked. Venom among the most toxic known but human fatalities not yet reported. **Range:** nw. Australia to New Caledonia; s. China to Thailand.

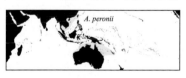

A. peronii

Olive Sea Snake <200 cm
Aipysurus laevis (<79 in)

Large head and robust body with ventral keel towards rear, 21–25 mid-body scale rows; juveniles usually brownish with narrow pale bars, adults uniformly grey to olive or purplish brown; fangs to 4.7 mm. ♀ gets larger than ♂. **Biology:** inhabits coastal and offshore coral reefs to 50 m. Common on many reefs of Coral Sea. Feeds primarily on fishes. Curious but not aggressive unless restrained or hit. May bite if provoked. Venom highly toxic, bite potentially fatal. **Range:** n. Australia and New Guinea to New Caledonia and Loyalty Is.

A. duboisii
A. laevis

Dubois' Sea Snake <114 cm
Aipysurus duboisii (<45 in)

Large head and robust body, laterally compressed with ventral keel towards rear, scales overlap along rear edges, in 19 mid-body rows; purplish brown with pale-edged scales, often with cream bars forming triangular lateral blotches. **Biology:** inhabits reef flats and coral reefs to 50 m. Often in water so shallow it must crawl. Feeds primarily in early evening on fishes, occasionally on fish eggs. Bites when handled. Venom among the most toxic known but human fatalities not yet reported. **Range:** New Guinea and n. Australia to New Caledonia.

Cogger's Sea Snake   <136 cm
Hydrophis coggeri   (<53 in)

Body cylindrical, head and forward part narrow, end of tail paddle-like, 29–34 mid-body scale rows; cream with 28–40 broad black bars, head dark in juvenile, cream in adults. ♀ gets larger than ♂. **Biology:** occurs on seagrass beds and shallow lagoon and coastal coral reefs to 40 m. Feeds primarily on eels at night. Aggressive, may attack when provoked. Bite potentially fatal. **Range:** Philippines and e. Indonesia to nw. Australian shelf; Coral Sea to Fiji, n. to Vanuatu.

Sea Kraits
Subfamily Laticaudinae

Yellow-lipped Sea Krait   <3.6 m
Laticauda colubrina   (<11.8 ft)

Body cylindrical, scales in 21–25 mid-body rows; blue to pale blue-grey with 20–65 black bars, snout and upper lip yellow. ♀ gets larger than ♂. **Biology:** occurs in mangrove swamps and on shallow flats and coral reefs to a depth of 60 m. Feeds exclusively on eels. A large moray can take up to 16 minutes to succumb to venom. Digestion, reproduction and egg-laying occur on land. Several males may mate with one female. Clutch of 4–20 eggs laid in crevices above high-tide line at traditional site, hatching in 2–3 months. ♂s mature during 2nd year of life, ♀s during 2nd and 3rd year. Extremely reluctant to bite, but may if provoked. Venom highly toxic, with high yield. **Range:** Sri Lanka and e. India to Tonga, excl. Australia, n. to Ryukyus; replaced by *L. saintgironsi* in New Caledonia. **Similar:** *L. frontalis* is a nearly identical dwarf species (Vanuatu, Loyalty Is); *L. laticaudata* has brown upper lip (136 cm; Sri Lanka to Niue, n. to s. Japan but not Australia).

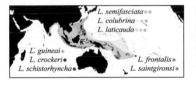

Sea Snakes
Subfamily Hydrophiinae

1. **Yellow-bellied Sea Snake** *Pelamis platurus* <110 cm <(43 in) Has caused human fatalities. (p.245).
2. **Olive Sea Snake** *Aipysurus laevis* <2 m (<6.6 ft) May bite if provoked or handled. Venom highly toxic, bite potentially fatal (p.246).
3. **Short Sea Snake** *Lapemis curtus* >100 cm (>39 in) In turbid coastal and estuarine waters to 15 m. Common near river mouths. Feeds on fishes, occasionally on squids. Can go into a biting frenzy when disturbed. Venom extremely potent, has caused fatalities. Arabian G. to PNG, n. to Hong Kong.
4. **Beaked Sea Snake** *Enhydrina schistosa* 1.6 m (5.2 ft) Venom potent, yield extremely high, enough to kill up to 53 people. Responsible for 90 per cent of fatalities by sea snake bites. Arabian G. to New Guinea and n. Australia, n. to Vietnam.
5. **Elegant Sea Snake** *Hydrophis elegans* 2.1 m (6.9 ft) In turbid coastal waters and deeper soft bottoms between reefs, usually below 30 m. Feeds on eels. Fangs moderately long, venom potent, yield high. Bite potentially fatal. n. Australia to s. New Guinea.
6. **Blue-banded Sea Snake** *Hydrophis cyanocinctus* 2.75 m (9 ft) On seagrass beds, shallow coastal reefs and soft bottoms. Feeds on eels and small fishes. Bites when molested. Venom yield high, has caused fatalities. Arabian G. to e. Indonesia, n. to Rykyus. Similar: Black-headed Sea Snake *H. atriceps* has smaller head, saddles in middle with spots below when large (1.2 m/3.9 ft; G. of Thailand to n.-central Australia, n. to Taiwan).
7. **Greater Dusky Sea Snake** *Hydrophis klossi* 1.3 m (4.3 ft) In shallow coastal waters. Rarely bites spontaneously, venom unstudied. G. of Thailand to Borneo and Indonesia. Similar: Slender Sea Snake *H. gracilis* has smaller head, broader bars and saddles (1.3 m/ 4.3 ft; Arabian G. to PNG, n. to s. China).

Sea Kraits
Subfamily Laticaudinae

8. **Yellow-lipped Sea Krait** *Laticauda colubrina* <3.6 m (<11.8 ft) Extremely reluctant to bite, but may if provoked. Venom highly toxic, with high yield (p.247).
9. **Brown-lipped Sea Krait** *Laticauda laticaudata* 1.36 m (4.5 ft) In shallow coral reef and coastal waters to 40 m. Digests food, mates and lays eggs on land. Feeds on fishes. Very docile. Venom highly toxic but yield low. E. India to Niue, n. to Ryukyus, not Australia.
10. **Broad-banded Sea Krait** *Laticauda semifasciata* 1.6 m (5.2 ft) On rocky and coral reefs and shores. Common. Very docile. Venom highly toxic, yield moderate. Widely used for food. Central Philippines to Ryukyus.

Harmless marine snakes
The Marine File Snake *Acrochordus grannulatus* (left) inhabits the same coastal waters as venomous sea snakes but is easily distinguished by its tail, which is not paddle-like. It ranges from India to the Solomon Islands, northern Australia and the Philippines. The Turtle-headed Sea Snake *Emydocephalus annulatus* (above) and two other species that feed only on fish eggs have weak venom and minute fangs. *Bali, MB; New Caledonia, MB*

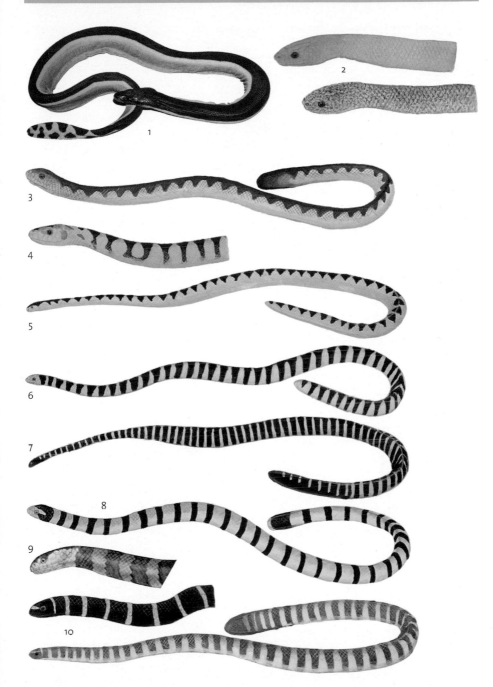

The Estuarine Crocodile *Crocodylus porosius.*

Crocodiles
Order Crocodylia, family Crocodylidae

A close encounter with a large crocodile is a life-threatening situation that one would never expect to happen in the ocean. Yet in some parts of the world it does. A few years ago, a well-known marine biologist was taken by surprise while scuba-diving on the Great Barrier Reef. He fought back and survived. The crocodilians are an ancient group that evolved with the dinosaurs more than 160 million years ago. Today, there are 23 species in three families. Three species occur in estuarine waters and the largest of all, the Estuarine Crocodile, can survive far out at sea.

Biology and life history
A crocodile is a perfectly designed amphibious predator with eyes and nostrils on top of its head. This enables it to remain unseen as it waits near the water's edge to surprise prey that comes to drink. In a flash, it explodes from the water to grasp its hapless victim, before dragging it under. Limbs and other large pieces are torn off when the crocodile spins in a high-speed 'death roll'. Larger prey may be stashed under-water for several days to soften up. Most crocodiles will eat just about any animal they can ambush, in the water and on land.

Crocodiles are surprisingly intelligent and have the most advanced maternal care of all the reptiles. The female constructs a large mound of leaves and soil to incubate her 20 to 60 eggs. When the eggs hatch after 10 to 12 weeks, she gently picks the hatchlings up, cradles them in her mouth and carries them to the water. Crocodilians are cold-blooded, with slow metabolisms that enable them to remain submerged for hours and live for months without a meal. Unlike alligators, they have salt glands that enable them to live in salt water.

Prevention
Avoid entering waters known to be inhabited by crocodiles. If diving near such areas, always be on

Massive jaws and teeth, and a bone-crushing grip

Crocodilians have powerful jaws lined with large conical teeth that enable some species to grasp and subdue prey as big as themselves. A bite force of several tonnes can break bones and prevent escape. The teeth are used to grasp or rip holes through tough hide rather than cut. Limbs and other large pieces are torn off when the crocodile performs a 'death roll' by spinning rapidly. The American Crocodile *Crocodylus acutus*, shown here, attains a length of 6 m (20 ft). *(Jamaica, JN)*

the lookout and stay with a group. Before approaching or entering the water, look for signs of a crocodile and keep a tall profile.

If taken by a crocodile

Try to poke the animal in the eyes or force a hand into its throat – this can cause the valve that keeps water out of the lungs to open. These are about the only methods to get a determined crocodile to release its grip. Medical help must be given as soon as possible, even for minor puncture wounds. Many who have survived the initial bite and trauma have succumbed to massive infection within days.

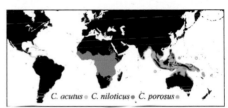

Distribution of three species of crocodile that enter salt water. Historically, the Nile Crocodile *C. niloticus* inhabited the upper Nile to the Mediterranean coast and *C. porosus* was in Fiji. Stray *C. porosus* have been found at Pohnpei, Cocos (Keeling) and Hong Kong.

Estuarine Crocodile >6.2 m; 1,100 kg
Crocodylus porosus (>20.3 ft; 2,425 lb)

♂ gets larger than ♀. **Biology:** resident in fresh waters of lower elevations, tidal rivers, mangrove swamps and estuaries. Regularly visits coastal coral reefs, where it has been found sleeping as deep as 12 m. Can survive open sea journeys of over 1,000 km. Feeds on any living creature it can take. Juveniles start with small fare such as insects, frogs, crabs and fishes, then move up to birds and mammals, including humans, as they grow. **Range:** s. India to Vanuatu, n. to Philippines, s. to s. Queensland; extinct in Fiji.

Turtles
Order Testudines

Sea turtles have sharp, powerful beaks capable of cutting through skin and flesh. While not normally dangerous, they are known to defend themselves vigorously against predators such as sharks and to bite humans when harassed. On rare occasions, amorous male sea turtles have confused a diver with a prospective mate. This can be dangerous, particularly for a novice diver – in such situations it is best to leave the water. Under normal circumstances it is safe to approach a sea turtle closely, but you should never touch it.

There are seven species of sea turtle, six in the family Chelonidae, which have hard shells, and the Leatherback Turtle of the family Dermochelidae, which has a tough leathery shell.

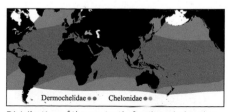

Distribution of the sea turtle families Chelonidae and Dermochelidae.

Hawksbill Turtle	1.14 m; 77 kg
Eretmochelys imbricata	*(3.7 ft; 170 lb)*

2 pairs of scales in front of eyes, upper jaw with distinct point; rear shell plates overlap to form serrated edge. **Biology:** inhabits all reef zones. The most common turtle on most tropical reefs. Omnivorous, feeds primarily on invertebrates, particularly sponges, which it breaks open with its beak. Its diet also includes sea anemones, jellyfishes, deadly box jellyfishes and Portuguese Man-of-war. Clutch size 53–206. The species most often used for 'tortoiseshell' products. **Range:** all tropical and subtropical seas.

Green Turtle	1.53 m; 150 kg
Chelonia mydas	*(5 ft; 330 lb)*

Single pair of scales in front of eyes. **Biology:** inhabits all reef zones. Young feed primarily on soft-bodied animals, adults primarily on plants, including mangroves and seagrasses. Nests every 2–3 yrs, laying 100–150 eggs per clutch at 10–15-day intervals. Incubation usually lasts 45–60 days, with nests cooler than 30°C producing mostly ♂'s, and warmer nests producing mostly ♀s. **Range:** all tropical and subtropical seas.

Leatherback Turtle 2.44 m; 867 kg
Dermochelys coriacea (8 ft; 1,918 lb)

Carapace leathery with 5 lengthwise ridges. **Biology:** the world's largest turtle. Pelagic, rarely near reefs. Feeds on jelly-fishes, salps and other soft-bodied animals. Known to ram boats and attack snorkellers. Dives to at least 1,500 m. Adults warm-blooded with core temperature up to 18°C above water temperature. Nests on only a few remote tropical beaches. Clutch size 50–170, but with many yolkless eggs. Incubation lasts 53–74 days. Often killed by ingesting plastic bags or by fishing lines and drifting nets. Numbers have declined precipitously in recent years. **Range:** all tropical to sub-polar seas.

C. mydas • E. imbricata •

Komodo Dragon
Order Squamata, family Varanidae

The Komodo Dragon, the world's largest lizard, not only preys on large mammals, including humans, but occasionally forages on beaches and in shallow waters. It therefore poses a small but real danger to anyone exploring a beach or snorkelling, particularly a child. Although Komodo Dragons are normally wary of humans in groups, they are known to stalk and ambush lone individuals. They have powerful jaws lined with sharp, serrated teeth that can cause severe wounds. However, the greatest danger is not from the immediate bite, but rather from the resulting infection. Their saliva is a veritable cornucopia of deadly pathogens and their toxins, comprising at least 50 varieties. This bacteriological soup, or toxic drool, is used like a venom. A Komodo Dragon normally bites and then releases large struggling prey. It then uses its long, forked toungue in the same way as a snake to follow the scent trail. Within 48 hours, the victim is usually near death due to massive infection. At this point the dragon finishes it off, or if the prey is very large it waits for it to die or even begin to rot before feeding. Komodo Dragons should not be approached by lone individuals, whether on land or in the water.

Komodo Dragon	<3.1 m
Varanus komodoensis	*(<10.2 ft)*

Massive body, broad head, small tubercle-like scales; juvenile with beige spots and bars, adults uniformly grey. **Biology:** juveniles in trees, adults on ground. Juveniles prey on insects and lizards, shifting to birds, large mammals and carrion with growth. Ambushes prey, then waits for it to be weakened by infection before finishing it off. Lays 8–27 eggs. Will cannibalise young. **Range:** Komodo, Rinca and w. Flores, Indonesia.

Touch-me-not Sponge *Neofibularia nolitangere*. Contact with the skin causes pain, numbness, swelling and a rash that can last several days. *Curaçao, RM*

Sponges: Toxic Chemicals and Spicules
Phylum Porifera

At present, approximately 8,000 species of sponge are known, nearly all of which live in the ocean. Newly recognised species are constantly being discovered, and marine biologists estimate the true number to be between 15,000 and 25,000. Sponges have no organs, only a small number of specialised cell types that form simple layers of tissue or meander about like ameoba. They are divided into three classes, based primarily on the material in their skeletons. Most species, including those harmful to humans, belong in the class Demospongia. They have skeletons of spongin, a flexible fibrous material, as well as spicules of either silica or calcium carbonate, and contain many noxious chemical compounds, some of which have been synthesised into anti-viral and anti-cancer drugs. Although most sponges do not cause any problems when humans come into contact with them, a few species can leave ink-like stains or

highly toxic sticky deposits, or cause unpleasant skin reactions that range from immediate burning pain to long-lasting rashes.

Behaviour and life history
Sponges grow on solid surfaces and feed on minute particles filtered from the surrounding water. The water is sucked in through tiny openings on the sponge's surface and pumped through a maze of canals and chambers by the collective action of special cells called choanocytes, which are equipped with a twirling whip-like filament (flagellum). These cells also filter and digest floating bacteria, single-celled algae and other organic material (detritus). The filtered water is then expelled through one or more larger excurrent openings. Some sponges contain symbiotic cyanobacteria, which manufacture sugars from the sponge's metabolic wastes.

Most sponges are permanently fixed to the bottom but a few can 'crawl' ever so slowly by lifting and redepositing spicules. Although sponges appear helpless, they have a variety of

The real danger of *Physalia* spp. lies underwater.

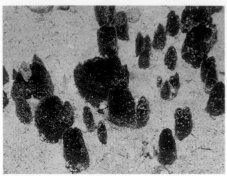

These Ehrenberg's Boring Sponges *Biemna ehrenbergi* seem to grow out of the sand but are actually attached to dead coral that they have bored into. The species may irritate or sting sensitive skin on contact. *Red Sea, JH*

weapons that protect them from predators and keep unwanted organisms from settling on their surfaces. These include sharp, indigestible siliceous or calcareous spicules and a large number of noxious and antibiotic chemical compounds. Some sponges produce chemicals that kill corals and other anchored animals so they can overgrow them. Some animals that feed on sponges, including certain nudibranchs, may sequester the sponge's noxious compounds for

use in their own defence. Sponges are hermaphrodites, producing both sperm (which is released into the water) and eggs. The eggs may be fertilised in the water or within the sponge. The resulting larvae either creep along the bottom or drift in the plankton until they settle on a suitable surface to grow.

Appearance
Sponges appear to be inanimate objects but are actually sessile animals that live permanently attached to solid surfaces. They come in a variety of sizes and shapes, including tubes, cups, balls, cones, vases, antlers, encrustations or amorphous blobs. Some species have characteristic and recognisable forms, but many others grow in a variety of shapes depending on their environment. Their colour may also be variable. This makes many species difficult or even impossible to classify by mere appearance. Many sponges are easily recognised by their porous surface and incurrent and excurrent canals and openings, but some appear solid and may be quite hard.

Typical accidents
Divers and snorkellers rarely suffer painful skin reactions when touching sponges, primarily because they are apt to do so only with their fingertips, which have relatively tough skin. Sticky deposits left by some sponges are generally harmless if washed off. Those who roughly handle or collect sponges are more likely to suffer a reaction. Oystermen on the eastern coast of the United States are particularly vulnerable because they often contact the venomous Red Moss Sponge *Microciona prolifera*, which grows among oysters. Adverse reactions can also be caused by other organisms growing on the sponges, such as the symbiotic stinging polyp stage of the jellyfish *Nasuithoe* spp. (p.286).

Prevention
The identification of sponges is usually difficult, and several species other than those included here can cause skin reactions, particularly to anyone with sensitive skin or if contact is made in sensitive areas. Therefore, no sponge should be touched or handled. If it is necessary to do so, wear gloves.

The venom: toxic and antibiotic chemicals
A sponge's tissue contains a high number of bioactive substances that offer excellent protection against most predators. These chemicals are also highly effective against harmful fungi, algae and bacteria, and keep unwanted

Treatment

First aid
Wash the affected area with either clear water or soap and water, and then dry carefully. Use tweezers to remove any skeletal needles stuck in the skin. Alternatively, if the needles are tiny and barely visible (often the case), it is usually better to remove them by placing sticky tape or a plaster over the wound and pulling it off.

What not to do
Do not rub the affected area with alcohol. This may cause the poisonous substances to penetrate deeper into the skin.

Ongoing medical management
A mild ointment or lotion can be used to soothe unpleasant or painful irritation. For predominantly allergic reactions, the use of corticosteroids may be advised. Antihistamines can be used to suppress itching.

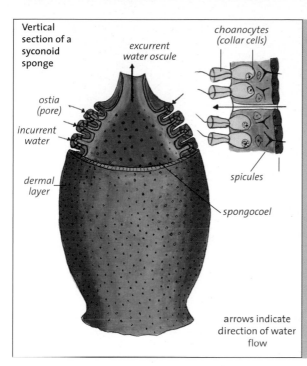

Vertical section of a syconoid sponge

excurrent water oscule

choanocytes (collar cells)

ostia (pore)

incurrent water

dermal layer

spicules

spongocoel

arrows indicate direction of water flow

Anatomy and venom apparatus

Sponges do not have a specialised venom-delivery system but contain tiny skeletal elements that are usually under a millimetre in length. These tiny siliceous or calcareous spicules can have many forms, but most are sharp and pointed. They can easily penetrate human skin, even if touched lightly. The resulting perforations allow the sponge's bioactive substances to enter the wound. When touched, some sponges leave a dark stain or noxious sticky deposit. *(Artwork: EL)*

organisms from settling on the sponge's surface. Generally, each sponge contains several often unique bioactive substances. Given the large number of sponge species, this means thousands, or tens of thousands, of such substances. Sponges thus represent a rich source of natural products of interest to chemists and pharmaceutical companies, who test them for their effects and potential suitability as medicine. The anti-viral herpes medication vidarabine was synthesised from a sponge. It is a wonder that, despite the large number of sponge species and their enormous variety of bioactive substances, there are only a few that cause painful irritation when touched. To date, the substances that cause irritation to human skin have not been isolated in any of the sponge species.

Envenomation and symptoms

When touched, the sponges in question produce reactions that are similar but vary in intensity. These include immediate reddening of the skin, tingling to sharp or burning pain, swelling, rash, blisters, stiffness and pain in the fingers. In some cases, an eczema can develop. The symptoms of a pronounced and painful skin reaction

(contact dermatitis) can last several days, and an itching, tingling or stinging feeling in particular can last for weeks. It is important to realise that dried sponges can cause these reactions when they are moistened. Even sponges preserved in formaldehyde have retained their toxic properties.

Species and distribution

Sponges occur in all seas as well as in a few freshwater areas. The 8,000 known species are distributed among about a hundred families in three classes based on skeletal make-up. Calcareous sponges (class Calcarea) have skeletons of calcium carbonate; glass sponges (class Hexatinella) have skeletons of silica; and demosponges (class Demospongia) have skeletons of spongin, a flexible fibrous material, and may also have spicules of either silica or calcium carbonate. The vast majority of species – including the noxious ones described here – are members of the latter. Sponges are notoriously difficult to identify and the classification of many families, as well as species, is in a state of flux. As a result, the distributions of many species are poorly known.

Fire Sponges
Tedanidae

Fire Sponge	<30 cm
Tedania ignis	*(<12 in)*

Orange to red irregular mass with excurrent openings in tall, volcano-like cones; surface clearly porous and transparent where thin. **Biology:** primarily in shallow protected areas, 1–11 m. Attached to rubble or rock, common in seagrass beds. Contact with skin causes burning pain, numbness, swelling and a rash that can last several days. **Range:** FL, Bahamas and Caribbean; possibly introduced to Hawaii. Red Moss Sponge (Redbeard Sponge) *Microciona prolifera* inhabits intertidal zone to shallow rubble, rock and oyster banks (North America from Nova Scotia to FL and TX).

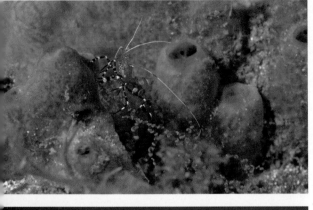

Touch-me-not Sponges
Desmacidonidae

Touch-me-not Sponge	<1.2 m
Neofibularia nolitangere	*(<4 ft)*

Dark reddish-brown lumpy mass with one or more large, irregularly rounded excurrent openings; has felt-like texture, often covered with small white polychaete worms *Haplosyllis* sp. **Biology:** inhabits shallow inshore waters and protected seaward reef slopes, 3–36 m. Shelters a wide variety of animals. Contact with skin causes pain, numbness, swelling and a rash that can last several days. **Range:** FL, Bahamas and Caribbean. **Similar:** *Neofibularia mordens* occurs in coastal waters of Australia.

Cnidarians: Radial Design with Toxic Darts
Phylum Cnidaria

There are over 8,000 species of cnidarians. Nearly all live in the ocean, while the remaining few inhabit fresh waters. Cnidarians are divided into four classes: class Hydrozoa, which includes fire corals, hydroids and siphonophores; class Scyphozoa, the true jellyfishes; class Cubozoa, the box jellyfishes; and the large class Anthozoa, which includes soft corals and gorgonians, sea anemones, stony corals, zoanthids, corallimorphs, black corals and tube anemones.

All cnidarians have two features in common: a radially symmetric body consisting of two layers of tissue around a stomach, with a ring of tentacles around the mouth; and a distinctive type of stinging cell, the nematocyst. All also have one or both of two basic body forms: the polyp, which is attached; and the medusa, which is free-swimming. Hydrozoans, scyphozoans and cubozoans alternate generations between medusa and polyp stages, while Anthozoans exist only as polyps. Although all cnidarians have nematocysts, most species are harmless because their nematocysts are too weak to penetrate human skin. Symptoms of contact with those whose nematocysts can penetrate human skin range from a slight skin irritation that clears up quickly to severe pain and life-threatening poisoning, depending on the species and, in some cases, on the sensititvity of the victim. A few species of true jellyfish, box jellyfish and the hydrozoan Portuguese Man-of-war are particularly dangerous and can kill a human.

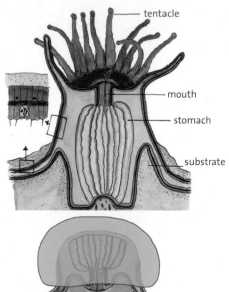

A polyp (top) consists of two layers of tissue around a stomach, with a ring of tentacles around a central mouth. The medusa stage (above) has basically the same structure but with the base modified into a bell that can contract to facilitate swimming. *Artwork: EL; RM*

The nematocyst

Cnidarians possess a unique 'high-tech' weapon, the nematocyst. This is a complex, specialised cell containing a hollow, coiled, spring-like thread with a trigger mechanism that is attached to a venom sac. There are at least are 25 varieties but all have the same basic structure. As with other capsule-like cells, a nematocyst has a double lining. On one end of the cell, the outside wall is turned inside and formed into an inverted, tightly coiled thread with stiletto-like barbs at its base that packed into a venom sac. A bristle-like process outside the capsule serves as a trigger. If it is aggravated, the outer capsule wall tears open and the thread-like tube rolls out with such explosive force that it pierces the victim. The tube enters the wound and injects the poison, and the barbs hold on. While the mechanism is extraordinarily clever, the speed of the explosion can only be described as spectacular. The entire process lasts less than three milliseconds and the crucial part, the outburst of the thread, takes less than one hundred-thousandth of a second! This extreme momentum results in the capsule's enormous penetrating force. Such acceleration is unique among all animal and plant life and is comparable to the acceleration of a pistol bullet. All nematocysts are used only once. After firing, they are replaced by newly formed capsules.

There are also non-venomous capsules called clinging capsules in the cnidarian's armoury. These do not have a powerful, tightly wound thread but a sticky one that is used to capture and hold onto prey. Very often, both varieties of capsule are located next to each other, in order to poison and detain the prey simultaneously.

Precautions

For any beach outing or dive trip, pack a first-aid kit that contains items appropriate for the creatures likely to be encountered: for cnidarian stings, it should include household vinegar, baking soda and concentrated magnesium sulphate.

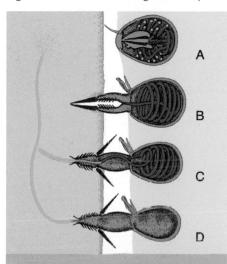

The nematocyst: nature's toxic dart

A nematocyst is a capsule-like cell with a double lining (A). At one end, its outside wall is turned inside to form an inverted, tightly coiled thread with stiletto-like barbs at its base that is packed into a venom sac. A bristle-like process outside the capsule, the cnidocil, serves as a trigger. If it is stimulated, the outer capsule wall tears open and the thread-like tube rolls out explosively with enough force to pierce the victim (B, C). The thread and venom are injected into the wound and barbs hold on (D). Not all nematocysts sting. Some non-venomous forms called clinging capsules glue or wrap their prey with a sticky thread. *(Modified from Mebs, 2002)*

First aid

With most venomous animals, the quantity of venom that enters the body is limited to what is injected during contact. In the case of cnidarians, the actions of the rescuers as well as the victim can result in further envenomation long after contact is broken. While contact results in immediate envenomation, numerous unfired nematocysts often continue to adhere to the skin. These pose an acute danger of firing with the slightest stimulation. It is therefore quite important that first-aid treatment prevents this from happening. Unfortunately, helpers or victims often take completely unsuitable measures, such as rubbing tentacles away. This actually forces the detonation of intact nematocysts. Appropriate first-aid treatment contains the damage by neutralising and removing unfired nematocysts, thereby preventing a far more severe poisoning.

What not to do

Do not rinse with fresh water or apply rubbing alcohol or formalin, and do not rub the affected areas or any adhering pieces of tentacle with a towel or any other object. These actions stimulate intact nematocysts to fire and worsen the victim's condition.

Recommended treatment

Remove the victim from the water immediately. Do not touch or disturb the affected areas in any way. In order to inactivate and remove unfired nematocysts and tentacle parts from the skin, the following measures are suggested:

box jellyfish (p.292): rinse with household vinegar (a 5 per cent solution).
compass and fire jellyfish (p.287): lightly wipe a paste made of baking soda (bicarbonate of soda) over the affected area.
fluorescent jellyfish (p.287): pour a solution of concentrated magnesium sulphate over the affected area.

If these resources are not immediately available, gently pour dry sand over the skin and then carefully scrape it off. Carefully use tweezers or a suitable substitute tool to lift away any tentacle parts still clinging to the skin. In the case of severe stings, seek immediate medical attention. These measures can mean the difference between life and death.

Divers soon learn to avoid brushing up against anything resembling a fern or feathers. This Fern Hydroid *Aglaophenia cuppressina* is common in nutrient-rich coastal waters of the western Pacific.

Hydrozaons
Class Hydrozoa

The class Hydrozoa includes about 3,200 species. They exhibit a great variety of forms, ranging from coral-like, feather-like or plant-like colonies, to jellyfish-like solitary and colonial pelagic forms. Most hydrozoans have both polyp and medusa stages, while others have only one or the other. Fire corals (p.273) and lace corals, the 'hydrocorals', are colonial forms with massive calcareous skeletons that superficially resemble stony corals. The hydromedusae are forms in which the jellyfish-like medusa stage is usually large and conspicuous and the colonial or hydroid stage is small and inconspicuous. The siphonophores (p.277) are quasi-colonial mid-water to surface forms that are divided into segments or sections that perform different functions. Many pack a nasty punch, and stings from the Portuguese Man-of-war can be fatal.

The term 'hydroid' as used here refers to an artificial assemblage of hydrozoans whose conspicuous life form resembles feathers, ferns, algae or fans. Some are actually more closely related to fire corals than to other more similar-looking hydrozoans. An exception is the hydroid stage of two species of the family Porpitidae (p.267), which are blue and float on the surface, and thus more closely resemble siphonophores. Hydroids range in size from tiny, inconspicuous, 1 cm-long strands to fan-like plumes 50 cm or more across. They are found in all marine waters from the poles to the tropics, and from the intertidal zone to the abyss.

Behaviour and life history

Hydroids are colonial animals consisting of a series of polyps attached to a wire-like stalk, which may be a single strand, branched or form a network. Colonies attach to almost any hard surface and are particularly successful on wrecks and other man-made structures that are not yet overgrown with other competing organisms. As with all hydrozoans, feather hydroids are filter-feeders that feed on plankton and other minute food particles brought in by the current. They therefore tend to be most abundant in turbid nutrient- and plankton-rich coastal waters than in clear offshore areas.

Hydroid polyps typically consist of two types, specialised either for catching prey or for reproducing. The reproductive stage is typically pelagic. Structures called buds develop, which are actually male and female medusae stacked like dishes. They detach and swim off to develop gonads and reproduce. The fertilised eggs develop into free-swimming larvae that eventually settle to the bottom and grow into new hydroids. Those of the Fern Hydroid *Aglaophenia cupressina* are pinecone-shaped cages of polyps called corbulae; these brood gonophores that drift to the bottom.

Most hydroids are short-lived but a few of the larger colonies probably persist for years. Their stinging power varies greatly, from imperceptible to a sudden and severe burning pain. Among the worst offenders are the Black-stemmed Hydroid *Macrorhynchia philippina*, Fern Hydroid, Seafan Hydroid *Solanderia gracilis*, and the Orange-stemmed Hydroid *Sertularella speciosa*.

Appearance

Depending on the species, hydroids can resemble tufts of feathers, ferns, algae or fans. They may occur as a single strand, be branched or form a network. They may be densely branched, robust and bushy, or sparsely branched and delicate. Like most of the hydrozoa, they have tiny polyps that attain a length of only 1–2 mm. Some are barely discernible to the naked eye, while others resemble a series of tiny but conspicuous bright dots or thick fern-like plumes. While the large, conspicuous species are easily seen and avoided, the inconspicuous ones can easily surprise even the most experienced diver.

Typical accidents

Most accidents occur when people inadvertently brush up against a hydroid. Swimmers

Venom apparatus

Many hydroids possess defensive polyps that are equipped with numerous nematocysts. These are often arranged in groups and distributed throughout the entire colony. The pinecone-like structures of the Fern Hydroid *Aglaophenia cupressina* (top) house reproductive gonophores. *(Bali, PM; southern FL, RM)*

never notice them, while inexperienced snorkellers and divers who are unaware of the danger often make no attempt to avoid them. Swimmers occasionally get stung by small hydroids attached to drifting seaweed. Divers typically get stung by inconspicuous hydroids as they accidentally or intentionally come in contact with the bottom. Most often affected are the exposed areas around the wrists and ankles. Fishermen get stung as they touch pieces of hydroids snagged by nets or fishing gear.

Prevention

Keep covered, as even light clothing provides a great deal of protection. If you need to touch any part of the bottom, look first and avoid brushing up against any unfamiliar fuzzy or feathery object.

Venom

Very little is known about hydroid venom. A small protein that supposedly weakens the

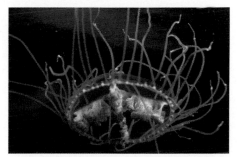

Looks can be deceiving. This hydromedusae *Olindias* sp. is not a jellyfish but the medusa stage of a hydrozoan. It can deliver a powerful sting and is wide ranging in tropical and temperate seas. *MK*

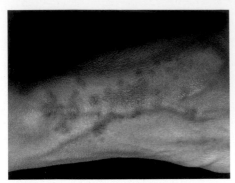

Contact with many species of hydroids results in a rash with small welts that may itch for more than a week. This rash was caused by the Fern Hydroid *Aglaophenia cupressina. MB*

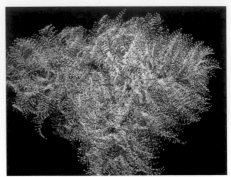

Hydroids are among the first organisms to colonise bare surfaces. This Christmas Tree Hydroid *Pennaria disticha* densely covers part of a shipwreck. *Mauritius, RM*

heart's circulatory system has been isolated from one species.

Envenomation and symptoms

Contact usually results in an immediate burning sensation. Depending on the hydroid as well as the sensitivity of the victim, the pain may range from a prickly itch to a severe piercing sting. Affected areas usually exhibit the following symptoms: redness of skin, swelling and hives. A blistery rash can form even hours after contact. Redness of the skin can last for several days or weeks. Severe itching may occur and last for sev-

eral days. In some cases, blisters can leave small lesions that take months or even years to disappear. People who suffer from allergies have more pronounced symptoms. Sensitisation and possibly anaphylactic shock can occur after repeated contact.

Classification and distribution

Most of the 3,200 known hydrozoan species have an attached hydroid stage. Their classification is based primarily on features that require microscopic examination as well as aspects of life history and can be quite bewildering. Many medusae and hydorid stages have never been matched but, when they are, their classification must be changed to reflect this and the oldest valid species name is retained. However they are classified, hydroids of one kind or another occur in all seas and at all depths, and many of them have the potential to cause painful stings or rashes. A few of the more conspicuous species are easily identified while many others are not. A relatively large portion of those species familiar to divers are widely distributed, with many occurring worldwide in tropical and temperate seas.

Treatment

First aid

No particular treatment is usually necessary. Where there is a slight skin reaction, a mild ointment can be applied. Over-the-counter anticortisone creams may be effective at easing itching. In cases where there is an unpleasant and persistent skin reaction or considerable pain occurs, consult a doctor.

What not to do

Do not scratch or disturb affected areas.

Ongoing medical management

It is recommended that people who have allergic reactions undergo a cortisone or antihistamine treatment. Antibiotic creams may help prevent infection of long-lasting open blisters.

Seafan Hydroid
Solanderiidae

Seafan Hydroid	<20 cm
Solanderia secunda	*(<8 in)*

Orange to red stem branches in a single plane; polyps white. **Biology:** inhabits caves and crevices of seaward reef slopes, 5–120 m. Usually hangs from ceiling. **Range:** Red Sea to Hawaii and Tuamotus, n. to s. Japan. **Similar:** *S. gracilis* occurs throughout the Caribbean.

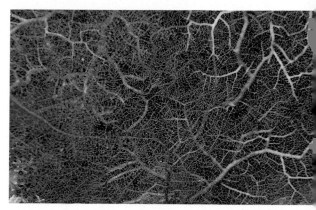

Pelagic Hydroids
Porpitidae

Blue Button	<4 cm
Porpita porpita	*(<1.6 in)*

Transparent blue disc with radiating branches that resemble tentacles; polyps blue. **Biology:** pelagic, floats on surface of open sea. Periodically washes ashore in large numbers during strong winds. Sting imperceptible to some, painful to others. **Range:** all warm seas.

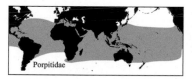

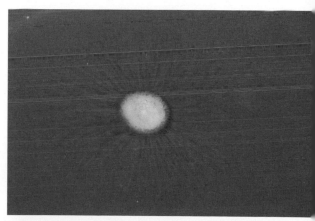

By-the-wind Sailor	<10 cm
Valella valella	*(<4 in)*

Transparent oblong disc with semicircular crest above and blue skirt with blue tentacles below. **Biology:** pelagic, floats on surface of open sea. May wash ashore in large numbers after periods of strong wind. Sting mild to unnoticed in most people. **Range:** all warm seas. **Similar:** *Physalia* spp. have a gas-filled float (p.280).

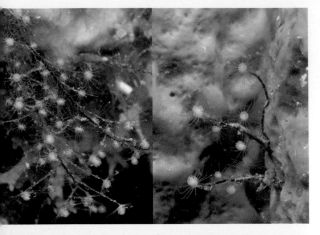

Solitary Hydroids
Tubulariidae

Solitary Gorgonian Hydroid	3 cm
Ralpharia gorgoniae	*(1.2 in)*

Large, solitary white polyp with long tentacles whose tips curl when disturbed; lacks medusa stage. **Biology:** inhabits seaward reef terraces, 5–20 m. Attached to tips of gorgonian branches, particularly of Sea Plume *Pseudopterogorgia* sp., which are dead for a length of <5 cm. Stings strongly. **Range:** Bahamas and Caribbean. **Similar:** other spp. of *Ralpharia* and *Tubularia* are often associated with other invertebrates.

Christmas Tree Hydroid
Pennariidae

Christmas Tree Hydroid	<8 cm
Pennaria disticha	*(<3.2 in)*

Single dark stems with alternating branches bearing white polyps on upper sides. **Biology:** in a variety of habitats, particularly bare surfaces of wrecks, buoys and drifting debris. Common in well-lit, nutrient-rich areas with moderate water movement. Can form clumps up to 30 cm across. Sting barely perceptible to some, but powerful to others, causing persistent burning pain. *Pennaria tiarella* and *Halocordyle disticha* are invalid names used in many books. **Range:** all warm seas.

Tuft Hydroids
Halopterididae

Yellow Tuft Hydroid	<15 cm
Antennellopsis integerrima	*(<6 in)*

Tuft of radiating single filaments, each with well-spaced yellow polyps on one side. **Biology:** inhabits reef outcrops exposed to currents, 1 m to over 20 m. Uncommon in most areas. **Range:** W. Pacific, n. to s. Japan. **Similar:** *Antennella* and *Nemertesia* occur in tropical and temperate waters around the world.

Fern Hydroids
Aglaopheniidae

Fern Hydroid   <60 cm
Aglaophenia cupressina   (<24 in)

Large, robust and repeatedly branching, with tiny polyps on one side of ultimate branches; forms thick straw-yellow to golden-brown fernlike clumps. **Biology**: inhabits coastal to offshore reefs, 1–30 m. Particularly abundant in nutrient-rich areas but also common and conspicuous on clear offshore reefs. Stings strongly, leaving extremely itchy rash with small welts that can last up to 3 weeks. Preyed upon by the nudibranch *Doto ussi*. **Range**: E. Africa to w. Pacific, n. to at least s. Japan.

Maroon Hydroid   <25 cm
Aglaophenia sp.   (<10 in)

Alternating secondary branches at shallow angle rather than on same plane; maroon. **Biology:** forms bushy clumps in shallow exposed areas. Probably stings strongly, as bad as *A. cupressina* (above) **Range:** w. Pacific; w. Papua and, possibly, Marshall Is.

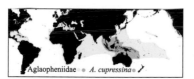

Aglaopheniidae ● *A. cupressina* ●

Graceful Feather Hydroid   <15 cm
Gymnangium graciliacaule   (<6 in)

Small groups of feather-like plumes, each with branches alternating along either side of central stalk. **Biology:** Stings strongly. **Range:** Red Sea to Marianas, n. to s. Japan, s. to w. Australia. **Similar:** Golden Quill Hydroid *G. hians* is smaller, golden brown; Golden Feather Hydroid *G. eximium* is similar but may be branched (both to 10 cm; Red Sea to Polynesia); other similar spp. occur in all shallow seas from the tropics to sub-polar regions.

Black-stemmed Hydroid   <20 cm
Macrorhynchia philippina   (<8 in)

Stem and main branches black, alternating terminal branches white with tiny white polyps (incl. terminal polyp) and curved. **Biology:** inhabits sheltered inshore to exposed offshore areas, 1–200 m. Forms small clumps to bushes of 20 cm height on exposed surfaces exposed to currents. Stings strongly. **Range:** Circumtropical; NC to Brazil in w. Atlantic. **Similar:** Black Hydroid *Lytocarpia niger* is uniformly dark brown to black, occurs in short clumps of <5 cm in crevices of exposed areas (Indo-Pacific).

White Stinger   <30 cm
Macrorhynchia phoenicea   (<12 in)

Clumps of feather-like branches in single plane; primary and secondary branches white, terminal branches dark reddish brown; resembles large flattened feather. **Biology:** inhabits exposed areas, 7 m to at least 35 m. Common in high-energy areas. Stings strongly. **Range:** S. Africa to Hawaii, incl. Marianas Is and ne. Australia.

M. philippina • *M. phoenicea*

Orange-stemmed Hydroids
Sertulariidae

Orange-stemmed Hydroid   <20 cm
Sertularia sp.   (<8 in)

Stout central stalk with alternating branches in one plane and large alternating polyps; stalk and branches orange, polyps pale yellow. **Biology:** often near the entrance to caves and on shipwrecks. Often with filamentous red algae growing among the hydroids. Sting mild, moderate in sensitive areas. **Range:** Red Sea (?) to Fiji. **Similar:** many spp. in all warm seas. Positive identification requires close examination of polyps. Orange-stemmed Hydroid *Sertularella speciosa* inhabits the Caribbean area.

Yellow-polyp Hydroid <8 cm
Cnidoscyphus sp. *(<3.2 in)*

Stout central stalk with alternating branches bearing alternating polyps; stalk and branches reddish orange, polyps pale yellow with tall stems. **Biology:** inhabits dead patches among corals, 1–40 m. Typically in small clusters and partially overgrown with filamentous algae. Sting mild, moderate in sensitive areas. **Range:** w. Pacific. **Similar:** many spp. in all warm seas. Positive identification requires close examination of polyps.

Stinging Bush Hydroid <30 cm
Sertularia sp. *(<12 in)*

Thick branching stem with secondary branches in one plane bearing small alternating polyps; stem and branches reddish orange. **Biology:** forms large bushes on exposed, well-illuminated surfaces, 6–30 m. Can sting, but virulence unknown. Misidentified as *Plumularia* sp. in one book. **Range:** w. Pacific. **Similar:** most *Sertularia* species form small, low clumps and occur in dark recesses.

Algae Hydroid <12 cm
Thyroscyphus ramosus *(<4.7 in)*

Tangle of stout stalks with branches in all directions bearing large alternating polyps; stalk and branches orange, polyps pale yellow. **Biology:** inhabits protected coastal to exposed offshore areas, 1–40 m. Can form large bushy masses on debris and wreckage. Often covered with fine algae and clogged with sediment. Sting mild, moderate in sensitive areas. **Range:** FL and Caribbean. **Similar:** many spp. of *Eudendrium, Bougainvillia,* and *Obelia*. All require close examination for positive identification.

Fire Corals
Milleporidae

Fire corals are often mistaken for stony corals owing to their similar hard calcareous skeletons. However, they aren't corals at all but belong to the class Hydrozoa, making them distant relatives of hydroids and harmless stylasterine lace corals. Like stony corals, fire corals play an important role in reef-building by overgrowing and binding together loose rubble and other objects while they are alive, and contributing to the reef framework after they die. Although they include only a handful of species, their abundance in shallow waters and innocuous appearance result in a disproportionately large share of painful injuries to swimmers, snorkellers and divers.

Behaviour and life history
Like the reef-building stony corals, fire corals incorporate zooxanthellae, symbiotic single-celled algae, in their tissues. It is a perfect partnership that profits both the algae and the fire coral. Through the process of photosynthesis, the algae use the energy in sunlight to synthesise oxygen and sugars from the coral's waste products. The coral feeds on the sugars and absorbs the oxygen during respiration, and in turn provides shelter and the nutrients in its waste to feed the algae. This requires that fire corals live in shallow reef areas exposed to strong sunlight. In clear, sunlit waters they can form massive colonies rivalling many of those of stony corals. Like stony corals, fire corals vary greatly in their growth form, which ranges from encrusting to massive to branching both within and between species. While most species have their greatest abundance in shallow areas of less than 6 m, some occur as deep as 40 m.

Appearance
Fire corals have hard calcareous skeletons that give them the general appearance of stony corals. However, at a distance they look much smoother since their polyps are nearly microscopic in size. On close inspection, one sees that the surface is covered by numerous minute pores, each housing a tiny polyp (the genus

Young fire coral colonies often encrust other objects and take on their shape. Here, a Branching Fire Coral *Millepora alcicornis* has overgrown a gorgonian. *Curaçao, RM*

name *Millepora* means 'thousand pores'). When the hair-like stinging polyps are extended, the fire coral has a slightly fuzzy appearance. Fire corals vary in form, from large upright sheets and blades to branching fans and bushes, as well as low encrustations. Although each species has a characteristic growth form, this can be affected by environmental conditions, so identification of some colonies is not always clear-cut. This is particularly true for young colonies, which simply take on the shape of the object they encrust. Whatever their shape, fire corals are always rather drab in colour – usually mustard-yellow to pale reddish brown with pale branch tips.

Typical accidents
Because fire corals are often found just beneath the surface, snorkellers, divers and swimmers alike are at risk of being stung. Most swimmers and novice snorkellers are unaware of the danger. In many areas frequented by swimmers and novice snorkellers, the high density of fire corals makes their sting one of the most frequent types of nematocyst poisoning. Injury usually happens simply by accidentally brushing against them. In some cases, waves or turbulence can actually detach polyps or branch tips and cause minor stings from a distance.

Prevention
Avoid contact, and take care to maintain a safe distance when swimming above a reef. Divers

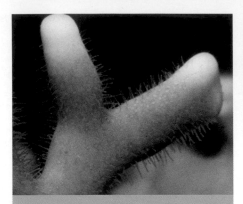

Venom apparatus

Fire corals are colonies of numerous tiny polyps of two kinds that serve different functions. The longer polyps are used for protection and are wellequipped with stinging cells. The shorter polyps are used for feeding. (*Millepora dichotoma*, Red Sea, MB)

should also take care to maintain proper buoyancy. Take special care when getting in and out of the water, as fire corals also grow around shallow reef margins. Wetsuits or light clothing offer good protection.

Venom
Fire coral venom contains a protein that affects blood cells and kills skin tissue.

Envenomation and symptoms
Contact with the fire coral causes an immediate intense burning pain, similar to that caused by

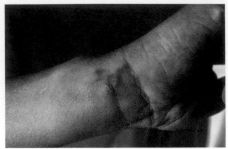

Typical rash and welts seen a few hours after contact with *Millepora dichotoma*. MB

Swimmers and snorkellers are the most frequent victims of contact with fire corals. *Red Sea, MK*

nettles. Although the pain subsides quickly, the skin often becomes red and swollen. In more serious stings, weals or blisters develop. Redness and itching can last several days to weeks.

Classification and distribution
There are only about 11 valid species of fire coral, all in the genus *Millepora*. Three occur in the tropical western Atlantic and eight in the Indian Ocean and east Pacific. With the exception of Hawaii and a few remote parts of Polynesia, fire corals occur in every coral reef area. In the species accounts, size refers to typical maximum heights of the living portion of colonies. Exceptional colonies or those overgrowing older dead portions can get much larger.

IF INJURED

Treatment

First aid
Avoid further contact and aggravation of affected areas. Skin irritations caused by fire corals rarely require medical treatment.

What not to do
Do not rub or scratch the site of injury.

Ongoing medical management
A mild salve or skin lotion may help relieve the irritation.

Distribution of fire corals, genus *Millepora*.

Net Fire Coral
Millepora dichotoma
<60 cm
(<24 in)

Narrow interlocking branches form fans, mostly in single plane. **Biology:** primarily along exposed reef slopes, 1–36 m. Abundant along clear shallow reef margins, also along edges of deep current-swept shelves. Grows transverse to current for optimal exposure to plankton. Contact results in intense burning pain followed by welts and rash. **Range:** Red Sea and S. Africa to Samoa and Johnston Atoll. **Similar:** *M. tenera* has branches that are primarily bifurcate; may be in single plane but often forms clumps (E. Africa to Samoa, n. to Ryukyus).

Plate Fire Coral
Millepora platyphylla
<60 cm
(<24 in)

Irregular interlocking plates in stands to several metres across; surface smooth to knobbly. **Biology:** inhabits upper margins of outer reef and lagoon slopes, as well as clear reef flats, 1–15 m. More common in less exposed areas than *M. dichotoma* (above). May overgrow corals. Small surface knobs are due to infestation of barnacles. Also hosts Christmas Tree Worm *Spirobranchus giganteus*, vermetid molluscs and the bivalve *Pteria aegyptiaca*. Sting is not severe. **Range:** Red Sea and S. Africa to Samoa and Johnston Atoll. **Similar:** *M. latifolia* forms thicker knobbly plates and has distinctly greener hue (w. Pacific).

Intricate Fire Coral
Millepora intricata
<1.5 m
(<5 ft)

Fine interlocking branches form mounds to 150 cm tall and 200 cm across; mustard-yellow to nearly white. **Biology:** inhabits outer reef flats and shallow protected slopes, 1 m to over 10 m. Common in Indonesia and Philippines. **Range:** Indonesia and Philippines to New Caledonia, n. to Ryukyus; e. Pacific. **Similar:** densely packed *M. tenera* (above) may be difficult to distinguish.

M. intricata ●●●
M. dichotoma ●●●   M. platyphylla ●●●

Branching Fire Coral   <60 cm
Millepora alcicornis   *(<24 in)*

Narrow cylindrical branches form fans to 60 cm tall in stands to 2 m across; fans usually in single plane but may randomly branch. May completely overgrow and take on the shape of gorgonians and other objects. **Biology:** primarily along exposed upper portions of reef slopes, 1–39 m. Abundant on clear outer reef slopes and shelves, usually deeper than *M. complanata*. Produces intense but short-lived burning pain, followed by welts and rash lasting several days. **Range:** s. FL, Bahamas and throughout Caribbean.

Blade Fire Coral   <1 m
Millepora complanata   *(<3.3 ft)*

Irregular interlocking plates to 1 m tall and 3 m across; blades usually thin, surface usually smooth. **Biology:** primarily along exposed upper portions of reef slopes, 1–14 m. Most common on shallow, semi-protected sandy terraces of outer reef slopes. **Range:** s. FL, Bahamas and throughout Caribbean. **Similar:** Box Fire Coral *M. squarrosa* has low, thick-walled, irregular chambers (Caribbean).

M. alcicornis & M. complanata

Red Fire Coral   <15 cm
Millepora tuberosa   *(<6 in)*

Forms inconspicuous, low, rounded encrusting knobs to 15 cm tall and 100 cm across; ochre to tan. **Biology:** inhabits exposed outer reef flats and upper slopes, below 1 m. Hosts vermetid molluscs. Sting is not severe. **Range:** Partly in the Indo-Pacific. **Similar:** *M. exaesa* forms massive knobbly encrustations up to 3 m or more across, and is mustard-yellow to greenish (E. Africa to e. Pacific).

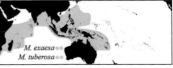

M. exaesa ●●●
M. tuberosa ●●●

Siphonophores
Subclass Siphonophora

Siphonophores are among the world's strangest creatures. They are best described as quasi-colonies of differently adapted polyps and medusae that collectively behave like a single organism. Some polyps are dedicated to catching prey, while others are involved in food digestion or reproduction. The latter develop medusae that remain attached and produce sperm and eggs or, in some species, provide propulsion. All parts share an interconnected digestive tube.

Siphonophores come in a variety of shapes and sizes, but generally have a gas- or oil-filled float or large swimming bell attached to a trailing string of polyps and tentacles. Most species remain beneath the surface and get about by contractions of their medusae or by changing the amount of gas in their floats. Men-of-war are unique in having a float that remains on the surface. They are well known for their powerful stings but little is known of the other siphonophore species. Many of them are certainly capable of stinging and all should be considered potentially dangerous.

Men-of-war
Physalia physalis and P. utriculus

Behaviour and life history
On the water's surface, only a pretty iridescent bluish bubble is seen. However, this is only the

Men-of-war consist of a clear float with bulbous polyps and tentacles that hang below. *Physalia utriculus* has a single very long tentacle. *Guam, RM*

tip of the iceberg. The largest portion, with the dangerous weaponry, lurks beneath. This is *Physalia*, the man-of-war, whose tentacles can extend 20 m below. *Physalia* is an active hunter whose contractile tentacles can be lengthened or shortened at will. It drifts with the wind, combing the upper surfaces of the ocean for prey. Anything small enough to be caught and held is immediately paralysed and then transported to special feeding polyps under the gas-filled float. Prey typically consists of small fishes. From a biological standpoint, *Physalia* is not a single animal like a jellyfish. Instead, it is a collection of differently adapted polyps and medusae that together behave like one. Each type is dedicated to a particular function, such as catching prey, digesting food or reproduction, and all share an interconnected digestive tube. *Physalia* is unable to swim or make any movement other than the contraction of individual polyps or tentacles. The gas-filled float remains on the water's surface and its sail-like crest enables it to drift with the wind. Converging winds can gather the colonies into vast swarms up to 12 km in length. When such swarms encounter land, long stretches of coast may be infested with men-of-war that wash ashore.

Appearance
To 17th-century European sailors, *Physalia* resembled a miniature warship, hence the name Portuguese Man-of-war. A *Physalia* consists of a

somewhat elongate asymmetrical float that tapers at one end, has a sail-like crest along its top, and has bulbous polyps and tentacles that hang on one side or the other, making it possible to distinguish between right-handed and left-handed colonies. The float is a shimmering pale bluish purple, and the polyps and tentacles are blue and purple. Two species have been described, distinguished primarily by size and number of elongate tentacles, and development of the sail-like crest, but otherwise identical. Both forms are more easily seen from the surface than from beneath. All other siphonophores live entirely below the surface.

Typical accidents
Swimmers are especially at risk, particularly during windy and choppy conditions, when *Physalia* is more difficult to see. Usually an unseen tentacle wraps partially around a victim, who often reacts by thrashing about. This leads to further contact with the tentacles and a more severe poisoning. Divers are also occasionally stung, not only at the surface but below, since the tentacles can extend by as much as 20 m. Although often unnoticed, the float is relatively easy to see, but the tentacles are nearly invisible, particularly when fully stretched. Fishermen are occasionally stung by pieces of tentacle that become entangled in their equipment. Waders are often stung around the legs, and even barefoot beachgoers get stung when they step on beached *Phyaslia*. The nematocysts are unusually robust and can remain active for some time after a beached colony dies and dries out, and detached tentacles can continue to drift and retain their stinging force. Most incidents are painful encounters with small *Physalia*, which do not require medical attention and leave no lasting damage. Occasionally, however, very large *Physalia* are encountered that can cause life-threatening envenomation.

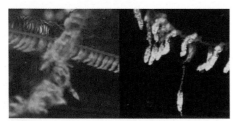

Most siphonophores live beneath the surface. Some, like these Swimming Bells *Praya* sp., have a gas-filled float. Many can deliver a powerful sting and so are potentially dangerous. *Southern FL, PM*

Venom apparatus

The diaphanous float is smooth and free of nematocysts. The blue parts – the bulb-like polyps and tentacles – bear dark blue clusters of nematocysts. The tentacles can be spirally contracted or stretched to a length of over 20 m in large colonies. A 9 m tentacle can contain more than 750,000 bulb-shaped nematocysts. *(PNG, MB)*

Prevention
Stinger suits (thin overalls made of synthetic fibres such as Lycra) and wetsuits provide protection only to the areas they cover. Divers and swimmers should keep a lookout for *Physalia* and maintain their distance, and if more than one is seen they should leave the water. Do not swim, wade or walk barefoot in areas with beached colonies, and avoid touching any stranded *Physalia*. Although the clear float can be handled safely, the slightest slip or gust of wind can cause contact with a tentacle.

Venom
Man-of-war venom is a complex mixture of various proteins, including physalia toxin. It causes intense pain and skin necrosis (death of skin cells), and may directly attack the heart muscle, producing irritation and unstable rhythm. Physalia toxin affects cell membranes, which results in a haemolytic reaction (damage to the red blood cells). The venom rapidly releases histamine and antibodies that are found in the connective tissue throughout the human body. This

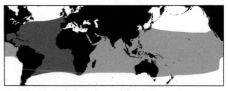

Distribution of *Physalia* and fatal encounters.

causes intense pain, an expansion of the blood vessels, and an allergic reaction in some.

Envenomation and symptoms

Contact with nematocysts results in immediate intense pain. If a large area is stung, the pain spreads rapidly and becomes unbearable. An itchy skin rash (urticaria) soon develops. Out-stretched tentacles leave narrow weal patterns, while contracted tentacles leave a characteristic pattern that resembles a string of beads. Severe envenomation leads to the development of blisters, ranging in size from a pinhead to several centimetres in diameter, and frequently results in skin or tissue necrosis. General symptoms include shock, vomiting, nausea, dimming of consciousness, fever, and breathing and circulatory disorders. The few known fatalities were caused by heart failure, circulatory stoppage or drowning due to sudden loss of consciousness.

Classification and distribution

About 150 species of siphonophores, distributed in three orders, are known. The two described species of men-of-war are the only ones with a surface float and are distinguished from one another by size and number of elongate tentacles alone. The Portuguese Man-of-war *Physalia physalis* gets up to 30 cm across, with several tentacles that can reach a length of over 20 m. It occurs primarily in the Atlantic but has also been

Sample cases

1) **Fatal case:** Off North Carolina, a 30-year-old recreational diver surfaced into the tentacles of a *Physalia*. He managed to shed his weightbelt and called for help. Three people quickly reached him but he was already unconscious. He remained unconscious despite immediate life-saving actions. He was airlifted to hospital but was dead on arrival. Although his body was protected by a neoprene suit, both his arms displayed severe stings.

2) **Non-fatal case:** Off the coast of Goa, India, a 31-year-old woman was stung by a *Physalia*. She managed to return to the beach on her own, then collapsed. She was treated at a local hospital but her condition remained critical. After four days she was flown home to Germany and treated in the intensive-care unit of a university hospital, where she subsequently recovered.

Treatment

First aid

Remove the victim from the water immediately since there is a danger of sudden loss of consciousness. The intense pain may cause irrational and very emotional behaviour, so try to calm the victim. Movement should be avoided since it could intensify the pain. Ensure that affected areas are not touched to prevent the detonation of unfired nematocysts. Monitor breathing, pulse and signs of shock. If breathing stops, immediately apply artificial respiration and, if necessary, external heart massage. Formerly, the recommended treatment of affected areas was the application of 5 per cent vinegar. However, in Australia it has been reported that vinegar did not deter the firing of nematocysts and may result in further envenomation. The current recommended treatment is to remove tentacles that cling to the skin carefully with a pair of tweezers or gloves. Dry sand can be poured over the area and then carefully scraped off. With the exception of minor encounters with small *Physalia*, medical care should be sought. In severe cases the victim should be swiftly transported to hospital.

What not to do

Do not rinse with vinegar or any other liquid including fresh or saltwater, since this may stimulate the detonation of unfired nematocysts. Do not rub the affected areas with sand, towels or any other object.

Ongoing medical management

Treatment with ointments, sprays or lotions containing lidocaine has shown varying success. Antihistamine or cortisone treatments are ineffective. There is no anti-venom for physalia toxin. Treatment must be in response to the symptoms. Be prepared for heart-muscle or circulatory problems, or even sudden respiratory stoppage. Shock should be treated normally by administering intravenous adrenalin.

found in parts of the Indo-Pacific. The Blue-bottle or Pacific Man-of-war *P. utriculus* reaches only 5–8 cm across, has fewer tentacles and usually only one long one that can reach a length of about 5 m. Until definitive genetic studies are carried out, the accurate assignment of *Physalia* morphs into distinct species remains unresolved.

Order Cystonecta
Man-of-war
Physaliidae

Portuguese Man-of-war   <30 cm
Physalia physalis   (<12 in)

Clear elongate float with large mass of short and long contractile blue tentacles hanging beneath that can stretch to 20 m. **Biology:** inhabits surface of open sea, with tentacles hanging below. Concentrates in wind-blown drifts, which occasionally wash ashore in large numbers. Large colonies often accompanied by several Man-of-war Fish *Nomeus gronovii*. **Range:** Tropical and temperate Atlantic and parts of Indo-Pacific. **Similar:** *P. utriculus* (below) is smaller, has single long tentacle.

Blue Bottle   <8 cm
Physalia utriculus   (<3.2 in)

Clear elongate float with clump of short blue tentacles and, usually, a single long contractile blue tentacle hanging beneath that can stretch to 5 m. **Biology:** inhabits surface of open sea, with tentacles hanging below. Concentrates in wind-blown drifts, which occasionally wash ashore in large numbers. **Range:** Tropical and temperate Indian Oceanand e. Pacific. **Similar:** *P. physalis* (above) gets larger and has multiple long tentacles. *Porpita porpita* and *Valella valella* (p.267) appear somewhat similar by having transparent floats and blue tentacles, but are hydroids rather than siphonophores.

Order Calycophora
Swimming Bells
Prayidae

Swimming Bells	<15 cm
Praya sp.	*(<6 in)*

Pair of bells trailing long contractile tentacle below, this bearing yellow feeding and stinging structures; tentacle can stretch to several metres. **Biology:** in open water with tentacle hanging below. When feeding, rotates in water to sweep tentacle in wide spiral pattern. Likely to be capable of delivering painful stings. **Range:** uncertain, probably in all warm seas. **Similar:** several spp. have similar bells with arrays of tentacles hanging below. Members of order Physonecta have an apical gas-filled float. All should be considered dangerous.

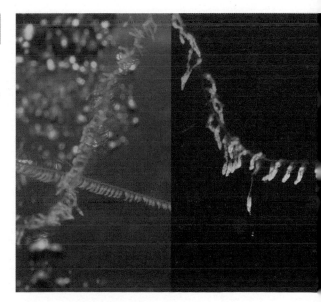

Many jellyfishes are quite beautiful. This Lung Jellyfish has a relatively mild sting. *Mediterranean, MB*

Jellyfishes
Class Scyphozoa

Jellyfishes have an evil reputation, and their appearance causes swimmers to leave the water and beachgoers to stay ashore. They are perhaps the most familiar of all the venomous ocean-dwellers. This is because they are often washed into coves or onto beaches, where they can be seen by even those who never enter the water. Jellyfishes are found in all seas, from the tropics to the poles. The 250 or so known species vary greatly in size and shape, from tiny 1 cm thimbles to 2 m-wide blobs with masses of tentacles. The result of contact with jellyfishes can vary considerably, both between species and between individuals of the same species. Many jellyfish species can cause violent and painful stings, and are justifiably feared. However, even contact with those species that are considered harmless can occasionally result in unpleasant consequences.

Behaviour and life history
Most jellyfishes move slowly through the water, propelled by the rhythmic pulses of their dome-shaped bells. They can occur anywhere between the surface and the bottom. Others migrate up or down at different times of the day or night, and some remain close to the bottom. Jellyfishes have considerable control over where they go but are helpless in strong currents or rough seas. At these times they may become concentrated in areas frequented by humans or even cast ashore.

Jellyfishes feed on any small organism unlucky enough to blunder into their tentacles. Their prey is stung and immobilised by batteries of nematocysts, then reeled into the bell by contractile tentacles, where it is drawn into a digestive chamber. Most species feed primarily on small fishes and pelagic crustaceans, as well as zooplankton. A few, including the Compass Jellyfish *Chrysaora hysoscella*, feed on other jellyfishes. Some jellyfishes incorporate symbiotic single-celled algae called zooxanthellae into their tissues, which may provide a portion of their nutrition. One group, the upside-down jellyfishes, takes this to the extreme by spending most of their time upside down in the shallows in order to expose their zooxanthelae to the maximum available sunlight.

Most jellyfishes alternate generations between polyp and medusa stages. The jellyfish that we are familiar with is the medusa stage, which is typically large and free-swimming. The polyp stage is usually minute – often only a few millimetres across and inconspicuous – and is attached to the bottom, where it remains unseen among the myriad of other organisms. Some jellyfishes, including the Luminescent Jellyfish *Pelagia noctiluca* and several deep-water species, do not have a sedentary polyp generation at all. The young medusae of these species hatch from eggs that are released directly into the water. Most jellyfishes are hermaphrodites and some, including the Compass Jellyfish, are capable of self-fertilisation, releasing their larvae directly into the water. Most jellyfishes have short lifespans of under a year. In many areas they appear seasonally or sporadically in large numbers and grow rapidly, feeding on blooms of plankton or the small fishes and other animals that feed on the plankton.

Appearance

Most jellyfishes have the familiar dome-shaped round 'bell', with tentacles trailing from the rim or oral arms, tentacle-like extensions of the mouth, hanging directly beneath the bell. Shape

Owing to their transparency, jellyfishes are often not recognised until it is too late and they have already stung their victim. This is especially true of sunny, shallow stretches of water like here, making this Moon Jelly *Aurelia* sp. hard spot.

Upside-down jellyfishes like this *Cassiopea xamachana* spend most of their time inverted to maximise their symbiotic algae's exposure to sunlight. If disturbed, they can release free-floating nematocysts, but their sting is usually mild. *Southern FL, RM*

and structure vary between the families. Bell shape varies from well rounded to conical and from high-vaulted to flattened. The bell of most species is smooth, but in some it is dotted with wart-like clumps of nematocysts. The jellyfishes' primary food-gathering weapons, the tentacles and oral arms, are armed with batteries of nematocysts. Tentacles may be long or short and wispy or robust. The structure of the oral arms ranges from frilly curtain-like ribbons and complexly branched clumps, to smooth and rope-like. Colour pattern varies considerably and is more useful for distinguishing species than families. Opacity also varies greatly, from highly transparent to opaque. Most species are slightly transparent, which usually makes their internal structure quite visible.

Typical accidents

Owing to the periodic appearance of jellyfish on all coasts, accidents involving them are relatively common. Swimmers and waders are most frequently affected since they usually don't see jellyfishes before being stung. Although divers

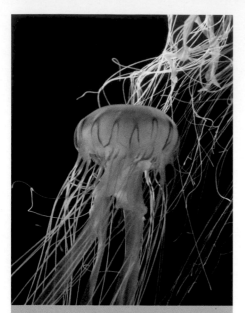

Venom apparatus

The venom of all jellyfishes is delivered exclusively through the firing of microscopic nematocysts. In many species, nematocysts occur only on the tentacles, where they are distributed along the entire length in well-ordered bands, rows or clumps. Other species, including this Luminescent Jellyfish *Pelagia noctiluca*, also have nematocyst-bearing extensions of the mouth called oral arms, which extend from the centre of the bell. Some, including *Pelagia*, have batteries of nematocysts in wart-like clumps over the outer surface of the bell. In general, areas of the bell that are smooth are free of nematocysts.

Prevention

Swimmers and waders should scan both the beach and water carefully for any signs of jellyfishes before entering. At the first sign of a jellyfish other than known, relatively harmless short-tentacled varieties, they should keep well clear, and if more than one or two are seen, they should probably leave the water. They should wear light clothing as this provides effective protection from most stings. Divers should take care to maintain sufficient distance from any jellyfish, particularly if they are viewing it from the underside, as virtually invisible tentacles may trail down. They should also become familiar with common jellyfish species in order to judge how close they can safely get. Beachgoers should avoid touching stranded jellyfishes and wear some sort of footwear when exploring. When large swarms appear, it is best to avoid the water altogether. Everyone should be aware that sting intensity can vary within a species and that 'harmless' species can have a sensitising effect. This means that a species that once caused no problems can suddenly be harmful. Anyone who is allergic to bee stings or other venoms should be particularly careful.

Venom

The venom of only a few species of jellyfish has been studied. In all cases thus far, it has been found to be a mixture of proteins or proteins and enzymes. The venoms of *Pelagia noctiluca*, *Cyanea capillata* and *Chrysaora quinquecirrha* attack the heart muscle. The primary toxin of *Cyanea capillata* has a molecular weight of 70,000. It disturbs the rhythm of the pulse and can cause tachycardia (sustained rapid heartbeat), which can lead to cardiac arrest. The venom of *Chrysaora quinquecirrha* has been particularly well studied. It also has neurotoxic components that change the permeability of cell membranes to calcium and sodium, as well as collagenase enzymes that cause skin necrosis. As the venom of more species is studied, it would be reasonable to assume that a greater variety of components will be found.

Symptoms

Symptoms of envenomation vary greatly between species and can also vary within a species. Contact with the tentacles of *Pelagia noctiluca*, *Cyanea capillata* and *Chrysaora quinquecirrha* results in an immediate piercing to burning pain that may be short-lived or can last for a few hours. Swelling may occur and red welts may appear. Contact with *Pelagia* tentacles

stand a better chance of seeing jellyfishes since they are more visible from beneath the surface, they too occasionally blunder into unseen tentacles. Fishermen also get stung when they encounter jellyfishes or pieces of them that break off on their nets or other equipment. Even dust from dried-out remains of jellyfishes can irritate the eyes, skin and lungs. Barefoot beachgoers can get stung when they step on jellyfishes or tentacles that are washed ashore.

may result in hives, as well as small blisters that may take a very long time to heal. Permanent scarring or traces of dark pigmentation can result. Swelling and welts caused by *Cyanea* may last up to two days. Severe cases of envenomation by *Chrysaora quinquecirrha* can result in skin necrosis, where areas of skin die and slough off. Especially widespread skin contact can cause general symptoms, including nausea, vomiting, a feeling of weakness, headaches, muscular pain and, rarely, unconsciousness. Sensitisation to the venom by repeated contact is possible and could result in anaphylactic shock. No deaths have been reported as a direct result of stings from these species, but severe stings have resulted in drowning. At least one death has been attributed to scyphozoan jellyfish in the Adriatic, but the authors could find no mention of the identity of the offending species. In northeast China, several deaths have resulted from massive envenomation by the metre-wide *Stomolophus nomurai*. These deaths were the result of cardiac arrest and pulmonary oedema (swelling and fluid in the lungs).

'Harmless' jellyfish
Many jellyfish sting only slightly on contact. Such encounters are unpleasant but not dangerous. Some jellyfish can even be touched without any effect. However, the stinging power of many jellyfishes of the same species can vary by location or time period. Furthermore, some people are more sensitive than others or are allergic to stings. Therefore, care is recommended even with those jellyfish that are regarded as harmless. Some of the jellyfish species considered harmless owing to their mild sting are the Compass Jellyfish *Chrysaora hysoscella*, the Lung Jellyfish *Rhizostoma pulmo*, the Moon Jelly *Aurelia aurita*, the Mediterranean Jellyfish *Cotylorhiza tuberculata* and the Cauliflower Jellyfish *Cephea cephea*.

Classification and distribution
The 250 known species of scyphozoans are distributed in four orders. They vary greatly in size and shape, from tiny 1 cm thimbles to 2 m-wide mop-like masses of tentacles, and occur in all marine waters at all depths. The stauromedusae are tiny semi-mobile attached forms that lack a free-swimming medusa stage and live primarily in cold waters. The three remaining orders, together known as 'scypho-medusae', are what we think of as jellyfishes.

Treatment
First aid
Leave the water immediately. If possible, for stings by *Pelagia* rinse affected areas with a solution of magnesium sulphate, and for stings by *Chrysaora quinquecirrha* apply a thick paste of baking soda (bicarbonate of soda). Otherwise, pour on dry sand and then very carefully scrape it off with a clean, fine edge such as the back of a knife. Remove any tentacle remains by lifting them with tweezers or any effective substitute. (For box jellyfish stings, see p.295.) In severe cases, seek medical attention.

What not to do
Do not rinse with fresh water, alcohol, urine or any other liquid. Do not rub the area with a towel. Such treatment stimulates the firing of intact nematocysts. The affected area may be cleaned with fresh water only after all traces of tentacles and unfired nematocysts have been removed.

Ongoing medical management
Clean the affected areas. Apply a skin ointment, such as lidocaine, as a local anaesthetic. Antihistamine or cortisone treatments are ineffective. In the event of circulatory problems, provide symptomatic treatment and monitor vital functions.

Members of the order Coronatae are small forms with a distinct concentric furrow on the outer layer of a relatively stiff bell and short, stiff tentacles. Most live in very deep water (>500 m) or cold surface waters. Members of the order Semaeostomeae, the 'typical' jellyfishes, have long, thin tentacles that extend from the rim of the bell, which is usually scalloped, and four or more frilly oral arms that extend like ribbons from the centre. Members of the order Rhizostomeae lack marginal tentacles and a central mouth. Instead, they have eight fused oral lobes at the base of the bell with numerous pore-like holes along their sides, and branched arm-like appendages that hang beneath, which can bear tentacles. Most species are tropical and many harbour zooxanthellae in their tissue. In the following species accounts, size refers to bell diameter.

Order Coronatae
Nausithoidae

Stinging Algae	<5 mm
Nausithoe spp.	*(<0.25 in)*

Polyp stage resembles algae, may be over-grown with blue grey or orange sponge; polyps at end of chitinous tubes, flash white when disturbed and close; small medusae (<5 cm) are rarely seen. **Biology:** in both protected and exposed seaward reefs, usually among the interstices of corals. Contact causes intense pain and blisters, which can last for weeks and ulcerate. Medusae rarely encountered, possibly responsible for 'swimmer's itch', an unpleasant rash. **Range:** *Nausithoe punctata* is circumtropical; validity and distribution of other spp. is uncertain.

Linuchidae

Thimble Jelly	<2.5 cm
Linuche unguiculata	*(<1 in)*

Thimble-shaped, tentacles few and very short, bell with distinct concentric furrow around top and covered with tiny clumps of nematocysts; inner layer contains brown clumps of zooxanthellae. **Biology:** occurs seasonally in swarms near the surface. Usually swims sideways. Feeds on plankton and on sugars manufactured by zooxan-thelleae. Contact can produce an itch and rash. **Range:** circumtropical.

Order Semaeostomeae
Pelagiidae

Compass Jellyfish   <20 cm
Chrysaora hyoscella   (<8 in)

Bell dome-shaped with 32 lobes and 24 tentacles to 2 m long; oral arms long and frilled; bell with radiating red to purple bands and streaks. **Biology:** pelagic, occasionally abundant in coastal areas. Feeds on other jellyfishes, small fishes, crustaceans and larvae. Eggs fertilised internally, then released as larvae. Sting generally mild. **Range:** N. Atlantic, N. Sea, Baltic Sea and Mediterranean Sea; to s. tip of Africa. **Similar:** several spp. primarily in temperate seas; Sea Nettle *Chrysaora quinquecirrha* has narrow reddish-purple radial lines, can sting severely (20 cm; scattered cosmopolitan, subsp. *pacifica* in Japan).

Luminescent Jellyfish   <10 cm
Pelagia noctiluca   (<4 in)

Bell dome-shaped, rim with 8 narrow tentacles to >1 m long; 4 long frilly oral arms; bell and arms covered with nematocysts; colour variable, usually purple or yellow. **Biology:** pelagic and oceanic, occasionally abundant in coastal areas. Lacks polyp stage, eggs transform directly into medusae. Sting slight to severe, rarely can lead to unconsciousness. **Range:** circumglobal, to high latitudes in summer. **Similar:** *Sanderia malayensis* gets larger, has 32 reddish-brown lobes, can sting severely (20 cm; Red Sea to w. Pacific).

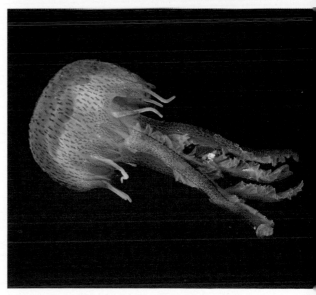

Cyaneidae

Lion's Mane	<2 m
Cyanea capillata	*(<6.6 ft)*

Bell slightly flattened, tentacles in 8 groups of 150, each of which can extend to 36 m; oral lobes short, densely packed; yellowish brown turning reddish purple with age. **Biology:** pelagic, seasonal in summer. Attains 900 kg. Strong sting can last 4–5 hours. Dust from remains in fishing nets can irritate eyes, skin and lungs. **Range:** circumpolar. **Similar:** Blue Lion's Mane *C. lamarcki* (25 cm; coastal tropical Asia); *C. nozakii* (25 cm; Japan); Fried Egg Jellyfish *Phacellophora camtschatica* has yellow gonad mass resembling egg yolk, mild sting (6 cm; circumglobal).

Ulmaridae

Moon Jelly	<50 cm
Aurelia sp.	*(<20 in)*

Bell low and transparent, rim with many short hair-like tentacles; oral arms as short frills. **Biology:** solitary or in groups, usually near surface, periodically in dense aggregations in plankton-rich coastal waters, reaching high latitudes during summer. Feeds on plankton trapped by surface mucus, which is drawn by cilia to stomach. ♀ carries developing larvae in inner edges of oral arms, ♂ carries trailing sperm filaments. Sting normally mild. **Range:** *A. aurita* has pread from Europe to most warm seas; *A. maldivensis* is violet with large curtain-like oral arms (25 cm; Red Sea and Indian Ocean); *A. labiata* (Hawaiian Is to se. AK and s. CA).

Order Rhizostomeae
Cepheidae

Mediterranean Jellyfish <35 cm
Cotylorhiza tuberculata (<8 in)

Bell domed; oral arms with many short
tubes ending in pale-rimmed purple discs.
Biology: Often accompanied by many juvenile jacks of the genera *Trachurus*, *Boops*
and *Seriola*. Sting normally mild. **Range:**
Mediterranean. **Similar:** *C. erythraea* has
smooth central dome without warts, oral
arms with stalked suckers (9 cm; Red Sea
to Indo-Pacific).

Cauliflower Jellyfish <15 cm
Cephea cephea (<8 in)

Outer part of bell flat to depressed, centre
white to purplish pink with clump of up to
60 finger-like processes; numerous short,
narrow tentacles extend from densely
branched oral arms. **Biology:** pelagic, often
drifts inshore. Sting normally mild to
unnoticeable. **Range:** Red Sea to Polynesia,
n. to s. Japan and Hawaiian Is. **Similar:**
C. octostyla has 8 bifurcated oral arms with
many short filaments, and 4–12 long,
tapering warty tentacles (Red Sea to w.
Pacific).

Cassiopeidae

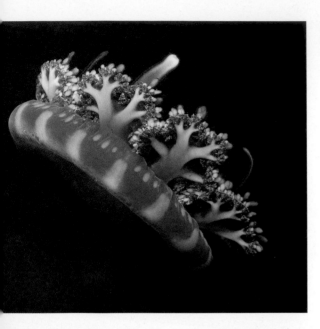

Upside-down Jellyfish	<12 cm
Cassiopea andromeda	*(<4.8 in)*

Bell disc-like; 8 branched oral arms with spatula-like attachments; colour pale grey to yellowish brown or olive-green. **Biology:** inhabits sheltered shallows to 15 m. Common in seagrass beds. Lies upside down to expose zooxanthellae to maximum sunlight and pulsates to draw water over its oral arms to filter zooplankton. Preyed upon by turtles and grapsid crabs. Can release free-floating nematocysts when disturbed. Sting normally mild but can be strong during breeding period. In Red Sea, breeds Apr.–Aug. **Range:** Red Sea to w. Pacific, introduced to Hawaiian Is; *C. xamachana* of W. Atlantic may be identical.

Stomolophidae

Canonball Jellyfish	<18 cm
Stomolophus meleagris	*(<7.3 in)*

Dome nearly spherical; pale olive above, grading to reddish brown, skirt with tiny white flecks; oral arms a short, thick folded mass, pale blue to white. **Biology:** coastal in summer. A strong swimmer. Feeds on zooplankton. Edible after treatment with salt and alum. **Range:** Atlantic, Chesapeake Bay to Argentina, incl. G. of Mexico and Caribbean; e. Pacific from San Diego and G. of California to Ecuador.

Mastigiidae

Lagoon Jellyfish	<13 cm
Mastigias papua	*(<5 in)*

Bell domed, olivaceous, usually with pale round spots; 8 stubby oral arms with finely branched clumps and knobs, may end in long, broad filament. **Biology:** coastal and inshore, usually near surface, occasionally in large aggregations. Feeds on zooplankton and on sugars produced by symbiotic zooxanthellae. Sting is mild, absent in some genetically distinct populations (e.g. Jellyfish Lake, Palau). **Range:** Indo-Pacific; introduced to Hawaiian Is. **Similar:** Australian Spotted Jellyfish *Phyllorhiza punctata* is reddish brown to pink with many tiny white spots (50 cm; Indo-Pacific).

Thysanostomatidae

Rope-armed Jelly	<20 cm
Thysanostoma loriferum	*(<8 in)*

Bell domed, pale with fine purple streaks and purple rim, can be finely sculpted with radial cracks; 8 rope-like oral arms with velvety texture. **Biology:** pelagic, usually near surface, occasionally drifts inshore. Often accompanied by juvenile jacks. **Range:** Red Sea to Hawaiian Is and Fr. Polynesia. **Similar:** *T. flagellatum* has purple bars around rim (widespread in Indo-Pacific); *T. thysanura* is yellowish brown (w. Pacific, n. to s. Japan); Lung Jellyfish *Rhizostoma pulmo* (Rhizostomatidae; p.282) is uniformly milky pale blue with purple rim and shorter oral arms (150 cm; N. Sea to se. Africa, incl. Mediterranean).

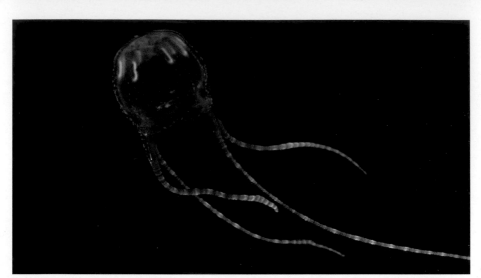

This Banded Sea Wasps*Carybdea sivickisi* shows the typical box-like bell of a cubozoan with tentacles extending from each corner. *Guam, RM*

Box Jellyfishes
Class Cubozoa

Box jellyfishes are among the world's most venomous and feared animals. They are the reason many beaches along the northern coast of Australia are deserted during the summer. When the 'jellyfish alert' has been sounded, affected beaches are closed and swimming is prohibited. And for good reason, as every year box jellyfishes are responsible for numerous fatalities in Australia and parts of Southeast Asia.

Box jellyfishes are a small group of about 21 species found throughout the world's tropical and warm-temperate seas. Three Australasian species are extremely dangerous and have caused many fatalities, and an Atlantic species has caused at least one fatality. The largest and best-known species, *Chironex fleckeri*, has killed in as little as three minutes and is considered by many to be the deadliest animal in the sea. Ironically, the other deadly species, the Irukandjis *Carukia barnesi* and *Malo kingi*, are among the tiniest, with bell diameters of only about 1 cm. Yet the stings of many close relatives, both large and small, are relatively mild. Most species of box jellyfish do not have a common name and as a group are generally known as box jellyfishes or sea wasps. The scientific name Cubozoa refers to the typical cube-like shape of the bell. We use the name Box Jellyfish for the most dangerous species, the infamous *Chironex fleckeri*, and adopt other names for some of the remaining species. The life history has only recently been worked out for the Box Jellyfish but remains unknown for most other species.

Behaviour and life history
Box jellyfishes are roving predators with well-developed eyes that are used to avoid potentially damaging objects and predators, as well as to hunt prey actively. They are excellent swimmers that can abruptly change direction and quickly cover great distances – *Chironex fleckeri* can reach speeds of 1.5–1.8 m/s (5.4–6.5kph)! It feeds on shrimps and small fishes, while some of the smaller species feed primarily on larval fishes and crustaceans. Their venom must be potent enough to instantly immobilise stronger and often hard-shelled or spiny prey that could easily damage them. However, their venom is useless against some predators. Both Green and Hawksbill turtles, for example, appear to be completely immune and hunt and eat *Chironex* with relish.

Like their distant scyphozoan relatives (p.282), box jellyfishes have short lives with alternating generations. During the late summer and autumn, at the end of the rainy season, adult *Chironex* gather in estuaries and river mouths to spawn, then die. The larvae, little bundles of cells called planulae, drift upstream on incoming tides to settle on rocks, where they transform into polyps. The polyps gather on the undersides of rocks, where they asexually bud additional polyps. In the spring, over a period of about 12 days before the onset of the rainy season, the polyps metamorphose into young medusae that migrate to adjacent coastal waters. There they feed in the sandy shallows and rapidly grow to maturity.

While *Chironex* has never been found far offshore, some of the other species occur in clear waters a long way from land. The medusa stages of the pelagic Winged Sea Wasp *Carybdea alata* and Warty Sea Wasp *Tamoya gargantua* occur in the open sea. Occasionally, large numbers drift inshore in concentrations great enough to close beaches. Some species of *Carybdea* are nocturnal. During the day, the Banded Sea Wasp *C. sivickisi* remains hidden on rock undersides, attached by a sticky pad at the top of the bell. At night, they emerge to hunt and feed. During the annual mass coral spawning of the Great Barrier Reef, this species emerges in droves.

Appearance

Box jellyfishes are transparent and bell- to cube-shaped, with one or more tentacles extending from projections called pedalia at each of the bell's four corners. They have four groups of eyes, one on each of the four sides. The central eye of each group is highly sophisticated, with both a lens and cornea. Depending on the species, tentacles may be banded or clear, and the surface of the bell may be smooth or dotted with small wart-like projections. *Chironex fleckeri* has a smooth bell and up to 60 finely banded ribbon-like tentacles in four bundles. Its bell typically attains a diameter of about 15 cm but may get as large as 30 cm, and its highly contractile tentacles attain a width of 6 mm and can stretch as far as 9 m. Despite its large size, *Chironex* can be nearly invisible when viewed from the surface over sandy shallows. The two deadly species of Irukandji, *Carukia barnesi* and *Malo kingi*, have a single tentacle extending from each corner of the bell. They are only 2–12 mm across with tentacles that may extend up to 2 m and are practically invisible.

Typical accidents, seasonality and risks

About 500 cases each of box jellyfish and Irukandji incidents have been compiled and analysed by Australian researchers. They occur only in the northern part of the country, primarily during the summer rainy season. Data for other countries is almost non-existent. Off tropical beaches worldwide, episodes of swimmers getting stung occur when large numbers of less virulent species such as the Wimged Sea Wasp *Carybdea alata* and Warty Sea Wasp *Tamoya gargantua* periodically concentrate.

Box jellyfish *Chironex fleckeri*: Box Jellyfish frequent sandy shallows, where their trailing tentacles can easily brush against waders and swimmers. Children in particular are at risk owing to their small size and habit of moving without looking. People have also been stung while engaged in other activities, such as launching a boat or operating a jetski. In Australia, Box Jelly incidents are highly seasonal but can occur at any time of the year. They are most frequent during the summer rainy season from October to May, and occur in shallow coastal waters, typically off beaches. They are virtually unknown in clear offshore waters. Over the past 100 years an average of about one fatality a year has occurred. In other areas such as the Philippines, where many people enter the sea for their livelihood and medical care is often non-existent, there are about 20 to 40 fatalities per year. These were once attributed to another species, *Chiropsoides quadrigatus*, but are now thought to be due to *Chironex*.

Irukandji *Carukia barnesi* and *Malo kingi*: In Australia, Irukandji stings are less seasonal and occur in a broader range of settings than Box Jelly stings. For years no one knew what was causing them because the small culprit was not seen and the initial sting is relatively innocuous. Irukandji stings were particularly alarming because some occurred within the 'safe' zones of beaches netted to exclude Box Jellyfishes. A recent fatality of a snorkeller attributed to an Irukandji occurred at a day facility on the outer edge of the Great Barrier Reef.

Prevention

The best prevention is to avoid entering the water in areas and during seasons in which box jellyfishes are prevalent. In northern Australia, avoid unprotected or unguarded coastal beaches during the October–May rainy season. Keep in mind that, although rare, *Chironex* can occur at any time outside of the 'season', and that Irukandji are less seasonal and are not

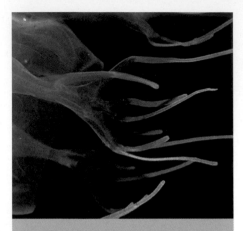

Venom apparatus

In most cubozoans the nematocysts are confined to the tentacles, but in others, including Irukandji, they are also distributed in clusters on the surface of the bell. In *Chironex*, the stinging capsules or nematocysts occur only in concentric bands on the tentacles. The ribbon-like tentacles may be up to 6 mm wide and stretch as far as 9 m. When touched, they contract and the nematocysts fire. The power of a nematocyst is considerable and the venom is instantly injected into anything that is penetrated. The considerable width of each tentacle allows it to cover a large area. About 3 m of tentacle contact is enough to deliver a fatal dose of venom to an adult human. With up to 15 tentacles per bundle and 60 per animal, this can easily occur. A large *Chironex* has enough tentacle length to kill as many as 60 people. To its normal prey of shrimps and fishes, death is instantaneous. *(Photo: Guam, RM)*

dead box jellyfishes on the beach, do not enter the water. Keep in mind that a single tiny sting from Irukandji can be life-threatening. Anyone compelled to enter areas with a high risk of encountering the Box Jellyfish or Irukandji should wear a hood and gloves and cover all exposed areas, including the wrists, ankles and neck, with duct tape. They should also dowse themselves with vinegar before removing the tape.

Venom

Box Jellyfish venom is a complex mix of various proteins with cardiotoxic, neurotoxic and highly dermatonecrotic (skin-killing) components that primarily damage cell membranes. Two major toxins have been identified in *Chironex* venom. The extremely quick, fatal effect of the venom seems to be based on one or more substances that attack the heart muscles and destroy red blood cells. The venom of some other box jellyfishes is clearly different. Irukandji venom causes little pain initially, yet has a delayed but profound systemic effect that spreads throughout the entire body.

Envenomation and symptoms

Chironex: envenomation causes instantaneous burning pain at the site of contact, this becoming excruciating within minutes. Symptoms

Sample case

Jiddah, Red Sea: During the winter, a large sea wasp tentatively identified as *Tamoya gargantua* appears in coastal waters. These 25 cm-long creatures usually float just below the surface. Thinking one of these animals was a plastic bag, a snorkeller allowed his forehead to come into contact with it. He immediately experienced extreme pain and was taken to hospital. His forehead swelled to the extent that it hampered his eyesight and took several days to subside. Marine photographer Hagen Schmid also accidentally came into contact with one, resulting in burning pain and a swollen hand. Only after several days of repeated treatment by bathing the hand in very hot water did he feel soothing relief. For several years thereafter, he continued to experience periodic extensive itching around the burned area, especially during cold weather. *(Communicated by Hagen Schmidt)*

excluded by netting. While the seasonality of *Chironex* and related species in other areas is not well known, it probably corresponds with the local rainy season. Obtain local knowledge of where it is safe to swim before entering the water, and avoid beaches where fresh water feeds into the ocean as this is a favoured habitat of *Chironex*. Wear protective clothing such as a Lycra skin or wetsuit when engaging in any aquatic activity where box jellyfishes occur. Although some nematocysts may penetrate a Lycra suit, it can be a life-saving layer. If there are include stinging, a burning sensation, vivid redness in the affected areas and swelling of lymph nodes. Visible manifestations include long, braided red welt lines that mirror the bands of nematocysts where tentacles have made contact. Depending on the severity of the sting, unconsciousness can occur within minutes or even seconds. Serious envenomation leads to death by respiratory paralysis and cardiovascular collapse. Badly stung children have died within three minutes. The symptoms and pain can last for weeks. Injuries heal slowly, and often remain permanently scarred.

Irukandji: the initial effects of envenomation are relatively minor and range from a barely noticeable prick to a minor wasp-like sting. A small lesion similar to a flea bite may be the only visible evidence. Then, anywhere from five to 60 minutes later, the pain intensifies and spreads throughout the body, soon becoming excruciating. This is accompanied by continuous and unrelenting backache, headache, pain in the back of the legs and knees, abdominal pain, nausea and vomiting, rapid and irregular pulse, coughing with mucus and tightening of the chest. This usually lasts one to two days but can continue for up to a week. Death can result from cardiac arrest, either indirectly from the effects of the pain or possibly as a direct effect of the venom itself.

Other species: effects of envenomation vary widely by species, ranging from a minor itch to a powerful sting with clearly visible welts. Although stings from other species have caused fatalities, none results in the extent of damage experseen with a *Chironex* sting.

Classification and distribution

Box jellyfishes occur throughout the world's tropical and warm-temperate seas. The 21 known species are distributed in three families on the baisis of number and arrangement of tentacles, distribution of nematocysts and other characters. Members of the Chirodropidae and Chriopslamidae have multiple tentacles extending from the pedalia at each corner. They are restricted to coastal waters of continental margins. The Chirodropidae includes the infamous *Chironex fleckeri*. The Chiropsalmidae includes the western Atlantic *Chiropsalmus quadrumanus*, which has caused at least one fatality, as well as other potentially deadly Indo-Pacific species. Members of the Carybdeidae typically have a single tentacle connected to each pedalium (except two or three tentacles per pedalium in two species of *Tripedalia*). Some of the

Treatment

First aid

Remove the victim from the water immediately. Pour domestic vinegar over the affected area as quickly as possible. This deactivates the nematocysts and allows the safe removal of adhering tentacles. It does not decrease pain or diminish the effects of the venom but prevents further envenomation. Vinegar is available on most beaches in Australia. If it is not available, carefully remove any remaining tentacles with tweezers. Keep the victim calm and avoid any movements that will intensify the pain. Monitor breathing and, if necessary, provide heart and pulmonary resuscitation. Get the victim to the nearest hospital or clinic. An antivenom is available in Australia and should be administered as quickly as possible. Irukandji envenomation is initially more difficult to detect. If a suspected sting is followed by intensifying and spreading pain, seek medical help immediately.

What not to do

Do not pour any other substance except vinegar on the affected area. Do not rub the affected areas with anything. Alcohol, fresh water and many other liquids, as well as any physical disturbance, stimulate the discharge of additional nematocysts.

Ongoing medical management

Hospitalisation should be essential for anyone stung by *Chironex* or exhibiting symptoms of Irukandji envenomation. Patients should be monitored until recovery is assured. Morphine should be administered to Irukandji victims, as the little relief it offers is better than none.

family's 12 species are circumtropical or widespread, while others – including the two deadly Australian Irukandji *Carukia barnesi* and *Malo kingi* – have restricted distributions.

Distribution of box jellyfish families and locations of fatal encounters.

Chirodropidae

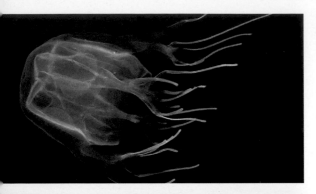

Box Jellyfish   <30 cm
Chironex fleckeri   (<12 in)

Bell smooth, each corner with up to 15 ribbon-like tentacles to 9 m long. **Biology:** highly seasonal in tidal creeks and shallow coastal waters during rainy season. Polyp stage cryptic under rocks during dry season, metamorphosing into young medusae shortly before rainy season then migrating to coast. Grows rapidly, lifespan <1 yr. Swims up to 1.8 m/s. Has well-developed eyesight, used to avoid obstacles and predators as well as locate prey. Feeds on shrimps and small fishes, which are killed instantly. Eaten with impunity by sea turtles. The world's most venomous animal, can kill within minutes. **Range:** tropical Australia, also Vietnam to Solomon Is, n. to Ryukyus.

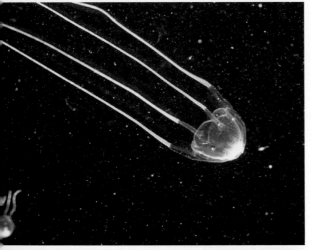

Raston's Sea Wasp   <2.5 cm
Carybdea rastoni   (<1 in)

Bell smooth, dome-shaped; 1 tentacle at each corner. **Biology:** inhabits primarily coastal waters, usually seen only at night. Burning sting may be followed by delayed itching 1–4 weeks later. **Range:** Indo-Pacific. **Similar:** Banded Sea Wasp *C. sivickisi* has taller bell with flattened top and banded tentacles; Irukandji *Carukia* and *Malo* spp. have clusters of nematocysts on bell (1 cm; tropical Australia).

Warty Sea Wasp   <11 cm
Tamoya gargantua   (<4.4 in)

Bell elongate with tiny white wart-like nematocyst clusters; 1 tentacle at each corner. **Biology:** juveniles inhabit coastal waters, hidden by day. Adults pelagic, occasionally drift inshore. Sting severe, may have long-lasting effects. **Range:** Indo-Pacific. **Similar:** Winged Sea Wasp *C. alata* has a smooth bell; other spp. have shorter bell or are much smaller.

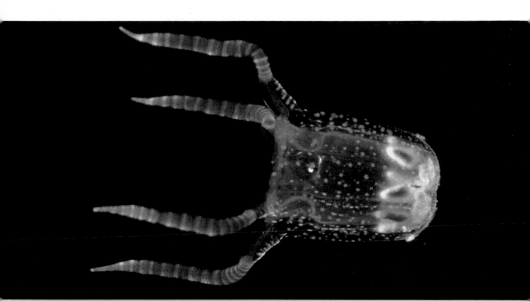

The Hell's Fire Anemone *Actinodendron arborea* can deliver a powerful sting that results in long-lasting blisters and scarring. *Philippines, MB*

Sea Anemones
Class Anthozoa

Sea anemones may resemble a flower, but like all cnidarians they are in fact predatory animals. Although some species live clumped together in groups, each is a fully independent polyp that does not share any living tissue with its neighbours. Sea anemones are quite soft and flexible to the touch, and most have long, conspicuous tentacles. There are about a thousand species, ranging in size from less than a centimetre to well over a metre across. Although all are equipped with stinging nematocysts, only a few are dangerous to humans. Contact with most feels sticky or causes only a slight burning sensation to sensitive areas of skin. However, contact with a small number of species can result in serious injury and leave permanent scars.

Behaviour and life history
Most sea anemones live attached to firm surfaces, usually rock or rubble. Those found in sand are usually anchored to a rock or hard piece of debris. Most anemones remain in the same spot for years, if not permanently. However, when necessary they can also creep along the bottom very slowly. A few can even break away and 'swim' for short distances. Most species are solitary, but some occur in groups. The latter are clonal but not colonial animals, because they do not share any common body tissue. Anemones are soft-bodied and, as such, are able to expand or contract. Many can quickly disappear into crevices or beneath the sand when disturbed.

Anemones feed on small animals that blunder into their tentacles. The prey is paralysed by their stinging nematocysts, then grasped and shunted into the mouth. Nematocysts on partitions inside the stomach may be called on to finish the job. Many species harbour symbiotic zooxanthellae in their tissues that provide much to nearly all of their nutritional needs.

Anemones lack a medusa stage. All can reproduce sexually and some can also reproduce asexually. Many are hermaphrodites, but more are either male or female. Sperm and eggs are released into the water through the mouth. Asexual reproduction occurs when anemones split in two, shed bits of tissue that regenerate into new polyps, or eject newly formed polyps from their mouths. Some small anemones can multiply and spread rapidly. Others, particularly the larger species, grow slowly and live a very long time, perhaps over a century.

Many anemones host a wide variety of symbiotic animals, including shrimps and anemonefishes. The latter may aggressively defend their host from potential predators such as sea turtles by attacking and biting them in the eyes.

Appearance
Sea anemones are solitary polyps that consist of a tubular body with a crown of tentacles surrounding a mouth. They vary greatly in appearance. Most look like a flower, while others resemble small bushes or shaggy carpets and may exceed a metre in diameter. Some anemones have long tubular bases while others have broad, squat bases that are rarely seen. Tentacles may be short or long, simple or branched, smooth or covered with knobs, and transparent or opaque. Some anemones have a complex 'two-in-one' structure consisting of a tall tentacle-bearing oral tube that emerges from the centre of a finely branched basal clump.

Typical accidents
Divers usually get stung when they brush against an anemone with unprotected parts of their bodies or place a hand on the reef. Swimmers and waders occasionally get stung by anemones that they don't even see, particularly some of the more dangerous sand-dwelling species.

Prevention
Avoid direct contact with skin and don't put fingers or hands into holes and crevices. Divers should wear a Lycra skin or wetsuit. Swimmers and waders should find out if there are potentially hazardous sand-dwelling species in the area and, if so, wear footwear and protective clothing. Avoid disturbing or even appoaching certain species. Hell's fire anemones (p.304) can release free-floating nematocysts.

Venom
Sea anemone venom contains toxic proteins. Some are neurotoxic and attack nerve cell membranes, while others cause pain and blistering by damaging cells. The neurotoxins are not particularly poisonous for humans. Some components may cause sensitisation.

Envenomation and symptoms
The tentacles of most anemone species feel sticky but do not sting through the thick skin of the hands. Contact with more sensitive areas causes a slight burning sensation and redness.

Venom apparatus – beware the pustule!

All sea anemones are well armed with nematocyst-bearing tentacles and many also have nematocysts around their basal column. Many of the more dangerous species have nematocysts concentrated in clearly visible clumps of pustule-like vesicles. In hell's fire anemones these may be on thick tentacles that may be branched (*Actinodendron*, at left; *Megalactis*) or simple (*Actinostephanus*). In berried anemones (*Alicia*, right), nematocysts concentrated in clusters of pustules on the basal column as well as on the relatively smooth tentacles can deliver a powerful sting. (*Sulawesi, RM; Red Sea, MB*)

Large anemones that host anemonefishes like this Magnificent Sea Anemone *Heteractis magnifica* are generally harmless to humans, with nematocysts that are strong enough only to penetrate sensitive areas of skin. *Maldives, MB*

Occasionally, weals develop within a few minutes, only to disappear soon after. A few species cause very painful stings, which may be short-lived or last for hours and can lead to blistering, skin necrosis and scarring. In some cases, contact with these species can produce general symptoms such as nausea, vomiting and fever. This is more likely in children or if a large area of skin is affected. Repeated stings can lead to sensitisation. At least one death has been reported from an anemone sting: in the Philippines, a fisherman badly stung by a Jack-in-the-box Anemone *Phyllodiscus semoni* died in 'horrible pain' a few days after refusing medical treatment.

Classification and distribution

There are about a thousand species of sea anemones distributed in about 20 families. Of those that inhabit warm waters, fewer than 20 species in four families pose a danger to humans. Members of the families Aliciidae and Actinodendronidae are among the most dangerous, while a few species in the families Actiniidae, Phyllactidae and Phymanthidae can cause painful stings. Many species can cause minor irritations when they come into contact with sensitive areas of skin. In the species accounts, unless otherwise stated, size is given as normal tentacle spread of large individuals.

IF INJURED

Treatment

First aid

If painfully stung, leave the water immediately. Remove any tentacles using whatever materials are available, including sand, clothing or towels, but preferably tweezers. Cleanse using sugar water, vinegar, plant juices or sodium bicarbonate. Further treatment is not normally necessary. However, if swelling, pain or general symptoms from more serious stings persist, prompt medical attention should be sought.

What not to do

Do not scratch or rub the affected area, particularly if blistering occurs.

Ongoing medical management

In more serious cases of injury, seek assistance from a doctor, who can provide appropriate treatment.

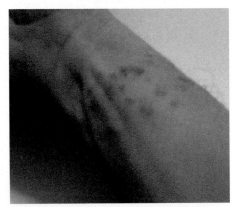

A slight brush against the hell's fire anemone *Megalactis griffithsi* resulted in an extremely painful sting and long-lasting itchy rash. *Tonga, LS*

Aliciidae

Berried Anemone
Alicia sansibarensis
base <10 cm (<4 in)

Semi-transparent body with clusters of nematocyst-bearing pustules; tentacles filamentous. **Biology:** on protected sand bottoms, 2–30 m. Contracts into warty knob by day. Feeds primarily on plankton, probably also on small fishes. Sting painful. **Range:** E. Africa to PNG.

Alicia spp. *Phyllodiscus* spp. death

Jack-in-the-box Anemone
Phyllodiscus semoni to 15 cm
<15 cm (<6 in)

A bushy clump of fuzzy-looking protuberances; at night, a tall, smooth tube with a crown of stringy tentacles emerges from centre; brown to green or lavender in colour. **Biology:** inhabits semi-protected coastal and offshore reefs, 1 m to over 20 m. Resembles a clump of algae or coral by day, looks like two anemones in one when fully emerged at night. Sting severe, followed by inflammation and long-term discoloration. Reported to have caused a human death in Philippines. **Range:** Indian Ocean to Indonesia, n. to Philippines.

Phyllactidae

Branching Anemone <25 cm
Lebrunia danae (<10 in)

Bead-like pseudo-tentacles with knobs of nematocysts surrounded by longer true tentacles. **Biology:** inhabits crevices among corals or rocks. Body remains hidden, leaving tentacles exposed. Can inflict a very painful sting. **Range:** w. Atlantic, incl. all Caribbean. **Similar:** Hidden Anemone *L. coralligens* has pseudo-tentacles with swollen dark tips, occurs in crevices of living corals (6 cm; s. FL, Bahamas and Caribbean); *Triactis producta* (8 cm; Indo-Pacific).

Actiniidae

Thimble Jelly <2.5 cm
Linuche unguiculata (<1 in)

Brown or green with purple-tipped tentacles. **Biology:** inhabits rocky bottoms, lower intertidal zone to 30 m. In clusters when in less than 5 m, solitary below 3 m. Sting weak, but can cause painful irritation to sensitive skin. **Range:** Mediterranean and e. Atlantic from Madeira to Norway.

Giant Anemone
Condylactis gigantea
<30 cm
(<12 in)

Tentacles usually with swollen tips and tiny, densely packed clusters of nematocysts, giving them a rough appearance; pale white to pink with pink to purple tips. **Biology:** inhabits semi-protected areas, 5–30 m. Usually on rubble in sand, also among corals. Hosts commensal shrimps. Sting weak, irritates sensitive skin. The largest Caribbean anemone but small by Indo-Pacific standards. **Range:** s. FL, Bermuda and all Caribbean. **Similar:** Golden Anemone *C. aurantiaca* is greybrown with dark-tipped tentacles (Mediterranean); an unnamed Indo-Pacific species has fewer tentacles.

Armed Anemone
Dofleinia armata
<30 cm
(<12 in)

Tentacles thick and tapered, diaphanous to opaque, densely packed with clusters of nematocysts. **Biology:** inhabits protected stretches of open sand or mud, below 3 m. Usually retracted into tight ball by day, often buried. Spreads tentacles over sand by night. Feeds on anything stung and retained. Stings severe, can take weeks or even months to heal fully. **Range:** Indo-Pacific, E. Africa to Australia, n. to s. Japan.

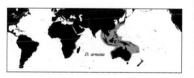

D. armata

Actinodendronidae

Hell's Fire Anemone <30 cm
Actinodendron arborea (<12 in)

Primary tentacles thick, secondary tentacles bear dense clusters of vesicles; from white to beige, olive or reddish brown in colour. **Biology.** on protected sand and rubble flats and slopes, 1–30 m. Hosts commensal shrimps and crabs. Symbiotic zooxanthellae produce most of its nutrition. Sting causes severe burning pain and blisters. All members of family withdraw completely into deep burrow when disturbed. **Range:** Red Sea to w. Pacific. *A. plumosum* is a synonym.

Globular Fire Anemone <30 cm
Actinodendron alcyonoidea (<12 in)

Primary tentacles thick and long, naked areas clearly visible through dense, widely spaced nodular clusters. **Biology:** on sand and rubble of protected shallows, 0.3 m to at least 20 m. Hosts commensal shrimps. Symbiotic zooxanthellae produce most of its nutrition. Sting causes burning pain and blisters. **Range:** Philippines and Indonesia to Tonga. *A. glomeratum* is a synonym.

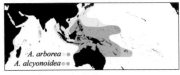

A. arborea ●
A. alcyonoidea ●●

Spider Fire Anemone <45 cm
Actinostephanus haeckeli (<18 in)

About 12 long, tapering tentacles with narrow conical tubercles, base to 8 cm; brown to green or black. **Biology:** on fine sand or mud of protected coastal reefs, 3 m to over 15 m. Often retracted by day, open at night. Feeds mainly on organic particles. Often hosts small symbiotic shrimp. **Range:** w. Pacific, at least in Philippines and Indonesia.

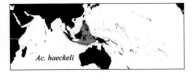

Ac. haeckeli

Bushy Fire Anemone   <20 cm
Megalactis sp.   (<8 in)

Primary tentacles long, may have green stripe along the top, their sides with secondary tentacles bearing clusters of vesicles. **Biology:** on sand and rubble of protected shallows, 0.3 m to at least 20 m. Common on seagrass flats. Hosts commensal shrimps. Symbiotic zooxanthellae produce most of its nutrition. Stings severely, causing burning pain and blisters. Withdraws completely when disturbed. **Range:** Indo-Pacific; replaced by *M. hemprichii* in Red Sea. Often indentified as *M. griffithsi* but this needs confirmation. **Similar:** *M. comatus* (Taiwan).

M. hemprichi
M. sp.
M. comatus

Phymanthidae

Knobbly Anemone   <11 cm
Ragactis lucida   (<4.5 in)

Tentacles filamentous and translucent, with numerus nematocyst-bearing knobs. **Biology:** inhabits clear fore-reefs, 1.5–30 m. Body hidden in crevice among corals or rubble, retracts when disturbed. Stings painful to bare skin. **Range:** s. FL, Bahamas and throughout Caribbean. **Similar:** Corkscrew Anemone *Bartholomea annulata* has twists rather than knobs on its tentacles and a mild sting (18 cm; w. Atlantic).

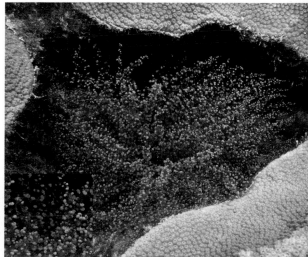

R. lucida

A large *Cerianthus* cf. *filiformis* extends its crown of grasping tentacles to capture plankton. *Indonesia, RM*

Tube Anemones
Order Ceriantharia

Tube anemones resemble sea anemones but are in fact more closely related to black corals. They are a small group of about 50 species that inhabit sand bottoms of all seas, from the shallows to abyssal depths. They occasionally occur in sandy pockets among corals, but are most common in open expanses. Tube anemones pack a powerful sting and can even sting from a distance by releasing free-floating nematocysts.

Behaviour and life history
Tube anemones have a long worm-like foot with a pointed base designed for burrowing in sand. They exude a slimy secretion that binds with sand and other particles to form a leathery parchment-like tube into which they retreat if disturbed. Tube anemones feed on current-born zooplankton snagged by their sticky tentacles. Many species emerge only at night, while others extend their tentacles during the day. Tube anemones spawn sexually as well as asexually and some species can live more than 100 years.

Appearance
Tube anemones have a crown of long, filamentous tentacles that emerge from a parchment-like tube. The outer clasping tentacles are the longest, while those around the mouth, the oral tentacles, are short and used to draw food particles down the pharynx. The tentacles come in a variety of colours, from white to deep purple, range in transparency from perfectly clear to opaque, and may be uniformly one colour, bicoloured or have bands or spots. The tentacles of some species lie flat on the sand, while others emerge in a full dome-shaped crown.

Typical accidents
While tube anemones are reported to pack a powerful sting, there is no information on incidents involving swimmers or divers. This is because tube anemones instantly withdraw into their tubes when disturbed. Some of the unsolved cases of people being stung at night by unseen culprits while on or close above sand are probably due to tube anemones.

Prevention

Always wear a protective Lycra skin or wetsuit. Keep a lookout when placing hands or any other exposed areas near the bottom. Avoid disturbing a tube anemone since it can sting from a distance by releasing free-floating nematocysts.

Venom apparatus and venom

The tentacles of tube anemones look smooth but are in fact packed with minute nematocysts. Nothing is known of the composition of their venom.

Envenomation, symptoms and treatment

Virtually nothing has been documented on the specific effects of envenomation by tube anemones. One of the authors (RM) was stung on two separate occasions by an unseen animal while engaged in photography over sand at night, once on the underside of the forearm and once on the thigh. In both cases he was jolted by a powerful stinging sensation, which persisted for several minutes and was followed by soreness and tenderness that lasted several hours. By the time he left the water, perhaps half an hour after each incident, a hard ruddy welt the size of a half a mango had developed at the site of the sting. The pain and swelling disappeared within 24 hours, but each site remained tender for some time thereafter. No treatment was taken.

Classification and distribution

There are only about 50 species of tube anemone. Only a few members of two famiIes are regularly encountered in warm, shallow waters. In the Cerianthidae, the tube often rises high above the surface of the sediment and the tentacles extend both above and around the rim of the tube. Some species have multiple rings of densely packed grasping tentacles, while others have only a single ring. In the Arachnactidae, the tube does not usually extend far above the bottom and there is a single ring of grasping tentacles that tend to lie flat, sometimes with their tips curled. In both families, identification to species level based on photographs or even live animals is unreliable since appropriate identifying characters have not yet been ascertained. Positive identification even to genus level is still based on internal characters. The identification details provided here are therefore provisional.

Cerianthidae

Greater Tube Anemone	<30 cm
Cerianthus cf. filiformis	(<12 in)

Dense crown of long, grasping tentacles in several rings around short oral tentacles in centre; colour varies from white to brown, blue or purple with pale oral tentacles; tube usually extends above surface of sediment. **Biology:** inhabits protected sand to mud bottoms, usually below 2 m. Common in nutrient-rich coastal waters. Emergent primarily at night, occasionally by day. Feeds mainly on plankton, probably also on small fishes. Sting painful. **Range:** widespread in Indo-Pacific, perhaps to Hawaii. **Similar:** *C. membranaceus* (e. Atlantic, Mediterranean); individuals with lime-green oral tentacles identified as *C. magnus* in some books.

Transparent Tube Anemone   <10 cm
Pachycerianthus cf. insignis   *(<4 in)*

Single garland of grasping tentacles in off-set row, each transparent with small white spots; tube usually flush with surface of sediment. **Biology:** inhabits protected sandy to muddy areas, usually below 2 m. Emergent mainly at night, occasionally by day. Feeds primarily on plankton, probably also on small fishes. **Range:** s. FL, likely widespread in w. Atlantic. **Similar:** *P. insignis* has distinct white spots (e. Pacific); *P. maua* has banded grasping tetacles (Indo-Pacific).

Arachnactidae

Banded Tube Anemone   <15 cm
Arachnanthus nocturnus   *(<6 in)*

Single ring of grasping tentacles in offset pattern, each pale with broad reddish bands. **Biology:** inhabits protected sandy areas, usually below 2 m. Emergent only at night. Feeds primarily on plankton, probably also on small fishes. **Range:** s. FL, Bahamas and Caribbean. **Similar:** *A. oligopodus* (circumtropical); *Isarachnanthus bandanensis* has fewer, shorter tentacles (w. Pacific to Hawaii).

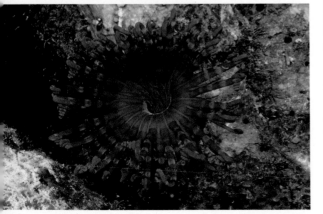

Wideband Tube Anemone   <10 cm
Arachnanthus unid. sp.   *(<4 in)*

Single ring of grasping tentacles in offset pattern, reddish brown with broad dark bands. **Biology:** inhabits protected sandy areas, usually below 2 m. Emergent primarily at night, occasionally by day. Feeds mainly on plankton, probably also on small fishes. **Range:** s. FL and Caribbean, likely widespread in w. Atlantic. **Similar:** other spp. in w. Pacific.

Disc Anemones
Order Corallimorpharia

Corallimorphs, also called disc anemones, are close relatives of the stony corals that resemble short-tentacled anemones but lack a skeleton. Like stony corals, most species contain symbiotic zooxanthellae, which provide nutrition by manufacturing sugars from waste metabolites. Some species are solitary while others form extensive mats. When disturbed, corallimorphs can extrude masses of thread-like filaments called acontia, which contain powerful nematocysts. The large platter-like *Amplexidiscus fenestrafer* is reported to deliver a painful sting. The mat-forming species *Discosoma rhodostoma* is more insidious, delivering a deceptively mild sting

that can penetrate a Lycra skin. This may be followed by a blistery rash resembling sand-flea bites. If a large enough area is affected, a dull muscular ache, accompanied by atrophication (loss of muscle mass), may ensue and last for weeks. Corallimorphs can also be highly toxic and deadly if ingested. When swimming or diving near disc anemones, wear protective clothing and avoid touching them. Definitely avoid prolonged contact even if no irritation is felt. There are about 50 species of corallimorphs distributed worldwide. Most are poorly known. The majority of those of concern to humans are in the family Discosomatidae.

Discosomatidae

Giant Corallimorph	<45 cm
Amplexidiscus fenestrafer	(<18 in)

Pancake-like with short tentacles; olivaceous brown or grey with a pale band inside rim and pale mouth. **Biology:** inhabits protected reefs, 10–30 m. Usually on rubble or dead coral. Most of its nutrition is provided by symbiotic zooxanthellae. Also feeds on zooplankton and perhaps small fishes by slowly enclosing itself into a ball. Prey are stung and then digested by gastral filaments extruded from the mouth. The entire upper surface thus becomes the inside of a digestive chamber. **Range:** Indo-Pacific.

Mat Corallimorph <12 cm
Discosoma rhodostoma (<5 in)

A small round pad with upper surface covered in short tentacles; beige to pale grey. **Biology:** forms extensive mats several metres across on protected reefs, 1 m to over 20 m. A secondary coloniser of rubble and dead coral rock. Lives primarily on sugars produced by zooxanthellae and on dissolved nutrients. Brief contact innocuous, but prolonged contact induces extrusion of stinging acontia. Resulting sting is mild but can lead to serious blistering and atrophication of flesh. **Range:** Indo-Pacific. **Similar:** numerous spp. in all coral reef areas distinguished by tentacle and disc structure as well as by colour.

Other Harmful Cnidarians

Most cnidarians lack the stinging power to harm humans by passive contact. However, rough contact can result in cuts or perforations that become infected with foreign matter or toxins, and many are highly toxic if ingested.

Stony corals and coral cuts

The stinging ability of stony coral nematocysts are normally too minor to be noticed by humans. Nonetheless, sensitive parts of skin, especially the lips and areas with mucous membranes, can react on contact. Redness of the skin, a faint burning sensation and, in rare cases, blistering can occur. Usually no special treatment is necessary for these skin reactions. The real problems caused by stony corals are cuts made by their sharp calcium carbonate skeletons. These wounds often contain bits of the coral, including soft tissue and nematocysts and their toxins, as well as mucus and particles of skeleton. All of this can delay healing and cause infection. All coral wounds should therefore be washed thoroughly with fresh or salt water as quickly as possible in order to remove any foreign material.

Soft corals

Many soft corals contain tiny sharp spicules in their skeletons. Hard or prolonged contact with species of *Dendronephthya* can cause them to puncture the skin and leave multiple openings

for the relatively weak nematocysts to inject their toxins. During such contact, the spicules feel like many tiny needles. Minutes later, an itchy rash appears, which may later blister and take several days to heal.

Zoanthids

Zoanthids are colonial anemone-like cnidarians that form slippery mats in shallow water or resemble small patches of mushrooms. Species of *Palythora*, *Protopalythoa* and, probably, others are deadly poisonous. They contain high concentrations of palytoxin (p.227), which is so powerful that a single microgram (one-millionth of a gram) can kill a 100 kg human. Touching zoanthids is harmless, but if the smallest amount of tissue or mucus enters a scratch or cut, it can greatly enlarge it by killing cells and can also be potentially deadly. The ancient Hawaiians rubbed their spears in *Palythoa* so that even slight wounds were made deadly.

Prevention

When walking on a coral reef, wear suitable shoes with solid soles. Do not trample, hold onto or lean against living corals whether they are soft or hard. When swimming near corals, take care to not bump into them, particularly when entering or leaving the water. If any cnidarians are handled, thoroughly wash off all traces of mucus as soon as possible.

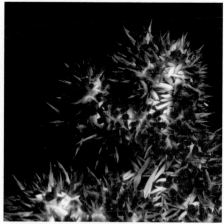

Stony corals can cause infection-prone cuts when accidentally stepped on or bumped into by divers. *Indonesia, RM*

Sharp spicules within the skeletons of soft corals such as this *Dendronephthya* can penetrate human skin during prolonged or hard contact. *Indonesia, RM*

A Bearded Fireworm *Hermodice carunculata* feeds on a gorgonian. The fuzzy-looking bundles on its sides are venomous brsitles. *MB*

Bristle Worms
Class Polychaeta

Unless eaten, the only marine worms that pose a danger to humans are certain kinds of bristle worms, all members of the large class Polychaeta. Over 10,000 species are known. Some live in mid-water as plankton, but most live on the bottom, in sand and mud as well as among rocks and corals. The few bristle worms that can be dangerous fall into two groups: those with fine toxic bristles that break off in the skin, and those that bite. The first group includes fireworms (families Amphinomidae and Hesionidae) and scaleworms (family Polynoidae). Those that bite include the venomous bloodworms (family Glyceridae) and bobbit worms (family Eunicidae).

Fireworms and Scaleworms
Families Amphinomidae, Hesionidae and Polynoidae

Behaviour and life history
Fireworms and scaleworms have tufts of fine bristles along their sides that break off and release toxic compounds when touched. The best-known species is the large Bearded Fireworm *Hermodice carunculata*, which has a worldwide distribution. On coral reefs it typically hides in fissures or under rocks by day and emerges to roam out in the open at dusk. In some situations, particularly when there is abundant food, it can be seen fully exposed during the day. It feeds on attached invertebrates such as coral and gorgonian polyps and anemones, as well as on carrion. Its eversible mouth contains numerous sharp structures used to scrape soft tissue. Other species occasionally occur in the open during the day, but most tend to be far less conspicuous.

Appearance
Like all bristle worms, the bodies of fireworms and scaleworms are divided into numerous

Stinging apparatus

The orientation of a fireworm's bundles of bristles are controlled by muscles. When the worm feels threatened, it tenses up to project them. Each bristle is a sharply pointed, brittle, hollow tube. Some also have barbs. The bristles easily penetrate human skin, then break off and release any substance that may be within.

nearly identical segments – up to 100 or more in some species. Each side of each segment has gills and a pair of small stump-like feet with an upper and lower limb. Each of these limbs bears a conspicuous bundle of bristles, which form a double row along the worm's side. Many fireworms are beautifully coloured, with upper surfaces of yellow, red, green or brown and, in some species, a metallic sheen. The uppermost side of the head has a short characteristic appendage, a nose-like proboscis. Members of the family Hesionidae have a pair of easily seen eyes. Scaleworms (family Polynoidae) have a double row of overlapping scales on their upper surfaces.

Typical accidents
Injuries often occur when a rock or other object is overturned, but can also happen when a

A Bearded Fireworm scavenges a dead sardine. Readily available food often induces nocturnal fireworms to feed during the day. *MB*

swimmer or diver accidentally brushes against an exposed fireworm. The bristles can penetrate thin gloves.

Prevention
Do not touch fireworms of any kind. Be careful when seeking support on the bottom or turning things over.

Venom
Although the bristles of fireworms are reputedly venomous and the effects of contact with them can be extremely painful, direct evidence of venom has not been found. Examination of three fireworm species revealed no toxic glandular cells. The symptoms may simply be the body's reaction to foreign elements, which may or may not contain a true venom.

Symptoms
Bristles that penetrate human skin cause an intense burning pain. The affected area reddens and becomes slightly swollen. Small blisters sometimes develop. The pain can be quite severe and continuous for several hours. The affected area can remain sensitive for a day or so thereafter, but there are usually no lasting ill effects.

Classification and distribution
The species most often encountered belong to the family Amphonimidae and are distributed worldwide in tropical and temperate seas.

Treatment

First aid
Where possible, remove any visible bristles. Although this is difficult, it is possible to remove at least some of them with tweezers or, in some cases, by grasping them with fingernails. Carefully applied adhesive tape can also be used to pull bristles from the skin. The affected areas should be disinfected with 40–70 per cent alcohol.

What not to do
Do not rub or scratch the affected area.

Ongoing medical management
No further treatment is usually necessary unless secondary infection occurs.

IF INJURED

Fire Worms
Amphinomidae

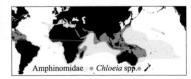

Amphinomidae ● *Chloeia* spp. ●

Yellow Fireworm   <10 cm
Chloeia flava   (<4 in)

Wide body with dense clumps of long bristles, giving it a furry appearance; bristles yellow. **Biology:** common on coastal flats and slopes, typically on open sand or rubble. A scavenger and predator that can swim above the bottom and may take a baited hook. Bristles cause extreme burning pain. **Range:** Red Sea and S. Africa to w. Pacific. **Similar:** *C. viridis* has red-tipped bristles (15 cm; e. Pacific and w. Atlantic).

Bearded Fireworm   <30 cm
Hermodice carunculata   (<12 in)

Sides with double row of bristles; colour variable, segments clearly visible. **Biology:** in a wide range of habitats, from sheltered inshore areas to offshore reefs, 1–40 m. Hides by day, emerging at dusk to feed on attached invertebrates such as coral and gorgonian polyps and anemones, as well as on carrion. When food is abundant, can be fully exposed during the day. Bristles cause extreme burning pain. **Range:** circumtropical. **Similar:** several spp., most less conspicuous.

Lined Fireworm   <20 cm
Pherecardia striata   (<8 in)

Sides with clumps of toxic bristles; upper surface with rows of dark dashes or stripes. **Biology:** all reef zones, often in open by day. Rises to surface to spawn in swarms at night on lunar cycle. A scavenger that will enter open wounds of starfishes to feed on them. Bristles cause extreme burning pain. **Range:** Indian and Pacific oceans.

Bloodworms and Bobbit Worms
Families Glyceridae and Eunicidae

Behaviour and life history
Bloodworms and bobbit worms live in mud and sand, where they actively prey on other worms and various soft-bodied animals as well as scavenge carrion. They have an eversible proboscis armed with strong jaws and, in the case of bloodworms, toxic venom. A bite from their claw-like grasping teeth can be quite painful.

The Bloodworm *Glycera dibranchiata* can reach a length of 38 cm and in North America is a favoured bait of anglers. In Maine, commercial diggers gather the worms from muddy shallows and deliver them to dealers. Once sorted and packed, they are sold to recreational fishers, either locally or shipped live to distant markets.

Bobbit worms grow quite large. For example, the Giant Bobbit Worm *Eunice aphroditois* reaches a length of 1 m and other species may reach 3 m or more. They occur among gravel, rocks and corals, as well as in softer sediments. They can occasionally be found under stones during the day and actively hunt in the open at night. Some are ambush predators that hold their head out of the sand with jaws wide open and sensory tentacles spread. They have been known to capture passing fish as large as 15 cm and pull them beneath the sand to be eaten.

Appearance
Bloodworms and bobbit worms have segmented bodies that vary in colour and transparency. Bloodworms get their name from the pink colour of their blood, which is clearly visible through their transparent bodies. Bobbit worms have opaque bodies that range in colour from beige to dark reddish brown, often with a metallic sheen. In all of these worms each segment has short, stiff protrusions on each side known as parapodia, which are tipped with bundles of fine bristles. Bobbit worms also have a single long cirrus on each side of their segments, as well as gills that project from segments near the front of the body. Bloodworms have four identical claw-like jaws in their proboscis, each projecting from a muscular base. Bobbit worms have five tentacles above five pairs of spiked jaws, two of them massive. The jaws are normally hidden. When extended, they resemble a spring-loaded trap that can span twice the width of the body – up to 5 cm in the largest species!

Typical accidents
Usually only fishermen and those who dig for these worms are bitten. Because the worms are quite cryptic and rapidly retreat when approached, it would be highly unusual for a diver, snorkeller or swimmer to be bitten. Reports of giant bobbit worms attacking divers are unsubstantiated. However, the potential exists for a serious bite to occur if one attempts to grab a large bobbit worm.

Prevention
Do not pick up or touch bristle worms of any kind that are not known to be safe. Be careful when turning over stones or other objects since dangerous worms often hide under them.

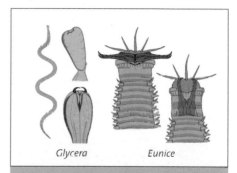

Glycera   Eunice

Venomous fangs and bear-trap jaws

Bloodworms (*Glycera* spp.) have an eversible proboscis, a tube that can be turned inside out like the finger of a glove. Their four claw-like mandibles are located at the end of the pharynx and are projected to the front of the proboscis when ready to be used. Each fang has a narrow canal that is connected to a venom gland (blue in the cross-section above). When the worm bites, the venom is injected into the wound. Bobbit worms (*Eunice* spp.) have five pairs of spiked mandibles, two of them massive. These are located at the end of the pharynx. When deployed, they are projected to the front of the proboscis and held wide open. Otherwise they remain completely hidden (above far right). *(After Halstead, 1965)*

IF INJURED

Treatment

First aid
Disinfect the wound with 40–70 per cent alcohol. No other treatment is normally necessary.

What not to do
Do not rub or scratch the wound.

Ongoing medical management
Usually there is no need for ongoing medical management. However, under certain circumstances secondary infection can occur and a doctor should be seen.

Venom
The venom glands of one species of *Glycera* contain a poisonous protein known as alphaglycera-toxin. It causes the neurotransmitters of synapses (the signal area at the juncture between nerve cells) to be released. Its biochemical effect is similar to, but much weaker than, the venom of a Black Widow Spider.

Envenomation and symptoms
Bites from these worms are normally only painful. The toxic effect is so weak that more serious consequences rarely occur.

Classification and distribution
Species of *Glycera* and *Eunice* inhabit soft bottoms of all tropical and temperate seas.

Bobbit Worms
Eunicidae

Giant Bobbit Worm	<3 m
Eunice sp. cf. aphroditois	(<10 ft)

Head with 5 tentacles above massive jaws; body cylindrical, reddish brown with metallic sheen, reaches diameter of 2.5 cm. **Biology:** inhabits course sand of sheltered reefs. Hidden by day. At night, extends head vertically from sand with jaws agape. Snaps at any suitable passing prey and drags it beneath the sand to be eaten. Can take fishes over 15 cm long. **Range:** Indonesia and Philippines to PNG, possibly also Australia; if *E. aphroditois*, then circumglobal in warm seas.

Long-bristle Bobbit Worm	<46 cm
Eunice longisetis	(<18 in)

Mottled reddish brown with metallic sheen. **Biology:** inhabits inner sheltered to offshore reefs, 2–30 m. Secretive, buried in sand, occasionally under rocks by day. At night, may extend head vertically from sand with jaws agape and snap at any suitable passing prey. Also forages around the bases of reefs. **Range:** s. FL, Bahamas and all Caribbean. **Similar:** *E. roussaei* is uniformly reddish brown (180 cm; s. FL, Bahamas and all Caribbean); many smaller spp. live within the reef framework and remain hidden from view.

The world's deadliest snail, the Geography Cone *Conus geographus*, in the process of engulfing a damselfish it has just killed. *Red Sea, AK*

Cone Snails
Family Conidae

Venomous molluscs

At first glance, cone snails seem to break nature's rules. Like most molluscs they are slow, yet they are active predators able to catch fast-moving prey such as fish. This is because nature has bestowed them with special hunting equipment, a venomous harpoon that quickly immobilises and kills their prey.

There are more than 500 species of cone snails, many with beautiful and complex colour patterns that have attracted people's attention for centuries. Most are relatively harmless, but a few are among the most venomous animals of the sea and have caused many human fatalities. Although many cones can be identified to species level only by specialists, those dangerous to humans are relatively easily recognised. They inhabit the tropical Indo-Pacific, although others that can give a mild to painful sting are found in all tropical waters. The danger posed to humans by many cone snail species is entirely unknown.

Behaviour and life history

All cone snails are carnivores that use venom to catch and kill their prey. They are rather specific about what they eat. Most, if not all, species feed on either worms, molluscs or small fishes. Regardless of diet, all cones have the same basic venom apparatus and predatory behaviour. A cone snail hunts by gliding across the bottom on a muscular foot with its tubular siphon extended to sample the water and 'sniff' for prey. Once prey is detected, the thread-like proboscis is deployed until it is very close to, or actually touches, the prey. Then the venomous dart is shot into the prey and the venom is injected. Even a fish that jumps remains tethered to the dart. Within a few seconds, the prey is paralysed or dead. It is then swallowed whole, engulfed in much the same way as a snake engulfs its prey.

Cone snails inhabit all tropical and warm-temperate seas, from tidepools to depths of hundreds of metres. They occur in a variety of

Many dangerous species of cone have a striking pattern of tent-shaped markings. This partially buried Textile Cone *Conus textile* is among the deadliest. *MB*

The harmless Strawberry Conch *Strombus luhuanus* superficially resembles a cone snail but is easily distinguished by the notches at the tip of its aperture and the bright strawberry colour inside. *MB*

habitats, on both soft and hard bottoms, with most species on or near coral reefs. During low tide, cone snails can often be seen on exposed reef flats. Most species are predominantly active at night, but some also roam the reef during the day. Most also bury themselves in sand or hide in crevices when they are not actively hunting.

Cone snails have separate sexes and internal fertilisation. The eggs are laid in pale pouch-like capsules, each containing anywhere from 80 to 1,000 tiny eggs (0.13–0.56 mm). These hatch into larvae that drift or swim in the plankton for several days to a month before settling on the bottom and metamorphosing into tiny juveniles that resemble adults. Some warm-temperate species skip out the larval stage altogether.

Appearance
All cone snails have the same basic shape: an oblong cone of overlapping whorls around a central axis forming a short spire at one end, with a narrow opening, the aperture, running along the remaining length of the shell. The spire can range from nearly flat to tall and pointed, but is often shaped like a parasol. The sides (outer whorl) may be slightly curved to straight, and the aperture is usually straight and narrow, but may be slightly flared. When active, the animal glides along the bottom on a foot that extends along the entire length of the shell. The narrow end of the shell is the front where the siphon, eyes and proboscis extend. The proboscis is the only dangerous part and remains hidden until it is about to strike. It is a long worm-like tentacle that extends from a thicker basal sheath. The shells of the living animals are covered in a chitinous layer, the

periostracum. It is thin and clear in most species but may be thick and nearly opaque in others. Species that spend most of their time exposed and visible often have thick shells that may even be overgrown with algae. For the most part these are worm-eaters and tend to be relatively harmless. The more colourful species tend to have more delicate shells. They are conspicuous when exposed but are often buried in sand when not hunting. Among them are many species with complex patterns of tent-shaped marks, the so-called 'tent cones'. Most of the species dangerous to humans are in this group. The colour patterns of cone snails vary greatly, not only between species but often also within species, making them difficult to identify. Most of those dangerous to humans are relatively easy to identify.

Typical accidents
Their beautiful colours make cone snails very popular with shell collectors and souvenir hunters. This attractiveness also leads the curious to pick them up, sometimes with tragic consequences. All documented accidents have happened as the animal was being handled or held in a pocket. In most if not all cases, the victim appeared to have been completely unaware of the danger.

Direct contact with a living cone snail is potentially and deceptively dangerous for two reasons: the animal can retract far into its shell, making it appear empty; and, more importantly, the proboscis and its venomous dart can reach any part of the shell. The so-called 'safe' or wide end, opposite the siphon and eyes, might appear to be beyond the animal's reach but is in fact within range of the proboscis. This is particularly true for the most dangerous species, whose long, thread-like proboscises are designed to hang onto a twitching fish.

Prevention

Although experts can and do pick up living cone snails of all species, the best advice for everyone else is to leave them alone. This is particularly true for the known dangerous species. Since many others are difficult to identify and the danger posed by them is unknown, the best advice is to avoid touching these too. Never carry a living cone snail in a pocket. For conservation purposes, refrain from collecting live cone snails.

Venom

Cone snail venom contains a multitude of pharmacologically active compounds, in some cases more than a hundred. They are among the most effective toxins known. The active components are small, highly constrained peptides, typically 10 to 30 amino acid molecules in length. The composition of the venom differs greatly

between species and even between individuals within a species, and each is optimally evolved to paralyse its prey. The cone snails that feed on fishes (at least 50 species) generally have the most toxic venom and are the most dangerous to humans. The toxic peptides of *Conus geographus* and *C. magus*, as well as those of the mollusc-eating *Conus textile*, have undergone intensive research. They are divisible into three groups: alpha-, omega- and mu-conotoxins. All of these conotoxins act by preventing neural communication, but each targets a different mechanism. Alpha-conotoxins target nicotinic ligand-gated channels, omega-conotoxins target voltage-gated calcium channels and mu-conotoxins target voltage-gated sodium channels. Neurons are thus disrupted in three places.

In addition to these three groups of peptides, cone snail venom contains several other peptides whose effects are not yet fully known. Cone snail venom is extremely lethal to their natural prey. The venom of *C. purpurascens*, for example, can completely paralyse a fish within

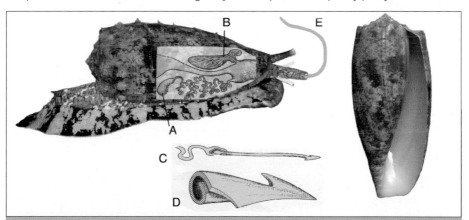

Venom apparatus

Cone snails have a highly developed and very sophisticated venom mechanism comprising a venom gland, a tubular duct, and a radular sac containing harpoon-like radular teeth. The venom is produced in a long tubular duct that is attached to a muscular bulb at one end (A). This serves as a pump, providing the necessary force to inject the venom through the tube, into the active radular tooth and, ultimately, into the prey. The radular sac (B) contains more than 50 spear-like chitinous teeth (C) made of

rolled sheets of chitin (D). Each tooth can be used only once and generally only one tooth is used at a time. Further teeth can be 'reloaded' as needed. The active tooth is located at the tip of the proboscis (E), a long worm-like tentacle that extends from a basal sheath. When it has located its prey, the cone snail impales the tooth into its victim and injects the venom. The siphon (F) is used to locate prey. In the Geography Cone shown here and other fish-eating species, the aperture is flared to enable the snail to take large prey. *(Based on Mebs. Photos: MH, RM)*

Sample case

Guam, Micronesia, 1960s: a 29-year-old spearfisherman found a large Geography Cone *Conus geographus* and tucked it in the sleeve of his shirt as he continued diving. Within an hour he experienced faintness, weakness and numbness throughout his body. He was immediately taken to hospital. When he arrived, he was semi-comatose and unable to speak. His left wrist was diffusely oedematous but there was no visible puncture mark. He was given 25 mg of the antihistamine benadryl and an intravenous drip of 10 ml of calcium gluconate and 500 ml of 5 per cent dextrose, and hot packs were applied to the wrist. As he was being transferred to another hospital, he suddenly stopped breathing and his pulse rapidly weakened. He was immediately given oxygen and artificial respiration but died within 25 minutes. The drugs used had no effect and artificial respiration came too late.

one to two seconds, making it one of the most effective toxins known.

Envenomation and symptoms

Symptoms can start immediately after a sting or the onset can be delayed for days. Typically, the first symptom is a severe pain, as if stung by a bee or wasp, but the actual spot of the sting can remain unnoticed. Numbness soon sets in and then spreads rapidly to the entire limb and, in some case, to the whole body. Muscular paralysis then sets in, the degree of which depends on the severity of the sting. Other symptoms include a progressive lack of coordination, weakness, blurred vision, trouble swallowing and, eventually, respiratory paralysis. If the sting is severe, unconsciousness can occur within an hour, followed shortly thereafter by death through respiratory paralysis.

Species and distribution

Cone snails evolved about 50 to 55 million years ago, at about the same time that 'modern' coral reefs similar to those of today first appeared. More than 500 species are known, all in the genus *Conus*, making it the most diverse animal genus of all. The true number of species will not be known until the full range of variation within

Representative Indo-Pacific cone snails

Specimens are shown to scale. The size given is the maximum recorded shell length.

Deadly species: stings often fatal

1. **Geography Cone** *Conus geographus* (p.323) 16.6 cm. Similar: Tulip Cone *C. tulipa* has multiple circular series of fine dashes (Indo-Pacific; common).
2. **Textile Cone** *Conus textile* (p.323) 15 cm.
3. **Striated Cone** *Conus striatus* (p.323) 13 cm.
4. **Marbled Cone** *Conus marmoreus* (p.324) 15 cm. Similar: Banda Cone *C. bandanus*.

Potentially deadly species: stings possibly fatal

5. **Omaria cone** *Conus omaria* to 8.6 cm. E. Africa to Fiji. Similar: Princely Cone *C. aulicus* (p.324) has taller spire.
6. **Magus Cone** *Conus magus* 9.4 cm. Common. Madagascar to Fiji. Similar: Striatellus Cone *C. striatellus* has fine circular lines.
7. **Ivory Cone** *Conus eburneus* 6 cm. Highly variable, usually black dashes in rings around shell. Common on sand of shallow reefs. E. Africa to Fr. Polynesia.
8. **Tesselate Cone** *Conus tessulatus* (p.324) 5 cm.
9. **Glory-of-the-seas Cone** *Conus gloriamaris* 16.8 cm. On sand and mud, 10–300 m. Uncommon. Feeds on molluscs. Philippines to Samoa.
10. **Admiral Cone** *Conus ammiralis* 9.7 cm.

Painfully stinging species: stings locally painful

11. **Obscure Cone** *Conus obscurus* 4.4 cm. Sand patches of shallow fore-reefs. E. Africa to Polynesia.
12. **Flea-bite Cone** *Conus pulicarius* 6 cm.

Unknown: stings likely painful, caution advised.

13. **Feathered Cone** *Conus pennaceus* 8.6 cm. Sand patches of shallow fore-reefs. Red Sea to Polynesia.
14. **Nusatella Cone** *Conus nusatella* 8.3 cm.
15. **Characteristic Cone** *Conus caracteristicus* 6 cm.
16. **Virgin Cone** *Conus virgo* 15 cm. Similar: Lettered Cone *C. litteratus* and Leopard Cone *C. leopardus* have rings of black dashes.
17. **Flag Cone** *Conus vexillum* 8 cm. (Juvenile). Common.
18. **Soldier Cone** *Conus miles* 8 cm.
19. **Crowned Cone** *Conus coronatus* 4 cm. On reef flats. Common. Similar: Cat Cone *C. catus* (4 cm).
20. **Abbreviated Cone** *Conus abbreviatus* 4 cm. Sandy areas to 60 m. Hawaii to Marshall Is.
21. **Hebrew Cone** *Conus ebraeus* 4.2 cm. On reef flats, common. Indian and Pacific oceans.
22. **Livid Cone** *Conus lividus* 8 cm. Variable, yellow to purple-brown. On reef flats. Common.
23. **Rat Cone** *Conus rattus* 5 cm. Abundant on reef flats.
24. **Morelet's Cone** *Conus moreleti* 6 cm. Under coral heads.

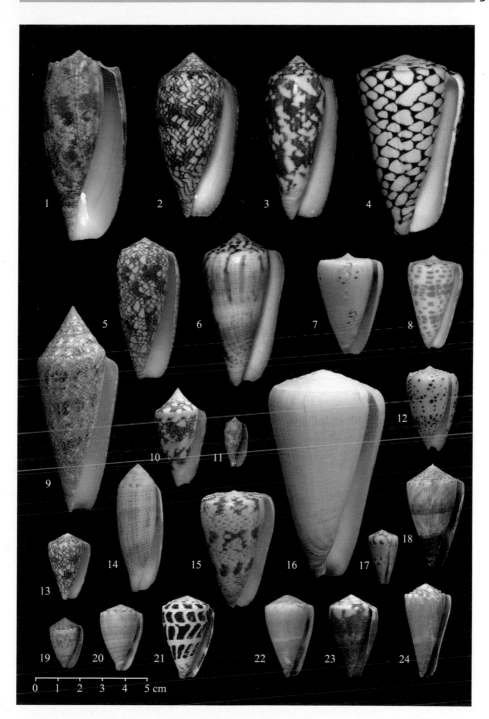

species is determined and studies of soft tissue DNA are carried out. Cone snails inhabit all warm seas from the intertidal zone to depths of several hundred metres, and occur in a variety of habitats on both soft and hard bottoms. They reach their greatest diversity on or near coral reefs of the tropical Indo-Pacific, where at least 318 species are known, including all those potentially lethal to humans.

Which cones are dangerous?
At least 18 species of cone snail are known to cause stings harmful to humans, and at least four of these have caused deaths. The fish-eating *Conus geographus* is by far the most dangerous, having caused more than 30 documented human deaths. At least two deaths have been attributed to the mollusc-eating *Conus textile*, and one each to the fish-eating *Conus striatus* and mollusc-eating *Conus marmoreus*. The mollusc-eating *Conus omaria* can also deliver a fatal sting: an eight-year-old girl stung by this species would have died were it not for artificial respiration. Laboratory tests on mice have indicated that two other fish-eating cones, *C. magus* and *C. tulipa*, may have the deadliest venoms of all, and at least one source claims that the latter has killed humans. Tests have also

shown that the venoms of three more species, *C. tessulatus*, *C. eburneus* and *C. purpurascens*, are deadly to fishes, so these should also be considered dangerous.

It is easy to see how cones that eat fast and strong prey such as fishes produce the deadliest venoms. Such prey needs to be immobilised quickly before it can escape. This is also true for cone shells that eat other molluscs that may be able to outrun, overpower or, in the case of cone snail prey, fight back. It is interesting that the two most dangerous mollusc-eating cones include other cone snails – even mollusc-eating ones – in their diet.

Since the danger posed by most cones has never been investigated, it is wise to assume that the closest relatives of known dangerous species should be considered just as dangerous. Among these are the so-called 'tent' cones, including *Conus aulicus*, *C. ammiralis* and the spectacular *C. gloriamaris*. All of these species feed on molluscs. Several other cone snails can cause severe local pain or numbness, which generally disappears within an hour. Among these are the fish-eating *C. catus* and *C. obscurus*, as well as the worm-eating *C. imperialis*, *C. litteratus*, *C. pulicarius*, *C. acutus*, *C. anemone*, *C. quercinus*, *C. lividus* and *C. sponsalis*.

Treatment

First aid
Remove the victim from the water immediately. Keep him calm and seek medical attention as quickly as possible. If the victim is unconscious, arrange him in the recovery position to avoid suffocation. Monitor all vital signs, especially breathing. If respiratory failure occurs, perform mouth-to-mouth resuscitation. If possible, take the shell with you since its identity can help determine the best treatment. Carefully transport it in a safe container as it can continue to sting.

What not to do
Do not make incisions where stung, and do not apply a tourniquet to the limb.

Ongoing medical management
There is no antivenom. Treatment depends on the symptoms, which include respiratory problems, paralysis and, possibly, allergic reactions. Even if the sting is minor, continue to monitor the victim for at least 24 hours.

IF INJURED

Distribution of cone snails and locations of some fatal and non-fatal stings to humans.

Geography Cone
Conus geographus <16.6 cm (<6.5 in)

Shell thin and rounded with low spire and wide aperture; orange-brown with small, pale tent marks in broad bands. **Biology:** shallow sandy areas, intertidal zone to 20 m. Usually partly buried or under rocks. Nocturnal, feeds primarily on fishes, occasionally on molluscs. Can eat fishes larger than itself. The deadliest cone, responsible for the most human deaths. **Range:** Red Sea to Fr. Polynesia. **Similar:** all fish-eating cones with similar shape should be considered potentially deadly.

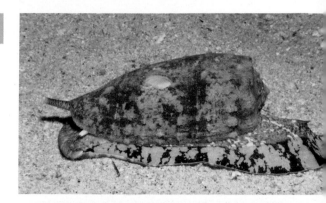

Textile Cone
Conus textile <15 cm (<6 in)

Shell slightly rounded; orange-brown with dark-edged tent marks and black squiggly lines. **Biology:** shallow sandy areas, intertidal zone to 50 m. Usually partly buried or under rocks. Nocturnal, feeds on cone snails and other gastropods, rarely on fishes, worms and carrion. Highly dangerous, sting can be fatal. **Range:** Red Sea to Hawaii and Fr. Polynesia. **Similar:** many spp., all potentially dangerous.

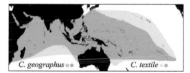

C. geographus ● ●   *C. textile* ● ●

Striated Cone
Conus striatus <12.9 cm (<5.1 in)

Shell rounded at shoulder; large, obscure, pale tent-like marks and thin striations over brown background. **Biology:** on rubble, dead coral and in sand patches, intertidal zone to 50 m. Feeds primarily at night on fishes. Preyed on by *C. textile* (above). Highly dangerous, blamed for at least one human death. **Range:** Red Sea to Hawaii and Fr. Polynesia.

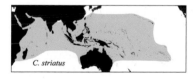

C. striatus

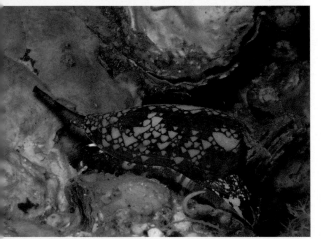

Marbled Cone   <15 cm
Conus marmoreus   (<6 in)

Shell thick with straight sides and low spire; dark brown to black with large white tent marks, these becoming more numerous and proportionately smaller with growth. **Biology:** on rubble, dead coral and sand, intertidal zone to 15 m. Feeds mainly on gastropod molluscs. Active by day, often in open on rising tide. Highly dangerous, sting can be fatal. **Range:** India to Marshall Is and Fiji. **Similar:** Banda Cone *C. bandanus* is nearly identical (15 cm; e. Africa to Hawaii and Fr. Polynesia).

Princely Cone   <16.3 cm
Conus aulicus   (<6.4 in)

Shell somewhat rounded and elongate with moderately wide aperture; dark brown with rows of distinct pale yellowish tent marks. **Biology:** on rubble, dead coral and sand, intertidal zone to 30 m. Nocturnal, feeds primarily on gastropod molluscs, occasionally on small fishes. Considered highly dangerous, sting potentially fatal. **Range:** Red Sea to Fr. Polynesia.

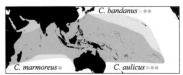

Tesselate Cone   >5 cm
Conus tessulatus   (>2 in)

Shell with nearly straight sides and low spire tapering to point; creamy with bands of yellow-orange rectangles, increasing in number with growth. **Biology:** on rubble, dead coral and sand, intertidal zone to 30 m. Common. Venom lethal to small fishes in lab tests. Should be considered dangerous. **Range:** Red Sea to Fr. Polynesia.

The bite of a blue-ringed octopus often goes unnoticed, leaving only a tiny skin abrasion.

This Greater Blue-ringed Octopus *Hapalochlaena lunulata* flashes its warning, a clear signal to stay away. *MB*

Blue-ringed Octopuses
Family Octopodidae

Deadly dwarfs

No other venomous animals seem as harmless and cute, yet are as deadly as the blue-ringed octopuses. They are among the smallest of the 200 or so members of the octopus family. Ironically, the larger octopuses – those demonised in horror stories – are for the most part harmless.

The extreme danger posed by blue-ringed octopuses was not really known until the 1950s, when the first death was linked to one. Since then, at least two other deaths and numerous near-deaths have been documented. Each death has been linked to a different species, and at least ten species have been distinguished, all in the genus *Hapalochlaena*. Yet in some areas there is no local knowledge of the danger and children play with these animals without incident. Until it is known for certain which species and areas are safe, the best recourse is to assume that all of them are potentially deadly.

Blue-ringed octopuses are not the only dangerous cephalopods. At least one other distinctively marked octopus and the small but spectacular Flamboyant Cuttlefish *Metasepia pfefferi* (p.333) are also known to possess a deadly toxin.

Behaviour and life history

Blue-ringed octopuses live on shallow rocky and coral reefs, from tidepools to a depth of 50 m or more. Like their harmless relatives, they are predators that feed on invertebrates and fishes. They use their tentacles to capture prey, which is then bitten and injected with toxic saliva. Octopuses have large salivary glands, these producing a mix of various toxins that quickly paralyse their prey. The saliva of blue-ringed octopuses also contains deadly tetrodotoxin (see p.198), which is produced by symbiotic bacteria and has the same effect on potential predators.

At rest, blue-ringed octopuses are a mottled brown to yellow and blend into their surroundings perfectly. When disturbed or excited, they instantly flash numerous electric-blue rings or streaks. These iridescent markings can be turned on or off at will. Some species squirt black ink into the water to aid their escape from predators. Others, such as the Southern Blue-lined octopus *H. maculosa*, lack functioning ink sacs. Perhaps the startling flash of their blue markings, backed by their deadly bite, has made other defences unnecessary.

Octopuses have short lives. Even the largest species live no longer than five years and many small ones such as the blue-ringed species may live for only a year. Females mate just once, then retire to a hole to tend their eggs. During this time they do not feed and slowly starve as they use all their energy to care for the eggs. Most octopuses lay thousands of tiny eggs, which hatch into larvae that are dispersed by currents. Others, including the blue-ringed octopuses, produce a few dozen relatively large eggs, which hatch into fully developed young that immediately crawl away. In blue-ringed octopuses even the eggs contain deadly tetrodotoxin, and the hatchlings are as fully functional as the adults, complete with electric-blue rings.

Appearance

Blue-ringed octopuses have the typical octopus form, comprising a sac-like body with eight arms surrounding a central mouth. Each arm has two rows of suction cups. Directly above the junction of the arms is the 'head' with two bulbous eyes at the top and the body hanging beneath. Like their relatives, blue-ringed octopuses can change the texture and colour of their skin as well as the shape of their bodies. At rest, they are nearly invisible as they blend perfectly with their surroundings, but when they feel threatened, they literally light up by 'turning on' electric-blue rings and become nearly impossible to overlook.

Typical accidents

All documented accidents with blue-ringed octopuses have happened when the animals were handled, usually with the victim being completely unaware of the danger. Found on the beach or in a tidepool, the 'cute' little octopus is picked up out of curiosity. The bite is so small that it is barely noticed but, once bitten, it is too late. Blue-ringed octopuses never attack humans. They are, in fact, shy animals that retreat when disturbed.

Prevention

Knowledge of the extreme toxicity of the venom, combined with appropriate behaviour, provides the best protection. Do not touch, pester or otherwise disturb the animal. Those kept in aquariums should be caught only by using a dip-net. Since blue-ringed octopuses at rest look like other harmless species and nothing is known of the effects of bites by many recently discovered ones, it is advisable to avoid touching any small octopus, particularly in an area where blue-ringed octopuses occur (Burma to Vanuatu, including southern Japan and all of Australia). Of course, one should be especially careful if iridescent blue rings are flashed.

Venom

The venom of blue-ringed octopuses (actually their saliva) contains tetrodotoxin, one of the most lethal substances known to man (p.198). When first isolated in 1970, the venom was identified as maculotoxin, named after the species of octopus examined, *Hapalochlaena maculosa*. In 1978, this was proven to be identical to tetrodotoxin found in puffers and various other animals. The toxin is not produced by the octopus but rather by bacteria living in the salivary glands. The bacteria and toxin are passed on from generation to generation via the eggs. This means that blue-ringed octopuses possess the venom from their very first day of life. Tetrodotoxin is an extremely effective poison, among the strongest found in any animal. As little as 0.009 mg per kilogram of body weight can be fatal, meaning that the minuscule amount of 0.72 mg (0.00072 grams) can kill an 80 kg man. Tetrodotoxin blocks sodium channels to nerves and muscles, causing motor paralysis and respiratory failure.

Envenomation and symptoms

The bite normally goes unnoticed and leaves only a tiny wound that is barely visible. Within a few minutes, however, weakness and tingling in the facial area, neck and, occasionally, the extremities set in. The tingling quickly turns to

When at rest, blue-ringed octopuses are difficult to see because their blue rings are 'turned off'. *MB*

numbness and is often accompanied by nausea and vomiting. Victims lose their sense of touch and speech as well as the ability to swallow, and are soon unable to move. Complete paralysis sets in within minutes, which ultimately leads to respiratory arrest and death from asphyxiation. Involuntary muscles such as the heart are not affected. In cases of non-fatal bites, victims have described themselves as being fully conscious and aware of their surroundings, with intact senses of sight and sound, but completely unable to move, react or respond, not even blink. The psychological torment is enormous.

Species and distribution
Blue-ringed octopuses, including blue-lined octopuses, are classified in the genus *Hapalochlaena*. They inhabit shallow inshore waters of the central Indo-Pacific from Sri Lanka to Vanuatu, including warm-temperate southern Japan

The Poison Ocellate Octopus *Octopus mototi* and other recently discovered species can flash a pair of electric-blue ocelli. *SM*

and all of Australia. At least ten species are known, but only three of them have been formally described and named. The others are still under study by specialists and will be given scientific names in the near future. Each species can be differentiated by the size and location of its blue rings or streaks, as well as by more subtle anatomical differences, including maximum size, distance between the eyes and presence or absence of an ink sac. Only one species, the Greater Blue-ringed Octopus *H. lunulatus*, is widely distributed. The rest have more restricted and mostly non-overlapping ranges, so that only one or two species are present at any given location.

The three confirmed human fatalities were caused by the Southern Blue-lined Octopus *Hapalochlaena fasciata* (Sydney); Robust Blue-ringed Octopus *Hapalochlaena* species 1 (Darwin); and the Greater Blue-ringed Octopus *Hapalochlaena lunulata* (Singapore; identity tentative, assumed to correspond with the only species known in the area). Serious non-fatal envenomations have been caused by the Southern Blue-ringed Octopus *H. maculosa* of temperate Australia. At least one other distinctively marked octopus, the Poison Ocellate Octopus *Amphioctopus mototi* of the Pacific, is known to deliver a non-fatal venomous bite.

IF INJURED

Treatment

First aid
Remove the victim from the water immediately and take him to a doctor or hospital as quickly as possible. If breathing stops, apply artificial respiration immediately. This is the only measure that can prevent death. There have been more than ten cases of victims being resuscitated and saved in this way.

What not to do
Do not scrape or cut the wound.

Ongoing medical management
There is no antidote for tetrodotoxin. The victim must be intubated and artificial respiration applied as soon as signs of paralysis set in. Monitor the cardiovascular system. In most cases the effects of the venom abate within a few hours and artificial respiration can be stopped once spontaneous breathing has resumed. Continue to monitor the patient for at least another 24 hours. There have been several cases of serious poisoning where the victim survived only due to the prompt and extended use of artificial respiration. Unlike poisoning by other venomous animals, surviving victims of blue-ringed octopus bites do not suffer any lingering effects. The nerves and muscles recover quickly and the tiny wound heals normally.

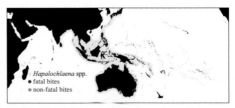

Hapalochlaena spp.
● fatal bites
● non-fatal bites

Distribution of blue-ringed octopuses and locations of some fatal and non-fatal bites to humans.

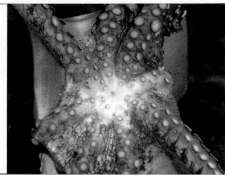

Venom apparatus

All octopuses have a small parrot-like beak tucked in the centre of the underside where the tentacles meet (A; right). Most have a pair of large salivary glands (B), connected via the salivary duct to the mouth. The saliva, which contains paralysing toxins as well as digestive enzymes, enters the wound produced by the beak. The saliva of blue-ringed octopuses contains deadly tetrodotoxin. The bite of most octopuses causes pain and some swelling, but is otherwise not dangerous to humans. This is definitely not the case with blue-ringed octopuses. Their beaks may be very small and the bite barely perceptible, but the tetrodotoxin in their saliva is extremely toxic and can be fatal to humans in as little as 30 minutes. *(MB; Guam, RM)*

Sample cases

Both cases below involved bites from the Southern Blue-lined octopus *Hapalochlaena fasciata*.

1) **Non-lethal envenomation near Stradbroke Island, Queensland, Australia:** On a rocky beach, a 43-year-old man discovered a tiny octopus and placed it on the back of his hand. After tossing it back into the water, he discovered two tiny specks of blood. This surprised him, as he did not feel the bite when handling the octopus. Shortly thereafter, he felt his chest tighten, called for help, then collapsed. He was immediately transported to the nearest hospital by seaplane. During the flight he became unconscious, stopped breathing and lost his pulse. Rescue personnel immediately performed resuscitation with the aid of oxygen. On arrival, the victim was completely paralysed and his pupils were fixed and dilated. He received external cardiac massage, and was intubated and ventilated. After five hours of treatment, he showed signs of spontaneous breathing, as well as slight movements of the hands and feet. Within 24 hours he was conscious but drowsy, and within 48 hours he was fully consciousness and able to walk. This is a typical pattern of events when resuscitation is successful.

2) **Deadly envenomation, Sydney, Australia:** During a camping trip to a beach, a 23-year-old soldier discovered a blue-ringed octopus in shallow water. He picked it up and placed it on the back of his hand to show his comrades. Ten minutes later he became dizzy and was unable to remove the octopus from his hand. His comrades removed it and threw it back into the water. A few minutes later the victim was no longer able to swallow or breathe, so his mates brought him to the main camp. Upon arrival he was unconscious and immediately received mouth-to-mouth resuscitation and heart massage. This continued as he was taken to hospital. Ninety minutes after envenomation, resuscitation efforts were discontinued. During the autopsy, two minute bruises were found on one of the knuckles of his left hand. These were the only evidence of the bite.

Greater Blue-ringed Octopus <5 cm
Hapalochlaena lunulata (<2 in)
arms <7 cm (<2.7 in)

Blue rings mostly larger than the eye.
Biology: inhabits protected and exposed coral reefs, intertidal zone to over 10 m. Forages over rubble and corals. Known to embellish rings with short lines to mimic coral polyps. Feeds on small crustaceans and fishes. During courtship, the male climbs on top of the female and may completely cover her eyes. The death of a 10-year-old boy in Singapore may have been due to a bite from this species. **Range:** Sri Lanka to Vanuatu, n. to Philippines.

Midring Blue-ringed Octopus <3 cm
Hapalochlaena species 4 (<1.2 in)
arms <6 cm (2<.4 in)

Blue rings mostly about the size of the eye.
Biology: inhabits shallow sandy or rubble bottoms covered in low algal turf. Little else known. Effect of the bite not known.
Range: Sulawesi. **Similar:** undescribed Western and Great Barrier Reef blue-ringed octopuses have smaller rings.

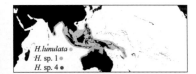

H.lunulata
H. sp. 1
H. sp. 4

Flamboyant Cuttlefishes
Family Sepiidae

Most divers are completely unaware of the potential danger of handling the spectacular Flamboyant Cuttlefish *Metasepia pfefferi*. Suspecting that its bright colours serve as a warning signal, reseachers tested for toxicity and recently found it. Like the blue-ringed octopuses, it has toxic saliva, most likely due to tetrodotoxin. It and its sister species, the Northern Flamboyant Cuttlefish *M. tullbergi*, should be considered just as dangerous and never be pestered or handled.

Flamboyant Cuttlefish	<8 cm
Metasepia pfefferi	*(<3.1 in)*

Has large knob-like projections; flashes bright yellow, red and white. **Biology:** inhabits shallow muddy and sandy areas. Hunts small fishes and crustaceans by day. May walk along the bottom on its lower arms and a pair of body flaps. Bright colours serve as a warning. Bite extremely venomous. **Range:** Indonesia and PNG to n. Australia; replaced by Paintpot Cuttlefish *M. tullbergi* from s. China to s. Japan.

Nudibranchs
Family Nudibranchia

Many nudibranchs are distasteful or toxic owing to chemicals they sequester from the organisms they eat. Some can kill other animals such as small fishes that are placed in the same container. However, they are generally harmless if handled. One exception is *Asteronotus cespitosus*, which secretes sulphuric acid in its mucus. Holding it out of water for even a short time can cause the outer layers of one's skin to peel away.

Clumpy Nudibranch	>22 cm
Asteronotus cespitosus	*(>9 in)*

Top with large warty protuberance; straw-yellow to brown; reaches 5 cm in Hawaii, possibly 30 cm at Guam. **Biology:** inhabits reef flats and lagoon and seaward reefs to >25 m. Feeds on sponges. Active primarily at night but occasionally crawls across exposed reef during the day. Sulphuric acid in its mucus can cause one's skin to peel. **Range:** E. Africa to Hawaiian Is.

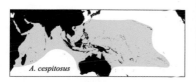

Swarming Crown-of-thorns Starfishes can strip vast areas of reef of all living corals. *Kenya, RM*

Crown-of-thorns Starfishes
Family Acanthasteridae

Venomous spikes

Starfishes are generally considered to be harmless. However, there is an exception to every rule. Of the 2,000 known species, the crown-of-thorns starfishes of the genus *Acanthaster* are the only ones with long venomous spines that can cause painful and sometimes debilitating wounds.

Behaviour and life history

Like most starfishes, the Crown-of-thorns Starfish *Acanthaster planci* has a planktonic larval stage that disperses it far and wide. Once the larvae have settled and transformed into juveniles, they are never seen because they live deep within the reef, 60 cm or more beneath coral rubble. By the time the juveniles reach a size of 8–5 cm, they resemble adults and emerge to feed on corals. Under normal conditions even

This purple morph of the Crown-of-thorns Starfish occurs in the Andaman Sea, with a few individuals as far west as the Maldives. *Similan Is, RM*

adult *Acanthaster* are secretive. They tend to hide under corals by day and emerge to feed at night. However, at irregular intervals *Acanthaster planci* gather in numbers so huge that they form a moving front that marches by day and night, leaving a vast wake of snow-white coral skeletons totally stripped of polyps.

The Crown-of-thorns Starfish is effectively protected from its enemies in three ways. First, its long, pointed spines provide effective physical protection; second, the spines are venomous; and third, the starfish's body tissue contains a high concentration of poisonous steroid glycoside. Steroid glycoside is a strong, sometimes deadly deterrent to many fishes. However, it is a passive defence that works only if part of the starfish is eaten and does not come into play through wounds caused by the spines. Despite these defences, the Crown-of-thorns does have enemies, most notably the Triton's Trumpet *Charonia tritonis*. Other predators include the Starry Puffer (p.155), Napoleon Wrasse (p.221), and the tiny but spectacular harlequin shrimps *Hymenocera picta* and *H. elegans*.

Appearance

The Crown-of-thorns is an impressive sea star. It is typically about 30 cm in diameter but can get to as large as 50 cm. It has a large body disc with relatively short arms, and its entire upper surface is covered with sharp, spike-like spines up to 5 cm long. The number of arms varies from seven to 23 but is usually 15 or 16. Its colour is variable, ranging from a pale tan to reddish brown and olive or purple. Most individuals sport a combination of colours, most often reddish brown and dark olive-green. The combination of large size, impressive spines and sometimes striking colours makes it instantly recognisable.

Typical accidents

Accidents occasionally happen when a careless diver or snorkeller brushes up against a Crown-of-thorns or foolishly attempts to handle it. Typically, one or two spines penetrate the skin and in some cases the tip of a spine may be left in the wound. Waders who venture onto the outer reef flat sometimes step on one, resulting in several spine wounds. The sturdy spines easily poke through gloves as well as the soles of most wading shoes. Injuries occur most frequently when divers attempt to remove the animals, a routine hazard when fighting a plague.

Prevention

Care should be taken when wading on the reef flat, particularly at night. It is especially important to look carefully before jumping from a boat onto the reef. Divers should always be aware of their surroundings and avoid accidentally touching the reef. When there is a large number or mass occurrence of the starfish, special care should be taken. When handling *Acanthaster*, it is important to wear thick protective gloves. Afterwards, the adhesive slime should be properly rinsed off all skin and swimwear.

A Triton's Trumpet *Charonia tritonis* eating a Crown-of-thorns. *Red Sea, KM*

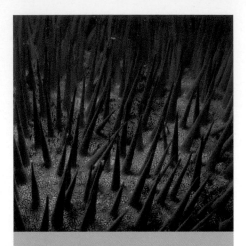

Venom apparatus

The entire upper surface of *Acanthaster* is densely covered with sharp, stout, tapering spines. These spines are tough, made of calcium and can reach a length of 5 cm. They are covered with an extremely slimy glandular tissue containing a protein-based venom. When a spine penetrates skin and flesh, the venomous covering is ripped off and enters the wound. *(West Papua, RM)*

Venom

The venom is a mix of proteins. It contains a relatively small glycoprotein that causes convulsions in mice, as well as the enzyme phospholipase A2, which damages muscle tissue.

Envenomation and symptoms

Wounds result in immediate sharp pain followed by oedema, tenderness and redness, and sometimes a blue discoloration near the point of puncture. The pain caused by many spines, particularly if particles are left in the wound, can be intolerable. Local pain from minor wounds generally disappears after a few hours. In more serious wounds, other symptoms such as nausea, vomiting and circulatory disorders often occur. Small calcareous particles left in the wound can cause granulomas, painful cysts that never heal.

Species and distribution

The Crown-of-thorns Starfish *Acanthaster planci* occurs throughout the entire tropical Indo-

Pacific and parts of the tropical eastern Pacific, from the Red Sea to Panama, including subtropical parts of Japan and Australia and nearly all tropical islands except the Galápagos. Regional differences (primarily in colour) are not genetically distinct enough to be considered separate species. The most spectacular of these is a purple form typical of the Andaman Sea. A second species, the Short-spined Crown-of-thorns *A. brevispinus*, which has short spines and more arms, is known from a few widely scattered areas of the Indian and western Pacific oceans. It is a rarely encountered inhabitant of deeper rubble and open hard bottoms. It is probably safe to assume that its spines are also venomous.

A plague of biblical proportions

From the late 1960s to mid-1970s, the sudden, nearly simultaneous mass appearance of the Crown-of-thorns in many parts of the Indo-Pacific made worldwide news. It was a plague of biblical proportions that devastated huge tracts of once pristine reefs. Dominant coral species were wiped out and the composition of recovering reefs remains altered to this day. A huge international effort was made to eradicate the starfish, as well as to research its life history and find effective ways of control. Shell collectors were blamed for depleting populations of its natural enemy, the Triton's Trumpet, but it was soon obvious that even the highest naturally occurring populations of this and other predators could have no effect on swarming *Acanthaster*. Years of painstaking research showed that these plagues occur naturally at irregular intervals averaging once every 400 years. It was also discovered that they often occurred three years after a major rain event and with unnatural frequency off the coasts of areas under intense agriculture, such as the sugar-producing regions of Queensland, Australia, and Okinawa, Japan. Nutrients in uncontrolled runoff somehow favours the survival of *Acanthaster* larvae over competitors and three years later the adults suddenly appear in vast numbers. Under natural conditions, infrequent *Acanthaster* plagues keep dominant species of corals from taking over and contribute to the diversity of the reef, but repeated occurrences can cause extreme and lasting damage.

Treatment

First aid

Leave the water immediately. Carefully remove any accessible spine remnants, preferably with a pair of tweezers. Great care must be taken as the brittle spine tips easily break and crumble. Disinfect the affected areas with alcohol (40–70 per cent).

What not to do

Do not attempt to extract any deeply embedded remnants by either cutting or squeezing.

Ongoing medical management

In most cases, ongoing treatment is not necessary. A local anaesthetic such as lidocaine can be used for intense pain. However, the effect is usually short-lived. As far as possible, remove any solid remnants – an X-ray may be useful for revealing deeply embedded particles. Remnants left behind may cause granulomas, encysted growths that are often sensitive and must be surgically removed.

This 8 cm *Acanthaster planci* may have spent three years deep in coral rubble before emerging to feed on living corals. *Guam, RM*

A. planci ● *A. brevispinus* ●

Distribution of the crown-of-thorns starfishes *Acanthaster planci* and *A. brevispinus*.

Clusters of long-spined urchins like these *Diadema setosum* are a hazard of shallow reef flats. *MB*

Sea Urchins
Class Echinoidea

A phalanx of spines

Many people who holiday along rocky coasts view sea urchins as their number one aquatic enemy. If an urchin is accidentally stepped on, its spines often break and leave their tips stuck in the wound. In most cases, such injuries are minor and the particles of spine dissolve or work their way to the surface. Urchins with extremely long, sharp spines, such as those of the genus *Diadema*, are especially feared. Their spines contain a slightly toxic substance that greatly increases the pain. Some tropical sea urchins, most notably the fire urchins (p.350) and flower urchins (p.346), have highly toxic venom with special delivery systems. In many areas sea urchins are harvested for their highly nutritious eggs.

Behaviour and life history

Most sea urchins are nocturnal. During the day they hide in holes and crevices, and at night they roam about. The spines of most species are flexible and can be directed towards approaching enemies. If the animals are disturbed, their spines may sway back and forth in hectic movements. Despite their spiny defence, sea urchins have many natural enemies, including triggerfishes, puffers and wrasses. These fishes are active by day and the urchin's respond either by hiding or crowding together to form an impenetrable phalanx of spines. In areas with few natural enemies, long-spined urchins of the genus *Diadema* may be abundant and remain fully exposed during the day. Except for accidental encounters, sea urchins are normally harmless and inoffensive. They feed mainly on algae, which they scrape from hard surfaces with five radial teeth located at the centre of the underside. Some species also eat various tiny sessile animals, including coral polyps.

Most sea urchins reproduce sexually. Males and females simultaneously release sperm and eggs through a hole at the top, which also serves as the anus. The fertilised eggs hatch into planktonic larvae that drift with the currents for several days to weeks. For this reason many species are widely distributed.

Appearance

The sea urchins that pose a danger to people all resemble a slightly depressed ball densely covered with long, sharp spines. Between the spines there are numerous transparent, flexible, tubed feet and stalked pincer-like structures called pedicellaria. The body of a sea urchin is covered in a calcareous exoskeleton called the test. It consists of interlocking plates arranged in a radial pattern. Species that bear spines have a round knob that fits into a socket at the base of each spine. Some sea urchins have a bulbous anal sac at the top of the test. Most sea urchins have rather stout spines that penetrate the skin only when some force is applied. However, the long-spined urchins of the family Diadematidae are not only sharp, but also delicate and brittle so that they easily break with the slightest touch and crumble under the skin. The primary spines of urchins of the genus *Diadema* are the longest of all and can reach lengths of over 20 cm. These urchins also have numerous very thin, shorter secondary spines. The Banded Urchin *Echinothrix calamaris* has relatively thick, blunt primary spines, as well as needle-like secondary spines that easily break off under the skin.

Typical accidents

Anyone entering the water where sea urchins occur is at risk. Most accidents happen when barefoot swimmers or waders bump into or step on unseen urchins. Even when it is hiding, an urchin's uppermost spines are usually exposed. *Diadema* urchins can be quite abundant and form clusters right along the shoreline or a jetty. Divers who make contact with the bottom also frequently fall victim to sea urchins. While wetsuits offer some protection, a forceful bump at the right angle can force spines deep into flesh. Divers, swimmers and waders are all at greater risk at night, when urchins are more active and exposed.

Prevention

Never touch sea urchins. Be especially careful when entering or leaving the water, or when walking on shallow flats. When doing so, wear shoes with thick, sturdy soles. Because sea urchins are nocturnal, the danger of injury is greater at night. The best protection for divers is to practice good buoyancy and maintain sufficient distance from the reef.

Venom apparatus: brittle spines, toxic fluid

The long, narrow spines of *Diadema* are very brittle (left). They have a rough surface, consisting of overlapping tapered platelets, and contain a dark blue watery substance that appears to have venomous properties. The spines pierce skin very easily, penetrate deeply, then break off and release the fluid into the wound. The primary spines of the Banded Urchin

Echinothrix calamaris appear blunt but are extremely brittle with a clear outer layer (right). They penetrate the skin and crumble with the slightest touch. In most cases, the particles dissolve within a few hours and the tenderness disappears within a few days. The spines of most other urchins do not crumble as easily nor are they venomous. *(Guam, RM)*

Diadema savignyi has a distnctive pattern of blue lines on its test. Each species has a disinct but variable pattern. *Guam, RM*

Venom

The dark blue watery fluid contained within the spines seems to have venomous properties. However, little is known of its composition or biochemistry, and scientists have not yet identified or isolated any individual toxins.

Treatment

First aid

Leave the water immediately. Remove the easily accessible particles with tweezers. The surface of the spines consists of tiny, backward-pointing hooks, so this can be difficult. Disinfect the affected area with alcohol or an iodine tincture.

What not to do

Do not attempt to remove deeply embedded spines on your own. A lack of suitable tools and/or surgical experience can worsen or enlarge the wound. Do not tap or press embedded spines. Doing so can cause them to crumble, and the body may then respond by encapsulating the fragments. Such knots under the skin can be very painful even when the slightest pressure is applied.

Ongoing medical management

Most sea urchin wounds, particularly those caused by *Diadema* and *Echinothrix* species, heal within a few days and do not require medical treatment. Sometimes even large, deeply embedded particles will work their way to the surface. Those that do not may require surgery.

Envenomation and symptoms

Injury by the spines of long-spined urchins of the family Diadematidae causes immediate severe pain, much more than one would expect, which suggests the presence of a toxin. Further symptoms are swelling and redness of the skin. Sometimes, the affected area becomes numb. These symptoms usually last only a few hours. The skin around the puncture turns blackish blue owing to the fluid in the spines. In severe cases, the discoloration can lasl several weeks. Fragments of spines that remain stuck in the wound pose the danger of becoming encapsulated by surrounding tissue, which can lead to the formation of pressure-sensitive granulomas. Secondary infection can also occur. Puncture wounds caused by urchins of most other families tend to be less painful and severe since their spines are less apt to crumble and do not contain venomous fluid.

Classification and distribution

About 900 species of sea urchin in more than 20 families are known. They range in shape from spherical to flat, and their spines vary greatly in length, thickness and texture. Sea urchins inhabit all bottom types, from rocky and coral reefs to sand and soft mud, and all depths, from tidepools to the abyss. Most of those that are dangerous to humans have sharp, needle-like spines. Long-spined urchins of the family Diadematidae inhabit all tropical and most warm-temperate seas. Most other urchins have spines that are stout enough for them to be handled safely but can cause painful wounds if forcefully pressed or stepped upon. Included in this group are members of the families Arbaciidae, Echiniidae, Echinometridae, Parasaleniidae, Stomopnuestidae and Temnopleuridae. Oddly enough, the most dangerous sea urchins of all are short-spined species of two families, the fire urchins (family Echinothurdae, p.350) and the flower urchins (family Toxopneustidae, p.346). In the species accounts, the size given is the diameter including the spines.

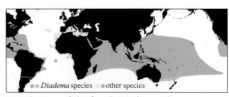

●● *Diadema* species ●● other species

Distribution of the family Diadematidae.

Long-spined Urchins
Diadematidae

Atlantic Long-spined Urchin   <45 cm
Diadema antillarum   (<18 in)

Spines very long and narrow, 3–4x test diameter; test black with white radiating lines, spines banded when small, white or black at intermediate sizes, and black in large adults. **Biology:** in most reef habitats, from inshore shallows to deep seaward slopes, 1–50 m. Usually partly hidden by day with spines protruding from holes or crevices, occasionally in clusters in open. Exposed and actively grazes on algae by night. Population crashed region-wide during a 1983–84 plague, but is slowly recovering. Sharp, brittle spines easily puncture skin and cause painful wounds. **Range:** Bermuda, n. G. of Mexico and FL to Brazil, incl. all Caribbean. **Similar:** Mexican Long-spined Urchin *D. mexicanum* (tropical e. Pacific); Ascension Urchin *D. ascensionis* (central Atlantic); *Centrostephanus longispsinus* (p.343) has shorter spines (20 cm; e. Atlantic, Mediterranean).

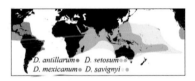

D. antillarum •   D. setosum •
D. mexicanum •   D. savignyi •

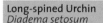

Long-spined Urchin   <50 cm
Diadema setosum   (<20 in)

Spines very long and narrow, 3–4x test diameter; test black with white to pale blue radiating lines, orange ring often around anus; spines banded when small, white or black at intermediate sizes and black in large adults. **Biology:** in most reef habitats, from shallow coastal waters to deep seaward slopes, 1 m to over 20 m. Usually partly hidden by day but may form huge clusters in open. Exposed and active by night. Occasionally hosts symbiotic cardinalfishes of the genus *Siphamia*. Sharp, brittle spines easily puncture skin and cause painful wounds. **Range:** Red Sea to Fr. Polynesia, n. to s. Japan, s. to Sydney.

Banded Urchin   <20 cm
Echinothrix calamaris   *(<8 in)*

Primary spines with blunt tips and banded when small, white or black when large, often clumped into spires; secondary spines very thin and sharp; anal sac with white and black spots; sutures of test green. **Biology:** inhabits most reef habitats, from shallow coastal waters to seaward slopes, 1 m to over 21 m. Usually partly hidden by day, exposed and active by night, when it grazes on algae. Primary spines are deceptively brittle and, along with the secondary spines, can easily puncture human skin and cause painful wounds. Rarely hosts symbiotic Urchin Cardinalfish *Siphamia fuscolineata*. **Range:** Red Sea to Hawaii and Pitcairn Is, n. to Ryukyus, s. to Lord Howe I. **Similar:** Blue-black Urchin *E. diadema* has velvety look, inhabits exposed seaward slopes (15 cm; Red Sea to Hawaii and Fr. Polynesia).

E. calamaris ●   E. diadema ●

Blue-spotted Urchin   <28 cm
Astropyga radiata   *(<11 in)*

Naked areas between spines with row of bright blue spots; young pale with banded spines, adults usually wine-red with darker spines. **Biology:** inhabits protected soft bottoms, 1–40 m. Young on shallow flats, often among seagrasses. Adults often in clumps on open sand below 6 m. Often hosts symbiotic Urchin Cardinalfish *Siphamia fuscolineata*, Twospot Urchin Cardinalfish *S. tubifer* and juvenile Emperor Snappers *Lutjanus sebae*. Spines cause painful wounds. **Range:** E. Africa and G. of Aden to New Caledonia, n. to s. Japan; Hawaii; replaced by Magnificent Urchin *A. magnifica* in tropical w. Atlantic.

A. magnifica ●   A. radiata ●

Diadem Urchin <20 cm
Centrostephanus longispinus (<8 in)

Spines very long and narrow, 2–3x test diameter, banded in juveniles, black in adults. **Biology:** inhabits rocky, coarse sand and coralline algae bottoms, 3–200 m. Spines easily puncture human skin and cause painful wounds. **Range:** tropical and warm-temperate e. Atlantic and Mediterranean, incl. Azores, Madeira, Canary, C. Verde and G. of Guinea Is.

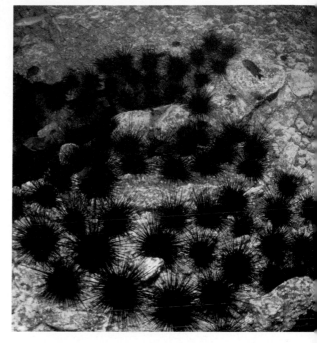

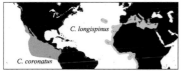

Family Arbaciidae

Black Sea Urchin <12 cm
Arbacia lixula (<4.7 in)

Spines sharp and narrow, about ⅓ the body diameter; uniformly black. **Biology:** inhabits exposed rocky reefs, 0–40 m. Common on shallow rocks, making it a hazard to waders. **Range:** Mediterranean. Subsp. *A. lixula africana* in e. Atlantic; replaced by *A. punctulata* in w. Atlantic.

Family Echinidae

Primary spines sharp and stout, smaller secondary spines in between; reddish brown. **Biology:** inhabits exposed rocky reefs, 0–50 m. Common on shallow rocks, making it a hazard to waders. **Range:** Mediterranean and e. Atlantic from Canary Is, Madeira and Azores to Ireland. **Similar:** other spp. in family (e.g. *Psammechinus*, *Echinus* spp.) have widely scattered primary spines and many more short secondary spines.

Dome Urchins
Temnopleuridae

Bald-patch Urchin   <5 cm
Microcyphus rousseaui   (<2 in)

Tall and dome-shaped with 5 undulating, spine-free bands radiating from centre; spines short and needle-like with pale tips. **Biology:** inhabits rubble and seagrass areas, 1–30 m. Rare. **Range:** Red Sea and G. of Oman to s. Mozambique. **Similar:** *Mespilia globulus* has straight dark pur-plish bald bands (India to w. Pacific); *Salmacis* spp. lack obvious bald bands Indian Ocean and w. Pacific).

Boring Sea Urchins
Echinometridae

Fine-spined Boring Urchin   <8 cm
Echinostrephus acicularis   *(<3.2 in)*

Spines narrow; dark reddish brown.
Biology: on rock or dead coral bottoms,
1–50 m. Common on exposed slopes. In
holes created by its teeth, with only upper
spines protruding. Poses a slight risk to
divers who contact bottom. **Range:** India
to Polynesia. **Similar:** *E. molaris* occurs
primarily in Indian Ocean.

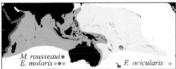

Rock-boring Urchin   <15 cm
Echinometra matthaei   *(<6 in)*

Spines stout; dark reddish brown, spines
usually lighter; green and lavender morphs
in Mauritius. **Biology:** on dead coral bottoms, 0–18 m. Common on rocky or limestone shorelines and exposed reef flats. In
holes, grooves or crevices by day, grazes
algae out in open by night. Requires some
force to puncture skin, posing a slight risk
to waders and divers, primarily at night.
Range: Red Sea to Polynesia.

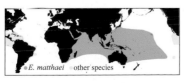

This Flower Urchin *Toxopneustes pileolus* has partially covered itself with debris. *Mauritius, RM*

Flower Urchins
Family Toxopneustidae

Behaviour and life history
Flower urchins occur predominantly in shallow water, where they prefer sand, gravel or dead coral bottoms. They are grazers of algae and occasionally feed on small attached invertebrates. They use their long, tubed feet to disguise themselves with algae and bits of debris. Although they look harmless, members of the genus *Toxopneustes* can be quite dangerous. They are unusual in having short spines but very large pincer-like pedicellaria. These are essentially three-pronged venomous graspers that are used for defence. They are capable of causing severe, possibly fatal stings, making *Toxopneustes* the most dangerous of the sea urchins. In most urchins, including other members of the flower urchin family, the pedicellaria are too small to puncture human skin. One species, the Collector Urchin *Tripneustes gratilla*, is widely collected for its edible eggs.

Appearance
The Flower Urchin *Toxopneustes pileolus* is covered completely with short but not particularly sharp spines. More conspicuous, however, are the numerous large pedicellaria. Each has three petal-like claws connected by a membranous tissue, which, when combined with their pink and white colour, gives them a flower-like appearance. Species of other genera of the family have smaller, less conspicuous pedicellaria.

Typical accidents
Injuries occasionally occur primarily through intentional contact. Flower Urchins look harmless and can easily be picked up without the spines causing problems. However, within a short time the handler receives a cluster of painful punctures from the urchin's venomous pedicellaria. There is one case of a female diver who passed out and subsequently drowned after she handled one. Other members of the family have smaller pedicellaria that do not normally cause problems, even though they may also be venomous.

Prevention
Do not touch flower urchins and never walk barefoot on shallow reef flats. A normal diving glove or wetsuit is thick enough to provide complete protection from the pincer-like pedicellaria.

Venom apparatus: toxic pincers

Stalked grasping organs called pedicellaria are distributed between the spines of many sea urchins. Those of the Flower Urchin *Toxopneustes pileolus* are huge, taller than the spines, and are clearly visible (left). They resemble small flowers, but the 'petals' are actually three sharply pointed, hinged pincers that form a claw. They are connected by a membranous tissue with venom glands at the base of each hinge. Very sensitive hairs on the tissue's surface cause the pincer to close when touched, and as the pincer penetrates the skin, the venom is injected into the wound. In most other members of the family, the pedicellaria are either too small to puncture human skin or too short to reach beyond the spines (Variegated Urchin *Lytenchinus variegatus*, right). *(Mauritius, RM; southern FL, RM)*

Venom
The venom of the Flower Urchin *Toxopneustes pileolus* contains a toxic protein. It has a molecular weight of 20,000 but nothing is known about how it works. A similar venom has been isolated from the Collector Urchin *Tripneustes gratilla*.

Envenomation and symptoms
Wounds from pedicellaria resemble a cluster of small red welts. They are very painful, but in most cases the pain subsides within an hour. Secondary muscular paralysis can occur, especially in the face and tongue, as well as in the limbs. This can last several hours.

Species and distribution
The family Toxopneustidae includes at least 13 species that inhabit shallow tropical and warm-temperate waters. All have short spines and large pedicellaria, but only species of *Toxopneustes* are normally dangerous to humans. All species can cause minor wounds if their spines are forcibly pressed into the skin. The size given in the species descriptions is the maximum diameter including the spines.

Treatment
First aid
Leave the water immediately. Accessible spine or pincer remains should be removed with tweezers. Disinfect the affected area with alcohol or an iodine tincture. Secondary infections can occur if the wound is not treated or occurred in polluted waters.

What not to do
Do not attempt to cut out, break or squeeze remains that have penetrated deeply.

Ongoing medical management
Spines that have penetrated deeply must be surgically removed – they can easily be identified on X-rays. If they have penetrated the joint capsules, there is a danger that the joints may become stiff. Secondary infections are rare but should be treated promptly. Anyone suffering muscular paralysis should be taken to hospital.

IF INJURED

Flower Urchin   <15 cm
Toxopneustes pileolus   (<6 in)

Pedicellaria flower-like, taller than most spines; white with pink centres. **Biology:** on coarse sand, rubble and dead coral of reef flats and protected slopes, 1–90 m. Often covered with algae and debris, may bury in sand during the day. Deceptively dangerous, pedicellaria highly venomous and can easily pierce human skin, causing extremely painful welts and secondary muscular paralysis. **Range:** E. Africa to Cook Is, n. to s. Japan; replaced by *T. roseus* in tropical e. Pacific.

Collector Urchin   <17 cm
Tripneustes gratilla   (<6.7 in)

Five double bands of short spines, may be obscured by overlying longer spines; pedicellaria shorter than spines; bluish black with black, white or red spines. **Biology:** inhabits reef flats and protected slopes to 25 m. Common on rubble and dead coral, and in seagrass beds. Often covered with bits of algae and debris. Harvested for edible eggs in some areas. Considered harmless, although pedicellaria are venomous. **Range:** E. Africa to Hawaii and Easter I., n. to s. Japan; subsp. *elatensis* in Red Sea (below).

Red Sea Collector Urchin   <17 cm
Tripneustes gratilla elatensis (<6.7 in)

Five double bands of short spines, may be obscured by overlying longer spines; pedicellaria shorter than spines but conspicuous; usually white or red. **Biology:** inhabits reef flats and protected slopes to 25 m. Common on rubble and dead coral, and in seagrass beds. Often covered with bits of algae and debris. Considered harmless, although pedicellaria are venomous. **Range:** Red Sea.

T. pileolus ●   *T. roseus* ●
Tr. ventricosus ●   *Tr. g. elatensis* ●   *Tr. gratilla* ●   *Tr. depressus* ●

West Indian Sea Egg <15 cm
Tripneustes ventricosus (<6 in)

Five double bands of short spines, may be obscured by overlying longer spines; pedicellaria short; reddish brown to black, spines white. **Biology:** inhabits protected coastal waters and reefs, 1 m to at least 10 m. On rubble and dead coral, common in seagrass beds. Often covered with debris. Harvested for edible eggs in some areas. Considered harmless, although pedicellaria are likely venomous. **Range:** NC to Brazil, incl. Bermuda, Bahamas and all Caribbean; replaced by *T. depresssus* in tropical e. Pacific.

Variegated Urchin <11 cm
Lytechinus variegatus (<4.3 in)

Five bands of short spines, pedicellaria shorter than spines; colour variable, typically white, maroon or green, sometimes pale with pink spine tips. **Biology:** inhabits protected coastal waters and reefs, 1 m to at least 50 m. Common on sand, rubble and dead coral bottoms, and in seagrass beds. Often covered with bits of algae and debris. Generally harmless, although pedicellaria are probably venomous. **Range:** NC to Brazil, incl. Bermuda, Bahamas and all Caribbean; replaced by *L. pictus* in tropical e. Pacific.

Violet Sea Urchin <13 cm
Sphaerechinus granularis (<5 in)

Short, blunt spines, areas between packed with pedicellaria shorter than spines; violet to brown. **Biology:** inhabits rocky reefs and adjacent coarse sand or rubble bottoms, 3–100 m. Common, often in clusters. May disguise itself with bits of algae and other debris. Harmless unless forcefully pressed. **Range:** e. Atlantic and Mediterranean.

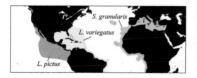

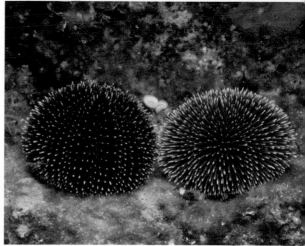

Fire Urchins
Family Echinothuridae

Behaviour and life history

Fire urchins live in semi-protected areas of rubble, coral, sand or mud, and have been found from the low-tide line to a depth of 285 m. They are predominantly nocturnal grazers of algae, but also eat small sessile animals such as coral polyps. During the day they usually hide in crevices or beneath overhanging corals. Fire urchins are named for the extremely painful stings caused by their venomous spines. They are also called leather or collapsible urchins because their shell, the test, is flexible. This allows them to change their shape and squeeze into narrow spaces.

Like many other large echinoderms, fire urchins host a handful of small creatures that live on them, including the beautiful Coleman's Shrimp *Periclimenes colemani*, the Long-armed Urchin Shrimp *Allopontonia iaini* and the Adam's Urchin Crab *Zebrida adamsii*, as well as the parasitic gastropod *Luetzenia asthenosomae*. The crustacean symbionts benefit by having a safe haven from their enemies, but it is unknown what benefits the urchin obtains in return. Perhaps the crustaceans remove certain parasites, although they do not interact with the parasitic gastropod that coexists with them.

Appearance

From a distance, fire urchins are immediately recognisable by the coarse, fuzzy look of their clusters of spines as well as their sometimes spectacular colours. Up close, one immediately notices that within these clusters each spine has globular swellings near its tip or along its entire length. The colour and sizes of the swellings differ by species. In the Red Sea Fire Urchin *Asthenosoma marisrubri*, the swelling near each spine tip is by far the largest and is pale, while in the western Pacific species Multi-coloured Fire Urchin *A. ijimai* and Variable Fire Urchin *A. varium*, the swellings are similar in size throughout the length of each spine and are dark with some electric-blue tips. Fire urchins also have numerous longer but narrower spines around their lower sides that completely lack these swellings. Fire urchins get unusually large – up to 20 cm in test diameter – and often appear somewhat flattened or misshapen owing to their flexibility.

Typical accidents

Injuries typically happen when fire urchins are accidentally touched or stepped on, or when they are handled. The slightest pressure on the

Venom apparatus: toxic globules

The venom apparatus of fire urchins consists of globular swellings associated with most spines. A thin layer of skin and muscle fibres covers each spine and encloses one or more large venom sacs. In the Variable Fire Urchin *Asthenosoma varium* (left) and Multicoloured Fire Urchin *A. ijimai*, these are located along the entire length of the spine. In the Red Sea Fire Urchin *A. marisrubri* (right), there is a very large sac located near the tip of the spine. The slightest pressure ruptures the skin and causes the venom to be injected into the wound. The long, thin, pale spines located around the base of the urchins lack these swellings. *(Sulawesi, RM; Red Sea, MB)*

spines causes the venom sacs to rupture and discharge their contents. Divers are most vulnerable to such injuries. Novices who fail to realise how delicate the spines are occasionally experience the painful consequence of touching them.

Prevention
Never touch a fire urchin! When diving, always look before leaning against or holding onto anything, particularly at night, when fire urchins can be completely exposed.

Venom
The composition of the venom is unknown. Attempts to isolate active components have so far failed, indicating that it may be extremely unstable.

Envenomation and symptoms
Puncture wounds from fire urchins are so small that they are practically invisible. However, a severe burning pain is immediately felt. This normally subsides within an hour, but in severe cases secondary symptoms such as nausea, shock or psychotic reactions may occur.

Species and distribution
Fire urchins inhabit all tropical and temperate seas, from the low-tide line to depths of over 800 m. However, only three shallow-dwelling Indo-Pacific species are normally encountered by humans. The size given in the descriptions is the maximum diameter including the spines.

Treatment

First aid
Leave the water immediately. Remove any easily accessible spines or particles with tweezers. Disinfect the wound with alcohol or an iodine tincture.

What not to do
Do not attempt to remove deeply embedded spines on your own.

Ongoing medical management
Secondary symptoms should be treated as they appear. Any deeply embedded particles that do not quickly work their way to the surface may require surgery.

IF INJURED

Red Sea Fire Urchin   <15 cm
Asthenosoma marisrubri   (<6 in)

Short spines with large, pale globular swelling near tips; reddish brown. **Biology:** inhabits seagrass beds and semi-protected reef slopes, 3 m to over 30 m. On sand, rubble or dead coral, hidden by day, active by night. Puncture wounds extremely painful, but pain usually short-lived. **Range:** Red Sea only.

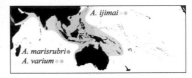

Variable Fire Urchin   <28 cm
Asthenosoma varium   (<11 in)

Short spines with globular swellings, some with blue tips; reddish brown, often with 5 broad, pale bands. **Biology:** inhabits mud, sand, rubble or dead coral bottoms of semi-protected reef slopes, 1–285 m. Usually hidden by day, more active and exposed by night. Stings by spines extremely painful. Often hosts small commensal shrimps or crabs, large individuals occasionally host the Twospot Urchin Cardinalfish *Siphamia tubifer*. **Range:** Oman to New Caledonia, n. to Ryukyus, s. to nw. Australia; also s. Baja California.

Multicoloured Fire Urchin   <15 cm
Asthenosoma ijimai   (<6 in)

Short spines with globular swellings; colour variable, in combinations of reddish brown, yellow, white or blue. **Biology:** inhabits primarily rocky and coral reef slopes, 1 m to over 30 m. On sand, rubble or among rocks and corals, hidden by day, active by night. Stings by spines extremely painful. Hosts small crustaceans, incl. Coleman's Shrimp *Periclimenes colemani*, Long-armed Urchin Shrimp *Allopontonia iaini* and Adam's Urchin Crab *Zebrida adamsii*, as well as the parasitic gastropod *Luetzenia asthenosomae*. **Range:** Indonesia and Philippines, n. to s. Japan, s. to w. Australia.

The Coconut Crab will aggressively defend itself with pincers strong enough to open a coconut. It uses snail shells only as a small juvenile and inhabits coral islands from Sumatra to French Polynesia. *Guam, RM*

Lobsters and Crabs
Order Decapoda

The most obvious danger posed by most large crustaceans is their ability to injure with their chelae, commonly known as pincers or 'claws'. Some of the largest species have pincers capable of severely injuring or even amputating a finger. Among those that could be considered dangerous are certain large-clawed lobsters, hermit crabs and 'true' crabs. Many decopod crustaceans also have sharp spines capable of causing painful puncture wounds. The spiny lobsters in particular rely on their spines for defence because they lack pincers altogether. The mantis

Assymetric pincers

The left pincer of a lobster is not only larger than the right one but also has bigger nodular teeth. This makes it better suited to crushing hard-shelled prey, while the narrower edge and smaller teeth of the right pincer are better suited to tearing or cutting. Either pincer can do considerable damage to a person's skin and flesh. *(Ireland, HS)*

Distribution of the two species of *Homarus*.

shrimps (order Stomatopoda) have highly specialised raptorial appendages that spear or smash their prey (p.358).

Lobsters (infraorder Astacidea)

The 'true' lobsters (family Nephropidae) are easily distinguished from spiny lobsters by the presence of chelae (claws) on their first three pairs of legs. The first two of these are massive and no longer resemble legs. The European Lobster *Homarus gammarus* and the slightly larger American Lobster *H. americanus* are among the largest decapods. They have the largest pincers, easily capable of causing severe injury to a finger or any other part of a person they are able to grip. Fortunately, accidents are rare since the animals are not particularly aggressive or fast, and most people who encounter them avoid such formidable-looking weapons. Both species support large commercial fisheries and are marketed live throughout the world. Once caught, their pincers are disabled by either a plug or rubber bands.

Lobsters inhabit hard bottoms of relatively cold waters. The European Lobster occurs from Norway to Morocco, including the Azores, the Mediterranean east to Crete and the Black Sea at depths of 1–90 m. It attains a length of 62 cm and a weight of 8.4 kg. The American Lobster occurs from Labrador to North Carolina and can weigh up to 20 kg.

Many smaller species of lobster found throughout the world are harmless. The spiny lobsters of warm-temperate and tropical seas are distant relatives of the family Palinuridae (infraorder Palinuridea) and lack pincers.

The Caribbean Spiny Lobster *Panulirus argus* and others in the family Palinuridae have sharp spines that can cause painful puncture wounds. *RM*

Some of the larger land hermit crabs of the same family, Coenibitidae, can also cause painful wounds. A few marine species of the family Diogenidae also grow large enough to fit a pincer around a finger. When disturbed, hermit crabs of this size don't always retreat within their shell. In one case, a diver was badly pinched by a White-spotted Hermit Crab *Dardanus megistos* that he approached with a pointed finger. He patched the wound without the benefit of sutures and missed the next dive. In members of both hermit crab families, the left claw is typically the largest and is used to plug the opening of their shell.

Hermit Crabs
Infraorder Anomura

Few people consider hermit crabs to be dangerous. However, a few species get large enough and aggressive enough to cause wounds that may require sutures. The largest of all, the Coconut Crab *Birgus latro*, can weigh more than 2.5 kg and has the strength to open a coconut. Its massive pincers can easily damage a finger to the point of requiring amputation – if it is not removed outright in the first place. Although the species is a land-dweller, we include it because it is potentially dangerous to those who venture into the vegetation beyond the beach.

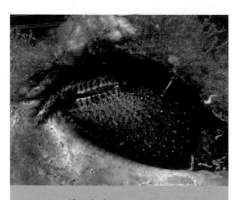

Saw-toothed claw

The major pincer of many hermit crabs has sharp toothed edges that can easily cut through skin and flesh. The left pincer is usually the largest. *RM*

Hermit Crabs
Diogenidae

Giant Hermit Crab   **<30 cm**
Petrochirus diogenes   *(<12 in)*

Pincers and legs with short spines and knobs; reddish brown. **Biology:** inhabits seagrass beds and sandy areas of sheltered inshore and seaward reefs, 0.3–30 m. Usually in conch shells. **Range:** NC, Bahamas and all Caribbean to Brazil: replaced by *P. californiensis* in tropical e. Pacific.

White-spotted Hermit Crab   **<30 cm**
Dardanus megistos   *(<12 in)*

Orange-red with dark-edged white spots. Grows larger than a man's hand. **Biology:** inhabits lagoon and seaward reefs, 0.3 m to over 30 m. Aggressive, may attack molluscs to eat as well as take over their shells. Large individuals usually use shells of the Triton's Trumpet *Charonia tritonis*. **Range:** Indo-Pacific, S. Africa to Fr. Polynesia and Hawaii, n. to Ryukyus.

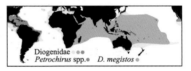

Diogenidae ●●
Petrochirus spp.●   *D. megistos* ●

Land Hermits
Coenobitidae

Coconut Crab   **<35 cm; 2.5 kg**
Birgus latro   *(<14 in; 5.5 lb)*

Purplish brown, turns blue with age. **Biology:** among coastal vegetation near shore. Primarily a nocturnal scavenger that also forages for fruit, particularly fallen coconuts. Hides under roots and in burrows by day. Will climb trees. When approached, will strike upwards. Capable of significant injury. Widely used for food. **Range:** Sumatra to Fr. Polynesia.

A Harlequin Mantis Shrimp *Odontodactylus scyllarus* strikes a curious mantis-like pose. *Sulawesi, RM*

Mantis Shrimps
Order Stomatopoda

The aptly named mantis shrimps look strikingly like underwater versions of a praying mantis, and their primary weapons, massive raptorial limbs, look and function in a similar way. There are two basic types of mantis shrimps: 'spearers', whose dactyls have a series of spikes; and 'smashers', whose dactyls are reinforced with a bony knob. Spearers strike up and under to impale and grasp soft-bodied prey, while smashers strike out to break the shells of armoured prey. Some species can strike with a force that approaches that of a small-calibre bullet and can break the glass of an aquarium! Many mantis shrimps also have sharp spines at the end of their tail. They will readily defend themselves with all their weapons and many can easily cut a finger to the bone. Wounds caused by mantis shrimps are genearally limited to deep lacerations that may require sutures or become infected. Occasionally, the damage is serious enough to require amputation.

Behaviour
Anyone who closely observes a mantis shrimp will soon be drawn to their amazing eyes. Constantly moving and complex, the eyes compliment their weaponry and are essential to their interesting and obviously intelligent behaviour. Mantis shrimps are highly territorial and engage in ritualised fights that may involve complex signalling behaviour. Spearers are primarily ambush predators that lie in wait, usually in a burrow with only their uppermost body parts exposed. Smashers tend to move about as they actively seek out and stalk their prey. Spearers and some smashers live in U-shaped burrows in sand, mud or gravel. Some smashers live in small cavities in coral rock and rubble.

In some spearers, the male maintains the burrow and cares for and brings food to his sequestered female. Female mantis shrimps carry their eggs in their first set of appendages (those normally used for feeding) and can put them down when needed. The eggs hatch into transparent larvae that drift in the plankton for weeks and grow quite large before settling on the bottom.

A *Oratosquilla oratoria*　B　C

Spears, hammers and spines

The raptorial limbs or dactyls of mantis shrimps fold under the cephalothorax and are used for both catching prey and defence, while the spiny tail is used for defence only (A). The dactyls of a typical spearer, the Banded Mantis Shrimp *Lysiosquillina maculata*, have a series of spikes designed to impale soft-bodied prey such as fishes (B and series at right). They are thrust up and under the prey. Each dactyl of a typical smasher is reinforced with a bony knob designed to break the shells of armoured prey such as molluscs and crustaceans (C). Smashers keep the last two segments folded as they strike in an action that can be completed in under five milliseconds. They may wedge prey even larger than themselves against a hard surface and systematically batter it to pieces, taking an hour or more if needed. *(Hawaii, RM; Indonesia, RM, MB)*

Appearance
Mantis shrimps resemble their terrestrial name-sakes the praying mantises. Aside from being crustaceans with completely different body parts, they are much wider, more heavily armoured and get considerably larger. Their dactyls also hinge in a different configuration: 'under-armed' rather than 'over-armed'.

Typical accidents
Accidents involvong mantis shrimps are invari-ably the result of handling or touching them. Shrimpers, who occasionally get injured as they remove them from their catch, refer to them as 'thumb-splitters'. Naive divers or aquarists

occasionally get cut when they handle them or touch a rock occupied by a cavity-dweller. Wounds are normally clean.

Prevention
Never attempt to touch or hold a mantis shrimp.

Species and distribution
Mantis shrimps evolved about 200 million years ago. There are now about 400 species in 19 fam-ilies. They inhabit shallow tropical and warm-temperate waters, from the intertidal zone to depths of a few hundred metres.

Treatment

First aid

If you are badly cut, leave the water immediately and disinfect the wound with alcohol (40–70 per cent) or an iodine tincture.

What not to do

Do not manipulate the wound.

Ongoing medical management

Deep cuts may require sutures and may also need to be monitored for infection.

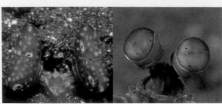

Mantis shrimp eyes are among the most advanced among living animals, providing trinocular vision. They are set high on stalks and can move independently in any direction. Spearer eyes are peanut-shaped (*Lysiosquillina lisa*, left) while those of smashers are round to oval (*Odontodactylus scyllarus*, right). Some spearers have only one visual pigment, specialised for low light, while smashers have up to 16 pigments and four filters that enable them to see ultraviolet and polarised light. *RM*

Smashing Mantis Shrimps
Odontodactylidae

Harlequin Mantis Shrimp	<18 cm
Odontodactylus scyllarus	(<7 in)

Usually <10 cm; eyes round, dactyls with reinforced knob; green with blue and red trim; ♂ darker green than ♀. **Biology:** in most reef habitats, from coastal shallows to offshore slopes, 1 m to over 50 m. Often in the open on sand, rubble or between corals. **Range:** E. Africa to Samoa.
Eyes round, dactyls with reinforced knob; paddle-like flaps and outer tail fans with

Blue-flap Mantis Shrimp	<8 cm
Odontodactylus latirostris	(<3.2 in)

lavender tips. **Biology:** inhabits sandy areas of shallow coastal waters. Common in Malaysia and Indonesia. **Range:** E. Africa to New Caledonia. **Similar:** *O. brevirostris* has pale white to grey 'flaps' and tail fan tips (7 cm; Indo-Pacific to Hawaii).

Odontodactylidae
O. scyllarus *O. latirostris*

Spearing Mantis Shrimps
Lysiosquillidae

Orange Spearer   <25 cm
Lysiosquilloides mapia   (<10 in)

Eyes peanut-shaped with conical top; dactyl spiked; bright orange, upper body with narrow yellow bars. **Biology:** inhabits sand patches of coastal and semi-protected seaward slopes, 2–30 m. Lives in monogamous pairs in U-shaped burrow. **Range:** Philippines and Sulawesi to Fiji.

Banded Mantis Shrimp   <38 cm
Lysiosquillina maculata   (<15 in)

Eyes peanut-shaped; dactyl spiked; pale with black bars; ♂ has larger eyes and dactyls than ♀, ♀ has salmon hue. **Biology:** inhabits sand patches of reef flats, coastal shallows and semi-protected seaward slopes, 1–20 m. Lives in monogamous pairs in U-shaped burrow up to 12 cm wide and 5 m long. Caps burrow entrances by day with mucus and sand, leaving room for eyes and antennules to protrude. ♂ does most of hunting, usually from uncapped burrow entrance at night. Widely fished and marketed in Asia. **Range:** E. Africa to Guam. **Similar:** *L. lisa* is reddish brown and white (right below); *Lysiosquilloides* spp. prefer more rubbly areas.

Lysiosquillidae ●●●
L. maculata ●●●   *L. lisa* ●●   *L. mapia* ●

Passively Poisonous Invertebrates
Invertebrates that are poisonous to eat

Deadly palytoxin was first isolated from the slippery mat-like zoanthid *Palythoa caesia. Guam, RM*

Many species of marine invertebrates are poisonous yet are considered harmless because they are unlike anything normally eaten. This is typically the case for actively poisonous species – those containing toxins that they produce or store. Included in this group are flatworms, sea hares, nudibranchs and soft corals, as well as some sea cucumbers. Passively poisonous species – those that occasionally acquire toxins from their environment or through their diet – are the ones that can be deceptively dangerous to eat. This is because they are similar or identical to things normally eaten and can, on occasion, be violently and deadly poisonous. Included in this group are bivalve shellfish, snails and crustaceans.

Vectors and their toxins

Many of the toxins that affect humans through seafood originate in things we do not eat. Deadly tetrodotoxin (p.198) is produced by bacteria that live symbiotically in a wide variety of species or is acquired by others through the environment or their diet. Palytoxin (p.227) is produced by anemone-like soft corals of the family Zoanthidae, as well as dinoflagellates and, possibly, bacteria. Saxitoxins and gonyautoxins are synthesised by microscopic dinoflagellates that either cause algal blooms or are associated with benthic red algae, and may even also be synthesised by bacteria. Ciguatoxin and maitotoxin (p.207) are produced by dinoflagellates associated with benthic algae. These toxins are incorporated in the tissues of normally edible species through the food chain, thereby rendering them toxic.

Major types of invertebrate poisoning

Poisonings involving bivalves are by far the most important types of invertebrate poisoning because they affect commercially harvested species and thus pose a major threat to public health. Snail and crab poisonings are less of a threat because they usually involve species harvested and consumed locally. In all of these groups, the symptoms and severity of poisoning depend on the source toxins involved.

Mytilus edulis filter algae from the water.

Shellfish Poisoning
Class Bivalvia

Bivalve molluscs, commonly called 'shellfish', are considered a delicacy throughout the world. There are about 20,000 known species but only a fraction of them are consumed by humans and fewer still are mass marketed. Bivalves are filter-feeders that sift planktonic organisms from the water. When they feed on microscopic algae that produce toxins – specifically dinoflagellates and diatoms – they absorb the toxins in their tissues. When these algae are abundant, the concentration of toxins in the bivalves that feed on them rises. Although the bivalves themselves are unaffected, the toxins concentrated in their tissues render them poisonous.

Distribution and occurrence
Shellfish poisoning occurs periodically throughout Europe, North America, Japan, South Africa, Chile and certain coastal areas of the Indo-Pacific such as Thailand and Papua New Guinea.

Outbreaks pose a major health hazard when they affect commercially important bivalves. Species occasionally affected include the Blue Mussel *Mytilus edulis* in Europe, and the California Mussel *Mytilus californianus*, Alaskan Butter Clam *Saxidomus giganteus*, Butter Clam *Saxidomus nuttalli* and Razor Clam (*Siliqua patula*) in North America.

Causative organisms
Shellfish absorb toxins via single-celled algae called dinoflagellates. Under the right circumstances, populations of algae can explode in a phenomenon called an algal bloom or red tide. Blooms involving certain types of dinoflagellates pose a health threat when their toxins enter the food chain and not only kill fish but also accumulate in shellfish eaten by humans.

Types of poisoning, associated algae and their toxins
There are four types of shellfish poisoning, caused by various types of dinoflagellate and at least one diatom. Each has its own set of symptoms, course of progression and degree of severity.

Paralytic shellfish poisoning (PSP): This is the best-known type of shellfish poisoning. It occurs all over the world, is often epidemic and can cause serious illness and death. Symptoms develop fairly rapidly – usually within 30 minutes of ingestion depending on the amount of toxin consumed. They are predominantly neurological and include tingling, burning, numbness, drowsiness, incoherent speech and respiratory paralysis. They can last several days and are accompanied by a general feeling of weakness, dizziness, stupor and difficulty with motor activity. Indications of severe poisoning are difficulty in swallowing and breathing, as well as paralysis in the face and eyes. Respiratory paralysis can result in death. Symptoms usually peak within the first 12 hours, and then weaken within two days. Nausea, diarrhoea and vomiting are not significant. The vectors of PSP are various types of dinoflagellates, including *Alexandrium tamarense, Alexandrium catenella, Alexandrium minutum, Alexandrium monilatum, Pyrodinium bahamense* and *Gymnodinium catenatum*. Scientists believe that more will be discovered. The toxin responsible is a derivative of saxitoxin,

Treatment

First aid
When the first symptoms of shellfish poisoning become apparent (prickliness or numbness in or around the mouth), induce vomiting immediately. However, do not do this if the poisoning has already reached an advanced stage, as suffocation may occur.

Ongoing medical management
There is no antidote to shellfish poisoning. Treatment must correspond to the symptoms. When the ingestion of contaminated food is recent, gut decontamination by gastric lavage and administration of activated charcoal or dilute bicarbonate solution is recommended. Care must be taken concerning aspiration with a neurologically compromised patient. Paralytic shellfish poisoning symptoms reach their peak a few hours after the ingestion of contaminated shellfish and usually subside after three to four days. In cases of severe diarrhoea, ensure the victim remains well hydrated. Depending on the symptoms and the course of the poisoning, the elderly, children and other high-risk patients should remain under medical observation for several days.

When toxic dinoflagellates are abundant, oysters that feed on them (like these Hooded Oysters *Saccostrea cucullata*) may become poisonous. *Bali, RM*

also known as gonyautoxin. It affects nerve cells, blocking the sodium channels and thus the transmission of nerve impulses, ultimately leading to muscular paralysis.

Neurotoxic shellfish poisoning (NSP): The eastern coast of Florida and the Gulf of Mexico often suffer from algal blooms of the dinoflagellate *Ptychodiscus brevis*. During these blooms and some time after, the harvest of shellfish in the affected areas and their sale are banned. The symptoms in NSP are similar to those in ciguatera (p.211), but are not as serious. They begin one to three hours after ingestion and include numbness, tingling in the mouth, arms and legs, lack of coordination, and gastrointestinal upset. As in ciguatera poisoning, some patients report temperature reversal. Death is rare. Recovery normally occurs in two to three days. People prone to allergies can suffer from asthma-like breathing problems when they inhale the aerosolised toxins from sea spray. *Ptychodiscus brevis* produces two types of lipid-soluble toxins known as brevetoxins. They affect the sodium channels that supply the nerve and muscle membranes, causing the muscles to be in a state of constant contraction.

Amnesic shellfish poisoning (ASP): This first came to the attention of public health authorities in 1987 when 153 cases of acute intoxication occurred as a result of ingesting Blue Mussels *Mytilus edulis* cultured off Prince Edward Island, Canada, and harvested when there was a large area affected by algal blooms. Twenty-two individuals were hospitalised and three elderly patients eventually died. What was unique about this type of intoxication was its effect on the central nervous system, specifically permanent damage resulting in memory loss. Marine biologists described the marine diatom *Pseudonitzchia pungens* as the main dinoflagellate involved. The toxin was identified as domoic acid, a natural amino acid and powerful neurotoxin. It attacks the glutamic acid receptors of the nerve cells, which results in a permanent condition of agitation and muscle cramps. In laboratory animals, the toxin caused brain oedema as well as other damage to certain areas of the brain.

Diarrhetic shellfish poisoning (DSP): This is observed primarily as a mild gastrointestinal disorder, i.e. nausea, vomiting, diarrhoea and abdominal pain, accompanied by chills, headache, and fever. The onset of the illness, depending on the dose of toxin ingested, may be in as little as 30 minutes and up to two to three hours, with symptoms lasting as long as two to three days. The first symptoms are nausea and vomiting with severe abdominal cramping, followed by diarrhoea. Recovery is complete, with no aftereffects; the disease is generally not life-threatening. The tingling and burning feeling in the face typical for PSP does not occur in DSP. At present, DSP has been registered only in Europe, Japan and Chile. This form of shellfish poisoning is caused by the dinoflagellate species *Dinophysis acuminata* and *D. fortii*. The toxins okadaic acid, pectenotoxin and yessotoxin have been isolated and identified. The specific effects of these toxins are not yet completely understood.

Prevention

In most developed countries government authorities routinely monitor commercially valuable shellfishes for any signs of toxicity, so eating shellfish from a supermarket or restaurant is relatively safe. However, those who collect and consume their own shellfish without any knowledge of current or past algal blooms, or seasonality of toxicity, are at great risk of being poisoned. Unfortunately, there is no way other than laboratory testing to detect if shellfish are toxic or not. Cooking does not destroy the toxins. It does, however, destroy illness-causing bacteria that may be present in seafood taken from polluted waters.

Snail Poisoning
Class Gastropoda

Marine snails are not eaten by most westerners, but throughout much of the world they an important food source. In Southeast Asia and across the Pacific islands, for example, a broad range of species are eaten, including venomous cone snails (p.317). Some species, including turban snails (family Turbinidae), top shells (family Trochidae) and abalones (*Haliotis* species) are commercially harvested and marketed.

The toxins that occasionally occur in snails include saxitoxin, neosaxitoxin, gonyautoxins and tetrodotoxin (p.198). Whether ingested by eating snails or by any other means, these toxins produce the same serious and sometimes deadly symptoms. There are also several other toxins specific to certain molluscs. Sea hares (family Aplysiidae) contain bromine compounds such as aplysitoxin, which are derived from their algae diet and stored in their digestive organs.

Unlike outbreaks of shellfish poisoning in bivalves, occurrences of gastropod poisoning tend to be rare or sporadic. This is because snails feed on bottom-dwelling organisms rather than the planktonic ones that cause algae blooms. Bottom-dwelling dinoflagellates and other vectors of toxins do not reach the same levels of abundance as planktonic ones during a bloom. As with any other unfamiliar food, the best way to avoid poisoning is to pay attention to local knowledge of what is safe.

The top shell *Trochus niloticus* is the most economically important snail in the tropical western Pacific. Occasionally it can become poisonous. *Palau, RM*

An Indian Volute *Melo melo* and other snails for sale in a Hong Kong market. *Hong Kong, RM*

In Borneo, five children died after eating Black Olive Snails *Oliva vidua* similar to this one. The snails contained saxitoxin. *Bali, RM*

Sea hares like this *Dolabella auricularia* contain toxic bromine compounds. When disturbed, they exude a violet liquid. *Guam, RM*

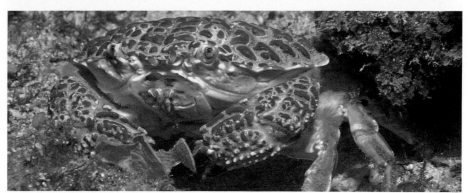

The stunning *Zosimus aeneus* is one of the most frequently poisonous species of crab. *Mauritius, RM*

Crab Poisoning
Class Crustacea

Most incidents of crustacean poisoning involve coral reef-dwelling crabs, perhaps because they are likley to feed on toxic organisms than those that occur in other habitats. The most frequently toxic species are certain members of the family Xanthidae: *Atergatis floridus, Atergatopsis germaini, Demania alcalai, D. toxica, D. reynaudii, Lophozozymus pictor, Platypodia granulosa* and *Zosimus aeneus*. Poisoning by these species is often fatal. Occasionally, normally edible species can be poisonous. These include the xanthid *Etisus utilus*, as well as members of the families Eriphiidae (*Eriphia sebuna*), Carpiliidae (*Carpilius convexus, C. maculatus*), Parthenopidae (*Daldorfia horrida*), Majidae, Grapsidae and Portunidae, and the land-dwelling Coconut Crab *Birgus latro* (p.356). Cases of poisoning involving these crabs are normally relatively mild. The Asian horseshoe crabs *Carcinoscorpius rotundicauda* and *Tachypleus gigas* (class Merostomata), which are actually more closely related to spiders than crabs, can also be toxic.

Typical circumstances
Cases of poisoning typically involve crabs caught on coral reefs and occur sporadically throughout the Indo-Pacific. In most cases, the crabs are cooked, often in soup – the dissolved toxins in such a dish can severely poison all who eat it. Rarely, the crabs and, more frequently, the eggs are eaten raw.

Toxins involved
A variety of toxins have been found in crabs. These come from various sources and occur in all body tissues. Most poisonous crabs contain high concentrations of saxitoxins and gonyautoxins, which cause paralytic shellfish poisoning (PSP; p.364). These toxins can be found in red algae that the crabs eat or may even be synthesised by bacteria living within the crabs. Deadly tetrodotoxin (TTX; p.198) has been found in *Lophozozymus pictor* and *Atergatis floridus*. In *A. floridus* it is synthesised by intestinal bacteria. Tetrodotoxin also occurs in Asian horseshoe crabs, in particularly high concentrations in the hepatopancreas and the eggs, which are occasionally eaten. The crabs *Demania alcalai, D. toxica, D. reynaudii* and *Lophozozymus pictor* often contain deadly palytoxin (p.227), possibly acquired by feeding on zoantharians of the genus *Palythoa* or dinoflagellates associated with algae. The unknown toxin in coconut crabs is probably acquired from plants in their diet.

Symptoms
Symptoms vary according to the causative agent. If poisoning is due to saxitoxins and gonyautoxins, they are identical to those of PSP (p.364) and are not usually fatal. If due to tetrodotoxin or palytoxin, symptoms are severe and often fatal. Symptoms due to tetrodotoxin, involving progressive paralysis, are identical to those of puffer poisoning (p.200), while those due to palytoxin (p.227) may involve severe

The Seven-eleven Crab *Carpilius maculatus* is widely eaten across the Indo-Pacific. Although considered safe, on rare occasions it can be toxic. *Guam, RM*

The horseshoe crab *Tachypleus gigas* is seasonally toxic and can contain tetrodotoxin. Usually only the eggs are eaten. *Hong Kong, RM*

gastointestinal distress, severe muscular pain, uncontrolled contractions, seizures and, ultimately, respiratory paralysis. If more than one toxin is involved, there may be a mix of symp-

toms. Symptoms of Coconut Crab poisoning are often delayed, may last several days and include nausea, abdominal pain, vomiting, diarrhoea, cold sweats, anuria and loss of consciousness.

Prevention
Avoid eating crabs caught on coral reefs if alternatives such as sand-dwelling species are available. Local knowledge is essential. Eat only known safe crab species that come from safe areas.

IF POISONED

Treatment

First aid
At the first signs of poisoning, induce vomiting, although not if paralysis of the mouth and throat has set in or if the patient has diffculty swallowing. Seek emergency medical aid immediately. Once breathing becomes impaired, artificial respiration is essential.

Ongoing medical management
Treatment is supportive and symptomatic, and is basically the same as for puffer poisoning (p.201). The patient must be ventilated throughout the course of paralysis. There are no antidotes.

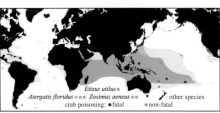

Distribution of crabs of the family Xanthidae, with locations of some poisonings.

Stone Crabs
Eriphiidae

Rough Red-eyed Crab	<6 cm
Eriphia smithi	(<2.6 in)

Shell heavy, rounded with small nodules; reddish brown, eyes red. **Biology:** among rocks and rubble, intertidal zone. Common in tidepools. Feeds on algae and molluscs. Potentially toxic for short periods. The close relative *E. sebana* is also ocasionally poisonous. **Range:** E. Africa to New Caledonia, n. to s. Japan; Hawaii. **Similar:** *E. sebana* has fewer granules and is a paler, more beige colour (Indo-Pacific).

Xanthid Crabs
Xanthidae

Granulose Reef Crab <15 cm
Zosimus aeneus (<6 in)

Shell granulose with network of blue to tan valleys between brick- to wine-red raised areas. **Biology:** among coral and rubble of reef flats and slopes. Moderately common on intertidal flats. Usually hidden by day, forages at night on algae. One of the most frequently deadly poisonous spp. of crab. **Range:** Red Sea to Fr. Polynesia, n. to s. Japan.

False Reef Crab <15 cm
Atergatis floridus (<6 in)

Shell heavy, smoothly rounded; pale brown with tan blotches, tips of claws dark. Resembles reef crabs (Carpiliidae). **Biology:** among coral and rubble of reef flats and slopes. Moderately common on intertidal flats. Forages at night on algae. Can be deadly poisonous owing to the presence of tetrodotoxin synthesised by intestinal bacteria. **Range:** Red Sea to Fr. Polynesia, n. to s. Japan. **Similar:** reef crabs (Carpiliidae) have a similar smoothly rounded shell but differ in colour pattern.

Sawedged Spooner <15 cm
Etisus utilus (<6 in)

Shell heavy, the front margin with 8 pointed teeth behind each eye; brownish red, tips of claws black. **Biology:** among coral and rubble of outer reef flats and slopes. Moderately common, usually hidden by day, forages at night on algae. Occasionally mildly poisonous. **Range:** SE Asia to New Caledonia. **Similar:** *E. splendens* and *E. dentatus* differ in details of shell sculpting and are brighter red (15 cm; Indo-Pacific, e. to Hawaii and Fr. Polynesia;).

This sea cucumber has extruded tubules that will instantly cling to anything it touches. *Guam, RM*

Sea Cucumbers
Class Holothuroidea

Sea cucumbers are rather unassuming relatives of starfishes and sea urchins. Unlike the latter, they are comparatively soft-bodied and, for the most part, are harmless. However, under the right circumstances they can harm a human in three ways: by emitting an irritating sticky thread-like substance, by poisoning when improperly prepared as food, and by piercing the skin with minute sharp spicules.

When disturbed, some species eject strings of an extremely sticky white to pink substance called Cuvierian tubules from their cloaca. These adhere to skin and swimsuits, and when in contact with mucus membranes can cause inflammatory reactions. They are otherwise only uncomfortable when they shrink and pull on skin and hair. At the earliest convenience, Cuvierian tubules should be removed and the affected area washed.

Although sea cucumbers contain toxic compounds, many species are widely harvested for the Asian *trepang*, or *bêche-de-mer*, fishery. They

are gutted, boiled, washed and dried, and then shipped to Asian markets for use in 'aphrodisiac' dishes. When improperly prepared, they can cause serious poisoning. When rubbed, the skin of at least one species, *Holothuria atra*, emits a toxic purplish-red fluid called holothurin, which is used by Pacific islanders to poison fish in tidepools. It does not affect the edibility of the fish. One group of holothurians, the delicate, highly contractile synaptids, have minute sharp-hooked spicules throughout their skin. In some of the larger species (*Opheodesoma* spp., *Synapta maculata*), these can break off when they are handled and cause considerable irritation.

Sea cucumbers are bottom-dwellers that occur in all seas and at all depths. They are nature's vacuum cleaners. Most feed by straining nutirents and detritus from bottom sediments. Those harvested for food are typically found in shallow tropical and subtropical waters. Overharvesting has depleted stocks in many areas.

Holothuroidea

Spotted Sea Cucumber	<25 cm
Bohadschia argus	*(<10 in)*

Beige to brown with dark-edged and dark-centred brown spots. **Biology:** on sand and rubble patches of shallow reef flats and lagoon and seaward reefs to 40 m. Extrudes sticky white Cuvierian tubules when disturbed. **Range:** Seychelles to Fr. Polynesia, n. to s. Japan. **Similar:** many spp. on rubble and sand, most emitting Cuvierian tubules.

Black Sea Cucumber	<45 cm
Holothuria atra	*(<18 in)*

Black with smooth skin that has sand stuck to surface. **Biology:** on sand patches of shallow reef flats and seagrass beds, tidepools to 30 m. Exposed, but covered with sand. Emits the toxic purplish-red fluid holothurin when handled and may eject viscera when severely disturbed. Reproduces sexually and by fission. **Range:** Red Sea to Polynesia. **Similar:** several spp., usually without sand sticking on them.

Synaptidae

Worm Cucumber	<2.5 m
Synapta maculata	*(<8 ft)*

Elongate with bubble-like rings; brown with darker bars and stripes. Highly contractile. **Biology:** on silty sand and rubble of protected flats and slopes to at least 10 m. Common in shallow lagoons. Feeds on detritus by inserting sticky oral tentacles in mouth. Skin feels prickly owing to small, sharp spicules, which can break off and irritate human skin. **Range:** Red Sea to Fr. Polynesia. **Similar:** several spp., all with small spicules.

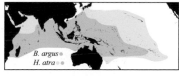

B. argus ●
H. atra ●

Index

Ablabys binotatus 64
  macracanthus 64
  taenianotus 64
Acalyptophis peronii 245
Acanthasteridae 335–7
Acanthocybium solandri 229
Acanthostracion polygonius 237
  quadricornis 238
Acanthuridae 169–83
Acanthurinae 173–80
Acanthurus achilles 175
  albipectoralis 178
  bahianus 173
  bariene 178
  blochii 177
  chirurgus 173
  coeruleus 173
  dussumieri 177
  guttatus 178
  japonicus 175
  leucosternon 175
  lineatus 174
  mata 178
  nigricans 175
  nigricauda 176
  olivaceus 176
  polyzona 174
  pyroferus 177
  sohal 174
  tennenti 176
  triostegus 174
  xanthopterus 177
Acrochordus grannulatus 248
Actiniidae 302–3
Actinodendron alcyonoidea 304
  arborea 304
Actinodendronidae 304–5
Actinostephanus haeckeli 304
Aetobatus narinari 27
Aetomylaeus 27
Aglaophenia cupressina 269
Aglaopheniidae 269–70
Agujon 161
Aipysurus duboisii 246
  laevis 246, 248
Algae, Stinging 286

Alicia sansibarensis 301
Aliciidae 301
Aluterus scriptus 229
Amberjack, Greater 219
Amphinomidae 312–14
Amplexidiscus fenestrafer 309
Anemone, Armed 303
  Banded Tube 308
  Berried 301
  Branching 302
  Bushy Fire 305
  Corkscrew 305
  Giant 303
  Globular Fire 304
  Golden 303
  Greater Tube 307
  Hell's Fire 304
  Hidden 302
  Jack-in-the-box 301
  Knobbly 305
  Snake-lock 302
  Spider Fire 304
  Transparent Tube 308
  Wideband Tube 308
Anemones, Disc 309–10
  Sea 298–305
  Tube 306–8
Anemonia sulcata 302
Anomura 355–6
Antennella 268
Antennellopsis integerrima 268
Anthozoa 298–310
Apistidae 36, 65
Apistops caloundra 65
Apistus carinatus 65
Aploactinidae 36, 81
Aprion virescens 220
Arachnactidae 308
Arachnanthus nocturnus 308
  oligopodus 308
  unid. sp. 308
Arbacia lixula 343
Arbaciidae 343
Ariidae 31–2
Arothron caeruleopunctatus 203
  diadematus 204

hispidus 203
  manilensis 203
  mappa 204
  meleagris 204
  nigropunctatus 204
  reticularis 203
  stellatus 155
Asteronotus cespitosus 333
Asthenosoma ijimai 352
  marisrubri 352
  varium 352
Astropyga radiata 342
Astroscopus guttatus 195
  sexspinosus 195
  ygraecum 195
  zephyreus 195
Atergatis floridus 369
Aurelia sp. 288
Auxis thazard 229

Bagre bagre 32
  marinus 32
Balistapus undulatus 152
Balistes capriscus 151
  vetula 151
Balistidae 146–52
Balistoides conspicillum 149
  viridescens 150
Barbfish 43
Barracuda, Blackfin 145
  Great 145
  Pickhandle 145
Barracudas 143–5
Bartholomea annulata 305
Batrachoididae 33–4, 235
Bells, Swimming 281
Belonidae 160–1
Belonoperca chabanaudi 235
Birgus latro 356
Bivalvia 364–5
Blenniidae 88–90
Bloodworms 315–16
Bohadschia argus 371
Bolbometopon muricatum 189, 222
Bottle, Blue 280
Bougainvillia 271
Boxfish, Longnose 239

Shortnose 239
Yellow 239
Brachypterois serrulata 62
Brachysomophis cirrocheilos
  141
    crocodilinus 141
    henshawi 141
Bristletooth, Goldring 179
Striped 179
Burrfish, Birdbeak 158
Bridled 158
Spotfin 158
Striped 158
Web 158
Button, Blue 267
By-the-wind Sailor 267

Calamus bajonado 226
Calycophora 281
Caracanthidae 36, 81
Caracanthus maculatus 81
    madagascariensis 81
    typicus 81
Carangidae 218–19, 224
Caranx hippos 224
    ignobilis 218
    latus 224
    melampygus 218
Carcharhinidae 112–18
Carcharhinus albimarginatus
  114
    amblyrhynchos 116
    falciformis 114
    galapagensis 115
    leucas 113
    limbatus 115
    longimanus 114
    melanopterus 116
    perezi 117
    plumbeus 115
Carcharias tauru 111
Carcharodon carcharias 111
Caringidae 82–3
Carpiliidae 369
Carpilius maculatus 368
Carukia 296
Carybdea alata 296
    rastoni 296

sivickisi 296
Cassiopea andromeda 290
Cassiopeidae 290
Catfish, Coco Sea 32
    Gafftopsail 32
    Giant Sea 32
    Hardhead 32
    Striped Eel 30
    Whitelipped Eel 30
Catfishes, Eel 28–30
    Sea 31–2
Centrostephanus longispinus
  343
Cephalopholis argus 216
Cephea cephea 289
    octostyla 289
Cepheidae 289
Cerianthus 306–8
Cerianthidae 307–8
Cerianthus cf. *filiformis* 307
    magnus 307
    membranaceus 307
Cheilinus undulatus 221
Cheilodipterus nigrovittatus
  90
Chelonia mydas 253
Chelonodon patoca 205
Cheroscorpaena tridactyla 65
Chilomycterus antennatus 158
    antillarum 158
    reticulatus 157, 158
    schoepfi 158
Chirodropidae 296
Chironex fleckeri 296
Chloeia flava 314
    viridis 314
Chlorurus microrhinos 222
Choridactylinae 75–9
Choridactylus multibarbus 79
    natalensis 79
    striatus 79
Chrysaora hyoscellu 287
    quinquecirrha 287
Clingfish, Urchin 237
Clupeidae 228
Cnidaria 262–311
Cnidarians 262–311
Cnidoscyphus sp. 271

Coenobitidae 356
Condylactis aurantiaca 303
    gigantea 303
Cone, Abbreviated 320
    Admiral 320
    Banda 320, 324
    Cat 320
    Characteristic 320
    Crowned 320
    Feathered 320
    Flag 320
    Flea-bite 320
    Geography 320, 323
    Glory-of-the-seas 320
    Hebrew 320
    Ivory 320
    Leopard 320
    Lettered 320
    Livid 320
    Magus 320
    Marbled 320, 324
    Morelet's 320
    Nusatella 320
    Obscure 320
    Omaria 320
    Princely 320, 324
    Rat 320
    Soldier 320
    Striated 320, 323
    Striatellus 320
    Tesselate 320, 324
    Textile 320, 323
    Tulip 320
    Virgin 320
Conidae 317–24
Conus abbreviatus 320
    ammiralis 320
    aulicus 320, 324
    bandanus 320, 324
    caracteristicus 320
    catus 320
    coronatus 320
    ebraeus 320
    eburneus 320
    geographus 320, 323
    gloriamaris 320
    leopardus 320
    litteratus 320

Conus cont.
 lividus 320
 magus 320
 marmoreus 320, 324
 miles 320
 moreleti 320
 nusatella 320
 obscurus 320
 omaria 320
 pennaceus 320
 pulicarius 320
 rattus 320
 striatellus 320
 striatus 320, 323
 tessulatus 320, 324
 textile 320, 323
 tulipa 320
 vexillum 320
 virgo 320
Coral, Blade Fire 276
 Box Fire 276
 Branching Fire 276
 Intricate Fire 275
 Net Fire 275
 Plate Fire 275
 Red Fire 276
Coralgrouper, Blacksaddled 217
 Squaretail 217
Corallimorph, Giant 309
 Mat 310
Corallimorpharia 309–10
Corals, Fire 273–6
Coronatae 286
Coryphaena hippurus 229
Coryphaenidae 229
Cotylorhiza erythraea 289
 tuberculata 289
Cowfish, Honeycomb 237
 Longhorn 239
 Scrawled 238
Crab, Coconut 356
 False Reef 369
 Giant Hermit 356
 Granulose Reef 369
 Rough Red-eyed 368
 Seven-eleven 368
 White-spotted Hermit 356
Crabs 354–7, 367–9

Hermit 355–6
Stone 368
Xanthid 369
Crocodile, Estuarine 251
Crocodiles 250–1
Crocodylia 250–1
Crocodylidae 250–1
Crocodylus porosus 251
Croucher, Spotted Coral 81
Crustacea 367–9
Ctenochaetus striatus 179
 strigosus 179
Cubozoa 292–6
Cucumber, Black Sea 371
 Spotted Sea 371
 Worm 371
Cucumbers, Sea 370–1
Cuttlefish, Flamboyant 333
Cyanea capillata 288
 lamarcki 288
 nozakii 288
Cyaneidae 288
Cyclichthys orbicularis 158
Cystonecta 280

Dardanus megistos 356
Dasyatidae 20–1, 23–6
Dasyatis americana 23
 centroura 23
 kuhlii 24
 say 23
Decapoda 354–7
Dendrochirus barberi 61
 bellus 61
 biocellatus 61
 brachypterus 61
 zebra 60
Dermochelys coriacea 254
Desmacidonidae 260
Devilfish, Spiny 78
Devilfishes 74–9
Diadema antillarum 341
 ascensionis 341
 mexicanum 341
 setosum 341
Diadematidae 341–3
Diademichthys lineatus 237
Diodon holocanthus 157

 hystrix 157, 158
 liturosus 157
Diodontidae 156–9
Diogenidae 356
Diploprion bifasciatus 235
 drachi 235
Discosoma rhodostoma 310
Discosomatidae 309–10
Doctorfish 173
Dofleinia armata 303
Dolabella auricularia 366
Dragon, Komodo 255

Ebosia bleekeri 62
 falcata 62
Echidna catenata 133
 nebulosa 139
 polyzona 138
Echiichthys vipera 87
Echinidae 344
Echinoidea 338–51
Echinometra matthaei 345
Echinometridae 345
Echinostrephus acicularis 345
 molaris 345
Echinothrix calamaris 342
 diadema 342
Echinothuridae 350–3
Echinus 344
Echiophis intertinctus 141
 punctifer 141
Eel, King Snake 140
 Napoleon Snake 141
 Snapper 141
 Spotted Spoon-nose 141
 Stargazer Snake 141
Eels, Moray 127–39
 Snake 140–1
Egg, West Indian Sea 349
Emperor, Longface 220
 Orangefin 220
 Smalltooth 220
Emperors 220
Emydocephalus annulatus 248
Enchelycore anatina 133
 pardalis 139
Enchelynassa canina 139
Enhydrina schistosa 248

Epinephelidae 185–8
Epinephelus cyanopodus 216
    fuscoguttatus 217
    itajara 187
    lanceolatus 187
    polyphekadion 217
    tukula 188
Eretmochelys imbricata 253
Eriphia sebana 368
    smithi 368
Eriphiidae 368
Erosa daruma 73
    erosa 73
Etisus dentatus 369
    splendens 369
    utilus 369
Eucrossorhinus dasypogon 123
Eudendrium 271
Eunice longisetis 316
    sp. cf. aphroditois 316
Eunicidae 315–16
Euthynnus affinis 229

Fangblennies 88–90
Fangblenny, Bicolour 90
    Canary 90
    Hairytail 90
    Lined 90
    Striped 90
    Yellowtail 90
Feroxodon multistriatus 155
Filefish, Scrawled 229
Fireworm, Bearded 314
    Lined 314
    Yellow 314
Fireworms 312–14
Fishes, Ciguatoxic 207–26
    Crinotoxic 233–9
    Gempylotoxic 231
    Hallucinogenic 230
    Palytoxic 227–9
    Poisonous 197–239
    Scombrotoxic 229–30
    Tetrodotoxic 198–205
    Traumatogenic 100–95
    Venomous 16–99

Galeocerdo cuvier 113

Gastropoda 366
Ginglymostoma cirratum 124
Ginglymostomatidiae 124
Glyceridae 315–16
Goatfish, Bandtail 230
Gobiesocidae 237
Grammistes sexlineatus 236
Grammistidae 235–6
Grouper, Black 223
    Brown-marbled 217
    Camouflage 217
    Giant 187
    Goliath 187
    Lyretail 218
    Peacock 216
    Potato 188
    Speckled Blue 216
    Tiger 223
    White-edged Lyretail 218
    Yellowfin 224
Groupers 216–18, 223–4
    Giant 185–8
Gymnangium eximium 269
    graciliacaule 269
    hians 269
Gymnosarda unicolor 222
Gymnothorax breedeni 135
    favagineus 135
    fimbriatus 136
    flavimarginatus 134
    funebris 132
    griseus 137
    isingteena 135
    javanicus 134
    meleagris 136
    moringa 132
    nudivomer 136
    pictus 137
    thyrsoideus 138
    undulatus 137
    vicinus 132
Gymnuridae 22

Halopterididae 268
Hammerhead, Great 119
    Scalloped 119
    Smooth 119
Hapalochlaena lunulata 330

Herklotsichthys
    quadrimaculatus 228
Hermits, Land 356
Hermodice carunculata 314
Hesionidae 312–13
Himantura fai 24
    granulata 25
    jenkinsii 24
    uarnak 25
    undulata 25
Hogfish 226
Holocentridae 162–5
Holocentrinae 162–5
Holocentrus adscensionis 165
    rufus 165
Holothuria atra 371
Holothuroidea 370–1
Houndfish 161
    Red Sea 161
Hydroid, Algae 271
    Black 270
    Black-stemmed 270
    Christmas Tree 268
    Fern 269
    Golden Feather 269
    Golden Quill 269
    Graceful Feather 269
    Maroon 269
    Orange-stemmed 270
    Seafan 267
    Solitary Gorgonian 268
    Stinging Bush 271
    Yellow Tuft 268
    Yellow-polyp 271
Hydroids, Fern 269–70
    Orange-stemmed 270–1
    Pelagic 267
    Solitary 268
    Tuft 268
Hydrophiinae 241–7, 248
Hydrophis atriceps 248
    coggeri 247
    cyanocinctus 248
    elegans 248
    gracilis 248
    klossi 248
Hydrozaons 264–76
Hydrozoa 264–76

Inimicus caledonicus 79
  didactylus 78
  filamentosus 78
  sinensis 79
Invertebrates, Venomous
  256–361
  Passively Poisonous 362–71
Iracundus signifer 48
Isarachnanthus bandanensis
  308

Jack, Crevalle 224
  Horse-eye 224
Jacks 218–19, 224
Jelly, Rope-armed 291
  Thimble 286
Jellyfish, Australian Spotted
  291
  Box 296
  Canonball 290
  Cauliflower 289
  Compass 287
  Fried Egg 288
  Lagoon 291
  Luminescent 287
  Lung 291
  Mediterranean 289
  Upside-down 290
Jellyfishes 282–91
  Box 292–6
Jobfish, Green 220

Katsuwonus pelamis 229
Kawakawa 229
Krait, Broad-banded Sea 248
  Brown-lipped Sea 248
  Yellow-lipped Sea 247, 248

Labridae 221, 226
Lachnolaimus maximus 226
Lactoria cornuta 239
Lagocephalus scleratus 155
Lamnidae 110–11
Lapemis curtus 248
Laticauda colubrina 247, 248
  frontalis 247
  laticaudata 248
  semifasciata 248

Laticaudinae 241–4, 247, 248
Leatherjacket 83
Leatherjackets 82–3
Lebrunia coralligens 302
  danae 302
Lethrinidae 220
Lethrinus erythracanthus 220
  microdon 220
  olivaceus 220
Linuche unguiculata 286
Linuchidae 286
Lionfish, African 60
  Blackfoot 62
  Bleeker's 62
  Clearfin 59
  Common 57
  Green 61
  Hawaiian 60
  Japanese 59
  Kodipungi 58
  Longspine 58
  Plaintail 58
  Pygmy 62
  Red 57
  Shortfin 61
  Spotfin 59
  Two-spot 61
  Zebra 60
Lionfishes 53–62
Lion's Mane 288
  Blue 288
Lobsters 354–5
Lutjanidae 219–20, 225
Lutjanus bohar 219
  cyanopterus 225
  jocu 225
  monostigma 219
Lysiosquillidae 361
Lysiosquillina lisa 361
  maculata 361
Lysiosquilloides 361
Lysiosquilloides mapia 361
Lytechinus variegatus 349
Lytocarpia niger 270

Mackerel, Indian 229
  Narrow-barred Spanish
  223

Mackerels 222
  Purgative Snake 231
Macrorhynchia philippina 270
  phoenicea 270
Mahimahi 229
Malo 296
Man-of-war, Portuguese 280
Manta birostris 189
Mastigias papua 291
Mastigiidae 291
Megalactis comatus 305
Meiacanthus atrodorsalis 90
  crinitus 90
  grammistes 90
  lineatus 90
  oualanensis 90
Melichthys indicus 152
  niger 151
  vidua 152
Melo melo 366
Men-of-war 277–80
Mespilia globulus 344
Metasepia pfefferi 333
Microcyphus rousseaui 344
Millepora alcicornis 276
  complanata 276
  dichotoma 275
  exaesa 276
  intricata 275
  latifolia 275
  platyphylla 275
  squarrosa 276
  tenera 275
  tuberosa 276
Milleporidae 273–6
Minoinae 80
Minous pictus 80
  pusillus 80
  trachycephalus 80
Mobula spp. 189
Monacanthidae 229
Monkeyfish 73
Moon Jelly 288
Moray, Barred 138
  Black-spotted 135
  Blackcheek 135
  Chain 133
  Dotted 133

Dragon 139
Fangtooth 133
Fimbriated 136
Giant 134
Green 132
Grey 137
Greyface 138
Honeycomb 135
Mediterranean 133
Peppered 137
Purplemouth 132
Snowflake 139
Spotted 132
Undulated 137
Viper 139
Whitemouth 136
Yellow-edged 134
Yellowmouth 136
Morays 127–39
Atlantic 132–3
Indo-Pacific 134–9
Muraena augusti 133
helena 133
Muraenidae 127–39
Mycteroperca bonaci 223
tigris 223
venenosa 224
Myliobatidae 22, 27
Myliobatiformes 17–27

Narcine sp. 194
Narcinidae 194
Nasinae 182–3
Naso annulatus 183
elegans 182
hexacanthus 183
lituratus 182
unicornis 182
vlamingii 183
Nausithoe spp. 286
Nausithoidae 286
Nebrius ferrugineus 124
Needlefish, Banded 161
Keeled 161
Needlefishes 160–1
Negaprion brevirostris 117
Nemertesia 268
Nemophini 88–90

Neofibularia mordens 260
nolitangere 260
Neoniphon marianus 165
sammara 165
Nettle, Sea 287
Netuma thalassinus 32
Nudibranch, Clumpy 333
Nudibranchia 333
Nudibranchs 333
Numbfish, Indonesian 194

Obelia 271
Octopodidae 326–31
Octopus, Greater Blue-ringed 330
Midring Blue-ringed 330
Octopuses, Blue-ringed 326–31
Odontaspididae 111
Odontaspis ferox 111
Odontodactylidae 360
Odontodactylus brevirostris 360
latirostris 360
scyllarus 360
Oligoplites palometa 83
saliens 83
saurus 83
Oliva vidua 366
Ophichthidae 140–1
Ophichthus bonaparti 141
rex 140
Orectolobidae 123
Orectolobiformes 120–5
Orectolobus sp. 123
Ostraciidae 237–9
Ostracion cubicus 239
meleagris 239
Oxycheilinus unifasciatus 221

Pachycerianthus cf. insignis 308
insignis 308
maua 308
Paracanthurus hepatus 179
Paracentropogon longispinis 64
vespa 64
Paracentrotus lividus 344
Paraplotosus albilabris 30

Parapterois heterura 62
macrura 62
Pardachirus marmoratus 237
pavoninus 237
Parrotfish, Bumphead 189
Pacific Steephead 222
Pastinachus sephen 25
Pelagia noctiluca 287
Pelagiidae 287
Pelamis platurus 245, 248
Pennaria disticha 268
Pennariidae 268
Petrochirus diogenes 356
Petroscirtes breviceps 90
Phacellophora camtschatica 288
Pherecardia striata 314
Phyllactidae 302
Phyllodiscus semoni 301
Phyllorhiza punctata 291
Phymanthidae 305
Physalia physalis 277–80
utriculus 277–80
Physaliidae 280
Plagiotremus laudandus 90
laudandus flavus 90
Platybelone argalus 161
Plectropomus areolatus 217
laevis 217
Plotosidae 28–30
Plotosus lineatus 30
nkunga 30
Pogonoperca ocellata 236
punctata 236
Polychaeta 312–16
Polynoidae 312–13
Porcupinefish 157
Black-blotched 157
Long-spine 157
Porcupinefishes 156–9
Porgy, Jolthead 226
Porifera 257–60
Porpita porpita 267
Porpitidae 267
Praya sp. 281
Prayidae 281
Prionace glauca 118
Prionurinae 181

Prionurus chrysurus 181
    scalprum 181
Psammechinus 344
Pseudobalistes
        flavimarginatus 150
    fuscus 150
Ptarmus gallus 81
    jubatus 81
Pteroidichthys amboinensis 50
Pteroinae 53–62
Pterois antennata 59
    kodipungi 58
    lunulata 59
    miles 57
    mombasae 60
    radiata 59
    russellii 58
    sphex 60
    volitans 57
Puffer, Bandtail 205
    Blackspotted 204
    Bluespotted 203
    Checkered 205
    Ferocious 155
    Guineafowl 204
    Map 204
    Masked 204
    Milkspotted 205
    Reticulated 203
    Silver 155
    Starry 155
    Striped 203
    Whitespotted 203
Puffers 153–5

Queenfish, Doublespotted 83
    Talang 83
Queenfishes 82–3

Rabbitfish, Brown-spotted 98
    Coral 97
    Double-barred 97
    Foxface 99
    Gold-spotted 98
    Lined 96
    Magnificent 99
    Masked 97
    Onespot Foxface 99

Orange-spotted 96
Rivulated 96
Scribbled 97
Starry 98
Streaked 99
Rabbitfishes 93–9
Ragactis lucida 305
Ralpharia gorgoniae 268
Rastrelliger kanagurta 229
Ray, Blotched Fantail 26
    Bluespotted Ribbontail 26
    Leopard Torpedo 193
    Manta 189
    Marbled Torpedo 193
    Spotted Eagle 27
Rays, American Round 22, 26
    Butterfly 22
    Eagle 22, 27
    Electric 191–5
    Torpedo 193
Redskinfish 64
Reptiles 240–55
Rhinecanthus aculeatus 152
    assasi 152
    rectangulus 152
Rhinesomus bicaudalis 238
    triqueter 238
Rhinopias aphanes 49
    argoliba 50
    cea 49
    eschmeyeri 49
    frondosa 49
    xenops 50
Rhizostoma pulmo 291
Rhizostomeae 289–91
Rhynchostracion nasus 239
    rhinorhynchus 239
Richardsonichthys leucogaster
    65
Rockfish, Small 44
Rockfishes 36
Rougefish, Whitebellied 65
Rypticus maculatus 236
    saponaceus 236

Salmacis spp. 344
Sanderia malayensis 287
Sanopus splendidus 235

Sapo Cano 34
Sardine, Goldspot 228
Sargocentron caudimaculatum
    164
    diadema 164
    spiniferum 164
Sawtall, Indonesian 181
    Scalpel 181
Scaleworms 312–13
Scaridae 222
Scat, African 91
    Spotbanded 91
    Spotted 91
Scatophagidae 91
Scatophagus spp. 91
    argus 91
    tetracanthus 91
Sciades felis 32
Scolopsis bilineatus 90
Scomberoides
        commersonianus 83
    lysan 83
Scomberomorus commerson
    223
Scombridae 222, 229
Scorpaena brasiliensis 43
    grandicornis 43
    inermis 43
    notata 44
    plumieri 43
    porcus 44
    scrofa 44
Scorpaenidae 36
Scorpaeniformes 36–81
Scorpaeninae 38–51
Scorpaenopsis barbata 47
    cacopsis 45
    diabolus 48
    eschmeyeri 46
    gibbosa 47
    macrochir 47
    neglecta 47
    orientalis 45
    oxycephala 45
    papuensis 46
    possi 46
    ramaraoi 45
    venosa 46

Scorpionfish, Ambon 50
Bandtail 47
Bearded 47
Black 44
Crested 81
Decoy 48
Devil 48
Flasher 47
Humpback 47
Japanese 50
Jenkins' 45
Lacy 49
Large-scaled 44
Leaf 50
Mushroom 43
Paddle-flap 49
Papuan 46
Plumed 43
Raggy 46
Spinycrown 46
Spotted 43
Strange-eyed 50
Tasselled 45
Weedy 49
Scorpionfishes 36–51
Indo-Pacific 45–51
Mediterranean 44
W. Atlantic 43
Scyphozoa 282–91
Sebastidae 36
Selenotoca multifasciata 91
Semaeostomeae 287–8
Sepiidae 333
Seriola dumerili 219
Serranidae 185–8, 216–18, 223–4
Sertularella speciosa 270
Sertularia sp. 270, 271
Sertulariidae 270–1
Shark, Blacktip 115
Blacktip Reef 116
Blue 118
Bull 113
Caribbean Reef 117
Galapagos 115
Gray Reef 116
Great White 111
Lemon 117

Nurse 124
Oceanic Whitetip 114
Sand Tiger 111
Sandbar 115
Silky 114
Silvertip 114
Small-tooth Sand Tiger 111
Tawny Nurse 124
Tiger 113
Whitetip Reef 118
Zebra 125
Sharks 101–25
Carpet 120–2
Hammerhead 119
Mackerel 110–11
Nurse 124
Requiem 112–18
Sand Tiger 111
Shellfish 364–5
Shrimp, Banded Mantis 361
Blue-flap Mantis 360
Harlequin Mantis 360
Shrimps, Mantis 358–61
Smashing Mantis 360
Spearing Mantis 361
Siganidae 93–9
Siganus corallinus 97
doliatus 97
guttatus 96
javus 99
laqueus 98
lineatus 96
magnificus 99
puellus 97
punctatus 98
rivulatus 96
stellatus 98
unimaculatus 99
virgatus 97
vulpinus 99
Siphonophora 277–81
Siphonophores 277–81
Snail, Black Olive 366
Snails 366
Cone 317–24
Snake, Beaked Sea 248
Black-headed Sea 248
Blue-banded Sea 248

Cogger's Sea 247
Dubois' Sea 246
Elegant Sea 248
Greater Dusky Sea 248
Horned Sea 245
Marine File 248
Olive Sea 246, 248
Short Sea 248
Slender Sea 248
Turtle-headed Sea 248
Yellow-bellied Sea 245, 248
Snakes, Sea 241–9
Snapper, Cubera 225
Dog 225
Onespot 219
Twinspot 219
Snappers 219–20
Soapfish, Arrowhead 235
Greater 236
Sixline 236
Snowflake 236
Spotted 236
Two-banded 235
Whitespotted 236
Yellowfin 235
Soapfishes 235–6
Solanderia gracilis 267
secunda 267
Solanderiidae 267
Sole, Moses 237
Peacock 237
Soleidae 237
Sparidae 226
Spearer, Orange 361
Sphaerechinus granularis 349
Sphoeroides spengleri 205
testudineus 205
Sphyraena barracuda 145
jello 145
genie 145
Sphyraenidae 143–5
Sphyrna lewini 119
mokarran 119
zygaena 119
Sphyrnidae 119
Sponge, Fire 260
Touch-me-not 260
Sponges 257–60

Spooner, Sawedged 369
Squamata 255
Squirrelfish 165
  Crown 164
  Longjaw 165
  Longspine 165
  Sabre 164
  Silverspot 164
  Spotfin 165
Squirrelfishes 162–5
Starfishes, Crown-of-thorns
    335–7
Stargazer, Brazilian 195
  Marbled 167
  Northern 195
  Pacific 195
  Southern 195
  Whitemargin 167
Stargazers 166–7
  Electric 195
Stegostoma varium 125
Stegostomatidae 125
Stinger, Caledonian 79
  Painted 80
  Spotted 79
  White 270
Stingfish, Dwarf 80
  Orangebanded 79
  Striped 80
  Three-stick 79
  Two-stick 78
  Weedy 45
Stingfishes 80
Stingray, Bluespotted 24
  Bluntnose 23
  Cowtail 25
  Honeycomb 25
  Roughtail 23
  Southern 23
  Yellow 26
Stingrays 17–27
Stomatopoda 358–61
Stomolophidae 290
Stomolophus meleagris 290
Stonefish, Estuarine 72
  North-west 73
  Red Sea 73
  Reef 71

Smallfin 72
Stonefishes 36, 67–73
Strongylura leiura 161
Surgeonfish, Black-barred 174
  Blackstreak 176
  Convict 174
  Doubleband 176
  Elongate 178
  Eyestripe 177
  Japanese 175
  Lined 174
  Mimic 177
  Ocean 173
  Orangeband 176
  Palette 179
  Powder Blue 175
  Ringtail 177
  Roundspot 178
  Sohal 174
  Whitecheek 175
  Whitefin 178
  Whitespotted 178
  Yellowfin 177
Surgeonfishes 169–80
Synanceia alula 72
  horrida 72
  nana 73
Synanceia verrucosa 71
Synanceiidae 36, 67–73
Synanceinae 71–3
Synapta maculata 371
Synaptidae 371

Tachypleus gigas 368
Taenianotus triacanthus 50
Taeniura lymma 26
  meyeni 26
Tamoya gargantua 296
Tang, Achilles 175
  Blue 173
  Indian Sailfin 180
  Pacific Sailfin 180
Tedania ignis 260
Tedanidae 260
Temnopleuridae 344
Testudines 253–4
Tetraodontidae 153–5, 198–205
Tetraroge spp. 64

Tetrarogidae 36, 63–5
Thalassophryne maculosa 34
  megalops 34
  nattereri 34
Thalassophryninae 33–4
Thunnus albacares 229
Thyroscyphus ramosus 271
Thysanostoma flagellatum 291
  loriferum 291
  thysanura 291
Thysanostomatidae 291
Toadfish, Coral 235
Toadfishes 33–4
Torpedinidae 193
Torpediniformes 191–5
Torpedo panthera 193
  sinuspersici 193
Toxopneustes pileolus 348
Toxopneustidae 346–9
Trachinidae 84–7
Trachinus araneus 87
  draco 87
  radiatus 87
Trevally, Bluefin 218
  Giant 218
Triactis producta 302
Triaenodon obesus 118
Triggerfish, Black 151
  Blue 150
  Clown 149
  Grey 151
  Indian 152
  Lagoon 152
  Orange-lined 152
  Picasso 152
  Pinktail 152
  Queen 151
  Titan 150
  Wedge-tail 152
  Yellowmargin 150
Triggerfishes 146–52
Tripneustes gratilla 348
  gratilla elatensis 348
  ventricosus 349
Trochus niloticus 366
Trunkfish, Smooth 238
  Spotted 238, 239
Trunkfishes 237–9

Tubularia 268
Tubulariidae 268
Tuna, Dogtooth 222
  Frigate 229
  Skipjack 229
  Yellowfin 229
Turtle, Green 253
  Hawksbill 253
  Leatherback 254
Turtles 253–4
Tylosurus acus 161
  choram 161
  crocodilus 161

Ulmaridae 288
Unicornfish, Bignose 183
  Bluespine 182
  Elegant 182
  Orangespine 182
  Sleek 183
  Whitemargin 183
Upeneus arge 230
Uranoscopidae 166–7, 195
Uranoscopus bicinctus 167
  sulphureus 167
Urchin, Ascension 341
  Atlantic Long-spined 341
  Bald-patch 344
  Banded 342
  Black Sea 343
  Blue-black 342
  Blue-spotted 342
  Collector 348
  Diadem 343

Fine-spined Boring 345
Flower 348
Long-spined 341
Mexican Long-spined 341
Multicoloured Fire 352
Red Sea Collector 348
Red Sea Fire 352
Rock-boring 345
Stone Sea 344
Variable Fire 352
Variegated 349
Violet Sea 349
Urchins, Boring Sea 345
  Dome 344
  Fire 350–3
  Flower 346–9
  Long-spined 341–3
  Sea 338–51
Urobatis jamaicensis 26
Urotrygonidae 22, 26

Valella valella 267
Varanidae 255
Varanus komodoensis 255
Variola albimarginata 218
  louti 218
Velvetfish, Crested 81
Velvetfishes 36, 81
  Orbicular 36, 81
Volute, Indian 366

Wahoo 229
Wasp, Banded Sea 296
  Raston's Sea 296

Warty Sea 296
Winged Sea 296
Waspfish, Bearded 65
  Cockatoo 64
  Longspine 64
  Spiny 64
Waspfishes 36, 63–5
  Longfin 36, 65
Weever, Greater 87
  Lesser 87
  Spotted 87
  Streaked 87
Weevers 84–7
Whipray, Jenkins' 24
  Leopard 25
  Mangrove 25
  Pink 24
Wobbegong, Indonesian 123
  Tasselled 123
Worm, Giant Bobbit 316
  Long-bristled Bobbit 316
Worms, Bobbit 315–16
  Bristle 312–16
  Fire 314
Wrasse, Napoleon 221
  Ringtail 221
Wrasses 221, 226

Xanthidae 369

Zebrasoma desjardinii 180
  veliferum 180
Zosimus aeneus 367, 369

The Authors

Dr Matthias Bergbauer is a distinguished marine biologist at Munich University. He has been diving for 28 years, using this to further his research, and has worked at research stations in the South Pacific, in Fiji and at the Great Barrier Reef, on the east coast of the United States, at a submarine laboratory in the Red Sea and also at sites in the Mediterranean. Alongside his research work, he also works as a journalist, regularly publishing scientific articles and has written several identification guides, diving books and reference works.

Robert F. Myers spent much of his childhood overseas, developing an intense interest in the aquatic and terrestrial animals at each posting. He began studying underwater life in high school and, for his BA in Zoology, surveyed the populations of coral reef fishes in Hawaii. Robert took his master's degree in Biology at the University of Gaum. Whilst there, he also spent time developing his underwater photography and working as a Government fisheries biologist. He has published numerous scientific papers on the fishes of the west Pacific and co-authored several books. Today he lives in Florida and is member of the Species Survival Commission for Coral Reef Fish of the IUCN.

Manuela Kirschner is a renowned underwater photographer and the recipient of several major international prizes for her work, which has been published in numerous newspapers, magazines and books. She runs seminars on underwater photography and has co-authored several books on diving. Her photo archive is based on more than 3,000 dives, which she has made all over the world: in local rivers and lakes in Germany, in the Baltic Sea, the Mediterranean, the Caribbean, and at many places in the Indian and Pacific Oceans.